Abraham Zvi Idelsohn, Johannesburg, c. 1930. *Unpublished photograph from the private collection of Mrs. Wendy Levine.*

Jewish Music
Its Historical Development

Abraham Z. Idelsohn

With a New Introduction
by Arbie Orenstein

DOVER PUBLICATIONS, INC.

NEW YORK

Published in Canada by General Publishing Company, Ltd., 30 Lesmill Road, Don Mills, Toronto, Ontario.
Published in the United Kingdom by Constable and Company, Ltd., 3 The Lanchesters, 162–164 Fulham Palace Road, London W6 9ER.

This Dover edition, first published in 1992, is an unabridged republication of *Jewish Music in Its Historical Development,* originally published by Henry Holt and Company, New York, in 1929 and reprinted by Schocken Books, New York, in 1967. The introduction by Arbie Orenstein was written for the Dover edition, and the new frontispiece was kindly provided by Mrs. Wendy Levine.

Manufactured in the United States of America
Dover Publications, Inc., 31 East 2nd Street, Mineola, N.Y. 11501

Library of Congress Cataloging-in-Publication Data

Idelsohn, A. Z. (Abraham Zebi), 1882–1938.
　　Jewish music : its historical development / Abraham Z. Idelsohn ; with a new introduction by Arbie Orenstein.
　　　　p.　　cm.
　　"An unabridged republication of Jewish music in its historical development, originally published by Henry Holt and Company, New York, in 1929 and reprinted by Schocken Books, New York, in 1967"—T.p. verso.
　　Includes bibliographical references and index.
　　ISBN 0-486-27147-1 (pbk.)
　　1. Jews—Music—History and criticism.　2. Synagogue music—History and criticism.　3. Folk music—History and criticism.　4. Folk songs, Hebrew—History and criticism.　5. Folk songs, Yiddish—History and criticism.　I. Idelsohn, A. Z. (Abraham Zebi), 1882–1938. Jewish music in its historical development.　II. Title.
ML3776.I3　1992
781.7'6—dc20
　　　　　　　　　　　　　　　　　　　　92-7643
　　　　　　　　　　　　　　　　　　　　CIP
　　　　　　　　　　　　　　　　　　　　MN

TABLE OF CONTENTS

Part I

THE SONG OF THE SYNAGOGUE

CHAPTER   PAGE

I. A HISTORICAL SURVEY OF RELIGIOUS AND SECULAR MUSIC IN ISRAEL AND ITS NEIGHBORING COUNTRIES THROUGHOUT BIBLICAL AND POST-BIBLICAL AGES UP TO THE DESTRUCTION OF THE SECOND TEMPLE .   3

II. SEMITIC-ORIENTAL SONG. TABLES I, II, AND III . .   24

III. THE OLDEST UNRYTHMICAL ELEMENTS OF JEWISH SONG. A: THE MODES OF THE BIBLE.—THE TA'AMIM (MUSICAL NOTATION) OF THE BIBLE. TABLES IV, V, VI, VII, VIII, IX, X AND XI   35

IV. THE OLDEST UNRHYTHMICAL ELEMENTS OF JEWISH SONG (CONTINUED). B: THE MODES OF THE PRAYERS. TABLES XII, XIII, XIIIa, XIV, AND XV . .   72

V. A HISTORICAL SURVEY OF THE SYNAGOGUE SONG AFTER THE DESTRUCTION OF THE SECOND TEMPLE UNTIL THE RISE OF ISLAM (70 C.E.–700 C.E.)   92

VI. RISE AND DEVELOPMENT OF THE PRECENTOR AND THE CHAZZAN FROM ANCIENT TIMES UNTIL THE EIGHTH CENTURY   101

VII. THE PHYTHMICAL SONG IN THE ORIENTAL AND SEPHARDIC SYNAGOGUE. TABLES XVI, XVII, XVIII, XIX, AND XX   110

VIII. THE SYNAGOGUE SONG OF THE "ASHKENAZIM." TABLES XXI, XXII, XXIII, XXIV, XXV, XXVI   129

IX. THE SONG OF THE SYNAGOGUE IN EASTERN EUROPE UP TO THE EIGHTEENTH CENTURY. TABLE XXVII   181

X. THE INTRODUCTION OF HARMONY AND POLYPHONY INTO THE SYNAGOGUE IN ITALY BY SALOMON ROSSI   196

CHAPTER   PAGE

XI. THE ASHKENAZIC SONG OF THE SYNAGOGUE IN THE
SEVENTEENTH AND EIGHTEENTH CENTURIES. TABLE
XXVIII 204

XII. THE INFLUENCE OF THE REFORM MOVEMENT ON THE
SYNAGOGUE SONG IN THE BEGINNING OF THE NINE-
TEENTH CENTURY. TABLE XXIX 232

XIII. THE INFLUENCE OF MODERATE REFORM UPON SYNA-
GOGUE SONG DURING THE NINETEENTH CENTURY
IN CENTRAL AND WESTERN EUROPE. BIBLIOGRAPHY 246

XIV. "CHAZZANIM" AND "CHAZZANUTH" IN EASTERN EUROPE
IN THE NINETEENTH CENTURY 296

XV. SYNAGOGUE SONG IN THE UNITED STATES OF AMERICA 316

XVI. COLLECTIONS OF AND LITERATURE ON SYNAGOGUE SONG 337

Part II

FOLK-SONG

XVII. THE FOLK-SONG OF THE ORIENTAL JEWS. TABLE XXX 357

XVIII. THE FOLK-SONG OF THE ASHKENAZIM. TABLES XXXI
AND XXXII 380

XIX. CHASSIDIC SONG. TABLE XXXIII 411

XX. BADCHONIM (MERRY-MAKERS) AND KLEZMORIM
(MUSIC-MAKERS); SONG AND SINGERS IN FOLK
STYLE. TABLE XXXIV 435

XXI. ARTISTIC ENDEAVORS 461

Part III

XXII. THE JEW IN GENERAL MUSIC 471

XXIII. HARMONY. TABLE XXXV 478

CONCLUSION 492

NOTES 495

INDEX 523

TABLES OF THE MUSICAL ILLUSTRATIONS

TABLE   PAGE

I. ARABIC TUNES: (a) SECULAR; (b) RELIGIOUS . . . 29

II. JACOBITE CHURCH SONGS: (a) UNRHYTHMICAL; (b) RHYTHMICAL 31

III. GREEK CHURCH TUNES 33

IV. PENTATEUCH: 1. BABYLONIAN; 2. PORTUGUESE-AMSTERDAM; 3. ASHKENAZIC-LITHUANIAN; 4. ASHKENAZIC; 5. KYRIE ELEISON (3RD TONE GREGORIAN); 6. CARPENTRAS.—COMPARATIVE TABLE OF ACCENT MOTIVES FOR THE INTONING OF THE PENTATEUCH 40

V. RUTH: BABYLONIAN-ASHKENAZIC. SONG OF SONGS: LITHUANIAN 48

VI. TUNES FOR THE POETRY OF THE PENTATEUCH: YEMENITE; PORTUGUESE 49

VII. PROPHETS: 1. YEMENITE-PENTATEUCH; 2. PERSIAN-SONG OF SONGS; 3. YEMENITE-PROPHETS; 4. BABYLONIAN-PROPHETS; 5. ASHKENAZIC-PROPHETS; 6. ASHKENAZIC-PROPHETS IN EASTERN EUROPE; 7. ASHKENAZIC CONCLUDING MOTIVE OF THE CHANT OF THE PENTATEUCH 52

VIII. LAMENTATIONS: 1. BABYLONIAN; 2. PORTUGUESE; 3. ASHKENAZIC; 4. SEPHARDIC-ASHKENAZIC; 5-6. GREGORIAN CHANT 54

IX. JOB: 1. SEPHARDIC-ORIENTAL; 2. ASHKENAZIC-PENTATEUCH FOR THE HIGH HOLIDAYS; 3-4. GREGORIAN 59

X. PSALMS: SEPHARDIC-ORIENTAL; ASHKENAZIC; MOROCCAN; YEMENITE; GREGORIAN 62

XI. ESTHER: 1. YEMENITE; 2. BABYLONIAN; 3. ASHKENAZIC 66

XII. TEFILLA MODE: 1. YEMENITE; 2. SYRIAC-ORIENTAL; 3. SEPHARDIC-EUROPEAN; 4. ASHKENAZIC; 5. GREGORIAN (4TH TONE); 6. GREGORIAN 75

XIII. COMPARATIVE TABLE OF SELICHA MODES: 1. PERSIAN; 2. YEMENITE; 3. ASHKENAZIC IN EASTERN EUROPE; 4. BABYLONIAN-SEPHARDIC; 5. PERSIAN; 6-7 ASHKENAZIC; 8. SEPHARDIC-ORIENTAL; 9. ASHKENAZIC (EASTERN EUROPE) 79

XIII a. COMPARATIVE TABLE OF VIDDUI MODES: 1. YEMENITE; 2. PERSIAN; 3. BABYLONIAN; 4. ASHKENAZIC . . . 82

XIV. MOGEN-OVOS MODE (STEIGER): 1-2. ASHKENAZIC; 3. SEPHARDIC-ORIENTAL 85

XV. AHAVOH-RABBOH MODE: 1. SEPHARDIC-ORIENTAL; 2-3. ASHKENAZIC 90

XVI. ARABIC METERS 115

XVII. MELODIES IN THE HAZAǦ METER: (a) YEMENITE; (b) BABYLONIAN; (c) SEPHARDIC 117

XVIII. (a) MELODIES IN THE RAǦAZ METER: 1. YEMENITE; 2. BABYLONIAN; 3. SEPHARDIC-ORIENTAL; (b) MELODIES IN THE MUTAKARIB METER: 4-5. YEMENITE; (c) MELODY IN THE KAMIL METER: 6. PERSIAN . . . 120

XIX. SEPHARDIC-ORIENTAL: (a) RHYTHMICAL MUSIC SET TO UNMETRICAL TEXTS; (b) UNRHYTHMICAL MUSIC SET TO METRICAL TEXTS 121

XX. ADONAY BEKOL SHOFAR: 1. SEPHARDIC-ORIENTAL; 2. MOROCCAN; 3. ITALIAN; 4. SEPHARDIC-LONDON; 5. CARPENTRAS 122

XXI. ASHKENAZIC MODES IN MINOR 138

XXII. ASHKENAZIC MODES IN MAJOR 145

XXIII. ASHKENAZIC TUNES FOR INDIVIDUAL PROSE TEXTS: 1. OLENU; 2. HAMMELECH; 3. OVOS I, II; 4. KADDISH I, II; 5. VEHAKKOHANIM I-III; 6. KOL NIDRE I-IV; 7. AKDOMUS 148

XXIV. MOTIVES OF THE GREGORIAN AND MINNESONG . . 163

XXV. ASHKENAZIC TUNES FOR INDIVIDUAL POETICAL TEXTS: OSCHOH EDROSH; EN AROCH; AAPID NEZER; EDER VOHOD; ESOH DEI; TUMAS TZUROM; SHOFET KOL HOORETS; ELI TZIYON; MOOZ TZUR; ADDIR HU I, II, III, IV 166

XXVI. MOTIVES AND TUNES OF GERMAN RELIGIOUS AND SECULAR FOLK-SONG 172

TABLE   PAGE

XXVII. (a) UKRAINIAN   SONG: SYNAGOGAL   AV-HORACHMIM
        MODE; UKRAINIAN MOTIVES IN "DORIAN"; UKRAIN-
        IAN MOTIVES IN "DORIAN" ENDING ON THE SECOND;
        (b) ROUMANIAN SONG   186

XXVIII. TABLE OF FOLK-SONGS COMPARED WITH THE YIGDAL
        TUNE: 1. SPANISH CANCIO; 2. JEWISH SEPHARDIC
        FOR TAL; 3. POLISH SONG; 4. ZIONIST HYMN HATIKVA;
        5. DORT WO DIE ZEDER; 6. YIGDAL; 7. BASQUE TUNE;
        8. BASQUE TUNE; 9. SMETANA   222

XXIX.   EN KELOHENU; ETZ CHAYIM   239

XXX.   FOLK-SONGS OF THE ORIENTAL JEWS: (a) HEBREW
        SONGS OF THE BABYLONIAN AND SYRIAC JEWS:
        BABYLONIAN;   SEPHARDIC-SYRIAN;   YEMENITE.   (b)
        JUDEO-SPANISH (LADINO) SONGS   372

XXXI.   TUNES OF ASHKENAZIC SONGS IN JUDEO-GERMAN OF
        THE SEVENTEENTH CENTURY: DER TOD ALS SCHNIT-
        TER; BRUDER VEITS TON; ES IST KEIN GRÖSSER
        FREUD   386

XXXII. TUNES OF THE EASTERN ASHKENAZIC FOLK-SONG . .   401

XXXIII. CABBALISTIC AND CHASSIDIC SONGS: (a) TUNES IN
        AHAVOH-RABBOH MODE;   (b)   TUNES   IN   MINOR;
        (c) TUNES IN MAJOR   421

XXXIV. MOSHIACHSZEITEN: 1. TUNE BY W. EHRENKRANZ; 2.
        TUNE BY E. ZUNSER   443

XXXV.   HARMONY: (a) AHAVOH-RABBOH: 1-7; (b) MINOR 8-9;
        (c) ADONOY-MOLOCH: 10-11   489

FACSIMILES

TABLE   PAGE

I. ACCENTS: PENTATEUCH (LEVITICUS 22.26-33; 23:1-7). ITALIAN MS. 15TH CENTURY 36

II. ACCENTS: PROPHETS (I SAMUEL 15:1-6). ITALIAN MS. . 15TH CENTURY 36

III. ACCENTS (JOB 3:2-14). MS. 13TH CENTURY 37

IV. REUCHLIN, DE ACCENTIBUS. PUB. HAGENAU, 1518 . . . 37

V. SALOMON ROSSI. PUB. VENICE, 1622 200

VI. ISRAEL JACOBSON HYMNAL. PUB. CASSEL, 1810 237

INTRODUCTION TO THE DOVER EDITION

A. Z. Idelsohn's *Jewish Music in Its Historical Development* was first published in 1929 and has been reprinted several times. Long considered a classic, it has been widely imitated but never superseded.[1] Of course, much has happened in the Jewish world since 1929, particularly the European Holocaust and the rebirth of an independent Jewish homeland. Furthermore, research in the field of Jewish music has burgeoned, mostly in the United States and in Israel. As the Jewish people enters its fifth millennium, the time is ripe for a comprehensive, up-to-date study of Jewish music. This study, no doubt, will modify some of Idelsohn's findings, just as it will build upon his many pioneering achievements. His life and work are summarized in this introduction, which concludes with suggestions for further reference in the multifaceted area of Jewish music.[2]

Abraham Zvi Idelsohn, the "father of Jewish music research," was born in Lithuania on June 11, 1882[3] and died in Johannesburg, South Africa, on August 14, 1938. He attended various yeshivas (religious academies), sang in synagogue choirs, studied cantorial music privately and continued his general music education in Berlin and Leipzig. Idelsohn's dual background of Eastern cantorial tradition and Western musicological discipline would play an important role in his personal odyssey from sacred singer to ethnomusicologist. In Leipzig, at age twenty, he married Zilla, the daughter of Cantor Hillel Schneider, one of his mentors. After serving briefly as cantor in Leipzig, Regensburg and Johannesburg (where he had relatives), Idelsohn, an ardent Zionist, moved with his family to the Holy Land in 1906. In an autobiographical sketch, he recalled this turning point in his life:

. . . the idea dawned upon me to devote my strength to the research of the Jewish song. This idea ruled my life to such extent, that I could find no rest. I therefore gave up my position and traveled to Jerusalem, without knowing what was in store for me. In Jerusalem, I found about 300 synagogues and some young men eager to study Chazanuth [cantorial music]. The various synagogues were conducted according to the customs of the respective countries, and their traditional song varied greatly from one another. I started collecting their traditional songs. [4]

This marked the genesis of Idelsohn's monumental *Thesaurus of Hebrew-Oriental Melodies*. [5] Volume 1 is devoted to the liturgical and paraliturgical songs of the Yemenite Jews. [6] Idelsohn's research was greatly facilitated by a grant from the Academy of Science in Vienna, which also provided him with a phonograph. He made over a thousand field recordings, in addition to his musical transcriptions and analyses. These proved to be a revelation, as they introduced the sounds of ancient traditional melodies of non-European communities into the purview of Jewish music. Blessed with a phenomenal memory and indefatigable zeal, Idelsohn's subsequent studies of comparative biblical cantillation, [7] the Near Eastern *maqams* (melodic frameworks found in Islamic music) [8] and the common elements found in Jewish and Christian liturgical-music traditions [9] proved equally pathbreaking.

Idelsohn's intense research was interrupted by World War I, during which he was drafted into the Turkish army, where he served as a hospital clerk and then as a bandmaster in Gaza. In 1921 he left Jerusalem, largely owing to the lack of a suitable academic position. Thus, following his Europe and Jerusalem sojourns, Idelsohn finally settled in the United States. In 1924, following an extended coast-to-coast lecture tour, he was appointed Professor of Liturgy and Jewish Music at the Hebrew Union College in Cincinnati. He taught, lectured and wrote with great distinction until 1934, when failing health forced him to retire; a series of cerebral hemorrhages led to virtually total paralysis.

An overview of Idelsohn's achievement would include, beside his *Thesaurus* and field recordings, almost 200 books and scholarly articles in English, German, Hebrew and Yiddish. His two most popular books, commissioned by Henry Holt and Company, were *Jewish Music in Its Historical Development* (1929) and its companion volume, *Jewish Liturgy and Its Development* (1932). In addition, he published Jewish songbooks, cantorial compositions and music for various synagogue services. The song "Hava Nagila" ("Come, Let's Rejoice") was adapted by Idelsohn and is listed in the *Thesaurus* as a "chassidic tune"; it would later become internationally popular.[10] His *Yiftah* ("Jephthah"), subtitled "A Musical Drama in five acts," was the first Hebrew opera ever written; the libretto was his own, and he partially based the music on traditional melodies. The first performance took place in Jerusalem in 1922 with an orchestra of authentic oriental instruments, and the piano-vocal score was published the same year by Breitkopf & Härtel.

January 1992   ARBIE ORENSTEIN
                          THE AARON COPLAND SCHOOL OF MUSIC
                          QUEENS COLLEGE

NOTES

[1]Idelsohn's survey is in fact an extract of a multivolume history of Jewish music that he wrote (in Hebrew) at the request of the great Hebrew poet Hayyim Nahman Bialik. Bialik's publishing firm, Devir, printed the first volume in 1924, but the remaining volumes are still unpublished.

[2]I wish to thank Dr. Israel J. Katz, who kindly read the introduction and made many helpful suggestions.

[3]According to Idelsohn's autobiographical sketch written in Hebrew (printed in *The Abraham Zvi Idelsohn Memorial Volume*, p. 17; see Suggestions for Further Reference). "I was born on the 24th of Sivan [in the Jewish calendar, corresponding to the 11th of June], but my birthdate was registered as July 1, 1882." This has given rise to incorrect birthdates (from reliance on the Gregorian rather than the Julian calendar) of July 13 *(Baker's Biographical Dictionary)* and July 14 *(New Grove Dictionary)*, among other sources.

[4]Ibid., p. 21.

[5]Published in ten volumes with commentary in German, 1914–32 (vols. 1–5, Jerusalem, Berlin, Vienna: Benjamin Harz; vols. 6–10, Leipzig: Friedrich Hofmeister). Several volumes have also been published in Hebrew (vols. 1–5) and English (vols. 1, 2, 6–10).

[6]Beginning with volume 6, Idelsohn expanded the scope of his *Thesaurus*, as may be seen from the titles: vol. 2: *Songs of the Babylonian Jews;* vol. 3: *Songs of the Jews of Persia, Bukhara, and Daghestan;* vol. 4: *Songs of the Oriental Sephardim;* vol. 5: *Songs of the Moroccan Jews;* vol. 6: *The Synagogue Songs of the German Jews in the 18th Century;* vol. 7: *The Traditional Songs of the South German Jews;* vol. 8: *The Synagogue Song of the East European Jews;* vol. 9: *The Folk Song of the East European Jews;* vol. 10: *Songs of the Chassidim.*

[7]See the commentary in the *Thesaurus*, particularly vols. 1–4.

[8]See "Die Maqamen der arabischen Musik" [The Scale Modes of Arabic Music], *Sammelbände der Internationale Musikgesellschaft* 15, no. 1 (October–December 1913), pp. 1–63. A summary of this article (in English) is found in the *Memorial Volume*, pp. 103–4.

[9]See "Parallelen zwischen gregorianischen und hebräisch-orientalischen Gesangweisen" [Parallels between Gregorian and Hebraic-Oriental Melodies], *Zeitschrift für Musikwissenschaft* 4, nos. 9–10 (June–July 1922), pp. 515–24. A summary of this article (in English) is found in the *Memorial Volume*, p. 125.

[10]The melody is printed in vol. 9, no. 716, and again in vol. 10, no. 155. Idelsohn discusses "Hava Nagila" as follows:

> This song may serve as an example of how a song becomes a popular folk-song, and particularly how a song becomes 'Palestinian'. The tune originated at the court in Sadigora (Bukovina) and was brought to Jerusalem. In 1915 I wrote it down. In 1918 I needed a popular tune for a performance of my mixed choir in Jerusalem. My choice fell upon this tune which I arranged in four parts and for which I wrote a Hebrew text. The choir sang it and it apparently caught the imagination of the people, for the next day men and women were singing the song throughout Jerusalem. In no time it spread throughout the country, and thence throughout the Jewish world. . . . Since then it has been printed in several songsters as 'Palestinian'.

(*Thesaurus*, English version, vol. 9, p. xxiv.) The words and tempo of "Hava Nagila" have recently been attributed to one of Idelsohn's pupils, Cantor Moshe Nathanson. (See Sheldon Feinberg, *Hava Nagila! The Story behind the Song and Its Composer* [New York: Shapolsky, 1988], pp. 15–18.)

SUGGESTIONS FOR FURTHER REFERENCE

The following suggestions for further reference are limited to recent publications in English. Space precludes listing many other important works, which can be found in the bibliographies cited here.

1. REFERENCES PERTAINING TO IDELSOHN'S LIFE AND WORK

Adler, Israel, and Judith Cohen. *A. Z. Idelsohn Archives at the Jewish National and University Library: Catalogue.* Yuval Monograph Series, no. IV. Jerusalem: Magnes Press, The Hebrew University, 1976.

Adler, Israel, et al. *The Abraham Zvi Idelsohn Memorial Volume. Yuval,* vol. 5. Jerusalem: Magnes Press, The Hebrew University, 1986.

Katz, Israel J. "Abraham Zvi Idelsohn (1882–1938): A Bibliography of His Collected Writings." *Musica Judaica* 1, no. 1 (1975–76), pp. 1–32.

2. BIBLIOGRAPHIES AND REFERENCE WORKS

Encyclopaedia Judaica. 16 vols. and yearbooks. Edited by Cecil Roth. Jerusalem: Keter, 1971. (Many articles on Jewish music and musicians, *passim.*)

Heskes, Irene. *The Resource Book of Jewish Music: A Bibliographical and Topical Guide to the Book and Journal Literature and Program Materials.* Westport, Conn.: Greenwood Press, 1985.

The New Grove Dictionary of Music and Musicians. 20 vols. 6th ed. Edited by Stanley Sadie. London: Macmillan, 1980. (Many articles on Jewish music and musicians, *passim.*)

Nulman, Macy. *Concise Encyclopedia of Jewish Music.* New York: McGraw-Hill, 1975.

Sendrey, Alfred. *Bibliography of Jewish Music*. New York: Columbia University Press, 1951.

Weisser, Albert. *Bibliography of Publications and Other Resources on Jewish Music*. New York: National Jewish Music Council, 1969.

3. Histories and Music Anthologies

Binder, Abraham Wolf. *Biblical Chant*. London: Peter Owen, 1960.

Cohen, Judith, ed. *Proceedings of the World Congress on Jewish Music* (Jerusalem, 1978). Tel Aviv: Institute for the Translation of Hebrew Literature, 1982.

Ephros, Gershon. *Cantorial Anthology of Traditional and Modern Synagogue Music*. 6 vols. New York: Bloch, 1929–1969.

Gradenwitz, Peter. *The Music of Israel: Its Rise and Growth through 5000 Years*. New York: W. W. Norton, 1949.

Hofman, Shlomo. *Miqra'ey Musika/Biblical References to Music* [in Hebrew, English, French and Spanish]. Tel Aviv: Israel Music Institute, 1974.

―――. *Hamusika Batalmud/Music in the Talmud* [in Hebrew-Aramaic, English, French and German]. Tel Aviv: Israel Music Institute, 1989.

Rosowsky, Solomon. *The Cantillation of the Bible: The Five Books of Moses*. New York: Reconstructionist Press, 1957.

Rubin, Ruth. *Voices of a People: The Story of Yiddish Folksong*. New York: McGraw-Hill, 1973.

Sachs, Curt. *The Rise of Music in the Ancient World, East and West*. New York: W. W. Norton, 1943.

Sendrey, Alfred. *The Music of the Jews in the Diaspora (up to 1800)*. Cranbury, N.J.: Thomas Yoseloff/A. S. Barnes, 1970.

Vinaver, Chemjo. *Anthology of Hassidic Music*. Edited with introductions and annotations by Eliyahu Schleifer. Jerusalem: Hebrew University of Jerusalem, 1985.

Werner, Eric. *The Sacred Bridge: The Interdependence of Liturgy and Music in Synagogue and Church during the First Millennium*. London: D. Dobson, 1959; New York: Columbia University Press, 1959.

————. *A Voice Still Heard . . . : The Sacred Songs of the Ashkenazic Jews*. University Park, Penn.: Pennsylvania State University Press, 1976.

4. JOURNALS

Journal of Jewish Music and Liturgy. The journal of the Cantorial Council of America. Edited by Macy Nulman. New York, 1976–.

Journal of Synagogue Music. The journal of the Cantors Assembly of America. New York, 1967–.

Musica Judaica. The journal of the American Society for Jewish Music. Edited by Israel J. Katz. New York, 1975–.

PREFACE

The aim of this book is to give a description and an analysis of the elements and characteristics of Jewish music, in their historical development, from the earliest times of its appearance as a Semitic-Oriental song, throughout the ages and countries. We follow its history as a tonal expression of Judaism and of Jewish life. We try to point out the influence that the foreign music of the environment exerted upon Jewish music, and seek to explain the principles according to which certain foreign elements were incorporated until they became organic parts of the musical body. In this music we find original elements and features, reflecting the spiritual life of the Jewish people.

The book presents the result of the author's research-work in the field of Jewish music during a quarter of a century, of first-hand collecting of Synagogue- and folk-songs in the Oriental and European Jewish communities, and of analyzing these into their elements. The amassed material the author classified, edited and has been publishing in his *Thesaurus of Hebrew Oriental Melodies,* five of the ten volumes of which have thus far been issued by Benjamin Harz, Berlin, 1922-28. Further, the author made a thorough study of all available old music manuscripts as well as of the vast literature of Synagogue- and folk-music published in both hemispheres—all of which is indispensable to an insight into the spirit of the music and its history. He has correlated all references to music scattered throughout Hebrew literature, from the Bible down to the latest works, in order authentically to assign to music the place that it occupied in Jewish religious and secular life. In addition, he found it imperative to acquaint himself in detail with the music of the many peoples among whom Israel lived or with whom the people came into contact during its 3,500 years of history, because only thus could he draw comparisons with Jewish song.

The book is written not only for technically trained musicians but for the intelligent lay public as well. The student will find technical details, a complete theory and in the notes at the end of the book, a clue to the most important sources; while the layman will gain a knowledge and an understanding of the history, development and character of the music. For clarity, the book is printed in two types: a large one for the nontechnical and a smaller one for the technical sections. All non-English terms are italicized and explained. For both groups of readers the book is liberally illustrated with every type of music discussed and with a table for each comparative study. Almost all the texts of the musical illustrations are either translated or paraphrased in English.

Hebrew transliteration throughout the book follows the system here listed as first in order after each vowel or consonant. The additional possibilities named are employed with the purpose of rendering certain texts as they are pronounced in specific localities:

Vowels:

ָ = a; Ashkenazic, Yemenite and Persian = o.
וֹ = o; Lithuanian = ej or oj.
וּ = u.
ִ = i.
ַ = a.
ֵ = e or ey.
ֶ = e; ȩ.
ְ = e, ĕ, or '.

Dagesh forte is indicated by the doubling of the letter.

Consonants:

א = a		ל = l	
בּ = b		ם, מ = m	
ב = v or b		ן, נ = n	
ג, גּ = g		שׂ, ס = s	
ד, דּ = d		ע = a or '	
ה = h		פּ = p	
ו = w, Ashkenazic = v		פ = f	
ז = z		ץ, צ = s, Ashkenazic = tz	
ח = h, Ashkenazic = ch		ק = k; q ;'.	
ט = t or ṭ		ר = r	
י = y		שׁ = sh or š	
כּ = k		תּ = t	
ך, כ = ch or ẖ		ת = th or ṯ, Ashkenazic s.	

Biblical names and terms are here given as they occur in the Bible translation issued by the Jewish Publication Society of America, Philadelphia, 1917.

Arabic, Syriac, Ukrainian, Ladino and Yiddish texts are transliterated with the one aim of making them pronounceable by the English reader. Technical phonetics is, therefore, not observed. Ǧ is to be pronounced like "dj" and "zh" like "zsh."

The author wishes to make acknowledgment of the valuable assistance of A. Irma Cohon in the presentation of the material of this book; to express his indebtedness to Professor Samuel S. Cohon for his reading of the manuscript and his helpful suggestions; and to record his gratitude to Dr. Joshua Bloch, chief of the Jewish Division of the Public Library, New York, for his furtherance of this work.

A. Z. IDELSOHN.

KEY TO INTERPRETATION OF
MUSICAL ILLUSTRATIONS

 / signifies ¼ flat.

x signifies ¼ sharp.

The signs ♭ ♮ ♯ in unrhythmical music: The "accidental" is noted (irrespective of motive divisions) only the first time that it occurs in a continuous series of the same note. Whenever other notes intervene, the note in question either is marked anew or should be understood to have resumed its tone value in the key employed.

Bar-divisions in unrhythmical music indicate motives. They should not be construed to determine accent.

Repeated notes on one syllable, in Oriental song, are not tied to make one prolonged tone, as in modern Occidental song. The Oriental musician or the singer of the old Church song holds the vowel or consonant of the word sung, while producing a throbbing repetition of the note in question.

PART I

THE SONG OF THE SYNAGOGUE

CHAPTER I

In surveying the development of music in ancient Israel it is essential to consider the music of Israel's ancient neighbors. In so doing we are enabled to draw a conclusion as to the extent to which Israel's music resembled that of the bordering countries of Palestine, during the period of Israel's development as a nation and thereafter, through the Second Temple until its destruction. From such comparison we likewise gain an idea of the features gradually developed in Israel's music, as an expression of its spiritual evolution. We discover the musical elements and tools held in common with the other ancient cultured peoples, and find how these were reshaped in conformity with Israel's spiritual concepts, and how the resultant music received an original form of expression.

We observe that as the song of the other ancient Oriental peoples, so Israel's music from earliest times was determined by its religious and social life, and the form of that music changed with the changes of Israel's religious attitudes and political conditions.

We turn first to the old EGYPTIAN MUSIC. As long as the Egyptian religion and culture were in their flower, music was developed as a tool of expression and drew its significance from its influence upon the sentiments of the gods in the higher regions, the gods in the lower regions, and not less upon the

3

evil spirits. The musicians were the priests, male or female, who were also the sacred dancers. Music was regarded as sacred and was credited with its own ETHOS—its divine power. But in the course of ages Egyptian culture outlived itself. When new ideas arose, revolutionizing the old-established ones, the aristocratic party clung desperately to its tradition, and forced the priest-musicians to fascinating expressions which they could no longer draw from the heart of their institution, since it now lacked vital influence.

Though we no longer know Egyptian music because, in the words of the music historian AMBROS, we did not have the opportunity of listening to it for even one minute in order to be able to judge its sound,[1] nevertheless, from our record of the manner of use of the musical instruments we may deduce that at the time of its height, Egyptian religious music had a certain dignity and holiness, inasmuch as those instruments employed were not held conducive to arousing sensuality. Thus, the religious musicians did not use the "profane" *Aulos* (pipe). Neither did they employ a great number of instruments of percussion, but usually they employed only one drum and one pair of cymbals in an entire religious orchestra. The main instruments were string instruments: the *Nabla* (different kinds of harps) and the *Kithara* (different kinds of lyres imported later by Semites). There were further the *double-flute* which was of an entirely different quality from the single flute or *Aulos,* and finally the *trumpet* and the *Sistrum*—both signal instruments only.

Plato says that the Egyptians accredited their sacred melodies to the goddess Isis. He praises them for their ability to create melodies which had the power to subdue the passions of man and purify his spirit. "This certainly must be the work of god or of a godly man," he exclaims. This might have been the reason that the Egyptians considered their religious melodies sacred and would not change them. Neither would they use foreign tunes, as Herodotus, the great Greek historian, states. He was, therefore, surprised to hear in Egypt a tune famous in Phœnicia, Cyprus and Greece—namely, the lamentation over *Linos* which the Egyptians called *Maneros*.[2]

At the beginning of the decay of Egypt, after the period of the Hyksos, we find that the flute was introduced for religious purposes, and that there was a marked increase of percussive instruments as well as of fascinating dancers and singers, as we see from the bas-reliefs representing processions of orchestras, etc., found in the tombs of the Egyptian kings. During the decay, the musicians carefully hid their products, both musical and poetic, allowing no one to see the "books of the songs." According to Pythagoras, who studied in Egypt around the sixth century B.C.E., the protests of the priests against virtuosity were of no avail, because artificiality had to cover the mummy of that great and powerful culture, until it was laid low by Cambyses and later cut off by Alexander. Did Egyptian musical expression die together with its religion? Not entirely; for some of the best human expressions in it were taken over by ISRAEL and GREECE.

The music of the PHŒNICIANS, whose close geographical and ethnological relationship to Israel should lead us to expect many features in common in the music of the two tribes, was nevertheless—according to the description of many Greek authors—in the sharpest contrast with Israel's, at least during the period of the Second Temple. The Phœnicians had the triangular *Kinnor* which the Greeks borrowed and called *Kinura*, and the *Neval*, known to the Greeks as the Sidonian *Nabla*, and which, according to their tradition, the Egyptians likewise adopted. But the arrangement of the religious orchestra, as well, apparently, as the contents of the music, was of a different nature, for it had an exceedingly sensuous and exciting character. It went to the extremity of joy on the one hand, and to the extremity of lamentation (especially for Adonis) on the other, resulting in a boisterous chaos of percussive instruments. Chief in the music of the Phœnician cult—whether for joy or lamentation—was the *Abobas* (pipe). By this instrument Adonis was lamented, and it therefore became synonymous with Adonis music. The fundamental difference between the music of Israel and Phœnicia affords the best proof for the contention that music was always a tool by which ideas were expressed. The fight of Elijah against the Phœnician Baal- and Ishtar-cult, which the Phœnician princess Jezebel introduced into Samaria, was one of the bitterest battles prophetic Israel fought. The Biblical description of the barbarous manner of the Baal worshippers: "they danced in halting wise about the altar . . . they cried aloud, and cut themselves after their manner with swords and lances, till the blood gushed out upon them" (1 Kings 18: 26-28), finds its confirmation in the statement of Lucian that at the Spring festivity in honor of Ishtar the noisy and exciting music of the double-pipes, cymbals and drums used so to stimulate the youths to a frenzied craze that they would emasculate themselves. "At the sound of pipes, cymbals and drums, and several other percussive instruments, those emasculated servants of the goddess Ishtar would march through the streets in procession, cut themselves with swords, and lash themselves until blood gushed forth." Isaiah's satire (23: 16) on Tyre, "Take a harp, go about the city, thou harlot long forgotten; make sweet melody, sing many songs, that thou mayest be remembered," finds an explanation in the statement of Horace, who says that "even during the time of the Roman Empire, Phœnician and Syrian female musicians, whose reputation for immorality was known, would be found in the *Ambubajarum Collegia* . . . and in the circus (Roman Arena) offering themselves."

Music in ASSYRIA and BABYLONIA was somewhat similar to that in Egypt. Only few bas-reliefs have been unearthed, presenting musical instruments. On the Ashurakhbal bas-relief a procession of an orchestra is reproduced.[3] In that orchestra there participate nine boys singing and clapping their hands; three men with big harps, of whom two are dancing; one man playing the double-pipe; one, an oblong harp; four women fingering the big harp; one woman playing the double pipe; one beating a small drum; one man striking the cymbals; six females singing, one of whom presses her cheek and throat with one hand. The composition of that orchestra gives us a clear idea of the character of the music in Assyria. We learn from it that the percussive instruments were of minor importance, and that in employing nine boys' voices and six female singers, stress was laid upon vocal music and sweet singing. Furthermore, there are seven string instruments, only two double-pipes, and no single-pipes at all. Considering that the procession was to meet the king upon his return from battle as a conqueror—and Assyrian kings were always supposed to be victorious—the two small drums and the one cymbal are too modest noise-makers even for our refined taste. This fact indicates a tendency toward refinement of musical expression. And the highly developed hymns and supplications, with their RESPONSIVE form sung by priests and confessors and offerers of sacrifices, which were in use in Babylonia long before Israel came into being, lead us to conclude that the Assyrian music ranks next to the Egyptian as a source out of which Israel drew its best elements of musical forms.

With regard to ancient religious music of the TEMPLE IN JERUSALEM, we have to apply the same words that Ambros did to Egyptian music: ". . . could we listen to it for but one moment!" However, from the composition of the orchestra of the First Temple, we learn that Israel accepted some of the

arrangements of the religious orchestra used in Egypt at the
time of its cultural height. The legend that when Solomon
married Pharaoh's daughter she brought with her a thousand
varieties of musical instruments [4] seems to be based upon historical facts, for we find that the instruments employed in the
First Temple and the arrangements of its orchestra bore similarity to those in Egypt.

The orchestra of the Temple of Jerusalem consisted of the
following instruments: *Nevel*, the big harp, originally without resonant body; *Kinnor*, the little lyre or harp, the Semitic
form of which was the square, and the Phœnician and Assyrian
form of which was mostly triangular. The *Kinnor* had no
resonant body. Both were STRING instruments. Their difference lay in the number of strings as well as in size, as the
Talmud explains. [5] These two instruments were the most important ones, without which no public religious ceremony could
be held. As to the number of their strings we have no
definite information. Whether *sheminith* indicates eight and
asor ten strings cannot be proved. [6] We do know, however, that
in Egypt and Assyria the number of the strings of the harps
and lyres, etc., varied from three to twenty-two. Neither have
investigations been successful in finding out the tonality, the
range and pitch, of the string instruments in Israel or Egypt.
We are rather more informed of the quality of their tone.
The tone of the *Kinnor* is described in the Bible as "sweet,"
"tender," "soft"—lyrical. The *Kinnor* was popular among
the more cultured classes in Israel. The tone of the *Nevel*
was naturally stronger because the instrument was larger than
the *Kinnor*, especially after it had received a resonant body.
According to Josephus, the *Nevel* had twelve strings and the
Kinnor ten. [7] And from him we know that on the *Nevel* they
used to play with their fingers, whereas for the *Kinnor* they
employed the plectrum. However, it is reported of King

David that he played the *Kinnor* with his hand—which means fingers. (1 Sam. 16: 16 and 23; 18: 10; 19: 9.)

There were likewise two kinds of WIND instruments, one of which was of no musical value, serving only for signaling purposes. To this class belongs (a) the *Shofar*—ram's-horn (in Assyrian *shapparu*—wild mountain-goat).[8] It produces a few tones approximating c—g—c, or any other equivalent intervals, e.g., 1—5—1, or 5—8—8; 1—4—8, and so on. The pitch, naturally, depends on the size of the *Shofar* and on the construction of its hollow. The instrument lends itself to the production of various rhythmical forms, from long notes to 1/32. But it is impossible to produce on it any melody whatsoever. Indeed, the Bible applies the terms "blowing"—*tekia*, meaning long notes, and "shouting"—*terua*, meaning short notes in staccato or tremulo form, but not *nagen*—"producing musical tones." It was used chiefly for announcements and signals, not only in secular life, but also in religious ceremonies to call on the god to remind him of his duties to his people, or to wake him from his sleep. To the *Shofar* was also attributed the magic power of frightening and dispersing evil spirits and gods of the enemies who helped their people in battle. This belief was current among all primitive tribes, and it was, likewise, accepted in Israel, as many Biblical stories and phrases testify. The blowing of the *Shofar* was even attributed to Yahve himself, in order to frighten his enemies and to gather the scattered remnants of his people to his sanctuary. Thus, Zachariah (9: 14-15) says: "And the Lord God will blow the horn. . . . The Lord of Hosts will defend them." Later, after the Second Destruction, the idea of blowing the "Shofar of Redemption" was transferred to the prophet Elijah, who is supposed to announce the coming of the Messiah.

During the latter part of the period of the Second Temple

two types of *Shofaroth* were in use: the curved (male) ram's-horn and the straight (female) mountain-goat's horn. The latter form with a gold mouthpiece was used in the Temple on New Year, whereas the first form, with a silver-covered mouthpiece, was used on fast days. After the destruction of the Temple no luxurious decorations were permitted.

The *Shofar* is the only instrument that retained its position in the Synagogue throughout the Medieval Ages up to the present day. On New Year's Day the *Shofar* was blown to remind God of His promise to Abraham, Isaac and Jacob, and especially of Isaac's sacrifice and of the ram that substituted him (Gen. 21: 13).[9] Later, Jewish philosophers, such as Saadia (tenth century), tried to interpret the custom of *Shofar* blowing by giving it a higher human idea, namely, that the sound of the *Shofar* stirs the heart to awe and reverence, and its purpose, therefore, is to remind us of our duties to God.[10] In like manner, Maimonides speaks of this custom.[11]

Of all musical instruments, it was the most unmusical of them, the *Shofar*, that was retained. Because of the religious reasons just mentioned, it was carried into the Synagogue. The term *tekia* of the Bible and Mishna was in the third century explained as a "long note," whereas concerning the term *terua* difference of opinion arose as to whether it meant short staccato notes or a tremolo on one sustained note. Finally, in the fourth century Rabbi Abahu in Cæsarea (Palestine) made a compromise that both ways should be used, the staccato (*shevarim*) and the tremolo (*terua*), and thus it remained to this day.[12]

(b) The *Chatzotzera*-TRUMPET seems to have been imported from Egypt, though it was also known to the Assyrians.[13] The trumpet was made out of silver and was used for signaling purposes (Num. 10: 1-10), for secular and religious functions. Only the priests were entrusted with the use of it, as was the custom in Egypt. *Chatzotzera* and *Shofar* are, as a rule, quoted together, and for both the terms "tekia" and "terua" are applied. From this we may deduce that their natures were alike. Both were handled by priests and not by Levites—the professional musicians of the Temple—a fact which proves that both served the same function of signaling. Josephus describes the *Chatzotzera* as being of approximately a cubit's length, its cylinder being somewhat larger than that of the *Halil* (pipe), its mouthpiece wide and its body expanding into a bell-like ending.[14] The form of the *Chatzotzera* is still preserved on the Jewish coins of the later part of the period of the Second Temple, and on the Titus arch in Rome.

As to the number of these two instruments employed in the Temple, we are informed that originally two *Chatzotzeroth* were ordered (Num. l.c.), which number remained as a minimum requirement for the Temple service. However, as a maximum, one hundred twenty trumpets might be used. And, indeed, at the dedication of Solomon's Temple, it is reported (2 Chron. 5: 12) that this number of trumpets was employed.[15]

The number of *Shofaroth* was restricted in the Mishna to one for New Year and two for fast days.[16]

We know of three kinds of *musical* wind instruments:

(a) *Uggav*—small pipe or flute. This instrument is not mentioned in the list of the musical instruments used in the Jerusalem Temple.[17] The only reference to *Uggav* is in Psalm 150: 4. In the later period of the Second Temple it was called *Abbub*—hollow reed,[18] and was identical, at least in name, to the Phœnician *Abobas*. Tradition reports of an *Abbub* which had been in the Temple since the time of Moses. It was small and of fine reed, and had a sweet tone.[19] It was, however, seldom used—only as a solo instrument for interludes "because it slides over softly." [20] Emphasis was laid upon reed instruments which alone produced, according to Jewish taste, a tender

and sweet tone.[21]   The *Uggav*, it is reported, "was one of the
two instruments retained from the First Temple, but when it
became defective it could not be mended." [22]   From all of
which we learn that the *Uggav* was an ancient instrument, once
in use in the First Temple; that it had gradually disappeared,
so that the last one which survived could not be mended when
damaged.

(b) *Ḥalil* or *Chalil*—big pipe; in Greek, *mono-aulos*.
Though in ancient Israel the *Ḥalil* was one of the most popular instruments in secular as well as in religious life, none the
less we do not find its name on the list of instruments of the
service throughout the First Temple.[23]   Later, at the time of
the Second Temple, the *Ḥalil* was permitted at the service but
only on twelve festal days during the year "to increase joy."
The number was set from a minimum of two to a maximum
of twelve.   On Sabbath no playing of the *Ḥalil* was permissible even at the Temple, because it was not held to be a
sacred instrument as the *Kinnor* and *Nevel*.[24]   The *Ḥalil* was
also considered by Jews at that time as an exciting instrument,
and was used for occasions of extreme joy and gaiety, such as
weddings or public processions of the pilgrims with their offerings of the first fruit.[25]   Likewise was it used to express extreme
sorrow, as, for example, during funerals, for which occasion
even the poorest man had to hire two *Ḥalilim*-players in
order to show his grief over the death of his wife.[26]

The structure of the *Ḥalil* was similar to that of the Greek
Aulos (i.e., with a mouthpiece), and, according to Maimonides,
similar to the Arabic *Muzmar*.[27]   Its tone was sharp and penetrating, like that of the oboe.[28]   The Mishna tells us, in a somewhat exaggerated way, that whenever the *Ḥalilim* were blown
at the Temple their tone carried as far as Jericho.[29]   For that
reason the *Ḥalil* was used for processions, as described by

Isaiah (30: 29), this custom prevailing as late as Mishnaic times.

The fate of the *Halil* in the Jerusalem Temple was similar to the fate of the *Aulos* in Greece. Olympus introduced it to Greece about 800 B.C.E. from Asia Minor, but the Greek philosophers opposed it because of its exciting sound and because it was tuned according to the four notes d½ ♯c₁½ b♭½ a, a tetrachord unfamiliar in Greece. On account of its strangeness (two half-steps and an augmented one) it was called "chromatic"; on account of its sadness, it was called "elegiac." The instrument was debarred from religious music and from the tragedy. But later, to the distress of the philosophers, Agathon, the virtuoso, at the beginning of the fourth century B.C.E., introduced the *Aulos* and its exciting scale into the tragedy. This scale is the most outstanding one in the Tartaric-Altaic and Ukrainian songs, and is of much importance also in Jewish music. It remained permanently in Greek music despite the dismay of the philosophers, and created a special type of song called *Aolodia,* an elegiac song with accompaniment of the *Aulos.* This scale survived even in the Greek-Catholic song to the present day after the *Aulos* has vanished and in spite of the strong opposition of the Church Fathers to "chromatic" scales.[30]

Of all the close relationship with the *Aulos,* we still cannot say with certainty that the *Halil* had the same scale as the *Aulos* or what kind of scale it had, because there is no record whatsoever.

(c) *Alamoth* seems to have been a double-flute. The name bears a similarity to the Greek *Elymos* which, as Pindar tells us, was produced in Phrygia from a certain kind of wood, and to Phrygia it was originally imported from Assyria. In this case, the name *Elymos,* too, is possibly of Assyrian origin. It may come from *elamu*—confronting—usually employed for two

bodies close together and yet parted, which precisely fits the
structure of the double-pipe, as seen on the ancient bas-reliefs
and wall-pictures.[31]

The double-pipe, which is always found in the old orchestras
in Egypt, Assyria, and Greece, was highly regarded. In the
list of instruments of the Jerusalem Temple it is mentioned
once (1 Chron. 15: 20) as being assigned to the *Nevel* group.
In the lists of the instruments employed in the Second Temple
the *Alamoth* does not appear at all.

About the beginning of the Common Era the name *Magrepha* (pipe-organ) occurs which, as described in Talmudic literature, was similar to the syrinx and was constructed of a skin-
covered box into which were fastened ten reeds each with ten
holes, each hole being able to produce ten different notes, so
that the instrument could produce a thousand notes. The description concludes with the statement that it was used solely
for signal purposes: to call the priests and Levites to their
duties. Its tone, too, was very strong, so that it was heard as
far as Jericho, and it was impossible to hear one talk when the
Magrepha played.[32]

It is recorded in the Talmud that there was no water organ
(*organon hydraulium*) at the Temple, because of its sweet and
powerful voice which was able to distract attention from the
traditional instruments.[33]

The third kind of instruments used in Israel was the PER-
CUSSIVE group. Of the many names mentioned in the Bible,
we know with certainty that *Tof* was the little drum, but we are
not sure of its exact form. It was the most primitive and popular instrument among the Semitic tribes from ancient times as
a rhythm-indicator, and it was used for dances and joyous occasions. In earlier times the *tof* was used for religious celebrations likewise. King David still employed it at the installation
of the ark into Jerusalem (2 Sam. 6: 5). Nevertheless,

despite its being mentioned in the Psalms three times (81: 3; 149: 3; 150: 4), the drum is not listed among the musical instruments either of the First or of the Second Temple.

The only percussive instrument permanent in the Temple orchestra was the *Metziltayim*, or as it was called later, *Tziltzal* —cymbal (derived from the Hebrew term *tzalal*—to sound). It was constructed of copper, and it had a very strong sound, penetrating "as far as Jericho."

In the time of David and Solomon much stress was supposed to have been laid upon the cymbal and percussive instruments. The chief musician of David, Asaf, was a cymbal player (1 Chron. 16: 5). David brought a great number of various instruments of percussive character to celebrate the dedication of the sanctuary in Jerusalem, such as *Mena'anim* and *Shali-shim*. Ezra restored one hundred twenty-eight cymbal players of the Asaf family to their traditional function (Ezra 2: 41; 3: 10). However, in the last century of the Second Temple the percussive instruments were restricted to one cymbal which was used to mark pauses only, but not to participate while the singing and playing were going on.[34] All of the other kinds disappeared entirely.[35]

Finally we have to mention another signal instrument, the *Paamonim* (little bells) which were attached to the skirts of the robe of the High Priest. "And the sound thereof shall be heard when he goeth into the holy place before the Lord, and when he cometh out, that he die not" (Exod. 28: 35). This custom reminds us of the Egyptian *Sistrum* which, according to Plutarch, had a double aim: to call the attention of the worshippers to the sacred function in the sanctuary, and to drive away the evil typhon.[36]

Dance—*Machol*—was considered an integral part of religious ceremonies in ancient Israel. Even in the time of the Kingdom we hear, "David danced before the Lord with all his

might" (2 Sam. 6: 14).   In the Psalms religious dancing is
mentioned twice only (Ps. 149: 5; 150: 4), and it seems that
this custom fell into disuse in the Jerusalem Temple.   At least,
it is never mentioned in the Bible or in the Talmudic sources.
Only at non-devotional public entertainments, such as the celebration of "Water libation" on the festival of Tabernacles,
prominent MEN would dance, displaying artistic skill in throwing and catching burning torches.[37]   But the custom of procession around the sanctuary or around the altar was retained in
the Temple (Ps. 26: 6), especially on the feast of Tabernacles, accompanied with singing, "We beseech Thee, O Lord,
save; we beseech Thee, O Lord, make us now to prosper!"
concluding with, "Beauty to thee, O Altar," or "To God and to
thee, O Altar!"[38]

This custom survived in the synagogue in various forms and
is still practiced on different occasions up to the present day.

Participation of WOMEN in the Temple choir is nowhere
traceable.[39]   The statements recorded in Ezra (2: 65) and
Nehemiah (7: 67) refer to the secular musicians of the noble
families who possessed among the 7,337 servants some 200 or
245 male and female musicians.[40]   No reference is made to
their being Levites, i.e., of the traditionally sacred cast of
musicians.   Even the boastful statement of Sennacherib, the
Assyrian king, that King Hezekiah of Judah had to send him,
as part tribute, male and female musicians,[41] would refer to
secular singers of the court only.   The same could be said with
regard to the female mourners mentioned in Chronicles (2, 35:
25) who were professional public singers for funerals and the
like.   They still existed in the Mishnaic time.[42]

The Mishna gives the number of the instruments employed
in the Temple as follows:

Nevel, minimum two, maximum six.

Kinnor, minimum nine, maximum limitless.

Cymbal, only one.

Ḥalil, minimum two, maximum twelve.

Thus the total minimum number required for the orchestra was twelve instruments, to which number two *Ḥalilim* were added on twelve festal days during the year.[43] Such was the actual composition of the Temple orchestra toward the beginning of the Common Era. Once a year, at the above-mentioned "Water libation," it is reported that all the instruments, "an innumerable mass," would be employed.[44]

We notice that the percussive instruments were reduced to one cymbal, which, as we have mentioned before, was not employed in the music proper, but merely to mark pauses and intermissions. We further learn of the absence of the drum, as well as of the dance and bodily movements and all means by which rhythm is created and marked and without which the rhythm of any music is weakened and diluted. This fact gives us a clue to the understanding of the nature of the music performed at the Temple. We get a full comprehension of it, however, when we learn about the construction of the whole body, the ensemble, i.e., the vocal and instrumental forces.

The chorus had to consist, so the same Mishnaic source reports, of a minimum of twelve adult male singers, the maximum being limitless.[45] The singer was admitted to the choir at the age of thirty, and served up to fifty, the age when the decline of the voice began. Before his admittance he had to have a five years' training.[46] In addition to the twelve adults, boys of the Levites were permitted to participate in the choir, "in order to add sweetness to the song." [47]

Thus we see that the choir equaled the number of instruments. Later, the tendency toward the superiority of the vocal music was pronounced by the regulation that for playing the instruments even non-Levites were permitted, whereas for singers Levites alone were admitted.[48] Furthermore, the opinion was pronounced that the importance of music lies in the singing.[49]

The predominance of vocal music naturally grew out of the attitude toward music as a tool for the conveyance of ideas. Vocal music, by its intimate association with words, carried and interpreted thoughts and feelings; while instrumental music, according to Semitic-Oriental conception, serves only as accompaniment and embellishment. On the other hand, the tendency to restrict percussive, stirring and signal instruments, as well as dances and the participation of women, gives evidence of the striving to evade all the forms of pagan worship in use in Phœnicia and in all the countries bordering upon Palestine.

Although Jewish spiritual life sought to elevate the form of its musical expression, it, nevertheless, could not stay the development of virtuosity among its musicians at the Temple. It is recorded that a certain *Agades* (Hagros) was a virtuoso singer, and that in applying some brilliant tricks he would produce tremolos in Oriental manner which would fascinate the people. He kept his "art" a secret, and did not want to teach it to others. His professionalistic spirit brought down the scorn of the sages.[50]

This is about all that our sources report of the Temple music. There are no descriptions of the tunes retained, nor is there any indication of scales and rhythm employed, such as the Greek philosophers and authors left us. In Israel music was seemingly taught and preserved in oral tradition only, as is the custom in the Orient to the present day. Yet with the scant information at hand, let us try to visualize a musical performance at the Temple service in the last century B.C.E. as it is depicted in the Mishna.[51]

After the priests on duty had recited a benediction, the Ten Commandments, the *Shema* (Deut. 6: 4-9), the priestly benediction (Num. 6: 22-26) and three other benedictions, they proceeded to the act of the offerings. And after they were through with the arrangement of the sacrifices, one of them sounded the *Magrepha* (see above) which was the signal for the priests to enter the Temple to prostrate themselves, whereas for the Levites that sound marked the beginning of the musical performance. Two priests took their stand at the altar immediately and started to blow the trumpets *tekia-terua-tekia* (see above). After this performance, they approached Ben Arza, the cymbal player, and took their stand beside him, one at his right and the other at his left side. Whereupon, at a given sign with a flag by the superintendent, this Levite sounded his cymbal, and all the Levites began to sing a part of the daily Psalm. Whenever they finished a part they stopped, and the priests repeated their blowing of the trumpets and the people present prostrated themselves.

The texts sung by the Levites were not Psalms alone, but also portions of the Pentateuch.[52]

The description gives us a picture of the service and its musical rendition as conceived by laymen, without indicating whether the instruments accompanied the singers, or whether choir and orchestra worked alternately.

A short time after the destruction of the Temple the entire art of the instrumental music of the Levites fell into oblivion; and two generations later the sages totally lost all technical knowledge and all sense of the reality of that silenced music. They either exhausted themselves in praising the music of the Levites or in homilizing on the musical terminology as well as on the names of the instruments. The VOCAL music, however, the intonations of the Psalms and the Pentateuch, as well as the recitation of the prayers (see above), was most likely retained and transplanted into the Synagogue, the *Beth-Hak'neseth* (House of Assembly), an institution established long before the destruction of the Second Temple. We are informed that in Jerusalem many synagogues existed, and that even in the Temple court there were synagogues in which priests, Levites, and laymen would worship.[53]

The vocal song of the Temple, like all religious song among the ancient and primitive nations, drew its sap from the folk-song, though foreign tunes may have occasionally crept in. These Temple songs—folk-tunes modified and sanctified—were in turn copied by the "representatives of the people," the *Anshe Maamad*, from all parts of the country, who used to be present at the Temple service.[54] They certainly learned the melodies together with the texts, and would carry them to their homes. Furthermore, many Levites would participate in public services in the synagogues and were naturally chosen to act as precentors or leaders in singing Psalms, portions of the Pentateuch and the Prophets.

The FORMS in which the Psalms and prayers were rendered were explained by sages who lived in the first century. Of these, Rabbi Akiba had still witnessed the service in the Temple. From them we learn that three forms of public singing were customary, which were based upon the principle of response. In form A the leader intoned the first half verse, whereupon the congregation repeated it. Then the leader sang each succeeding half-line, the congregation always repeating the same first half-line which thus became a refrain throughout the entire song. This was the form in which ADULTS used to sing the "Hallel" (Ps. 113-118), and, according to Rabbi Akiba, this form was also employed for the Song of the Sea (Exod. 15). This form of singing the *Hallel* is still in use among the Jews in southern Arabia. In form B the leader sang a half-line at a time, and the congregation repeated what he had last sung. This—Rabbi Eliazar, son of Joseph Hagalili, said—was the form in which the children used to be instructed at school. Form C was responsive in the real sense, i.e., the leader would sing the whole first line, whereupon the congregation would respond with the second line of the verse. This was the form, as Rabbi Nehemiah explained, in which the *Shema* was recited in public; and it is still used by the Babylonian Jews for chanting the *Hallel* on Passover.[55]

We know that the ancient Assyrians and Babylonians had already used the responsive form, notably form A (refrain), in their laudations and supplications.[56] In ancient Israel, too, that form was popular. Refrains, as *Amen, Halleluyah, Hoshianah* (Oh, help!), *Anenu* (Answer us!), etc., were mostly used in public worship. And in accordance with the spiritual development of the people, we can follow a certain development in this form. While in ancient times, the people —in that they were primitive—were able to participate by responding with but one word, as those mentioned above, in later times we find a higher development of the people as shown in their response with phrases, for example, *Ki leolam Chasdo* (Ps. 118: 1-3; 136).

Besides the responsive form, the UNISON and SOLO forms were used. To antiphonal singing, i.e., to the alternate singing of balanced groups, we have but few references in the Bible (Deut. 27: 21-26), and it is described in the Mishna.[57]

Thus far we dealt with the SACRED music only. All we can gather about the SECULAR music in Israel indicates that it was of the same nature as the music of the neighboring nations in the Near East. As the many references in the Bible to the music performed in secular life testify, Israel enjoyed life through music both vocal and instrumental, and associated music with dance and wine in which men and women participated. The drum and cymbal, the harp and lyre, the small and the big pipe, were used. Rhythm played an important part, and in order to emphasize it, hand-clapping was employed. As a whole, we may say that in its FORMS, the secular music was similar to the Arabic music still used in Palestine and the Near East.

We learn that toward the beginning of the Common Era Greek song penetrated into Palestine,[58] and that people of education cultivated a great liking for it,[59] a fact which aroused the dismay of the pious spiritual leaders.[60]

As already stated above, all the explanations thus far give us no clue as to the TONALITY—scales and modes—of ancient Jewish song. We have no reference to its theoretical basis, for so far as we know, there never was written, as in the case of Greek music, a theory of Hebrew music.

There is, however, one authentic source preserved and at our disposal. And this is oral tradition!

Long before the destruction of the national sanctuary in Jerusalem, large Jewish settlements were established throughout the ancient world, from Persia to northwest Africa, and from Arabia to Rome,—settlements which cultivated spiritual values. After the complete ruin of the national center in Palestine, the remnants of Judea were scattered. They were taken into captivity, sold into slavery, and dispersed throughout the Roman Empire as far as the Pyrenean peninsula, the Rhine, and the Danube. They had lost their country, their independence; they had been robbed of their possessions, even of their human rights. But their spirit, their God, could not be taken away from them. Their spiritual values became their only treasure, a recompense for country and independence. And just as they had once defended their country against giants like Assyria, Egypt, Greece, and Rome, so they stood henceforth ready to give their life for their God and their culture—their spiritual creation embodied in a TRADITION! From that tradition we justly draw our information as to the nature of Jewish music and its history.

This musical tradition is preserved in memory and practice

in various Jewish centers in the East and in the West—centers whose existence continued since the destruction of the Second Temple, and in some instances from even before that event, throughout the ages up to this very day. These centers are:

YEMEN in South Arabia, historically known from pre-Mohammedan times, a community that lived practically in seclusion for thirteen hundred years, and evidence of whose contact with other Jewish settlements we have but scant sources;

BABYLONIA, historically the oldest Jewish settlement, dating from the destruction of the First Temple, never ceasing to exist despite changes of conditions;

PERSIA, almost as old as the Babylonian community. SYRIA, NORTH AFRICA, ITALY, and the so-called SEPHARDIM, i.e., the Spanish Jews expelled from Spain in 1492, who, despite dispersion, did preserve their SPANISH tradition;

The GERMAN JEWS, whose settlement in southwestern Germany dates back to the fifth century;

And the Jewish settlement in EASTERN EUROPE, the largest center of all in number, whose tradition comes partly from Germany and partly from the Oriental communities.

The results of our investigations of the traditional song of these communities enable us to construct the features of Jewish song; and the analysis of that tradition reveals to us its elements, its originality, its development, and its growth—in a word—its history.[61]

CHAPTER II

Jewish music is the song of Judaism through the lips of the Jew. It is the tonal expression of Jewish life and development over a period of more than two thousand years. To place that song into its ancient and original setting, we must seek the beginning of the people itself. In so doing, we see that just as the Jew, being of Semitic stock, is a part of the Oriental world, so Jewish music—coming to life in the Near East—is, generally speaking, of one piece with the music of the Orient. It takes its trend of development through the Semitic race, and retains its SEMITIC-ORIENTAL CHARACTERISTICS in spite of non-Semitic—Altaic and European—influence. Jewish song achieves its unique qualities through the sentiments and the life of the Jewish people. Its DISTINGUISHING CHARACTERISTICS are the result of the spiritual life and struggle of that people.

Hence, in order to recognize the Oriental elements in Jewish song, it is indispensable that we assure ourselves of a common understanding of the basic elements of Semitic-Oriental music.[1]

In the first place, Oriental music—whether Semitic, Altaic, or Hindu—is based on the modal form.

(a) A MODE (in Arabic and Persian: *Makam* or *Naghana*) is composed of a number of MOTIVES (i.e., short music figures or groups of tones) within a certain scale. The motives have different functions. There are beginning and concluding motives, and motives of conjunctive and disjunctive character. The composer operates with the material of these traditional

24

folk motives within a certain mode for his creations. His composition is nothing but his arrangement and combination of these limited number of motives. His "freedom" of creation consists further in embellishments and in modulations from one mode to the other.[2] Sixteen of these modes are most widely known throughout the Near East.

(b) The next element is the emphasis upon ORNAMENT. Oriental music is unthinkable in long sustained tones. On the contrary, it is of a vivid tonal character. Either a note is short, or if long, it quavers in a tremolo and is adorned with ornaments.

(c) Oriental music is chiefly UNRHYTHMICAL (in Arabic: *Tartil*—narrative or recitative). It is mostly rendered by a solo voice with accompaniment of the *Ud*, a kind of lyre or mandolin, or *Kanun*, resembling a guitar. The accompaniment is only a repetition of the melodic line rendered by the singer with some variations. Rhythmical music (in Arabic: *Anshada*) is used for dancing and bodily movements, and is considered inferior to the unrhythmical *Tartil*.

(d) The TONALITY in the Oriental music is based on a quarter-tone system. Thus a scale of an octave has twenty-four steps. The perfect consonance of the octave is known to the Oriental musician by the Arabic term *jewab* (answer, echo, repetition). However, seldom does the melodic construction show the tendency of the octachordal line, for the folk-tunes are usually built on the tetrachordal or pentachordal range.

As a result of the quarter tones there are a great variety of scales in existence, many of which are rather artificial inventions and subtle combinations which are not used often. The most popular scales are: I. d¾—e¾—f¼—g¼—a¾—b¾—c¼—d, which corresponds to the ancient Greek Phrygian (the medieval Dorian): d¹—e½—f¹—g¹— a¹—b½—c¹—d; and has the character of minor. II. e¾—f¾—g¼— a¾—b¾—c¼—d¾—e; which corresponds to the ancient Greek Dorian (the medieval Phrygian): $e^{1/2}$—f^1—g^1—a^1—$b^{1/2}$—c^1—d^1—e; and is no longer used in modern music. III. $f^{1/4}$—$g^{1/4}$—$a^{3/4}$—$bb^{1/4}$—$c^{1/4}$—$d^{3/4}$—$e^{3/4}$—f, which is similar to the ancient Greek Lydian with b flat; and has almost the character of major, with the exception of the seventh (e) which is a quarter flat. IV. $d^{3/4}$—$eb^{3/4}$—$f^{\#3/4}$—$g^{1/4}$—$a^{3/4}$—$b^{3/4}$—$c^{1/4}$—d is in its first tetrachord (d-g) similar to the scale of the *Aulos* (see Chapter I), and corresponds to the *Ahavoh-Rabboh* scale (Chapter IV): $d^{3/4}$—$eb^{3/4}$—$f^{\#3/4}$—$g^{1/4}$—$a^{3/4}$—$bb^{1/4}$—$e^{1/4}$—d. On each of these scales several modes are based.[3]

The Oriental musicians have the habit of mixing scales to combination-scales, as for example the mode called "Sabba" which is based on the scale: d—e—f—gb—a—bb—c—db—eb—f, which is merged of scales I and IV. Or some scales receive a different order in the higher octave, as in the case of scale IV, which continues in the octave as follows: d—e—f—g.

Whether or not Jewish music, in its *origin,* was based on or even affected by a quarter-tone system, we have not sufficient data to prove or disprove. Only these facts are incontrovertible: (1) that the four scales just explained are those on which practically all Jewish song is based; (2) that in the ORIENT the Jews sing in those scales, using the quarter-tone steps of their neighbors, while (3) the Jews of the OCCIDENT employ the same scales with steps of the semi-tone system; (4) that despite the resultant variance, Synagogue song remains identical the world over, because these differences in tonality are of sufficiently minor importance not to change the character of the music. Compare the technical differences listed in the preceding paragraph.

(e) The Oriental musicians and laymen are fond of IMPROVISATION. Even set tunes are largely varied and modified. The improvisation occurs in a certain mode, and the improviser has to operate with the traditional motives therein.

(f) Oriental music is WITHOUT ANY HARMONY. The only beauty the Oriental finds is in the melodic line and in the intricate ornamentation. Occasionally in unison singing of a group there are fourths or fifths, due solely to the range of the voices, but not to harmonic instincts, because the people sing frequently in seconds or in any other "discord."

(g) Oriental music has retained the FOLK CHARACTER. Therefore, unlike the art music of Europe, which can be understood by the few only, the song of the Orient is understood by all.

(h) The folk-character is pronounced also in the FORM. Most of the set tunes consist of very short phrases. Only a few have two or three phrases. The most compound form seems to be the *Bashraw* (Turkish *Pashraw*), a Rondo form in the scheme a—b—a—c—a

(i) Music is never written down, but transmitted ORALLY. Consequently, "EAR"-MARKS were developed by which music is recognized. The entire theory of Oriental music is based upon these "ear"-marks,[4] i.e., signs for musical patterns learned by ear.

All these elements and features are to be found in the religious and secular music of the Mohammedans and of the Oriental Christian churches: the Greek, the Jacobite, the Nestorian, and the Maronite.

"Music" is primarily vocal. Instrumental music, never rising above accompaniment, does not present an art in itself. It is forbidden in Mohammedan and Christian Oriental worship.

Women are excluded from participation in religious music.

This brief description holds true particularly of the Semitic-Oriental music. It distinguishes itself from the music of the other Oriental races by its preference for the scales cited above and the modes built on them.

In addition, it should be mentioned that minor—scale I— is not considered SAD, nor is major—scale III—considered joy-

ous. Quite the contrary, the first scale is the basis upon which
very joyous tunes are built, while scale III serves for serious
music. Moods are rather expressed by the rhythmical construction of the motives. Scale IV is described by the Greek
Church musicians as "sad," and is employed for supplications
and occasions like funerals; whereas to the Turks the same
scale lends itself to the expression of fervent, passionate sentiments. Since music is mainly vocal, its rhythm, when there is
any, is not like that of European music divided in small measures such as ⅜, ¾, ²⁄₄, ⁴⁄₄, ⁶⁄₈, etc., but is derived from the meter
of the text. In other words, the metrical text leaves the impress of its meter upon its tune.

As a rule, a tune is constructed according to the length of a stanza
of two lines (in Arabic *baith*), and since most folk-songs are syllabic,
each syllable having one note (embellishments are not counted), the
number of the time-units of a tune must be equal to the number of
the syllables in the stanza. These time-units (in Greek: *chronos
protos*) run from three to thirty-two. There are LONG units, similar
to the European whole measure ○; HALF unit— ♩; SMALL unit— ♩;
and HALF-SMALL unit— ♪.

In Oriental music provision was also made for the desig-
nation of tempo, as slow, vivacious, sad, moderato, soft, and
so forth.[5]

Of the account thus far given, the musical examples in the
tables I-III will offer sufficient illustration. Table I contains
examples of Arabic folk-tunes (a) secular (1-6, 8), popular in Palestine and Syria, (b) religious, of which example 7
is the tune in which the Muezzin calls the people to prayer, beginning with the familiar formula: "Allah is great, there is
no God besides Allah and Mohammed is the messenger of
Allah. Hasten to prayer, hasten to service!" This musical
version is customary in Palestine. It is in unrhythmical MODAL

TABLE I
Arabic Tunes
a) Secular

b) Religious

Mode: Hedjaz

(Mohammedan)

7. Al-la - huakbar, al-la - - hu akbar! Al-la-hu

ak-bar, al-la - - huakbar! ish-ha-du la i - la-ha il-

la l-la.____ ish-ha-du la i-la-ha il-la l-la.

ish-ha-du anna Mu-ham-ma dar-ra-sul Al-la.____ ish-ha-du

il - la. Mu-ham-ma dar ra-sul Al-la.

ḥay-ya a-laṣ sal-lat.
- - - lfa - lah

a-las sal-lat.____
- lal-fa-lah.____

Al - la-hu ak-bar, Al-la - - huakbar, la i - la il la Al-la.

As-sal-latu____ was-sal-la____ mu a-la-yik,

ya aw-wela hal-kil - lah ____ wa-ḥa-ta-ma rús sul Al-lah.

Mode: Huseni

I   II

8.

TABLE II
Jacobite Church-Songs
a) Unrhythmical

5. Ey _____ sham-li_ fe - ro-so de_ men ke - - - - - dim. do - - - - wid ____ it - na - - - - - - - bi. do - wid ___ it - - na - bi we - - - - - mar.

b) Rhythmical

Andante

6. Ka-bel - lo mo-ran le-fir-mo ho - no min i - dayn, ach fir-mey de - ah-run dak-lo mu-to min a - mo.

Mode: sh'bioyoh (Seventh tone)

M.M. ♩=132

7. *Fine* D.F.

Maronite Song

Moderato

8. Ka - dish ka - dish - at, Ka - dish bkhul e - don, a - blo - ho insha-bho mka - dash lka - di - she.

TABLE III
Greek Church Tunes

Al-le-lu-i-a al - le-lu-i-a, Al le-lu - i-a.

form, in the so-called *Makam Hedjaz*. The secular tunes are likewise based upon MODES (*Makams*).

The illustrations are in *Bayati* (1-3), the most popular Arabic mode; in *Siga* (4), *Sasgar* (5), *Nawa* (6), and *Huseni* (8), which are also popular throughout Palestine and Syria, as well as in Arabia and Mesopotamia. In No. 7 we recognize motives which repeat themselves with some variations.[6]

Table II gives a selection of religious songs of the Syriac-Orthodox Church, called the "Jacobite Church." We see that they have the same scales, forms, and modes as the Arabic song. They are mostly unrhythmical (1-5) in syllabic form (1-4), in free modal form (5); and only part of them indicate strict rhythm similar to European measures (6-8). The last tune (8) is from the Maronite Church of Lebanon, and is used for various texts. The custom of adopting tunes for different texts is general in the Orient.

The Arabic scales and modes used in the Jacobite Church received other names ("first" to "eighth tone"). Example 4 gives a Psalm-tune (91:1) in a tetrachordal line, and example 5 is a solo in the *Hedjaz mode*, resembling the modal form of table 1 (7).[7]

Table III furnishes us with some examples of the Greek Church tunes. They, too, have the same characteristics in scales, modes, forms, as the Mohammedan and the Christian song. We note that 2 and 7 have the "chromatic" scale, or the *Hedjaz*; 1 and 3 have scale I; 4 and 5 have scale II; and 6 and 8, scale III. Their form is MODAL, partly syllabic, partly embellished (8).[8]

These illustrations will later serve the purpose of comparative study with the Synagogue song. At present they may enable us to familiarize ourselves with the essential elements of the song of the Near East, the song of that spot which constituted the cradle of the Jewish people.

CHAPTER III

The public reading of the Bible as performed in ancient times, and as still done in the Orthodox Synagogue, was not according to the manner now employed in the Reform Synagogue (since 1815). In the latter it is simply spoken or declaimed without any musical flavor, whereas the manner of reading, according to tradition, is a cantillation, a chanting of the text, a recitation in which music plays a great part. This way of reading the Bible is mentioned in ancient times—at least as far back as the first century. It was not the general manner of public reading, for in the Orient the usual public reading is done in declamation as in the Occident. There may be more flavor in the voice, but it is without musical tone. This usage is true of the Arabs to the present day, whereas the reading of the Koran is done in the same manner as the traditional reading of the Bible. There is, therefore, no foundation for the current notion that the cantillation of the Bible is derived from the Oriental manner of reading in public. It seems rather to indicate that it was introduced in order to arouse the interest of the hearers through the setting of the text to music. The Talmud says that the Bible should be read in public and made understood to the hearers in a musical, sweet tune. And he who reads the Pentateuch without tune shows disregard for it and the vital value of its laws.[1] A deep understanding can be achieved only by singing the Torah (naturally, in the traditional tunes), and "whoever intones the Holy Scriptures in the manner of secular song abuses the Torah." [2]

These statements of the Talmud from the first centuries C.E. prove that the musical performance of the reading of the Bible in public was intentionally instituted. This becomes more evident through observation of the fact that only those books of the Bible are provided with tunes the public reading of which was obligatory. These books are: the Pentateuch, the Prophets, Esther, Lamentations, Ruth, Ecclesiastes, Song of Songs, Psalms, and, in some communities, Job; whereas Proverbs,

FACSIMILE 1.

Accents: Pentateuch (Leviticus 22:26-33; 23:1-7)
Italian MS. 15th Century. Hebrew Union College Library.

FACSIMILE 2.

Accents: Prophets (1 Samuel 15:1-6)
Italian MS. 15th Century. H. U. C. Library.

וַיַּעַן אִיּוֹב וַיֹּאמַר · ﬞ · · יֹאבַד יוֹם אוּלַּד בּוֹ

וְהַלַּיְלָה אָמַר הֹרָה גָּבֶר · הַיּוֹם הַהוּא הָיָה יְהִי חֹשֶׁךְ

אַל יִדְרְשֵׁהוּ אֱלוֹהַּ מִמַּעַל · וְאַל תּוֹפַע עָלָיו נְהָרָה

יִגְאָלֻהוּ חֹשֶׁךְ וְצַלְמָוֶת תִּשְׁכָּן עָלָיו עֲנָנָה יְבַעֲתֻהוּ כִּמְרִירֵי יוֹם

הַלַּיְלָה הַהוּא יִקָּחֵהוּ אֹפֶל אַל יִחַדְּ בִּימֵי שָׁנָה בְּמִסְפַּר יְרָחִים

אַל יָבֹא הִנֵּה הַלַּיְלָה ﬞי· · הַהוּא יְהִי גַלְמוּד

אַל תָּבֹא רְנָנָה בוֹ · יִקְּבֻהוּ אֹרְרֵי יוֹם

הָעֲתִידִים עֹרֵר לִוְיָתָן · יֶחְשְׁכוּ כּוֹכְבֵי נִשְׁפּוֹ

יְקַו לְאוֹר וָאַיִן וְאַל יִרְאֶה · בְּעַפְעַפֵּי שָׁחַר

מִלֹּא אָסַנְגֹר דַּלְתֵי בִטְנִי זֵ · וַיַּסְתֵּר עָמָל מֵעֵינָי ;

לָמָּה לֹא מֵרֶחֶם אָמֻת · מִבֶּטֶן יָצָאתִי וְאֶגְוָע ;

מַדּוּעַ קִדְּמוּנִי בִרְכַּיִם ; וּמַה שָּׁדַיִם כִּי אִינָק ;

כִּי עַתָּה שָׁכַבְתִּי וְאֶשְׁקוֹט · יָשַׁנְתִּי אָז יָנוּחַ לִי ;

עִם מְלָכִים וְיוֹעֲצֵי אָרֶץ · הַבֹּנִים חֳרָבוֹת לָמוֹ ;

FACSIMILE 3.
  Accents: (Job 3 : 2-14)
  MS. 13th Century. H. U. C. Library.

FACSIMILE 4.
  Reuchlin, De Accentibus. Pub. Hagenau, 1518. H. U. C. Library.

Ezra, Nehemiah, and Chronicles have no tunes, because they
were not read in the public service.

The obligation to read these books is very old. We know,
for instance, that EZRA was the first to introduce the reading
of the Pentateuch in public (fifth century B.C.E.). Psalms,
as is known, were sung in the Temple in Jerusalem. And we
have testimony that the Prophets were read in public service
as Haftara—the concluding portion after the reading of the
Pentateuch—during the latter part of the existence of the
Second Temple, for we know that Jesus was asked to read from
the Prophets in the Synagogue service.[3] The Book of Esther
has been read since about the time of the Maccabees [4]; Lamentations, at least since the destruction of the Second Temple;
while as to the Song of Songs, Ruth, and Ecclesiastes,we have
evidence that they were read as far back as the first century.[5]
Thus, we see that this ancient usage had its origin in Palestine
during the time when the bulk of the Jewish people still lived
there.

As proof of the antiquity of the traditional tunes in which
the Scriptures are chanted, we cite their Oriental origin. They
bear the distinctive marks of the Semitic-Oriental song explained in the second chapter. They have the modal form
and character; they are furthermore unrhythmical and are
based upon three of the four scales usual in the song of the
Semitic Near East.

Though this ancient part of Jewish song has much in common with the song of the East, its motives and consequently its
expression distinguish it from the rest of the body of Oriental
song.

In the Bible the predominance of the motive is the most outstanding characteristic. The motives of the Biblical modes are
regulated in a strict syntactical order. They are arranged not
only in disjunctives and conjunctives, as closing or binding

motives (in Hebrew *mafsikim*—disjunctives, *mesharethim*—conjunctives), but these two groups are subdivided into primary and secondary disjunctives; motives which express the ending of a complete verse, and those which indicate the conclusion of its parts. Originally, the motives were classified also as to their TONAL, DYNAMICAL (forte or piano), and TIME value (allegro or lento, etc.). There are rules governing the succession of motives into a musical phrase, a melodic line within a certain mode.

But before describing the THEORY of the MOTIVES, it is necessary to familiarize ourselves with the MODES, in order to see the practical application of the motives, how by their stratification and musical phrases, specific melodic lines are created which mark the distinctive characteristics of a certain mode.

(a) THE PENTATEUCH MODE is founded upon the scale e—f—g—a + b—c—d—e which is identical with the ancient Greek Dorian and with scale II of Oriental music (chapter 2nd). Its chief feature is its tetrachordal basis, for the scale is constituted of two tetrachords: e—a + b—d in disjunctive form, which means that between the tetrachords there is an interval of a whole step (a—b).

For the better understanding of the nature and development of Jewish song, we give numerous illustrations to assure a clear view of the most essential elements. The "bars" in the unrhythmical examples do not mark rhythm, but indicate the motives of the modes. This procedure enables us to grasp the way the motives are employed within the modes.

We give an example of the mode of the Pentateuch according to the tradition of the Babylonian Jews (table IV, 1). A comparison of this reading with the tradition of the Amsterdam Portuguese community (written down by David Pinna at the end of the seventeenth century [6]) proves: first, that the two chants are identical, despite the geographical distance between the people who employ them; secondly, that the tonality of the Amsterdam version is remolded according to the European system of half and whole steps, whereas the Babylonian version shows the Oriental tonality of ¾ steps instead of whole steps, as indicated in table IV, 1, (Chapter II). Furthermore, we learn from

TABLE IV
Pentateuch

Exod. 18, 1-2 (Babylonian)

1. Way-yik-ra mo-she.___ le-chol zik-ne yis-ra-el wa-yo-mer a-le-hem.

mi-she-chu___ uk-hu la-chem___ son___ le-mish-pe-ho-the-chem,

we-sha-ha-tu hap-pa-sah. ul-ka-tem_____ a gud-dath e-

zob___ ut-bal-tem___ bad-dam a-sher bas-saf, we-hig-ga-tem

el ham-mash-kof we-el she-te ha-me-zu-zoth min haddam a-sher bas-saf.

we-at-tem___ lo___ the-se-u___ ish mip-pe-sah be-tho ad bo-ker.

Genesis 48, 15-16 (Portuguese-Amsterdam)

2. Way-ba-rech eth yo-sef way-yo-mar. ha-e-lo-him___ a-sher___

hith-ha-le-chu a-bo-thay le-fo-naw ab-ra-ham we yis-hak. ha-e-lo-him

ha-ro-e o-thi, me-o-di ad hay-yom haz-ze. ham-mal-ach___

hag-go-el o-thi mik-kol ra ye-ba-rech

eth ha-ne-a-rim we-yik-ka-re ba-hem she-mi we-shem a-bo-thay

ab-ra-ham we-yis-hak, we-yid-gu la-rob be-ke-rob ha-a-res.

Song of Songs 1; 1-2; 3, 2   (Ashkenazic-Lithuania)

Shir hash-shi-rim a-sher lish-lo-mo. yish-sho-ke-ni mi-ne-shi-kos.

pi-hu, ki to-vim,do-de-cho miy-yo-yim. o-ku-mo no va-a-so-va-voh

vo-ir, bash-vo-kim u-vo-re-cho-vos, a-vak-sho

es she-o-ha-vo naf-shi. bik-kash-tiv ve-lo me-tso-siv.

(Ashkenazic)

Exod. 18, 1-2

Vay-yik-ro mo-she le-chol zik-ne yis-ro-el vay-yo-mer

a-le-hem. mish-chu u-ke-chu lo-chem tson.

le-mish-pe-cho se-chem ve-sha-cha-tu hap-po-sach.

ul-kach-tem   a-gud-das   e - zov   ut-val-tem

bad-dom   a-sher bas-sof,   ve-hig-ga-tem   el ham-mash-kof

ve-el she-te ham-zu-zos,   min-had-dam   a-sher bas-saf.

ve-a - tem   lo   se-tse-u   ish mip-pe-sach be-so   ad-bo-ker.

Exod.15. 3

a - do-noy   ish mil-chô-moh,   a - do -noy   she-mo.

Kyrie eleison (Third tone, Gregorian)

5

Ky - ri-e   e - lei - son,   Do-mi-ne   mi - se - re - re

Chris-tus⸺⸺   Do-mi - nus. Fac-tus est   o - be-di - ens

us-que ad 'mor-tem.Qui pas-su-rus   ad-ve - nis-ti prop-ter nos

Exod. 15. 1-2   (Carpentras)

6

Az ya-shir mo-che   ub-ne yis-ra - el   eth ha-shi - ra

ha-zoth la-do-nay   va - yo-me-ru   le-mor   a - shi-ra

la-do-nay ki-ga-o   ga-a,   sus ve-ro-che-vo ra - ma   ba-yam.

the Amsterdam example that since the seventeenth century no changes in the Pentateuch mode are noticeable.

This mode is common in all Oriental and Italian synagogues with the exception of the Yemenite and Spanish-Oriental. Neither does it occur in the Ashkenazic synagogues.

Example 3 (table IV) shows the same mode used for the Song of Songs by the Ashkenazic communities in Eastern Europe and notably in Lithuania, with the one difference, that through German influence the MAJOR scale was applied and the tonic became c instead of e. This procedure of changing the ancient Dorian scale (scale II in Chapter II) to the major is typical in the Ashkenazic song of the Synagogue, and we will witness it repeatedly in the course of our discussions.

Another peculiarity we notice in example 3 is the transfer of the mode from the Pentateuch to the Song of Songs. The transfer of a mode of one text to another text in the Bible is to be found in other cases, as we shall see later.

Of quite different character is the Pentateuch mode of the Ashkenazic communities. Its scale is: f—g—a♭—b—c—d—e—f, i.e., the Lydian, and it has major character, though several motives are identical with motives of examples 1-2, as evidenced by the "Comparative Table" of this mode's motives in their forms in the different communities. In this table we notice that the essential motives of the Babylonian (1), Bokharian (2), Persian (3), Syriac (4), Moroccan (5), Gibraltarian (6), Italian (7), Sephardic in France (8), Sephardic in Amsterdam (9), Sephardic in Egypt and Palestine (10), and the Ashkenazic for Canticles (13) are practically alike. In contrast to these evident similarities, example 11 shows the variants in the Ashkenazic tradition. These variants, however, are of no recent date, for their inclusion in the table of motives of the Pentateuch mode printed in 1518 in the Hebrew Grammar of Johann Reuchlin [7] (see example 12) proves that the mode in this form was already at that time considered traditional by the German Jews.

The Ashkenazic mode is similar to that in use in the Jewish communities in Southern France, in Carpentras and Avignon (example 6).[8] Now history tells us that the Ashkenazic tradition is the youngest, that spiritual life in the Jewish settlement in southwestern Germany starts about the ninth or tenth century, and that some of its prominent au-

Comparative table of accent motives for the intoning of the Pentateuch

talša gědola   zarqa   pazer   gereš

talša qĕṭana

zarqa

zarqa

zarqa

tĕren qadmin   zarqa   azla gereš

šalšelet

pašta kefulla

thorities were natives of Southern France or Provence [9] or of Italy.[10] These facts may explain why so many similarities between the Ashkenazic (German) and the Southern French and Italian songs of the Synagogue are to be found. In Chapter VIII we shall have some examples of them.

At the same time, much similarity is to be found between the mode of the Pentateuch in its Oriental version and the third Gregorian mode (the ancient Greek Dorian), for which example 5 (Kyrie eleison) may offer evidence. It is quite certain that the Synagogue did not borrow that mode from the Church, since it is the tradition of those communities, which, like the Babylonian, never came into contact with the Roman Church. Quite to the contrary, we know that the Christian Church in the first centuries took over many elements from the Jewish song, as repeatedly testified to by ancient authors and reaffirmed by historians of our day.[11] The Gregorian song, by establishing for "Plain Chant" the rule of equal time-value for all notes of the chant, robbed the song, which it had borrowed from the Synagogue, of its distinctive features: the unrhythmical, free character of improvisation, and the embellishment, which is the very color of Oriental life.

The mode of the Pentateuch expresses dignity and is elevating in spirit. It has not lost its vitality and elasticity, nor its attractiveness to the Jew of the old school, and if rendered in a proper way,[12] also to the modern Jew, despite its antiquity.

(b) The mode of RUTH is built on the same scale as that of the Pentateuch, but its motives are of a different nature, for we hear a pronounced lyric strain in them (table V). The comparison between the Babylonian and Ashkenazic versions clearly shows their identity. In the Ashkenazic version we notice the European influence in changing the scale from Dorian to major, by making "c" the tonic instead of "e," a change similar to what we saw in the mode of the Pentateuch and the Song of Songs.[13]

(c) ECCLESIASTES is chanted in the mode of Ruth in most communities.

Thus far we have discussed the regular mode of the Pentateuch and closely related modes.

(d) For the POETICAL PORTIONS of the Pentateuch special modes are employed in several communities. These poetical versions are, ac-

TABLE V
Ruth

Ruth 1, 1-2 (Babylonian-Ashkenazic)

1 Babyl.

way-hi, bi-me she-fot hash-shof-tim way-hi ra-ab ba-a-res

2 Ashkenaz.

1 way-ye-lech ish mib-beth le-hem ye-hu-da

2

1 la-gur bis-de mo-ab hu we-ish-to ush-ne ba-naw

2

Intonation of the Song of Songs

(Lithuanian)

Šir ha-ši-rim ă-šer liš-lej-mej. Ji-šo-ke-ni mi-ně-ši-kejs pi-hu

ki tej-wim dej-de-ho mi-jo-jin O-ku-mo no vă-ă-sej-wě wo wo-

ir baš-wo-kim u-vo-rě-hej-vejss a-vak-šo

ejs še-o-há-vo naf-ši bi-kaš-tiv vě-lej mě-tso siv. Ad še-jo-fu-ah

ha-yejm ve-no-su ha-tze-lo-lim sejw dmej lě-ho dje-di litz-

vi ej lě-ej-fer ho-ă-jo-lim al ho-rejvo - ser.

TABLE VI
Tunes for the Poetry of the Pentateuch

(Yemenite)

Exod. 15. 1

1. Oz yo-shir mo-she uv - ne yis - ro - el   es

hash-shi-roh haz-zoth   la - do - noy,

way - yo - me - ru   le - mor.

Exod. 20. 2

2. O - no - chi   a - do-noy e - lo - he -

choh,   a - sher ho - se - si - choh

me-e - res mis-ra - yim,   mib-beth a - bo - dim.

(Portuguese)

Exod. 15. 1

3. Az ya-shir mo-she uv - ne yis-ra - el   et hash-shi-ra haz-

zot   la - do - nay   way - yo - me-ru le - mor.

cording to tradition: the Song of the Sea (Exod. 15), the Ten Commandments (Exod. 20:2-17) (Deut. 5:6-18), and the Blessing of Moses (Deut. 33). They are marked by the special way in which they are written in the scroll, the verses being set in this form: ───── ───────── ───── ───────── called in the Talmud *ariach all gabbe levena* = a log (long line) upon a brick (short line), like the structure of a wall.[14] Deut. 32 is not considered a poem because it is not of a joyous nature and, therefore, it is not written in the poetical form, but the lines are divided in two straight columns, called "log upon log," [15] ═══ ═══.

The Yemenite and Persian communities have a special tune for the "poems," as given in table VI, 1-2. The Moroccan, Italian, Portuguese, and Southern French communities have rhythmical tunes for the Song of the Sea alone. Some of the communities, as the Southern French, have a special tune for the Song of the Sea, for every festival. The best known tune is given in table VI, 3. It reminds one of the second part of example 6 in table IV given for the same text. The tune may be a creation out of the Psalm mode of which we shall speak later, or even of the Pentateuch mode, according to the French-German version.

(e) THE MODE OF THE PROPHETS, like the mode of the Pentateuch, is based upon a tetrachordal system, on the scale d—e—f—g plus a—b—c—d. This scale is the same as the ancient Greek Phrygian, or the first Gregorian mode or scale I, discussed in Chapter II, and it is identical with the scale of the Arabic mode *Bayati* (Chapter II). In some instances it is changed to the scale: d^1—$e^{1/2}$—f^1—g + g^1—$a^{1/2}$—bb^1—c, the scale of the plagal of the first Gregorian mode, called the second mode (Hypodorian). This is the standard scale in Jewish music, not only in Synagogue song but also in folk-song. Nearly eighty per cent of all Jewish folk-song is based upon it. This scale expresses what in Hebrew is called *hishtapchuth hannefesh*—the outpouring of the soul, and it is, therefore, used for the exhortation of the Prophets as well as for Lamentations and for a part of the Psalms, that is, for those emotional texts the contents of which are pleading or fervent. It seems that the Prophetic mode is one of the chief strains in Semitic music, and was even more at home among the Hebrew people in ancient times than later, for the Yemenite and Persian Jews use the Prophetic mode for the Pentateuch also. Although the mode has the character of minor, it is, nevertheless, not melancholy because it has a note of hope—of promise. It expresses a fine and tender sentiment, and turns frequently to a bright and even joyous mood. Of course, according to West European and especially Anglo-Saxon feeling, the mode sounds sad, for these peoples prefer the major; and to them any minor tune is melancholy.

The Prophetic mode has been well preserved through the obligatory chanting of a portion of the Prophets—*Haftara*—after the reading of the Pentateuch. This mode is built of motives just as is the mode of the Pentateuch. See the illustrations in table VII. We recognize in 1 and 2 the same mode. While the Yemenites use it for the Pentateuch, it was transferred by the Persians to the Song of Songs. A similar procedure we found in the application of the Pentateuchal mode for the Song of Songs by the Ashkenazim in Eastern Europe. In example 3 we see the single tetrachordal range of the Yemenite mode, while in 4-6 we recognize a double tetrachord in a heptachord, which scale corresponds to the Hypodorian mentioned above. Example 6, the East European tradition, is closer to the Yemenite and Persian modes given in 1-2.

The Ashkenazim employ a special motive as an ending motive of the reading of the Pentateuch (see 7). This motive leads over to the parallel minor scale, and was apparently invented to lead the reader into the scale of the mode of the Prophets, the chanting of which follows immediately thereafter. Later we shall meet the same motive employed in like capacity in other modes. It is most likely derived from the Ashkenazic *athnah* motive of the Prophets, as may be clearly seen in example 5 (*eved adonoy*).

(f) In the scale of the Prophetic mode, there is also the mode of LAMENTATIONS which has the same tetrachordal character, except among the Ashkenazim, with whom the tradition was so modified by European influence as to give special emphasis to the third and fifth tones, a distinctive characteristic of the eight-tone scale.

The lamentative character of the mode of Lamentations is expressed mainly through the melodic line which is short and produces the effect of depression. Especially the verses of the third chapter are short and remind one somehow of the pentameter in which the Greeks wrote lamentations. Though the mode of Lamentations is common to all communities, yet each has peculiarities of its own. For instance, the

TABLE VII
Prophets

TABLE VIII
Lamentations

Lam. 5. 1-2
Sephardic Sephardic-Ashkenazic

4 Ze-chora-do-nay me ha-ya la-nu hab-bi-ta ur-e eth her-pa-the-nu.

Ashkenazic

na-ha-la-the-nu ne-hef-chale-zo-rim, ba-te - nu le - noch -rin

Lam. 4. 16. Gregorian Chant

5 phe 16.Fa-ci - es Do - mi-ni di -vi-sit e - os.

non ad-det ut re - spi - ci - at e - os. Fa-ci - es sa-cer-do -

tum non e - ru - bu-e - runt. e - que se-num mi-ser - ti sunt.

Gregorian Chant (Prima lectio)

6 In - ci-pit la - men-ta - ti - o Je -re-mi-ae pro-phe - tae.

A - leph.

Babylonian mode has a local concluding motive which is to be found also in the traditional song of the Jacobite Church and in the Song of the Copts in Egypt.[16]   Striking similarity to the mode of Lamentations is to be found in the Gregorian chant.   In table VIII we illustrate the Babylonian (1), the Portuguese (2), and the Ashkenazic (3) tradition, and we give a comparative example (Ashkenazic-Sephardic) (4).   Further we present two examples of the Gregorian chant for Lamentations, as they are rendered on the night of Easter (5-6). The first is more similar to the Jewish Oriental mode, while the second comes near to the Portuguese and Ashkenazic version, though its scale is that of the first mode (Dorian), and the Jewish scale is based upon the Hypodorian.

The Book of Lamentations is chanted in the Synagogue on the ninth of Ab, in the evening and in the morning, in commemoration of the destruction of the Temple in Jerusalem.

(g) The mode of Job.

The three books of the Writings, Job, Proverbs, and Psalms, have the peculiar construction of short two-part phrases.   Of the reason for this form we are not certain, but it gives the impression that its purpose was to make the verses suitable for public singing and response.   In Job, out of 1,070 verses, 1,000 are two-part; 67 have three or four parts; and only three verses have five parts.   But these four and five part verses are only in the first two chapters and in the last one, which are in prose, while the verses of the poetic portion of the book from Chapter III to Chapter XLII, 7, are of two parts. Likewise with the Book of Proverbs: out of 915 verses, 870 are two-part; 30 three-part; and only a few in four and five parts.   In Psalms, all chapters which were designated for public singing—for unison, or for solo and choral response, or for the antiphonal response of two alternating choirs (see Chapter I) are likewise in two-part verses.

The short two-part form of these books shaped the form of their modes by moulding melodic structure into a two-part period, and for the three-part verses into a three-part period.

The mode of Job is based on the scale f—g—a—b♭, identical with the Ionian or modified Lydian scale which is a tetrachord.   The character of the scale is major in so far as it has a major third; but its tetrachordal form prevents it from being a real major in the modern sense in which the major character is pronounced by the fifth and the seventh tones, and the elevating melodic curve to the eighth, the octave. In this ancient Oriental form this scale received a serious and meditative complexion. The same scale is utilized in the Oriental mode called *Rehaw*, a corruption of the name of the Oriental city *Raha*, which meant in ancient Assyrian "the West." According to the Arabic tradition, whenever this mode is sung, the angels as well as the devils gather to listen, because it influences the good as well as the evil spirits.[17]

Among the Oriental and Sephardic Jews, Job is read on the ninth of Ab, immediately after Lamentations. Therefore, among these groups its mode has been preserved, while the Ashkenazim—not having this custom—have forgotten the tradition of this mode as the "Job mode." Instead, they employ it for the reading of the Pentateuch on the High Holidays—a usage in which the Ashkenazim are the exception, as only they have a special mode for the Pentateuch on these days, while all the other communities read it in the same mode as is used during the year. The reason for changing the tune for the High Holidays and for employing especially the Job mode may be this: The *Zohar* (a cabbalistic homiletical commentary to the Pentateuch, compiled in Aramaic from old sources of mystical literature in the thirteenth century by Moses de Lion) says (Lev. 16) that while reading on the Day of Atonement the portion Leviticus 16 in which the sudden death of the children of Aaron is mentioned, every one should shed tears, and that whoever expresses his sorrow over the death of the children of Aaron may be sure that his own children will not die during his life. Because of these instructions old editions of the Ashkenazic *Machzor* (prayer-book including poetical insertions for the entire year), like that of Salonica, 1550, carried a mark on this portion, in order that this text be read in a tune different from the usual one, a tune which expresses complaint and sadness. The search for such a tune led to the mode of Job which had had no function in the Ashkenazic rite and suited these requirements. The Ashkenazim took this mode at first for the reading of the Pentateuch on the Day of Atonement; later they extended its use also to the days of Rosh Hashana (New Year). It is interesting to notice that in the ancient communities of Germany, like Frankfort-on-the-Main, only the main portions read from the first scroll are chanted in the Job mode, while the portions read from the second scroll (the contents of which is a description of the sacrifices for these days) are chanted in the usual Pentateuch mode.

The Job mode was utilized by the Ashkenazic Jews also for prayers. We shall find the mode in the supplications (Chapter IV).

Like the modes of the Pentateuch and Lamentations, the mode of Job has its derivative in the Gregorian chant for Lamentations, according to a manuscript of the thirteenth century.[18] But this mode is to be found in the Gregorian Graduale in much closer form. In table IX, 1, the Job mode is illustrated according to the Sephardic-Oriental tradition. In some communities local changes of minor importance have crept in. Example 2 gives the Ashkenazic version of the mode. Upon closer study of both examples we find that the Oriental version is the simpler one. It consists of two motives, one ending on the second (g), marking the first part of the period, and the other concluding on the tonic (f) and indicating the ending of the second part of the period and of the whole melodic line. In case the verse has three parts, as in verse four of example 1, two parts are intoned by the first part of the musical period, and the third part by its second part. In the Ashkenazic version the same principle is observed. There is, however, a motive which is inserted before the ending motive and which makes a melodic curve to the third. The Ashkenazic is richer in motives than the Oriental. The additional motives were taken over from other modes, from the Pentateuch (for the words: *Moshe dabber el aharon ochicho*) and from the Prophets (*vay'yomer adonoy*). The custom of borrowing from other modes is characteristic of the Ashkenazic traditional song—a custom which we shall discuss later at greater length. Example 3 is from the above mentioned manuscript of the thirteenth century, which has more resemblance to the Oriental version, whereas example 4 reminds one more of the Ashkenazic mode, and is commonly used in the Catholic Church. The Job mode, too, exercised a considerable influence upon the later creations of the Synagogal song.

(h) THE MODES OF THE PSALMS.

The Book of Psalms has come to be the standard collection of hymns and prayers of the Jewish and Christian faith. It is the fountain from which millions of souls have drawn their inspiration and through which they have voiced their devotion for more than two thousand years. It has provided thousands of religious spirits with a means of

TABLE IX
Job

expressing their sentiments to their Creator. So many Jews and Christians, highly gifted and filled with holy devotion, have created wonderful hymns and prayers in the last two thousand years; yet the Psalms still stand supreme. The reason for their power is well explained by many of the Church Fathers, especially by Athanasius, Bishop of Alexandria (295-373). "The Psalms," he says, "embrace the entire human life, express every emotion of the soul, every impulse of the heart. When thy soul yearns for penance and confession, when thy spirit is depressed or joyous, when thou art become master of thy sins or thy sins have overpowered thee, when thy soul is yearning to express its thanks to God, or its pains—for all these, the Psalms completely satisfy our needs." St. Jerome advises a monk "that the Psalter shall be in his hand and he shall learn it by heart." He ordered the nuns in Jerusalem to memorize the Psalms, or leave the convent. Ambrosius gives testimony "that the women sing the Psalter well. And verily its songs are sweet and suitable for every age and sex. . . . It unites the people in the bond of unity, wherever they sing (the Psalms) in unison." [19]

For the Jews, it is indeed quite readily understood why the collection of the Psalms was the songster of their faith centuries before the Christian era, and why these Psalms were sung not only at the Temple with the musical apparatus of the Levitical choir and orchestra, described in Chapter I, but also outside of the Temple throughout Palestine and, perhaps, in other countries likewise, forming an integral part of Synagogue worship. When we go through the one hundred fifty Psalms, we see at once the variety not only of their contents but also of their forms.

We spoke already of the predominance of the short two-part verses in the Book of Psalms. But besides this form, the Psalms have also other forms. And it is quite natural that, in accordance with contents and form, different modes were used to intone them. The occasion— joyous or sad, feast or fast day—influenced their musical rendition. And finally, stylistic considerations were decisive. If, for example, a Psalm was used as an introduction to or interlude between prayers in a certain mode, that mode was, as a rule, transferred also to the Psalms—a procedure called by the precentors *meinyana*—in the same subject or THEME. The musical intonations or modes used for the chanting of the Psalms are based on the Dorian, the Gregorian or

Hypophrygian, and on the Lydian scale.   In table X we give examples of the modes mostly used in the various communities.   Group A (1-3) presents modes in Dorian.   These modes are common in the Sephardic congregations, whereas in the Ashkenazic tradition (3) they are disappearing, due to the predominance of the major and minor scales.   In example 15 a comparison with the Gregorian chant of the Epistles is given.[20]   Group B (4-8) offers examples for modes in Phrygian or Hypophrygian.   Some of them have the tetrachordal structure (4-5, 1), some the pentachordal line (6, 8), and one example (5) is rhythmical ($\frac{3}{8}$), though the rhythm is frequently interrupted to suit the rhythm of the text.   We compare these modes with some Gregorian psalmodies, as for example 16 with 4, 17 with 7-8.   Group C (9-14) is based on the Lydian or Hypolydian scale. The Sephardic-Oriental congregations chant Proverbs 31: 10-31 in the same mode as 11-12.   The similarity of 18 (Gregorian) with 9-10 (Yemenite and Persian) is apparent.

From the comparative examples thus far given, we learn that the tradition and history of the Catholic Church are justified in claiming that at least a considerable part of its traditional song was adopted from the Synagogue, due to the continuous endeavor of the Church Fathers in the first centuries.   At least in Spain it was believed that the Hallelujah tunes were of Jewish origin.   Thus Isidor of Sevilla testifies, *"Laudes, hoc est Alleluja canere, canticum est Hebraeorum"*— "The tunes of Laudations, that is Halleluyah-singing, is of Hebrew origin." [21]

From the examples we likewise learn that several modes are common in the various countries, as 1 Sephardic-Oriental; 3, Ashkenazic; 7, 11, Moroccan; 8, 12, Ashkenazic; 13, Sephardic-Oriental; and 14, Carpentras.

Aside from the modes thus far treated, there are some modes not generally in use, as the mode of PROVERBS which book is chanted in Oriental congregations on the Sabbath afternoons between Passover and the Feast of Weeks, but its public reading is not obligatory.   The mode is a variation of the Psalm mode, group A.   There is, likewise, a mode for the reading of DANIEL in use in the Sephardic-Oriental congregations only, but it is not used in public services.   This mode is based on the Lydian scale.   In like manner, we find local modes for some parts of the Bible used by one or the other com-

TABLE X
Psalms

Ps. 21, 1-2 (Ashkenazic)

Solo   *Cong.*

12

Lam-nats-tse - ah miz - mor le - do - vid a - do -

noy be-oz-cho yis-mah me-lech, u - vi shu-os-cho ma yo - gel me - od.

Prov. 31, 10- (Sephardic - Oriental)

13

E-sheth ha-yil mi yim-sa, we-ra-hok mi-pe-ni-nim mich-ra.

Ps. 49, 1-2 (Carpentras)

14

Lam - nas - se - ah lib - ne ˙ ko - rah miz - mor.

shim-u zoth kol ha -am-im, ha-a-zi-nu kol yosh-be the - bel.

(Gregorian)

15

Lec-ti-o E-pis to-lae be-a-ti Pau-li A-pos-to-li ad Ro-ma-nos.

(Gregorian)

16

De - us in - di - ci - um tu - um re - gi - da.

et jus - ti ti - am tu - am fi - li - o re - gis.

(Gregorian)

17

Lau-da-te Do-mi-num de coe-lis; lau-da-te e-um in ex-cel-sis.

(Gregorian)

18

E - ruc - ta - vit con me - um ver - bum bo - num;

di - co e - go: Lin-gu-a me - a ca - la-mus scri-bae.

munity—modes which have no originality but are derivations of the chief modes presented.[22]

(i) There is a mode which, though developed by one community and, hence, stamped with local characteristics, yet by reason of its influence on the creation of the later songs of that community and the charm it exercised through many centuries, deserves special treatment here. It is the MODE OF ESTHER. The Book of Esther has been read in public on the 14th day of Adar since long before the destruction of the Temple (see above), but its reading was very plain—like the reading of a letter or a historical document, which manner the Oriental Jews employ to the present day. The Esther-mode in the Orient is, therefore, simple, really only a speaking tone with some elevated points, especially at the half and full stops. Some Orientals employ the Phrygian, others the Dorian, as the examples in table XI, 1-2 evidence. The Ashkenazim, however, combined the two modes, and—what is of more significance—introduced into the reading of Esther motives of different modes, such as Pentateuch and Lamentations. The reason for enriching the reading of Esther was that in the reading of this book, the German Jews found opportunity to give vent to their bitterness against their oppressors. They, therefore, interpreted the *Megilla* (Scroll) of the story of Esther and Mordecai and the struggle of the Jews in Persia as the story of their own life. Their abuse of Haman was but a disguised attack on their contemporary enemies, and an opportunity to mock them, at times even in a vulgar manner. For that reason they drew into the mode popular street tunes, snatches of marches current at different ages in Middle Europe. A more detailed description of these tunes we shall give later when we come to relate the story of the Medieval Ashkenazic song (Chapters XVIII and XX). At present we wish to point out the Ashkenazic Esther mode, the form that was shaped through enrichment by motives of other modes. In example 3 the borrowed motives are marked. The motives 2, 9, 10, are taken from the Lamentations, because the text relates of trouble and affliction; while the motives 7, 8 are borrowed from the Pentateuch and are employed whenever the text needs an emphatic expression. The motives 2, 4 and 11 were utilized to a great extent as material for tonal creations about which we shall speak later (Chapter VIII).

THE *Ta'amim* (MUSICAL NOTATION) OF THE BIBLE.

TABLE XI
Esther

The Biblical intonations preserved in the memory of the people, were transmitted orally from generation to generation. Yet an attempt was made in the early centuries to find a way by which these intonations could be preserved. Similar attempts, as we know, were also made by all the other ancient nations, such as the Indians and the Greeks; and were the beginnings of musical notation, which, after a long development, resulted in the modern system of writing music. The earliest system was the notation of the rise and fall of the voice and the curves made by the voice in producing a motive. These were ear-marks. With the ear-marks the "hand-signs," in Greek *cheironomia*, made by the teacher or musical leader to indicate the rise and fall of the voice, were developed among the ancient nations.[23] We notice this custom in ancient Egypt, shown on the wall-pictures of the pyramids. The Talmud gives evidence of the custom of using finger-motions in the air in Palestine and Babylonia in the beginning of the Common Era.[24] We know that it continued for many centuries, for Palestinian precentors in the eleventh century on their visit to France and Germany still used to make these finger-signs while they were chanting the Pentateuch.[25] In some countries, like Yemen, the custom is still in vogue. For these movements of the hand descriptive names were invented. For example, the ascending tone was marked by raising the finger. This movement was called *Kadma*—ascending. The falling of the voice was marked by the falling of the finger and was called *Tifha*—descending. A sustained tone was marked by keeping the hand uplifted and was called *Zakef*—upright, and so on.

During the Talmudic period only three names were known, marking the beginning, half stops, and end of the verse. In like manner we find among other nations: *udata, svarita,* and *anudata* among the Hindus; *acutus, circumflex,* and *gravis* among the Greeks; and *shesht, kurr,* and *butu* among the Armenians. The names employed by the Jews were *kadma*—ascending, *athnah*—resting half-stop, and *sof*—conclusion. Gradually, there developed the system of naming each detail of the nuances marked by voice and hand. But not satisfied with the *cheironomia,* every nation mentioned above invented WRITTEN SIGNS independently which were IMITATIONS of the HAND-MARKS. And remarkably enough the signs or accents of the three mentioned tonal motions are identical among all the nations. These three ac-

cents are constructed of the diagonal line in various positions. Thus
pashta or *acutus* is a diagonal line upward (⸍) and *tifha* or *gravis* the
same line placed downward (⸌), while the *athnah* or *circumflex* is a
combination of the two positions (⌃). In the accents invented thereafter for further tonal lines filling out between beginning (*kadma*)
and half-stop (*athnah*) or end (*sof*), the point was introduced in addition to the line. The development continued for several centuries
until the system received its finishing touches in Tiberias and was introduced in the Bible in the ninth century as a means by which the
Scripture should be chanted. However, the use of an accented Bible
for public reading in the service was not permitted. For this purpose
only the original Scroll without vocalization or accents had to be used.

Two systems of accents were employed in the Bible, one for twenty-
one books and the other for the three books: Psalms, Proverbs, and
Job. The first system has thirty accents,[26] the second only twelve.
The reason for the large number of the first is accounted for by the
various syntactical forms occurring in the twenty-one books, for which
musical interpretations were provided through the various tonal nuances; whereas the three books mentioned above have mostly the short
two-part sentences, as has already been explained.

The first man known to furnish the Bible with a complete system
of accents was Aaron ben Asher, in Tiberias, of the ninth century.
His manuscript became the standard code, though a second scholar, Ben
Naftali, prepared another code with some variations. Ben Asher also
wrote a treatise, describing the tonal value of the accent-marks. In
Babylonia, too, attempts were made to invent a system of accents, but
they did not prove successful.

The so-called Tiberian system, on examination, will be found to
have a great deal in common with the Greek *prosodia*, which came to
be known about the second century, C.E.,[27] and especially with the
neumes-system of the Byzantines and Armenians in the forms that it
took on in the ninth century.[28] Aside from the identical figures, the
classification and valuation of the accents are alike.[29] Like the Greek-
Byzantine accents, so also the Jewish, are divided into con- and disjunctives. Furthermore, they are classified in *tonoi*—Hebrew *rum*,
marking tonal value, *chronoi*—*shehiya*, marking time value, *pneumata*—*gova*, specifying dynamic value.[30]

The Hebrew accents agree with the Greek system in their general outlines, but not in detail. The reason for the variance is, apparently, that the Jewish scholars had to adjust the accents to the traditional modes of the Bible. In their anxiety to preserve the modes, they made use of this system as the only musical notation which existed at that time. While the Byzantian system was adopted by the Latin Church and later developed more and more into a notation of intervals and steps (by Guido of Arezzo, 995-1050), the Hebrew system remained in its ninth century form. Our modern system of writing music, we know, is still incapable of expressing many nuances regarding tonality (less than half-tones) and many time and dynamic features. In that primitive system of the Biblical *ta'amim*, or *neginoth* (notes, tunes), we must, therefore, expect but poor indication of even the most elementary and basic musical values. And, indeed, the accents indicate small patterns with their approximate intervals but they show neither notes nor exact intervals. Only for those who know the mode and its motives and characteristics do the accents serve their purpose. They are rather reminders of the motives. The fact that the same accents are set for all the twenty-one books, irrespective of the different modes, proves that they are only primitive reminding-signs of the rising and falling of a tune. They indicate neither scale nor rhythm, neither tonality nor tempo, neither intervals nor steps. Even at the time when they were introduced, people who did not know the modes beforehand could learn nothing from this system. This is another proof that the Biblical modes were popular among the scattered communities long before the accents were introduced.

We give here a list of the accents and their classification, according to the oldest sources: [31]

A. DISJUNCTIVES

I. *Tonoi:*

Figures and names:

- ⁎ ᴬ *Zarka—segol*—Scatterer
- ⁎ *Rebia*—Square
- ⌐ *Tifha*—Hand-breadth
- ˋ *Kadma*—Preceder

- ʟɪ *Legarme*—Disjunctive-rester
- ⸴ *Tebir*—Broken
- ɪ *Silluk*—Cessation
- ⸱ *Sof pasuk*—Period

II. *Chronoi:*

Figures and names:

- ˂ *Yethib*—Staying
- ʌ *Ethnachta*—Rester

- ⸱ ⁞ *Zakéf*—Raising

III. *Pneumata:*

Figures and names:

- ᴬᵁ *Pazer*—Dispersed
- ˮ *Tarsa (gereshin)*—Expulsion

- ᴾ ᵠ *Talsha*—Plucked

Of later date:

- ⸦ *Shalsheleth*—Chain

B. CONJUNCTIVES

Figures and names:

- ᵤ *Shofar mehuppach*—Reversed horn
- ᴶ *Shofar Munach*—Resting horn
- ⸝ *Agala*—Round
- ⸲ *Maarich*—Lengthener

- ⸲ *Darga*—Steps

We gain a clear idea of the loose relationship between the motives and accent signs upon examining the COMPARATIVE TABLE. The comparative table of the Pentateuch mode shows how inexactly the names of the accent signs describe the impression made by the music for which they stand. But the same table gives evidence of the close relation between the motives of the various traditions, though some of these communities, due to their geographical situation and their political condition, never, or very seldom, came into contact with one another. Some of these communities, on the other hand, never stood under the influence of the Roman Catholic Church, and yet several modes are found in both Synagogue and Church. Both this uniformity of tradition and the independence of Church influence prompt us to adopt the opinion that the Biblical modes treated thus far, are of an ancient age, probably preceding the expulsion of the Jewish people from Palestine, and older than the Christian Church. They are the remainder of the Jewish-Palestinian folk tunes, representing the Jewish branch of the Semitic-Oriental song.[32]

CHAPTER IV

THE OLDEST UNRHYTHMICAL ELEMENTS OF JEWISH SONG
(CONTINUED). B: THE MODES OF THE PRAYERS.

Simultaneously with laudation and adoration, Israel likewise cultivated supplication. The Bible contains a considerable number of prayers composed by outstanding men and women in Israel (Chapter VI). The Psalter is not merely a book of songs and praises. An appreciable part, approximately one-third of it, is supplication and petition. This fact justifies the conclusion that prayers, like songs and laudations, were chanted in the Temple service in Jerusalem. The popular refrain *Hoshiannah*—"Oh, help!" indicates prayer.

At first supplications in public were voiced only in time of need and distress. But gradually, in the later period of the Second Temple, these occasional prayers developed into a set ritual, performed at certain times with certain stipulated texts in a certain order.

The Mishna reports the texts and order of the daily ritual used at the Temple. It consisted of reciting the Ten Commandments, which was later replaced by the *Shema*, the Song of the Sea, and the priestly benedictions.[1] All of these selections were taken from the Pentateuch. As introductions to these readings, benedictions were composed based on verses from the Prophets and the Writings. And in addition Psalms were chanted.

Identical in content and spirit, as well as in style and form, with the prayers of the Bible, were those composed by prominent rabbis during the Talmudic period and accepted into the ritual for daily service and for feast and fast days. Up to the end of the seventh century the ritual was continuously enriched. Its parts fall into several classifications: *Tefilla* (prayer), *Hallel* (laudation), *Techinna*, *Tachanun* (petition), *Selicha* (intercession for pardon), *Viddui* (confession), *Kina* (lamentation), and *Zemiroth* (hymns).

By reason of their sources, we should be led to expect that the musical rendition of the prayers was taken over from the Biblical modes, together with the texts. And in fact, we do find the modes of the Bible reechoed in the modes of the prayers, though with variation and additions of motives. We shall examine the main modes used in the service.

(1) THE TEFILLA MODE, OR ADONOY-MOLOCH STEIGER

This mode is originally derived from the Pentateuch mode, carried along with the Pentateuch texts which constituted the chief parts of the *Tefilla*. The scale is the Hypodorian, instead of the Dorian as in the Pentateuch mode, and the melodic line has the tetrachordal form. In table XII we furnish examples: (1) is the Yemenite mode for daily service, whereas examples (2) and (3) illustrate the *Tefilla* mode which the Oriental and European Sephardim use for the High Holidays only. (5) offers a similar chant of the Gregorian song in the "fourth tone." In the Ashkenazic, example (4) we recognize the European influence (as in the case of the Pentateuch mode in Chapter III), by the addition of two steps below the tonic (a-g), through which change the scale becomes identical with that of the Gregorian Mixolydian mode. Consequently the modern Ashkenazic cantors designate as *mixolydian* the mode originally called *Adonoy-Moloch Steiger* after the first text (Psalm 93) in the order of the Friday evening service, for which it is used.[2] During the medieval period many variations in scale and motives, as well as in modulations, were developed by the Ashkenazic cantors, the nature of which we shall discuss in Chapter VIII in detail. In example (6) a Gregorian chant is given for Daniel (*Prophetiæ XII^ae in officio matutino*), which has striking similarity especially to the Ashkenazic mode of the *Tefilla*.

The *Tefilla* mode in its Oriental setting, as we saw, has striking similarity to the Gregorian fourth mode. The latter is described as

having a soulful, almost dreamy, character, suitable for devout prayer.[8]
It expresses profound emotion and yet solemnity and is used for various
prayers and texts which voice an optimistic and sound view of
life.   Therefore in the Sephardic-Oriental and Occidental communities, the *Tefilla* on the High Holidays is chanted in this mode mostly.
The Ashkenazic communities use it for the introductory selections of
Sabbath and for a great part of the morning service on Sabbath and
for Holiday prayers.

(2) THE SELICHA MODE

The *Selicha*, that is intercession for pardon, *Techinna*—emotional
outbursts of repentance, *Bakkasha*—intense pleading for a definite
boon, and *Kina*—lamentation, are the expression of the soul in its
distress.   As is generally known, Israel's prayers are not exclusively
in the singular form; they are not prayers for individuals only, but
prayers for the household of Israel.   The same needs, hopes, wishes,
and ideals motivate the entire community.   The individual is a part
of the community.   He does not stand by himself; he could not exist
by himself.   He is incorporated into the community, and is influenced
by the moral strength of the community.   At the same time—although in the plural—Israel's prayers interpret the life of the individual.   To be aware that a whole community has the same wishes
and hopes as he has and shares the same troubles and distress, is in
itself a consolation for the individual.

The four types of penance mentioned, although their roots reach to
a very early period of antiquity, received their important place in
Israel's service after the destruction of the Second Temple (Chapter VI).   With the increase of pain and the persecutions inflicted not
only upon him as a man and a Jew, but especially upon his convictions and ideals—in a word, upon his Judaism, these four types of
penance multiplied.   As did no other people or creed, Israel created
lamentations over the destruction of religious institutions and the
burnings of religious books, because these books held the contents of
his life, and these institutions were the backbone of his existence.

Selicha, Techinna, Bakkasha, and *Kina* sound the vibrations of
Israel's tortured soul; they are the reflection of its inmost despair and
longing.   Yet they do not end in complete despair, for in every supplication or lamentation there is a bright note of hope in a better fu-

TABLE XII
Tefilla Mode

ture; there is the repeated voicing of the lovingkindness of the Almighty. It is quite natural, therefore, that these types of supplications should be expressed in the modes of the Prophets and the Psalms. We find these modes, which we call *Selicha* modes, in all the communities of the Diaspora—their importance depending upon the economic and political conditions of the respective localities. In those communities which enjoy freedom and equal rights, the *Selicha* modes are diminished in number, but in those communities which suffer from oppression, these modes are the most outstanding in the service and their usage is extended even over the prayer texts—the *Tefilla*. Thus the *Selicha* becomes the measure by which we can estimate the well-being of the different communities. The Italian and German Jews, who had a rich *Selicha* literature and, consequently, a great number of *Selicha* modes and tunes, have gradually abandoned them with the increase of their emancipation since the middle of the nineteenth century. The Spanish Jews, who, while living in Spain, had a small *Selicha* liturgy, developed it to a great extent in the Orient after their expulsion from Spain. The Polish and Ukrainian Jews took over the German *Selicha* and increased it after the pogroms in 1648-1660. But the community richest in *Selicha* modes is the Persian, because of its sufferings for many centuries from the fanatic and brutal *Shiites*, the predominant Mohammedan sect in Persia.

The *Selicha-*and*-Kina* mode is founded, as stated above, upon the Prophetic mode, and it is strongly influenced by the Psalms (table X B) and by Lamentations (table VIII, 8). Table XIII, 1-4 gives a comparison of the *Selicha* mode in its Persian, Yemenite, Ashkenazic (Eastern Europe), and Babylonian versions. 1-3 have the same text (of the High Holidays), whereas 4 is set to another text. The mode in this table is presented in the form used on High Holidays with the ending on the fourth c, whereas on other occasions the mode ends on tonic g, as shown by examples 5-6. In this mode the melodic line seldom rises above the sixth, the melody dwells upon the third (XIII, 9), and modulates to the fourth. In the Eastern Ashkenazic version (3) the third is frequently elevated to a major, by which procedure the step between second and third becomes augmented, thus creating the scale of the *Ahavoh-Rabboh* mode. (See further on *Hedjaz*, Chapter II.)

The Ashkenazim in addition utilized motives of the Prophetic

mode, such as the motive of *athnah* and *kadma veazla*, as evidenced
in example 7, 2-3. The *athnah* motive was taken over for the concluding of the Pentateuch mode (Chapter III a). The various phases
of the *Selicha* mode created by the Ashkenazim, we shall treat in
Chapter VIII. The responsive forms of the Psalms were likewise
carried over to the *Tefilla* and *Selicha* (table XII, 1-3; XIII, 8-9).

(3) THE VIDDUI MODE

We have already mentioned the *Viddui*, the confession, as a part of
the penitential prayers. Its mode, however, is a derivation from the Job
mode, that is, it has the major tetrachord as its foundation. This fact
is significant of the characteristics of Synagogue song, which expresses
sentiments and pain, desires and longings, wishes and hope in minor.
But as soon as it strives to express or confess *truth*, it turns to the emphatic sound of the major third. It matters not whether that truth be
the proclamation of the Almighty's glory or the self-humiliating decla-
ration of our own sins; for one of Judaism's chief features is its
staunch adherence to and fearless proclamation of the truth, however
painful to personal vanity that truth may be. Therefore, Synagogue
song expresses confession in the emphatic manner of the major scale.
Table XIIIa gives a comparison of the Yemenite, Persian, Babylonian
and Ashkenazic versions of the *Viddui* mode, which evidences the
similarity between them. The Persian version shows an inclination
to the parallel minor, because of the influence of the *Selicha* mode in
that song, as stated above.

The mode does not rise above the fifth or sixth, so that the melodic
line never climbs up to the octave. Consequently, it lacks the ener-
getic ascent of the seventh step, the tone leading to the eighth. In
consequence thereof, the mode acquired a sternness and dignity of
character.

(4) THE MOGEN-OVOS MODE

This mode, though it can be traced in the song of other countries,
received its development primarily in the song of the Ashkenazim.
Its name is derived from the prayer *Mogen-Ovos*—a summary of
the seven benedictions of the *Amida*—composed in the third century
in Babylonia for the benefit of the late comers to the Friday evening
service, to enable them to hear, at least, the essentials of the service.

TABLE XIII
Comparative Table of Selicha Modes

1.
Persian

U - bĕ - ḥên tên paḥ dŏ ḥa ă - do - nay ĕ -

2.
Yemenite

Ub - ḥen   tên paḥ-dŏ - ḥa

3.
Ashkenazic
in Eastern
Europe

Ub - ḥên   tên paḥ-dĕ - ḥo ă - do-noy e - lo - he -

4.
Babylonian
Sephardic

Ā - do - nay   ša ma-ti šim - ă - ha   ya -

1.

lo - hê - nu 'al kol ma-a s'e - ḥo wĕ - ê - mot - ḥa

2.

ă - do-nay ĕ - lo-hê - nu al kol ma-a se - ḥa wĕ-ê-ma-

3.

nu al kol ma-a se - ḥo wĕ-ê - mo - te - ho 'al kol

4.

rê - - ti yom bo tif qĕ dê - - - ni hoš-pal-ti

1.

al kol šĕ - bo - ro - ta   wĕ - yi - ro - u - ḥa

2.

tĕ - ḥa al kol ma se - ba - ra - ta wĕ-yi-ra-u - ḥa kol ha

3.

ma - se - bo - ro - to   we - yi - ro - u - ho kol ha

4.

we - nib - hal - ti pen bĕ - a - pe ḥa tam - 'i - te' - - -

1.
kọl ha-ma-a-sim wĕ-yiš-ta-ḥa-wu lĕ-fọ-ne-ḥa kọl
2.
ma-a-sim wĕ-yiš-ta-ha-wu lĕ-fa-ne-hă kọl
3.
ma-a-sim we-yis-ta-ha-wu le-fo-ne-ho kọl ha-
4.
- - ni ki ga-dol yom ă-do-nay.
1.
ha-bẹ̆-ru-im wĕ-yê-ạ-su hu-lọm ă-gu-dọ ẹ-
2.
ha-bẹ̆-ru-im wĕ-yê-'ạ-su hu-lam a-gu-dọ ẹ-hat
3.
bẹ-ru-im we-ye-ọ-su hu-lọm ă-gu-dọ ẹ-
1.
hot la-a-sot rĕ-so-nĕ-họ bĕ-lê-bọb sọ̆-lĕm.
2.
la-a-sot rĕ-so-nọh bĕ-lê-bạb šạ-lĕm.
3.
hot la-a-sot. rĕ-so-ne-họ bĕ-lê-bọb šo-lĕm.
Persian
5.
Shaw-o-the-nu ta-a-le li-she-me me-ro-mim,
el me-lech yo-shev al kis-se ra-cha-mim.

TABLE XIIIᵃ
Comparative Table of Viddui Modes

For the same purpose *Vaychullu* (Gen. 2: 1-3) was repeated.[4] In the eleventh century it was customary to chant *Vaychullu* and *Mogen-Ovos* in a "fine and long tune." [5]

This mode in its Ashkenazic version is founded on the minor scale. As to the characteristics of the mode, we mention first its pentachordal form, for the melodic line ascends to the fifth which is predominant in the mode. Furthermore, there is noticeable an inclination toward the third, i.e., the parallel major. The ending occurs on the fifth, employing the ending motive (*sof pasuk*) of the Prophetic mode.

The *Mogen-Ovos* is identical in many features to the *Bayat-Huseni* mode of the Arabic song. (See table I.) It has a tender and lyrical strain, and became, therefore, the basis for many Jewish folk tunes of religious and secular character, as we shall see later in Chapter XVIII. In table XIV, 1-2, the Ashkenazic version of the *Mogen-Ovos* mode is given. Example 3 illustrates the Sephardic-Oriental version. The latter differs from the Ashkenazic mode in some basic features, for it has the tetrachordal form and the fourth (g) as the dominating tone on which note it ends. The Orientals call that form *Bayat-Nawa* (see table I); in Greek music it was called Hyperphrygian.

We mentioned above (Chapter III) that the closing motive of the *Mogen-Ovos* mode was taken from the mode of the Prophets. On examination, we find that the mode as a whole is a derivation from the Prophetic and Pentateuchal modes. We see it best in XIV, example 2, in which the motives 1, 3, 4, 5, 6, are to be found in both modes (compare table IV), while the motives 7, 8, are from the Prophets only. Motive 2 is a sequence of 1. The Oriental version (example 3), however, does not show this relationship.

Motive 1 is related to *rebia*-oriental; 2, to Pent. *gereshin;* 3, to *tebir*-orient., and Pent. *gershayim*-Ashken.; 4, to *rebia* Pent. and Proph.-Ashken.; 5, to *telisha,* Pent.; 6, to *darga* and *tebir,* Pent. and Proph.

(5) THE AHAVOH-RABBOH MODE

The prayer modes thus far treated show connections with the Biblical modes. They either are a derivation from them or have at least absorbed some motives of these modes. They have to be considered originally Jewish, even though their scales are to be found in the music of the classic and Oriental nations, for, as we have empha-

TABLE XIV
Mogen-Ovos Mode (Steiger)

Gen. 2. 1-3

(Ashkenazic)

Va - ye - chu - lu hash-sho-ma - yim ve - ho - o - rets

ve - chol   tse - vo - om.   va - ye-chal e - lo-him bay-yom

hash-vi - i me-lach-to a - sher o - so.   vay-yish -

bos bay-yom hash vi - i   mik-kol me-lach-to   a-sher o - so.

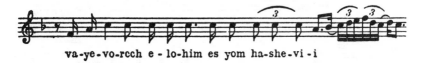

va-ye-vo-rech e - lo-him es yom ha-she-vi - i

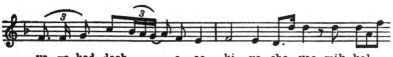

va - ye-kad-desh   o - so. ki vo sho - vas mik-kol

me - lach - to   a - sher bo - ro e - lo-him la - a - sos.

Moderato   (Ashkenazic)

Congregation

2.

Mo - gen o - vos bi - de - vo - ro, me-cha - ye me-sim bema - a - mo - ro, ho - el hak-ko-dosh she - en ko-mo-hu, ham-me-
ni - ah le - am-mo be-yom shab-bas kod-sho, ki - vom ro-tso

Precentor

le - ho - ni - ah lo-hem... u - me - ni - ach bik-du-sho le - am
me-dush-ne o - neg, ze - cher le-ma - a - se ve - re-shis.

Gen. 2. 1-3   (Sephardic - Oriental)

3.

Way-chu-lu hash-sha-ma-yim we - ha - a———— res we-
chol se - ba-am way-chal e - lo-him bay-yom hash-bi-
i me-lach-to a - sher a - sa. ki bo sha-bath mik-kol me-lach-
to a - sher ba-ra e - lo-him la - a -soth.

sized several times, the originality of a national music is not dependent upon an original scale, but upon original motives and melodic curves which above all express the characteristics of a nation, a group, or a people. At the same time, one particular mode or *Steiger*—the so-called *Ahavoh-Rabboh*—must be especially considered. It is not to be met with in the Biblical modes.

The mode is based on the tetrachords e—f—g#—a + b—c—d—e, or their equivalent steps in other notes. The augmented second step of this scale does NOT exist in the scales of the Biblical modes and of their derivations in the prayer modes. It is the same scale which Olympus was supposed to have introduced into Greece about 800 B.C.E., with the *Aulos* and which innovation, as we have seen, aroused strong opposition in Greece. (See Chapter II.)

If we investigate the traditional songs of the various communities, we find the interesting fact that this mode is not at home in all of them. Proceeding geographically, we find that the Yemenite, Persian, Babylonian, Moroccan, Italian, Portuguese, and Western German communities do not use this mode at all, while those communities which are living in environments that are or were predominantly Tartaric-Altaic use it very much; for example, in Egypt, in Palestine, in Syria, in Asia Minor, on the Balkan, in Hungary, Roumania, in Ukraine, and Volhynia. Going further north to Poland, Lithuania and Northern Germany, we find that the usage of this mode diminishes gradually.

The fact that this mode is not used for the Bible and the ancient prayers nor in the ancient communities in the Near East for the prayers or for the old *piyyut*, created in the period 800-1000 C.E., leads us to the opinion that this mode was originally unknown to the Jewish people, and that only later was it adopted as a result of the influx of the Mongolian and Tartarian tribes into Asia Minor, Syria, Palestine, and Egypt, as well as on the Balkan, beginning with the thirteenth century. With the expansion of the Tartars in Southern Russia, reaching as far west as Hungary, their song was carried with them and nestled itself in the fertile soil of the receptive Jewish soul. Whether or not the Chazarian proselytes on the Caspian Sea sang in the same mode we are not certain. However, being a Tartaric tribe, they probably did so. Thus after they amalgamated with the Jews, they may have transmitted to the latter their characteristic racial song.

Be that as it may, this mode came to be much liked by the Jews of the
countries mentioned above, so that it became a real channel of Jewish
expression, especially for moods of excitement, for the stirring passion
of pain, of love, and faith in God. The more the Jewish people in
those countries were persecuted for their religion, the more passionate
became their expression of love for it. For such intense sentiments
they adopted this Tartaric Oriental mode, full of fire and romanticism.

For certain parts of the prayers on Sabbaths and Festivals, but foremost on the High Holidays, the *Ahavoh-Rabboh* mode is employed in
those countries. Especially in Ukraine and Volhynia it became the
vehicle of tense emotion. We can perceive the power of this mode
only when we study the compositions of the *chazzanim* in Eastern
Europe of the eighteenth and nineteenth centuries.

The name *Ahavoh-Rabboh* is derived from a prayer in the morning
ritual, with which, on the Sabbath, the precentor usually introduces
this mode into the service. Out of this mode were created a number
of rhythmical melodies not only for religious but also for secular purposes about which we shall speak in the sections on Folk-song (Chapters XVII-XX).

The characteristic of this mode may be gathered from table XV.
Example 1 is Sephardic-Oriental from the *Musaf Kedusha* on Sabbaths and Festivals, which is sung responsively. Example 2 is Ashkenazic from Eastern Europe. Its text is likewise from the Sabbath
Musaf service. In both examples we find the same features. The
sixth is flat (in example 2—e♭) when used ABOVE the tonic; whereas
when BELOW the tonic, it is natural. The same peculiarity we saw in
the scale of *Hedjaz* and the Greek "second" tone (see Chapter II).
The resting points of the motives are: the fourth, the seventh below
the tonic, the third, and the tonic. The descending line from the seventh above to the seventh below the tonic is a chief feature and appears as a rule before the end. Example 3 furnishes an illustration
of the same mode when used for the expression of tense emotion. It
climbs in tetrachordal curves, first to the fourth, then it changes to
Ahavoh-Rabboh on the fourth, and from there it modulates to the
fifth according to the same scale, whereupon it turns back to the original tonic, using the same motives in tetrachordal curves. But here
we touch the modulation of Jewish song, a subject which we shall

treat in detail in Chapter **XXIII**. At present it is our aim to familiarize ourselves with the elementary characteristics of this mode.

There are some modes branched off from the *Ahavoh-Rabboh*.
These are of much later date and of local significance. We, therefore, defer discussion of them to Chapter **IX**.

These are the oldest elements of the modes of the prayers
preserved in the Jewish communities. They are mostly derived from the modes of the Bible: the *Tefilla* mode from
the Pentateuch mode, the *Selicha* and *Mogen-Ovos* from the
modes of the Prophets, Lamentations, and Psalms, and the
Viddui mode from the Job and group C of the Psalms modes.
Both Biblical and prayer modes constitute the oldest, the most
genuine and the most Oriental-Semitic part of Jewish music,
upon which the later creations were based.

TABLE XV
Ahavoh-Rabboh Mode

(Sephardic - Oriental)

Congregation

1.

Ka-dosh ka-dosh   ka-dosh a - do-nay se - ba - oth,

me - lo chol ha - a - res ke - vo - do.

Precentor

ke - bo-do ma-le o - lam,   me-sha-re-thaw   sho-a-lim.

Congregation

ay-ye   me-kom ke-bo-do. le-ha-ri-so.

(Ashkenazic)

2.

Tik-kan-to shab-bos ro-tsi-so kor-be-no-se-ho, tsiv-vi   so

pe-ru-she-ho im sid-du-re ne-so-che-ho,   me-an-ge-ho

le-o-lom ko-vod yin-cho-lu,   to-a-me-ho cha-yim zo-chu,

ve-gam ho-o-ha-vim de-vo-re-ho   ge-du-lo bo-cho-ru.

oz   mis- si-nay nits-tav-vu o- le-ho, vat-tsav-ve _____ nu

a-do-nay e-lo-he-nu le-hak-riv bo kor-ban mu-saf shab-bos ko - ro-uy.

(Ashkenazic)

3. Hi-ne-ni he-o-ni mi-ma-as.   af al pi she-e-ni che-

day ve-ho-gun le-chach.   lo-chen a-vak kesh mim-cho, e-lo-

he av-ro-hom, e-lo-he yits-chok   ve-lo-he   ya-a-kov,

a-do-noy, a-do-noy, el ra-chum ve-chan - nun, e-lo-he yis-

ro - el. shad-day o-yom ve-no-ro,   he-ye no mats-

li - ach dar - ki   a-sher o-no - chi ho-lech ve-o -

med le-vak-kesh ra - cha-mim o-lay ve-al shol-choy.

CHAPTER V

A HISTORICAL SURVEY OF THE SYNAGOGUE SONG AFTER
THE DESTRUCTION OF THE SECOND TEMPLE UNTIL THE
RISE OF ISLAM (70 C.E.–700 C.E.).

In the first centuries after the destruction of the Temple
in Jerusalem and after the failure of the last attempt of the
Jews to regain their independence in Palestine, it seemed
that music was doomed to be silenced forever among the Jewish people. Already before the Destruction, secular music
was considered a bad influence upon the people.[1] Greek song
especially was regarded harmful,[2] and the spiritual leaders
tried to fight against it by urging the people to sing religious
songs at festivities.[3] This attitude grew out of religious-
ethical considerations. For example, among the transgres-
sions of the apostate "Acher" (Elisha ben Abuyah) was
counted his continuous singing of Greek songs. People who
had musical ability and sweet voices were exhorted to make
a pilgrimage to Jerusalem, there to join in the singing of
sacred songs; and he who did not offer his talent for holy
service was doomed to divine punishment. It is related of
a certain Naboth who went regularly to Jerusalem to perform
his songs in public that, because he refused to do so once, he
was punished.[4] The challenge of the sages to all singers was
this: "If you have a sweet voice, glorify God with the gift He
bestowed upon you, chant the *Shema*, and lead the people in
prayer."[5] They went to the extreme in saying that profane
songs of love and lust are sufficient cause to destroy the world,
and that Israel's religious songs save it.[6] Whenever God
hears Israel's song He calls the Heavenly host to listen.[7]

But after the Destruction, all instrumental music, even for religious purposes, was prohibited, as a sign of national mourning over the Temple. The attitude, "Rejoice not, O Israel, unto exultation, like the peoples" (Hos. 9: 1),[8] became prevalent. Hence national mourning strengthened that antagonism to secular music which existed already before the Destruction.

That antagonism cannot be credited to the exaggeration of moralists only. If a great man like Abba Areka (Rab), at the beginning of the third century, was of the opinion that "an ear which listens to (secular) music shall be torn out," though he himself was a fine singer and one of the greatest liturgists, then there must have been something in the current songs to justify that statement. Nor was he the only one to issue protests against "music." A generation later Raba said, "Music in a house must bring that house to destruction," and his colleague Rab Joseph expressed the opinion that "if men sing and women respond, the result is licentiousness, but if women sing and men respond, the end is like a flame in hatcheled flax." [9]

The clue to the attitude here reported we find in the condition of secular and pagan music of a decadent civilization about the beginning of the Common Era. Greek art and culture, which had become international, degenerated to mere virtuosity, empty of any ideal. Hence, Greek music became a means by which to stimulate voluptuousness. It became synonymous with obscenity and was chiefly used for carnal purposes at frivolous occasions. No wonder then that Judaism opposed "profane" music.

But in this regard Judaism was not unique. Christianity, too, fought the heathen music bitterly. We read in the writings of Clement of Alexandria: [10]

"Let revelry keep away from our national entertainers, and foolish virgins, too, that revel in intemperance. For revelry is an inebriating pipe, the chain of an amatory bridge, that is, of sorrow. And let love, and intoxication, and senseless passions, be removed from our choir. Burlesque singing is the boon companion of drunkenness. A night spent over drink invites drunkenness, rouses lust, and is audacious in deeds of shame. For if people occupy their time with pipes, and psalteries, and choirs, and dances, and Egyptian clapping of hands, and such disorderly frivolities, they become quite immodest and intractable, beat on cymbals and drums, and make a noise on instruments of delusion; for plainly such a banquet, as seems to me, is a theatre of drunkenness. . . . Let the pipe be resigned to the shepherds, and the flute to the superstitious who are engrossed in idolatry. For, in truth, such instruments are to be banished from the temperate banquet, being more suitable to beasts than men, and the more irrational portion of mankind. For we have heard of stags being charmed by the pipe, and seduced by music into the toils, when hunted by the huntsmen. And when mares are being covered, a tune is played on the flute—a nuptial song, as it were. And every improper sight and sound, to speak in a word, and every shameful sensation of licentiousness—which, in truth, is privation of sensation—must by all means be excluded: and we must be on our guard against whatever pleasure titillates eye and ear, and effeminates. For the various spells of the broken strains and plaintive numbers of the Carian muse corrupt men's morals, drawing to perturbation of mind, by the licentious and mischievous art of music.

". . . 'Praise Him on the chords and organ.' Our body He calls an organ, and its nerves are the strings, by which it has received harmonious tension, and when struck by the Spirit, it gives forth human voices. 'Praise Him on the clashing cymbals.' He calls the tongue the cymbal of the mouth which resounds with the pulsation of the lips. Therefore He cried to humanity, 'Let every breath praise the Lord,' because He cares for every breathing thing which He hath made. For man is truly a pacific instrument; while other instruments, if you investigate, you will find to be warlike, inflaming to lusts, or kindling up amours, or rousing wrath.

"In their wars, therefore, the Etruscans use the trumpet, the Arcadians the pipe, the Sicilians the pectides, the Cretans the lyre, the Lacedæmonians the flute, the Thracians the horn, the Egyptians the drum, and the Arabians the cymbal. The one instrument of peace, the *Word* alone by which we honor God, is what we employ. We no longer employ the ancient psaltery, and trumpet, and timbrel, and flute, which those expert in war and contemners of the fear of God were wont to make use of also in the choruses at their festive assemblies, that by such strains they might raise their dejected minds. . . .

"Further, among the ancient Greeks, in their banquets over the brimming cups, a song was sung called a skolion, after the manner of the Hebrew psalms, all together raising the pæan with the voice, and sometimes also taking turns in the song while they drank healths round; while those that were more musical than the rest sang to the lyre. But let amatory songs be banished far away, and let our songs be hymns to God. 'Let them praise,' it is said, 'His name in the dance, and let them play to Him on the timbrel and psaltery.' And what is the choir which plays? The Spirit will show thee: 'Let His praise be in the congregation (church) of the saints; let them be joyful in their King.' And again he adds, 'The Lord will take pleasure in His people.' For temperate harmonies are to be admitted; but we are to banish as far as possible from our robust mind those liquid harmonies, which, through pernicious arts in the modulations of tones, train to effeminacy and scurrility. But grave and modest strains say farewell to the turbulence of drunkenness. Chromatic harmonies are, therefore, to be abandoned to immodest revels, and to florid and meretricious music."

The effort succeeded. Within a short time no instrument was used in any Christian service.[11] The Greek art music was abolished not only from religious but also from secular life, and, with the addition of a few simple sentences of common prayers, the Book of Psalms became the standard prayer-book in the Church.

Hence, Synagogue and Church adopted the tendency toward striking simplicity in text and music. Of the elaborate Temple music the Synagogue retained only the chants in Palestinian folk-modes, which remain to the present day, for Bible and prayers (as explained in Chapters III and IV). All customs regarding heathen worship, such as instruments and bodily motions (dances), vanished. When Athanasius found the congregation in Milet accompanying song in the church with handclapping and bodily motions, he became very much upset. This is proof that at his time (fourth century) all traces of heathen and Greek art had perished from the Church.[12]

The strict order of the Church Fathers that only one instrument should be employed, i.e., the human voice, has been observed in the Syriac, the Jacobite, the Nestorian, and the Greek churches to the present day. So also the Synagogue did not use any instrument in the service up to 1810, in which year the organ was introduced in the first Reform Temple in Seesen, Germany (see further Chapter XII). The reason for abolishing instrumental music from the Church was the ethical concept of that day that instrumental music led to licentiousness. Therefore, in those countries in which the conception of ethics changed regarding the use of instruments in worship, the prohibition was annulled. In the Synagogue, on the other hand, the prohibition had a national motive, the idea being that no musical instrument be used in the Synagogue until the restoration of the Temple when the Levitical music would be revived. In addition, the playing of musical instruments on Sabbaths and festivals was regarded a desecration (see Chapter I). Later, from the time the organ became permanent in the (Catholic) Church (twelfth or thirteenth century), the view was entertained that the organ had become a "Christian" instrument (more in detail in Chapter XII). From this attitude we may deduce that the Jewish sages did not consider the instruments as such, harmful, but rather the music performed on them. A proof of their insight and sound judgment regarding music, we find in the episode related about Rab Huna, who in his zeal, prohibited all secular music in the Jewish community in Babylonia. The prohibition caused the suspension of festivities and social affairs, resulting in a complete paralysis of social and commercial life. It brought about a crisis in the market, for without music nobody cared to arrange festivities, and there was in consequence no sale of products. Becoming aware of the danger of the execution of the decree, Rab Hisda cancelled the extreme ruling.[13] Nonetheless, restrictions were made as to the occasions appropriate for instrumental music and the degree to which they should be used. Thus, instruments were forbidden, not only on Sabbaths and festivals but also on week days; they were permitted only at joyous celebrations, such as weddings. And even then, to prevent over-indulgence in hilarity, a dish would be thrown and broken in front of the bride and groom to remind them of the destruction of the Temple ('in the spirit of the phrase of Psalm 136: 6, "If I set not Jerusalem above my chiefest joy").[14] It is told of some prominent sages in the Talmudic period that as soon as they noticed that the gaiety at the wedding was becoming extravagant, they would suddenly break the most costly dishes in order to shock the guests and thus tone down the joy. Likewise, in order to turn the minds of the hilarious guests to seriousness, they would start singing a responsive song, the subject of which was death and the earnestness of life.[15]

The restrictions applied to everybody, regardless of social standing. Therefore, even the Exilarch Mar Ukba, who in his love for music made extensive use of it in his home, was rebuked by the spiritual leaders, who dispatched a special delegation to him to remind him of the restriction.[16]

No wonder, therefore, that the song in the first centuries was simple, and that only religious song was tolerated and cultivated. The music served only to interpret the text; it was consequently limited in its form, and after becoming closely associated with particular texts, it was cut off from further development. Solo recitation, like the Arabic *Tartil* (see Chapter II, c), excluded rhythmical development, and the strict adherence to the interpretation of the word caused a certain stagnation in the music.

But what seemed impossible in the Bible was permissible in the prayers. There the Jew found a free field for creative song. Out of elements of the Biblical modes new modes were formed, as we have seen in Chapter IV. Indeed, at first the principle of subduing the music to the text, keeping it a mere interpretation of the words, as we find it in the Biblical modes, continued in the prayer modes. But soon the very purpose of prayer defeated this restriction, for the purpose of reading the Bible was INSTRUCTION, whereas the aim of prayer was INSPIRATION. In texts of instructive nature tunes must be subordinate to the text, while for the outpouring of the heart in prayer-texts musical embellishments offer added power of interpretation, and the solo-recitative insures freedom for the expression of rising devotion. Much stress was laid also upon unison congregational singing "in one tone, with one mouth and in one tune." [17] The prayer-modes were, as we saw in

Chapter IV, as a rule unrhythmical, and in the form of unison or responsive singing. There was a syllabic rhythm, based on the accentuated words. Indeed, there was no stimulus to the creation of strict rhythm, such as bodily motions or instruments of rhythmical nature or metrical texts.

This condition obtained not only in the Synagogue but in the Church as well. Not two centuries passed before Christian spiritual leaders in the Orient became conscious of a feeling of stagnation. The completeness of the Psalms that "express all the different sentiments of the human heart in every mood," [18] did not prevent the natural human longing for innovation. Therefore, when Bardaisan of Edessa (150-222) wrote one hundred fifty hymns in the form of the one hundred fifty Psalms to be used as interludes between the Psalms and not as substitutes for them, his verses were accepted with great enthusiasm in the Syriac Church. They became popular throughout the whole Orient, and remained so for about a century and a half, not because they were superior to the Psalms but because they were an innovation, a change. The Christian Church, tiring of its simplicity, began to long for intricate tools of poetical and musical expression, especially after it succeeded in becoming the state-religion of the Eastern Roman Empire. Therefore, when the greatest Syriac Church poet, Ephraim of Nisibis (406-473), started creating his poetry, it spread rapidly throughout the Old World, and was translated into all the languages of the various converts to Christianity. Bardaisan had been accused by Ephraim because he had adapted secular folk tunes for his one hundred fifty imitations of the Psalms, but Ephraim followed in the same practice. His poetry he based on meters of a certain number of accented syllables to the line, for the musical rendition of which rhythmical tunes were required.[19] This was the first step toward

metrical poetry and rhythmical music in the Oriental Church,
yet the poetry was still far from being in strict meter.

Inspired by the spirit of Ephraim, toward the end of the
fifth century, a Jew of Homs in Syria, who had been converted
to the Greek Church and had renamed himself Romanos, became the greatest of the Greek Church poets, by composing for
his adopted creed one thousand poems of different forms. The
new music for this new Greek poetry, too, was not in strict
rhythm, as the examples, furnished in the tables II and III,
will prove.

In Jewish worship, also, a general craving for new expression gradually came to be felt. In the fifth and sixth centuries
poems based on "verbal" meters were created. The meters
were formed according to a certain number of words, three or
four words to a line, a scheme already employed in several parts
of the Bible.[20] Yet no special music for those poems is recorded. We do not know whether at that time they caused any
innovation in the traditional song, for at present they, too, are
chanted in the modes of the prayer-texts of old. Only when
sung in unison or in responsive form the music of these poems
shows a marked syllabic rhythm (Chapter IV).

During the sixth and seventh centuries, the Jews created no
new forms in poetry and music. In those periods of persecution, as in all times of distress, the Jew found the modal form,
the free outpouring of his troubled soul and aching heart, the
most appealing and consoling song. Until around 700 C.E.,
he cultivated the *Selicha* and *Tachnun* modes, the supplica-
tional and petitional song. From the time that the Jews in
the above-mentioned countries were permitted to breathe again,
i.e., after the rise of Islam and its conquest in the Near East,
they interested themselves in new artistic forms in poetry and
music created by their new neighbors, the Arabs, and began
adding to their song metered verse and rhythmical music.

CHAPTER VI

The history of Synagogue song and its development cannot be fully understood without the consideration of the functionaries who were the bearers and preservers of this treasury of folksong, and who became the creators of that song throughout the medieval ages. A traditional song is unthinkable without professional executors. It cannot be abandoned to the good will and memory of the community. Furthermore, the song, inasmuch as it is closely connected with the text of the ritual, was surely determined by the precentor or by the priest, who, already in ancient times, recited the prayers to and for the community.

The ancient nations, such as the Assyrians, Babylonians and Egyptians, many centuries before the establishment of worship in Israel, had an organized service with responsive prayers in which the priest functioned as reader and precentor; and the priestly choir and, occasionally, also the public participated with responses, very similar to the forms which, as we explained, were in practice in ancient Israel.[1] Yet there is one important principle which differentiates the Jewish worship from that of these ancient peoples. In the latter, it was the priest, who simultaneously with his offering of the sacrifices, acted as precentor. He recited the prayers and was the only mediator between the people and their God. In Judaism the idea became prevalent, through the influence of the Prophets, that God is near to everybody, and that everybody is worthy

101

of approaching Him. *Yahveh* as "Our Father" occurs first in Isaiah (63: 16; 64: 7), and "Our Father in Heaven" became a common expression in Palestine about the beginning of the Christian Era.[2] The relation between God and Israel, as between father and children, entitled everybody to pray to God without priestly mediation. But as the people had not sufficient education to express their wishes, usually a prominent man—"one of the people"—used to be the intercessor. It is an interesting and important phenomenon in the history of Judaism that from the very beginning the spokesmen were men of the people. Sometimes even women were chosen to pray for the people; but we seldom find that the people chose a professional priest to pray for them. The latter occasionally prayed while sacrificing, but he never prayed for the people merely as an expression of human need in time of distress.

Such a spokesman was called in ancient times in Hebrew *mithpallel*—lead oneself to pray. He became the intercessor for the people because he was recognized as one endowed with the rare power of praying. This is a unique Hebrew expression. The act of precentorship, which would usually call for a transitive verb, in this instance employs the reflexive.

With the further development of the institution of worship as a regular daily ritual, there arose in the last centuries before the Common Era the need of having a person to recite the very simple and short forms of prayers and laudations used at that time. At the Temple in Jerusalem, as we have already seen (Chapter I), this function was exclusively in the hands of the priests and Levites; but in the houses of worship, in the Synagogues, the office was occupied by a layman, the precentor, at that time called *shaliach-tsibur*—the messenger of the community. It was an office of honor. It was a distinction to be chosen by the elders of the Synagogue for this function. Naturally, the man selected was well versed in the prayers and their meanings. After reciting the first benedictions, the precentor had to improvise prayers according to the need of the hour, and then to close with the final benedictions during which the community listened silently and participated only with short responses, the form of which has already been explained in Chapter I. The progress of education increasingly enabled larger numbers of the community to function as precentors. Moreover, we find that the people visiting from other communities were honored with this function. Since everybody participated in the service, and everybody might be the precentor provided only that he knew the texts, and since even visitors could come to any synagogue and without any preparation chant the prayers, we conclude that the modes of the prayers were generally known and of a popular character, that is, folk-song. And not only were the modes generally known, but even in the way the prayers were offered, there was uniformity, at least in Palestine. Hence, special notice is taken of an exception. It is reported that the community in Jericho had the local tradition of reciting the *Shema* in unison, thus differing from the general custom which held to the responsive form.

The reading of the Bible, too, was in the hands of the precentor. Though we know that Ezra was the first to arrange the public recitation of the Pentateuch, yet the urgent advice given by a Palestinian authority not to read the Bible without singing, dates from the third century C.E. Therefore, the reader had to be familiar with the text of the Scriptures, with all its traditional variants as well as with its musical rendition, the traditional modes. The knowledge of the Scriptures grew to the extent that almost every congregant was able to read from the Pentateuch and the Prophets, whereas for the parts less in use, such as the "five scrolls," a scholarly man, a scribe (*sofer*), had to be sought. However, for the reading of the Pentateuch and

Prophets the custom developed that the congregants would be called upon to chant a portion, while the community reader (*koré*) was there only to help out in case the layman made a mistake. This custom lasted for centuries and is still prevalent in Yemen. This is historical proof of the widespread familiarity with the ancient traditional modes, of their simplicity and of their folk-character.

The list of prominent precentors did not cease with the Bible. Names of famous *mithpallelim* throughout the ages have been preserved in honor and esteem, men who distinguished themselves not only as scholars, but primarily by their ethical and democratic personality.[3] They enriched the Jewish ritual with wonderful prayers which they improvised in moments of inspiration. This custom of improvising prayers continued throughout the Talmudic period until about five hundred C.E. The most striking of these products of momentary inspiration were preserved. They spread among the people and became popular.

In the course of time, the collection of prayers grew into a ritual, preserved by memory, inasmuch as the writing of prayers was prohibited.[4] Therefore, it became a hard task for the precentor to memorize the ritual and to recite the prayers according to their order. For this reason, two assistants to the precentor were ordered, and it soon became a rule that no precentor should function unless he had at least one assistant.[5] The task of the assistants was originally that of prompters. Gradually that post developed into that of a musical assistant. The two *tomechim* or *mesayim*, as the assistants were called, did not only help the precentor occasionally as reminders, but aided him in singing all the prayers. Although the writing of the prayers was later permitted (seventh century) and the assistants therefore became superfluous, the institution none the less continued and became the nucleus of the synagogal choir-singers. The first statements of the existence of assistants go back to the third century.[6]

The qualifications required of an honorary precentor were fixed in the second century by Rabbi Judah ben Illai in Palestine. It was the general opinion that though scholars and prominent men were present, only men familiar with the prayers and qualified for precentorship should be invited to officiate. Rabbi Judah described the one who could meet the requirements to be [7] "a man who has heavy family obligations, who has not enough to meet them, who has to struggle for a livelihood, but who none the less keeps his house clean (above reproach), who has an attractive appearance, is humble, pleasant to and liked by people, who has a sweet voice and musical ability, who is well versed in the Scriptures, capable of preaching, conversant with the *Halaka* (Law) and Jewish folklore (*Agada*), and who knows all the prayers and benedictions by heart." The possesson of a sweet voice, however, was regarded the most essential requirement. It was even considered as a heavenly gift bestowed upon the person through which to inspire the people to devotion.[8]

Much stress was laid upon the good pronunciation and distinct articulation of the precentor. Therefore, people with certain defects of speech were not allowed to function.[9] A proper and clean garment was likewise required.[10] Physical deficiencies, such as blindness or deformities, were no cause of objection.[11]

As indication of reverence and humility in worship, the sages insisted that the precentor should stand on a lower level than the other worshippers, as the psalmist prays, "Out of the depths I cry to Thee" (Ps. 130: 1). Therefore, the platform from which the precentor officiated was lower than the floor of the synagogue.[12] This custom has been retained in many synagogues. Only for the reading of the Scriptures was there a

Bema (elevated platform) in the center of the synagogue.[13]

Persecution and oppression changed the face of the Jewish world. In Palestine the severity of the Eastern Roman Empire was followed by that of the Christian Church. In Babylonia, the fanatical Magi caste, which controlled the Persian Rulers, laid its heavy hand upon the Jew also. Old centers of Jewish culture were ruined. The sages were killed in part and in part dispersed, and the continuation of study was interrupted, so that a short time after the conclusion of the Talmud, ignorance was prevalent in many of the communities in which, some generations before, Jewish wisdom and knowledge had flourished. No wonder that in the course of time there was scarcely a man to be found in some communities who was able to officiate as honorary precentor; and the need of a professional *shaliach-tzibbur* became more and more urgent.

Later, another development tended toward professionalizing the post of precentor. The simple style of the ancient prayers continued, as we have already seen, until the sixth century, when attempts were made to introduce more intricate poetical forms. After Islam's conquest, the metrical poetry called *piyyut* was created. This *piyyut* stimulated the creation of intricate music, both rhythmical and modal, the rendition of which required more musical talent than did the simple modes in use before. It necessitated rather professional singers who should devote themselves to studying and cultivating both the new texts and their tunes—a task which was impossible for the lay-precentor. Thus, on the one hand, ignorance, and on the other, the new artistic demands, created the professional precentor who received the name *chazzan*.[14]

This name is an old one transferred from the secular post of government officer, later care-taker (beadle) of the court of law or of communal affairs in general. Etymologically, *chazzan* is derived from the stem *chazah*—to oversee. In the last period of the second Temple, care-takers or beadles in general were called *chazzanim*. After the fall of the Temple and the collapse of political independence, the communal functions of *chazzanim* melted away; and only the Synagogue retained the *chazzan* as a beadle. Little by little, there was relegated to him the recitation of minor parts of the service. Yet, during the Talmudic period, the *chazzan* was never permitted to function as precentor or reader of the Bible in the public service, unless he was a learned man, conversant with the prayers, and might, like everyone else, be thus distinguished. But the time of distress in the sixth and seventh centuries compelled many communities, for lack of able men, to entrust the *chazzan*-beadle with the function of precentorship, inasmuch as he was always present in the synagogue. He was first permitted to read the weekly portions of the Pentateuch and Prophets and translate them into the vernacular, the Aramaic idiom spoken in Palestine and Babylonia at that time. For some time a distinction was drawn between the function of reading the Bible and that of leading in prayer. And still in the ninth century the partaking of the *chazzan* in the prayer was of a subordinate character.[15]

At the same time *chazzanim* reached an honored position and climbed high in popular esteem by merit of their personality and knowledge. Already toward the end of the first century, the *chazzan* Rabbi Zenon was recorded as having been an important personage in the court of Rabban Gamaliel in Jamnia.[16] At times, a special benediction was inserted for the *chazzan* as one of the distinguished men in the community.[17] A prominent *chazzan* was often compared to an angel, as he faced the congregation with the Scripture in his hand.[18] These utterances and many others prove that the advance of the *chazzan* from beadle to precentor was due not exclusively to emergency, but also to the virtues of some of the leading *chazzanim*.

Small congregations were only too glad to acquire a man who could occupy all the religious offices. In the eighth and ninth centuries, for lack of adults suitable for the post, congregations were compelled to entrust youths of seventeen or eighteen with the office of precentor. Amran Gaon, the author of the oldest ritual (*siddur*) known, in the ninth century, decided that in case of emergency even boys of thirteen should be permitted to assume this office.[19]

Early in the Talmudic period the service was divided between two officers. One was invited to recite the *Shema* including the benedictions connected with it. He as a rule used to sit among the congregants. After he was through, another man was invited to stand up before the pulpit facing the direction of Jerusalem to recite the prayer proper, i.e., the *Amida* (seven benedictions on Sabbaths and holidays, and eighteen on week days). On Sabbaths and Festivals the first precentor recited the morning-prayer (*Shachrith*), and the second the additional-prayer (*Musaf*).[20] The office of the second precentor was regarded superior to that of the first.[21] This custom has survived to the present day, and has influenced the song, in so much as the music of *Musaf* is greater in quantity and more elaborate than that of *Shachrith*.

The professional *chazzan*, even after he became the permanent precentor, could never replace the honorary precentor. The latter never vanished altogether from the Synagogue. Throughout the medieval ages and in some places down to our time, at special occasions, on fast days and High Holidays, prominent men of high ethical standing, rabbis or laymen, functioned as spokesmen and intercessors for their people. Concerning the outstanding of these we shall speak later (Chapters VIII and IX).

Together with the Psalms and parts of the Jewish ritual, the early Christians transplanted the institution of the precentor

from the Synagogue into the Church.[22]   Just as in the Synagogue so also in the Church the solo recitation of the precentor
became the chief part of the service.   Similarly, the responsive
form used in the Temple and Synagogue was adopted by the
Church, especially short refrains such as *Amen, Hallelujah,
Hosanna.*   The singer was called cantor, præcentor, *pronunciator psalmi.*[23]   Originally, in the Church, too, there was the
reader (lektor) and the singer (cantor).   The latter did not
officiate in the Mass.   As in the Synagogue so also in the
Church an elevated stand was erected for the lektor from
which place he read the Scriptures.   However, gradually the
precentor gave way to the choir; the choral and antiphonal song
replaced the solo recitation.   Thus, the precentor has vanished
completely in some churches, and in some churches his rôle
has been reduced to an insignificant function;[24] whereas in the
Synagogue, the precentor preserved his importance in the
service.

CHAPTER VII

THE RHYTHMICAL SONG IN THE ORIENTAL AND SEPHARDIC
SYNAGOGUE.

Music developed in two parallel lines: one accompanying
bodily motions, such as marching, laboring, and dancing, for
which it had to mark strict rhythm; and the other, the recitative
or mode, independent of bodily motions, serving only as an
interpretation of text. We find both types in the music of all
nations, cultured and primitive. Some peoples, notably the
Orientals, such as Hindus, Tartars, Arabs, and Jews, considered
the free music, the modes, superior to the rhythmical; while
Northern European nations developed the rhythmical music to
a high degree, neglecting altogether the modal type. Though
we do not know the state of the folk-song of the Northern
European peoples before the eleventh century, we see clearly,
beginning with that period and afterwards, the tendency to
rhythmize even the unrhythmical modes. As an illustration
we have the Gregorian chant, originally unrhythmical, taken
partly from Jewish-Oriental song and partly from other
Levantine sources, gradually reworked according to the taste
of the European peoples through the moulding of it into some
rhythmical forms, and finally through the use of its elements
as themes for rhythmical art music. In the first centuries of
their conversion to Christianity, these peoples, greatly influenced by the Gregorian chant, retained the modal forms
for the songs that they created;[1] but gradually they emancipated themselves from the Catholic Church chant and started
creating, in accord with their nature, the Northern European

music. Even at so small a distance south as Southern Italy and Spain, not to speak of the Southern Slavs (Ukrainians, Bulgarians, Serbians), likewise, modern Greece, we find the free modal form more and more predominant. The folk-singers of these localities are able to improvise according to a certain modal scheme, while this ability is unthinkable in a Northern folk-singer. This phenomenon is due to the continuous large Semitic-Oriental influx that these countries received for many centuries.

From the psychological point of view it is questionable whether the rhythmical form is better suited to express the emotions of our soul than is the modal form. Rhythm leads inevitably to a fixed succession of measured tones, to a firm structure—to a stable *logical* expression of a sentiment—to *melody*. The hard encrusted mould of melody in which none of the tones can be changed is a means of *preserving* a sentiment. It may serve rather to reawaken a mood to which the composer gave a musical expression. It lacks the spontaneity of the improvisation of the modal form. "The continuous mechanical, pendular motion of rhythmical music was always annoying to the people. Although it was appropriate for marching and riding, yet at no time was it suited to and liked for expressive vocal music. Therefore the recitative is the beginning and the end of all genuine song, from the Psalmody of the Hebrews to the Gregorian chant, and from the Greeks to Richard Wagner." This statement is by Franz M. Boehme, an authority on German folk-song.[2]

Fixed forms of worship were considered by the Jewish sages of old a constraint upon the free stream of our sentiments. Thus they say: Do not make your prayers a fixed form, for he whose prayer is routine, can never attain the pulsating emotion of genuine supplication.[3] Free, improvised prayers, such as were customary in Jewish worship (Chapter V), without artistic forms of meter and rhyme, could not but be intoned in free, improvised modal music. This circumstance and the general Oriental inclination to unrhythmical song explain the predominance of the modal form in the Synagogue; while the complete absence of rhythmical music was, as we saw in Chapter I, due to the abolition of bodily movements and percussive instruments from the service.

The lack of the rhythmical element, though that element was accounted inferior, was certainly intuitively felt by the people all along. But as in so many similar circumstances in history, there was needed a stimulus from without to help the inner longing to express itself. Though already prior to the Arabic invasion attempts were made to compose prayers and hymns in certain metrical forms (Chapter V), yet, due either to lack of a model or to lack of inspiration, those efforts fell like sterile seed.

The Arabs, as a Semitic-Oriental people, were not differentiated from the Jews in their preference for modal music. Yet at the same time they developed secular rhythmical music for those of their poems which were accompanied by bodily motions. This poetry and this music made a great impression upon the Jews. The influence was enhanced by the political freedom which the Jewish people received from the same source. Gradually the Arabic type of verse and music was introduced not only into Jewish secular life but also into the Synagogue, so that by the tenth century we find poetry in Arabic meter together with Arabic melodies in the Synagogal service in Babylonia, Syria, Morocco, and Spain. Hence, rhythmical song among the Jews of the Orient became synonymous with Arabic music from that time on until the present day. An exception to this tendency to fall under the influence of rhythm, we find in the Yemenite Jews, who, though living in Arabic environment, accepted very few Arabic melodies.

They seldom employ rhythmical music in their Synagogue song, altogether about nine tunes. They recite even those poems in the ritual which are based upon Arabic meter in the same traditional modes employed for the ancient prayers. On the other hand, in their home-songs (though these are religious in content) they have a rich treasury of melodies in strict rhythm, because these are accompanied by handclapping, dancing, and the beating of rhythm on little drums (Chapter XVII). This description holds also for the song of the Persian Jews.[4]

In the Eastern and Balkan countries, which remained under Christian influence and had but little or no contact with Arabic culture, the poetry continued to develop in the forms used prior to the Arabic era, namely in meters based on the number of words or accented syllables. (See Chapter V.) The highest development this type of poetry attained was in the compositions of Eleazar Kallir, who in all likelihood lived in Palestine or Syria in the eighth or ninth century. His poetry was carried over to Italy and Germany where it became a model and was imitated in form and style by local poets. (See Chapter VIII.)

Arabic meter—so Arabic tradition claims—sprang from the rhythm of bodily motions, such as the pendular beating of the blacksmith and the trot of the horse and the camel.[5] Arabic philosophers and grammarians, however, coined names for the meter derived from grammatical terminology: such as *mu-fa-i-lun*, *fa-u-lun*, *fa-i-la-tun*, etc. These terms were confusing, because, when correctly pronounced, their accents did not correspond to those of the verses that they designated. Hence, they conveyed the idea that it was the NUMBER of their syllables that determined the type of poetic form. The musicians, however, or the poets who were at the same time musicians, instinctively abided by the MUSICAL time value of the meter and cultivated those meters which lend themselves to strict time, while the other intricate meters were neglected.

Table XVI presents the musical formulæ of those meters with strict time: 1. *Hazag* U＿＿⊥. This foot has the first *chronos* (time-unit), a half syllable followed by three syllables, the last being prolonged. For *Hazag* meter, the foot occurs twice. In case it occurs three times, the meter is called *Wafir*. The foot is called "Mŭ-fā-ī-luñ." Its musical value is given in table XVI, 1. The musical rhythm of the meter can be rendered in 4/4 measure.

2. *Ragaz* U＿U＿, repeated three times: mŭs-tāf-ĭ-lūn. This meter takes on the triplet character and is rendered in 6/8. (XVI, 2), having the character of the Greek iambic meter (twice).

3. *Mutákarib* U＿⊥ repeated four times: fă-ū-lūn. Its musical rhythm is 3/8, and has, likewise, the triplet character. (XVI, 3.)

4. *Ramal* is a compound meter of ⊥U＿＿, which occurs twice, and ⊥U⊥; its formula being: fă-ĭ-lā-tūn (twice), fă-ĭ-lăn. The musical rendition of this meter, however, is in 2/4. (XVI, 4.)

5. *Tawil* is likewise a compound meter of ＿＿⊥, which occurs twice and ＿＿＿＿; its formula being: fā-ū-lŭn (twice) and mū-fā-ī-lūn. The musical measure is 4/4. (XVI, 5.)

6. *Saria*, compound: U⤳U＿ twice and ＿U＿, i.e., mŭs-tăf-ĭ-lūn twice and fā-ĭ-lūn. The difference between the *Ragaz* formula and that of *Saria* lies in dividing the second time-unit (the syllable *tāf*) into two halves (ta-f), while the musical value of the unit remains the same as before. (XVI, 6.)

7. *Kámil* has the basis of UU⊥U＿ occurring twice, its formula being mŭ-tă-fă-ĭ-lūn. This meter is a combination of anapæst (UU＿) and iambus (U＿). Yet its musical rendition is in 4/4. (XVI, 7.)

8. *Basit* is a compound meter of UUU＿ and UU＿, using the terms mŭs-tăf-ĭ-lūn, fă-ĭ-lūn in a different time value than in the previous meters. This meter must be rendered in the musical scheme of 5/8-4/8. (XVI, 8.)

Of these meters it was chiefly the first five that were adopted and used in Hebrew poetry, while of the others but little use could be made, because the Hebrew language does not lend itself to their forms. Even these five meters were frequently

TABLE XVI
Arabic Meters

altered to facilitate their application to Hebrew. The *Hazağ*
meter (and *Wafir*) became the most popular one in Hebrew
poetry, and it was the poetry in this meter most often selected
for music. Many melodies in the *Hazağ* meter are retained
in the Oriental Synagogue and we give in table XVII a few
of the most popular tunes known in the Oriental and Sephardic
ritual. The TIME of the tunes in the illustrations Nos. 1, 2, 6,
7, 9, 10, 11, 12, 14, 15, 16 corresponds exactly to the *Hazağ*
meter of the poems, whereas in Nos. 3, 4, 8, 13 the TIME of
the music bears no relation to the strictly *Hazağ* meter of the
poems. The poem in 5 is in the *Wafir* meter. Nos. 5 and 8
have the same text, yet the melodies are based upon different
rhythms. Especially the poem in 1 (the famous hymn *Adon
olam*) is set to innumerable melodies of various rhythms. The
same is true of the text of 14-16 (the famous hymn *Lechoh
dodi*), a poem which received about two thousand musical
settings. Table XVIII furnishes melodies to the well-known
hymn *Yigdal*.

From the illustrations Nos. 1-3 we see that the poem which holds
strictly to *Rağaz*-meter (altered) is set to music unrelated in time.
Likewise, the *Mutákarib* meter of 4 and 5 is ignored in the musical
setting, as is the *Kamil*-meter of No. 6.

From these examples we learn that only melodies for poems
in *Hazağ* bear the impress of its meter, and even there, in only
a few cases; while in the case of melodies set to poems of other
meters, no relation between the meter of the text and the
rhythm of the music is traceable. Moreover, we find that
PROSE texts are set to RHYTHMICAL music, as the illustrations
in table XIX evidence. No. 1 is set to the *Kaddish*, No. 2
to *Hashkivenu* (a prayer in the evening service), No. 3 to
Psalm 29, and No. 4 to a *Selicha* with alphabetical acrostic and
WORD-meter (two words to the line). In this connection we

TABLE XVII
Melodies in the Hazag meter

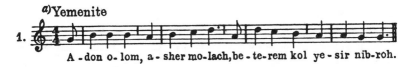

a) Yemenite

1.

A -don o-lom, a- sher mo-lach, be- te-rem kol ye-sir nib-roh.

2.

Le-choh e-li   te-shu-ko-thi; be-choh hesh-ki we-a-ha-bo-thi.

3.

She-e el-yon be-kol eb-yon   we-shaw-o - thi al yib - ze.

4.

De-ror yik - roh le-ben im   bath,   we-

yin - sor - chem   ke - mo bo - bath.

b) Babylonian

5.

Ge - u - le el te-nu she-bah   we - ho - da -oth,

le - sam o - thoth   be - mis - ra - yim we - nif - la - oth.

6. Le-choh e - li te-shu-ka-thi, be-choh hesh-ki we-a-ha-ba-thi.

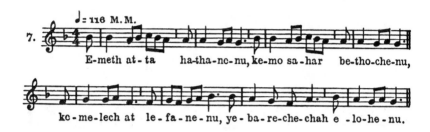

7. E-meth at-ta ha-tha-no-nu, ke-mo sa-har be-tho-che-nu,

ko-me-lech at le-fa-ne-nu, ye-ba-re-che-chah e-lo-he-nu.

8. Do-ror yik-ra le-ben im bath we-yin-sor-chem ke-mo ba-bath.

c) Sephardic

Lento

9. Be-rith nif kad a-sher ne-kad le-ha-a-loth le-fa-ne-chah

Moderato

Solo

10. Ye - de ra - shim ne-he-la-shim me-has-sig ye-

I   II   *Unison*

de chof-ram. ro-me-moth êl. le-hak-dish eth ke-

dosh ya-a-kob wo-eth e-lo-he yis-ra-el.

11.
Sephardic-Italian

Ye - de ra-shim ne-he-la-shim me-has-sig ye-de chof-ram.

12.
Sephardic-London

13.

A - zam-mer bish - ba - hin le-me - al go pi-the-hin de-

ba - ha-kal tap-pu - hin, de - in-nun kad - di - shin.

14.
Sephardic-Oriental

Le - cha do - di lik - rath kal-la, pe -

15.
Sephardic-Italian

16.
Sephardic-Amsterdam

14.

ne shab - bath ne - ka - be - la.

15.

16.

TABLE XVIII
a) Melodies in the Rağaz meter

b) Melodies in the Mutakarib meter

c) Melody in the Kamil meter

TABLE XIX

a) Rhythmical music set to unmetrical texts

Sephardic-Oriental

1. Yith-gad-dal we-yith kad - dash she-me rab - ba.*etc.*

2. Hash-ki - be - nu a - bi - nu le - sha - lom we-ha-
a - mi-de-nu mal ke - nu le-ha-yim to-bim u-le-sha-lom.

3. Ha - vu la-do-nay be-ne-e-lim, ha-vu la-do-nay ka-vod wa-oz.

4. A - don ha - se - li-hoth, bo - hen le - ba-both.
...ha - ta - nu le - fa-ne-cha ra - hem a - le - nu

b) Unrhythmical music set to metrical texts

5. She-fal ru-ach, she-fal be - rech we-ko-ma. *etc.*

6. *Solo* Eth sha-a - re ra - son le-hi - pa-the - ah,
yom e - he-ye chap-pay la - el sho-te ah.
Unison o - ked we-ha-ne - kad we-ham-miz-be - ah.

TABLE XX
Adonay bekol shofar

Sephardic - Oriental

1. *Solo*

A-do-nay be-kol sho-far   yash-mi-a

ye-shu-a le-kab-bes se   fe-zu-ra   be-vo hez-yon te-shu-a.

Unison

a-la e-lo-him bith - ru-a, a-do-nay be-kol sho-far.

Moroccan

2. *Solo*

A - do-nay be-kol   sho-far yash-mi - a ye-shu-a le-

kab-bes   se   fe-zu - ra be-bo hez-yon te-shu - a,

Unison

a-la e-lo-him bith - ru-a, a-do-nay be-kol sho-far.

Italian

3. *Solo*

A-do-nay be-kol   sho-far,   kol   mi-sha-ma-yim, al

har hak-ko-dosh ve-al ye-ru-sha-la-yim, ve-az kan-nath

ye-mi-ne-cha te-hi ke-me-rosh   ne-tu - a,

Unison

a-la e-lo-him bith-ru - a,   a-do-nay be-kol sho-far.

may refer back to table VI, 3, where the "Song of the Sea" is illustrated, set to rhythmical tune, based upon the Pentateuch mode.

It is therefore quite obvious that the Arabic meter, though it opened the way for rhythmical music in the Synagogue, did not remain the only moulding and determining creative power of rhythmical song. Rhythmical music, once established in the Synagogue, gained more and more ground; and rooted itself in Jewish song. It emancipated itself from the metrical impress of the poetry. It was Arabic tunes which were first adopted for the Hebrew poems based upon Arabic meters. This very procedure of adopting tunes, originally set to OTHER texts, developed in the people an appreciation of the MUSICAL value of the melodies, apart from the text. There arose an esteem for music not merely as a tonal interpretation or echo of a certain text, but as a human expression independent of any text. Thus music attained in the eyes of the people a place equal to that of the text. Soon a melody was no longer adopted for a text, but on the contrary, a text was set to a popular melody and sometimes even, especially, composed for it. In this wise, the music became of greater importance than the text. Frequently poets would be inspired by a certain melody to write a poem according to its rhythm; others would adjust their verses to favorite tunes then in vogue, even when the poetical meter did not exactly fit the musical rhythm. There were many instances of attractive tunes originally for secular texts to which some rabbis, in their zeal to prevent the people's singing words of doubtful morals, would supply substitute texts of religious content, imitating the meter and even the sounds of the vowels of the secular texts.[6]

The chief factor in supplying rhythmical music and metrical poetry was the *chazzan*. His was the task to fascinate his congregation with new material. The week-day services, because of the brief time that could be allowed them, permitted no poetical and musical embellishments. On Sabbaths and holidays on the other hand, when the people were free from work, it was the task of the *chazzan* to entertain them and to display his twofold art of poet and singer. Most of the *chazzanim*, from the tenth down to the fourteenth centuries, were like the "bards," the Arabic "singers" (*Shuar*), the French *Trobadors*, and the German *Minnesinger*, poet-musicians.

Gradually the traditional unrhythmical modes ceased to hold first place in the hearts of the people, who became interested mainly in singing, which now became synonymous with rhythmical song. A twelfth-century observer states [7] that the prayers were recited by the precentor only, but that as soon as he started the *Chazzanya* (the *chazzanic* art, i.e., poetry and its music), the entire congregation joined in loud singing. Similar testimony reaches us from several authors before and after that time. So Yehuda Charizi, a Sephardic scholar and poet, who visited Mossul (Mesopotamia) at the beginning of the thirteenth century, leaves a satiric description of the "art" of the *chazzan* there, counting all his grammatical mistakes in the prayers as well as in his poetry; relating how the *chazzan*, self-satisfied with his artistic performance, exhausted himself and the congregation and wasted the time through his "art," so that no time was left for the ritual proper. When Charizi called the attention of the *chazzan* and his adherents to the mischief, they declared that his poetry and his music were more important than the prayers themselves. [8]

An opposition to this exaggerated emphasis on the poetry was inevitable. In fact, already early in the eleventh century we hear the opinion of great men like Hay Gaon (himself a poet), Isaac Alfasi, and Jehuda of Barcelona [9] against too much use of poetry and Arabic melodies in the Synagogue. The op-

position increased more and more, so that Maimonides was extremely antagonistic to all poetry and "music." [10]   The most
that the opposition could effect was a check upon the poetry, to
prevent its gaining a permanent upper hand in the service.
Numerous poems and their tunes remain in the Synagogue to
the present day.   Among a vast number of aspiring poets there
arose in Spain some very gifted ones: Solomon ibn Gabirol,
Jehuda Halevi, who in theory opposed the Arabic meter,[11]
Moses and Abraham ben Ezra in the eleventh and twelfth
centuries.   They enriched Synagogal poetry with their deep
religious spirit, some of their hymns reaching a height equal
to that of the Psalms.   And even as late as the sixteenth century some poets in Northern Palestine: Isaac Luria, Solomon
Alkabetz, and Israel Najara were successful in making worthy
contributions to Synagogal poetry.   Najara was both poet and
singer (*chazzan*).   For some of his poems he composed his
own melodies, but most of them were written according to
the rhythm of popular Arabic, Turkish, and Spanish tunes.   He
was the last Synagogal poet (Chapter XVII) writing in
Hebrew.

On the other hand, we see that rhythmical music not only
did not displace modal music, but also lost out to its older
sister, for the settings of even many metrical poems were intoned according to traditional modes or to Arabic *Makams* in
free modal form.   Aside from the above-mentioned Yemenite
and Persian communities, even the Sephardic and Syrian communities sing poems based upon strict meter in free modes.
The Synagogue song in Syria (Aleppo, Damascus) was
Arabized more than that of other Mohammedan countries; and
yet in these very Syrian communities, not only were the Biblical
and Prayer modes carefully preserved, but more than that,
even metrical poems were interpreted in the genuine Semitic-
Oriental modal form.   Two illustrations of unrhythmical music

set to metrical poems may suffice. The one (5) is a poem by the above-mentioned Solomon ibn Gabirol *Shefal berech*, which is founded upon the *Wafir* meter (altered). Its musical setting, however, is in the *Tefilla* mode (Chapter IV). The second (6) is a poem known in the Sephardic-Oriental ritual (*Eth Shaare ratzon*), of the twelfth century, in the *Ragaz* meter, while its music is in the *Selicha* mode (Chapter IV). In like manner we find many modal unrhythmical chants in the Oriental and even in the Italian tradition, which were molded in the Northern European communities of the Sephardim into rhythmical tunes, most likely influenced by the style and spirit of Northern European music.

The custom of adopting tunes from local Arabic or other music made a breach in the unity of Synagogue song, for until the rise of the *piyyut* (poetry) the traditional modes prevailed in the worship of all communities in the Diaspora. But since poets arose in various localities who composed poems, they selected local tunes for their products, or composed tunes in the style of the music of the people of their environment.

Nonetheless we find a number of tunes common in the various Sephardic communities in the East and the West, though with some variations. Table XX illustrates one of these common tunes for the poem *Adonay bekol shofar*. Whether these common tunes originated in the Orient and from there were carried by *chazzanim* to the scattered Sephardic congregations, or originated in Spain before the expulsion in 1492, it is impossible to find out with certainty. At any rate nothing proves that these rhythmical tunes are Jewish creations, for though they have the general Semitic-Oriental features, they have no specific Jewish characteristics. No elements of Biblical modes are traceable in them, as in the earlier Ashkenazic tunes, which we shall treat in Chapter VIII. It is only in the SELECTION of the tunes that the Jewish spirit manifested itself, in choosing tunes based primarily on the minor and Dorian scales, expressing tender warmth and a calm dignity. We note no harshness; and we find but very few tunes in the *Hedjaz* mode. In the phlegmatic Orient, the Synagogue song of the Sephardic-Oriental communities remained stagnant in the last three centuries. Only the Italian Jews were stirred by the Italian Renaissance to renewed activity and creation. And this, indeed, for a short time only (Chapter X), leaving their attempt to be continued by the youngest and strongest of all Jewish groups—the *Ashkenazim.*

CHAPTER VIII

THE SYNAGOGUE SONG OF THE "ASHKENAZIM."

Ashkenazim are Jews living in Western, Central, and Eastern Europe and those Jews in America, Africa, Asia, and Australia who are descendants of them. Originally, only German Jews were called *Ashkenazim* (*Ashkenaz:* Gen. 10: 3 was considered Germany).[1] The oldest Jewish settlement in Germany was in the Southwestern part, on the banks of the Rhine and Main. At the time of Charlemagne there already existed several Jewish communities in the German districts of his Empire. According to tradition, Charlemagne settled the Italian Kalonymos family in Mayence in the eighth century.[2] He likewise imported a Jewish sage from Bagdad, Rabbi Machir, and placed him in Narbonne, Southern France.[3] From that time on Jewish learning and tradition were transplanted into France and Germany. The Kalonymos family had a tradition that its ancestors came from Palestine and descended from Simeon Happakoli (who had phrased the eighteen Benedictions for Rabbi Gamaliel in Jamnia c. 100 C.E.).[4] Similarly, another Rabbinical family in Southern Italy (Oria) preserved the tradition that its ancestors came to Italy from Jerusalem. Among the members of that family were poets and liturgists of importance.[5] During the tenth and eleventh centuries the immigration of rabbis of the Orient into France and Germany, and from Italy into Germany, was considerable. These carried with them their Oriental traditions, which became the basis of the religious practices in both Germany and France. Thus "previous to 1000 C.E. almost no difference

129

existed between the Old French and the Old German rituals, because both were founded upon the Amram ritual." [6]   The great commentator Rashi of the eleventh century says that "all our (religious) customs are according to Babylonian tradition." [7] The same may be assumed with regard to the status of the Synagogue song, for, as we saw, the Biblical and prayer modes of the Ashkenazim are essentially the same as those of the Oriental communities.   However, the close relations between the Jews and Gentiles in early centuries and especially during the reign of Charlemagne and his son Louis the Pious brought about a cultural reciprocity in which at first the Jews were more frequently those to exert the influence than those to be influenced.   We learn this fact from the campaign which Bishop Agobard of Lion in his letters to Louis the Pious started in 825 against the Jewish influence upon the Christians, which in his opinion endangered the Christian faith.   He complains that the Jews teach the Christians the principles of their religion; that Christians attend Jewish services and prefer the blessings and prayers of the Jewish rabbis; that Christians attend Jewish meals on Sabbaths and that Christian women rest on Sabbaths [8] and work on Sundays; that Christians openly declare that they would like to have a lawgiver such as the Jews have; and that Christians have the audacity to announce that the Jewish religion is the only true one.   In view of this fact, Agobard demanded that a prohibition should be issued to the effect that no Christian man or woman should attend Jewish services, nor observe the Sabbath, nor participate in Jewish festal meals, and that Christian people should stay away from the Jews.   He demanded from the Emperor that he send out orders to all the bishops and priests in the Empire urging them to exert the utmost energy that with united effort the menace be removed from the Church. [9]

Judging from the zealous tone in which Agobard's letters

are written, we may deduce that the Jewish influence was strongly felt; gradually penetrated into the mind of the clergy, and bore fruit. From that time on restrictions against the relations between Jews and Christians were issued, or old ones dating from the fourth to the seventh centuries were renewed, and at the same time the civil and human rights of the Jews were reduced until the Jews were declared strangers and dangerous individuals.

Of the song of the Germans, there are reports from the fourth century. Armianus Mercelinus (330 C.E.) calls their song whistling, squeaking, or a sound like that of wheels. In like manner Emperor Julianus (356-360) described the German song.[10] And John Diaconus in the seventh century says that the Gauls and Germans are of all European peoples the most industrious in their study of art (Gregorian) song; but despite all their effort, they are the least capable of performing it, because of their barbarous state, their lack of ability to grasp it precisely, and their vulgar loud voices hoarse from drinking. They always mingle into the art song elements of their own folk-song. Their singing resembles the rumbling of a loaded wagon running down the slope of a hill.[11] Charlemagne was the first prince who tried to cultivate art singing among his people, for which purpose he brought music teachers from Rome who established the singing schools in St. Gallen and Metz, both of which became centers for fostering and cultivating Gregorian chant and for developing music in Germany. Charlemagne issued the order in 789 that the people should be instructed to sing the Doxology, and Louis II in 856 urged the people to participate in responsive singing. Hence, on various religious and secular occasions and at daily occupations, the people intoned the *Kyrie eleison* in tunes improvised of Gregorian and folk elements, or they indulged in what was called Jubilations, i.e., protracted improvised singing without words, on the last

syllable of "Halleluja." In 799 a decree was issued warning
the people not to corrupt the Church song.[12] Such was the
beginning of the creation of German and Gallic music, a combination of Gregorian chant and folk-song, out of which the
song of the Troubadours and Minnesinger sprang, about the
eleventh century.

Thus we see that prior to the tenth century the standard of
music in France and Germany was still low. It is, indeed, no
wonder that in the early centuries the Jews exerted an influence
upon their Gentile neighbors, for their cultural standard was
infinitely higher than that of the latter. We hear that about
that time Christian clergy studied Jewish literature and
Hebrew, and were instructed by Jews in the principles of
Judaism as well as in the song of the Synagogue. Against this
practice Archbishop Odo issued a prohibition in 1197.[13] Also
from the Jewish side there arose opposition, in the twelfth century, against the exchange of Synagogue and Church melodies
or hymns.[14] A Jew was forbidden to teach a priest or a gentile
layman a tune of the Synagogue. In like manner, it was strictly
forbidden to let a Christian nurse sing to a Jewish child a
Church song lullaby.[15] We learn from the same source that
Jews used to study Christian liturgical books and to sing from
them.[16] We hear also that Rabbi Simeon the Great in the
eleventh century adopted a hymn for himself, the tune of
"Magdala," which he was taught in his dream and which was
supposed to be similar to the song of the angels.[17] On the
other hand, we hear that even in the fifteenth century Christians and even dukes with their courts used to attend services
in the Synagogue.[18] From these facts we see that restrictions
and prohibitions, crusades and persecutions could not stop the
reciprocal relation which persisted between Jew and Christian
from the ninth down to the seventeenth century. Joseph
Hahn, a rabbi and cantor in Frankfort in the seventeenth cen-

tury, complained that Jews adopt Christian tunes for their Sabbath home songs and justify their act with the excuse that the Christians had borrowed these tunes from the Temple of Jerusalem.[19]

In view of all evidences presented, it is quite natural that motives of German folk or sacred songs crept into the song of the Synagogue in Germany. Especially since and during the development of the Minnesong (eleventh-fourteenth centuries), in which art Jews took part (see below), it was inevitable that German music should leave its impress upon the song of the Jew, that the Jew's spirit should be imbued with the musical scale and style of his surrounding.

With regard to scale we have pointed out on several occasions the German influence in re-shaping it, as in the case of the Pentateuch, Ruth, Song of Songs, and *Tefilla* modes (Chapters III-IV). Likewise, German music affected the re-shaping of the tetrachordal form of the mode of Lamentations into a melodic line in which the third and fifth are pronounced (Chapter III). The influence went much deeper; it touched the very marrow of Jewish song. As already mentioned, German elements penetrated into the Semitic-Oriental song of the Jews and, by amalgamating with it, became an organic part of it. Thus a new type of music was created in the course of time, a Judeo-German song, which became the genuine expression of the German Jew. Here for the first time since the Hellenistic period two conflicting elements met and were merged and moulded into one. In such cases, the stronger element usually gains supremacy. Here, both being powerful, gave birth to a new creation: the unique *"Ashkenazic* song," while the Oriental Synagogue, continuing to draw musical nourishment from Semitic-Oriental sources, was spared a similar clash.

The Oriental rabbis who settled in Germany, coming via

Italy and France, were also precentors, *chazzanim*, and *pay-tanim* (poets). For example, there were Kalonymos and his son Meshullam from Italy and Simon bar-Abbun from France. Kallir's poetry (Chapter VII) was introduced into Germany and served as a model in style and meter for new creations. Almost all the rabbis in the period of the tenth-fourteenth centuries composed poems and hymns for the Synagogue and functioned as precentors either permanently or, at least, on feast and fast days. They would create or adapt tunes for their poetry in a FOLK-MANNER, that is instinctively. Some of these tunes would gain popularity and spread throughout the German congregations; others, of less attraction, would fall into oblivion. The popular tunes, as a rule, would conquer the heart of the Jew by reason of the preponderant proportion of the Jewish over the German elements of which they were composed. In very rare cases pure German tunes without any Jewish flavor became popular in the Synagogue, at least in the earlier period mentioned. As soon as a tune succeeded in becoming popular, it would be imitated; and generally other texts would be written according to its rhythm—a procedure customary in the Occident as well as in the Orient.[20] As a result of this practice, the Synagogue, like the Church, has infinitely more poems and texts than tunes.

Aside from the tunes of metrical texts, i.e., of poetry, the Ashkenazim created special tunes for several prose-texts of the old prayers. In the Oriental Synagogue, these prayers were and still are chanted in the traditional modes (Chapter IV). Indeed, in the Ashkenazic Synagogue, too, these texts are chanted in the same modes in the daily service. However, for religious reasons the idea was conceived by the Ashkenazic rabbis, to express the significance of every holy day by distinctive tunes, and to consecrate special melodies to each occasion in order to create the distinctive atmosphere for that day.

To achieve that aim the regular daily prayers were set to special tunes or modes for various distinguished days, with the aim of giving tonal expression to the underlying idea of the day by a LEADING MOTIVE or mode or tune assigned to it. Thus, the leading motives for New Year express reverence and awe for the Day of Judgment; those for the Day of Atonement—pleading and contrition; those for the Three Festivals —joy and hope, liberty, exultation and thanksgiving; those for the Day of Destruction express mourning; and so on. Upon entering the house of worship on one of these days, the Jew was inspired by the dominating mode or melody which reminded him of the purpose of the day.

Of course, it is impossible and futile to pass judgment as to whether these tunes are capable of calling forth in our days the ideas and sentiments they are supposed to express, since so many centuries have passed from the time of their creation, and inasmuch as they have become traditional to the Ashkenazim, deeply rooted in their soul and associated with religious sentiments in general and with the holy days in particular. The fact that only these out of many tunes became traditional and popular would point to their combination of Jewish and German material as the reason for their preservation. Those tunes were selected which appealed to the German-Jewish taste. They were singled out of a multitude of tunes which the rabbis-*chazzanim* throughout the centuries attempted to introduce into the Synagogue.

The idea of special modes and tunes for prayers in prose to be used on holidays is not an original Ashkenazic one, for the Oriental Synagogue, too, practices the same custom. The Yemenites have a special mode for the High Holidays, which is a variation of the *Selicha* mode (table XIII); the Sephardim use the *Tefilla* mode for the High Holidays only and possess several tunes for various festivals, as pointed out in Chapter

VII.　However, none of the communities succeeded in creating
a new musical genre of "special tunes" as did the Ashkenazim.
These tunes were sanctified and were called "sacred melodies"
or *scarbove*—a corruption of the Latin *sacra*.　They were also
called *Missinai*-tunes, which means "received by Moses on
Mt. Sinai.[21]　The birth-place of these *Missinai*-tunes was
Southwestern Germany in the old communities of Worms,
Mayence, Speyer, and the Rhineland, those places which were
for several centuries the center of Judaism, and from which
Talmudic Judaism was spread throughout Central and Eastern
Europe.　There was the cradle of the so-called Ashkenazic
ritual, and there lived those sages who were also poets and
chazzanim.

In Chapters III and IV we have treated those Biblical and
prayer modes common in the Ashkenazic as well as in the Oriental and Sephardic tradition and we have pointed out the
changes the Ashkenazim introduced into them.　Therefore we
shall deal here with the part of Synagogue song which the
Ashkenazim created.　On examination we find that this musical
material can be classified in (I) Modes, (IIa) in set tunes partially rhythmical and partially unrhythmical, and (IIb) in
rhythmical melodies.　We shall make an attempt to explain
their elements and characteristics and the time of their composition.

Early Hebrew literature makes but scanty reference to its
authors.　Seldom is mention made of the name of the writer,
and more rarely of the incidents of his life.　It seems that
Jewish sages did not consider it very important to acquaint the
public with their personal affairs.　From the eighth or ninth
century on, the custom arose for poets to weave their names into
their poems in acrostics.　In the melodies there is no hope of
finding any names, because Synagogue music was preserved by

memory, and only beginning with the sixteenth century were attempts made to write it down (Chapter XVI).

However, if there is no prospect of discovering the names of the composers, there is a way of finding out the time that the songs were created, taking into consideration their style and the elements out of which they were composed. This we can achieve by means of comparison and analysis.

I. Modes or *Steiger* in Minor (Table XXI)

a. In character and form these Ashkenazic modes or *Steiger*, as they were called,[22] are similar to the old Oriental modes. They are constituted of a group of motives, and are used in free fluid form for the intonation of certain texts. We differentiate modes as follows:

Mode 1 (XXI) is founded upon the Prophetic and *Mogen-Ovos* modes, and it is used for the evening service of the Three Festivals, including the *Hakafoth* (procession) service of *Simchath Torah* (Rejoicing in the Torah). It has five motives; 1, 2, and 4 are from the *Mogen-Ovos* mode (table XIV, 1-2); 3, in its beginning is from *Mogen-Ovos*, while the ending is derived from the Prophetic mode— the *athnach-motive*—and 5 is taken from the *sof pasuk*-motive of the same mode.

(2) The *Tal- and-Geshem* (dew and rain) mode is closely related to 1, and consequently to *Mogen-Ovos*. It has practically all the motives of 1, and it has two motives (4-5) in addition.

(3) The mode for SABBATH *Mincha* (afternoon) service is likewise related to 1 and 2. It has besides, the *tebir*-motive from Esther (3) and the *zarka-segol* motive from the Prophets (4-5). These last three motives are very much in use in the Ashkenazic modes and tunes, and we shall meet them often in the course of our discussion.

(4) The *Tefilla* mode for the High Holidays has motives 1, 3, and 4, found in the modes already explained, and is derived from the Prophetic mode, from which source also 5 (*darga*-motive) is taken,

TABLE XXI
Ashkenazic Modes in Minor

u - me - lech o - lom. e - me-choh no-so-si chin b'or-chi,

be - mal - a - chus   am. - choh be - rech be-vor-chi.

Bo-ruch sho · o - mar ve - ho-yoh ho - o - lom.... bo-ruch at-

toh a - do-noy, el me-lech go-dol bat-tish-bo-chos, el ha-ho-do-os,

a - don han-nif-lo-os, hab-bo-cher be-shi-re zim - roh, me lech

el chey ho - o - lo-mim...kul-lom a - hu-vim, kul-lom be-ru-rim,

kul-lom gib-bo-rim...ve-chul-lom pos-chim es pi-hem bik-du-shoh

uv-to-ho-roh.... u-ma-a - ri-tzim u-mak-di-shim u-mam-li-chim.

L. SÄNGER

She-ma yis - ro-el a - do-noy e - lo-he-nu, a- do-noy e-chod.

She-ma   yis-ro-el a - do-noy e - lo-he-nu, a-do-noy e-chod.

11. Glo-ri-a laus et ho-nor ti-bi sit, rex chris-te re-demp-tor, cu-i pu-e-ri-le, de-us promp-sit, Ho-sa-na pi-um.

12. Golt von a-ra-bye ist gut, Daz darb auch ne-man stra-fen Swe-lich her-re tu-gent un-de ver-dich-heit von kun-de hat furt la-sen. Kant ich in by na-men ich wolte in schel-ten daz iz klvu-ge.

13. Wer das e-lend ba-wen wil, der mach sich auff vnd zich da-hin, wol auff sant Ja-cobs stras-se, Zwey par schuh die muss er han, ein schüs-sel vnd ein fla-schen.

14. Ki she-sheth ya-mim a-sah a-do-nay eth ha sha ma yim ve-eth ha-a-retz, u-ba-yom ha-she-bi-i sha-bath va-yi-na-fash.

while 2 is somewhat of a variation of (1) (motive 4) or (2) (motive 6). The concluding motive (6) is found also in the *Selicha* mode (XIII, 6).

(5) The *Yotzer* mode for the Three Festivals is composed of the concluding motive of the Prophetic (1) and that of the Esther mode (2).[23]

(6) The *Yotzer* mode for the High Holidays is constructed out of the same motives as utilized in 5 plus the *darga-tebir* motives of the Pentateuch mode (3). 5 is a variation of (1), 5.

(7) The *Tefilla* mode for the Three Festivals is likewise composed of the same material: Motive 2 resembles (6), 3; motive 3, is a fusion of (6), 4, (6), 1, and (5); 2 is employed as a concluding motive. Motive 1 is a condensation of (3), 4-5. A similar motive (6) (b) we find in a song of the fourteenth century on the birth of Jesus (XXII, 10).[24]

(8) The *Yotzer* mode for weekdays and Sabbaths is a variation of (1)-3, or vice-versa, and, at any rate, a variation of the *Mogen-Ovos* mode.

(9) The tune for *Shema* for Sabbath has the concluding motive of (7), while (10) the tune for "Shema" for the High Holidays has been worked out from (2), or directly from the *Mogen-Ovos* mode.

The eight modes and the two tunes treated have all a minor character, being chiefly constructed out of the Prophetic, Esther, *Selicha*, and *Mogen-Ovos* modes, with but a few motives from the Pentateuch mode. No German elements are to be found in these creations.

Of interest in this connection is the existence of similar tunes (not modes) in the earliest song of the Catholic Church in Germany.

Example 11 (Gloria) is sung on Palm Sunday during the procession.[25] Its close resemblance to the Arabic *Bayati*-tunes (table I, 2-8) is obvious.

Example 12 is from the "Minnesong," composed by *Meister Gervelyn* (thirteenth century),[26] and it is identical to the

"Gloria" cited. Example 13 is the so-called St. Jacob's tune, used for the pilgrimage to the grave of that saint in Campostella (Spain) in the sixteenth century.[27] These examples of Semitic-Oriental elements in the old German religious and secular song are not to be taken as mere incidents, but as a continuous influence which came from two sources: first, from the Judeo-Moorish source in Germany and Spain. Tunes like that of St. Jacob, the German pilgrims evidently learned while in Spain. We know that after the Christianization of Spain and expulsion of a number of Moors and Jews, a great many of them embraced Christianity and remained in the country. Their tunes were set to Spanish texts of a religious or secular nature,[28] which spread over France and Germany. The other source of Semitic-Oriental influence came through the crusaders to Palestine, who brought back tunes which they had picked up while in the East. Already in Chapter IV, 4 (table XIV, 3) we showed that the *Mogen-Ovos* mode, upon which the greater part of all these songs is based, is also found in the Oriental Synagogue. In XXI, 14, we offer an example for that mode from the Italian Synagogue [29] which, likewise, proves that there are common musical elements between the Italian and the German Synagogue song.

II. Modes or *Steiger* in Major (Table XXII)

Of modes with major character the Ashkenazim possess but two. In example 1 the Oriental *Tefilla mode* (see table XII, 4) is still retained. 2 illustrates the *Adonoy-moloch* mode (Chapter IV, 1) as it was used for Friday evening in *Germany* in the eighteenth century, and 3, another form of the *Tefilla* mode (example 1), presents the Psalm mode used for the introduction to the Friday-evening service. Its equivalent we find in the Gregorian 5th mode (example 4), which has the same text (p. 95) as has 3, and is called *invitatorium* (invitation for prayer, because the Psalm starts, "Oh, come let us sing"). This example is taken from a MS. from 1640. However, this Psalm-tune was already in use in the Church in the eleventh century.[30] That the Ashkenazim did not borrow that mode from the Church is proved by its genuine Jewish source for which example 5 from the Yemenite Synagogue song gives evidence. Here, the concluding motive shows that this *Adonoy-moloch* mode was originally based upon the Dorian scale and remained so in the Yemenite tradition as well as in the MS. of the eleventh century of Gregorian song (4, 6),[31] while later, through the influence of the German inclination toward Major, both in the Synagogue and Church tradition, the scale of the mode was changed to major, i.e., two tones below the tonic of the ancient Dorian.[32]

The Friday-evening mode, another form of *Adonoy-moloch* (example 2), enriched with a special tune or theme, is used also for the evening service of the High Holidays. Example 7 gives the insertion. The first four bars are found in an old hymn by Paulus Diaconus at the court of Charlemagne (lived 720-799) and go back to Gregory I (d. 604).[33] The motive in the bars 3-4, as well as the concluding motive, are frequent in the Minnesong, as evidenced in examples 8-9.[34]

III. Tunes for Individual Texts

The modes or *Steiger* thus far treated were composed out of old elements of Jewish-Oriental song, with but very little non-Jewish additions. And it seems that these modes were created in an early age, at a time when German music was still in its infancy, and therefore incapable of exerting an influence to compete with Jewish song, i.e., before or about 1000 C.E. Hebrew literature of the eleventh and twelfth centuries men-

TABLE XXII
Ashkenazic Modes in Major

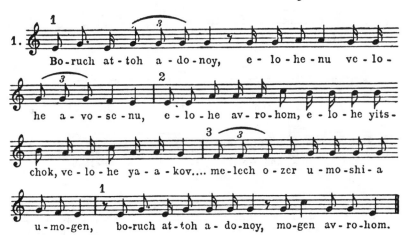

1. Bo-ruch at-toh a-do-noy, e-lo-he-nu ve-lo-
he a-vo-se-nu, e-lo-he av-ro-hom, e-lo-he yits-
chok, ve-lo-he ya-a-kov.... me-lech o-zer u-mo-shi-a
u-mo-gen, bo-ruch at-toh a-do-noy, mo-gen av-ro-hom.

2. U-ma-vir yom u-me-vi loy-loh, u-mav-dil
ben yom u-ven loy-loh, a-do-noy tzvo-os she-mo.
êl chay ve-kay-yom, to-mid yim-loch o-le-nu le-o-lom
vo-ed, bo-ruch at-toh a-do-noy, ha-ma-riv a-ro-vim.

Ps. 95

3. Le-chu ne-ra-na-noh la-do-noy, no-ri-oh le-tzur yish-e-nu.

4. Ve - ni - te ex - sul - te - mus Do - mi - ne,
Ju - bi - le - mus De - o sa - lu - ta - ri nos - tro.

5. Yis-mach mo-she be-mat-nath chel - ko, ki e - bed ne -
mon ko - ro - thoh lo.... way-yin - no - fash.

6. Glo - ri - a pat-ri *etc.* el in sae-cu - la sac-cu - lo - rum. A - men.

7. Bor - chu' es a-do - noy ha
ha ___ m'vo - roch.

8. I - ste con - fes - sor do - mi - ne co - len - tes.

9.

10. Ma-ri - en ward ein bot ge - sant, vom hi-mel-rich in kur-zen stunt...

tions already the special modes for the different services for Sabbath and festivals.[35]

The tunes composed for the individual texts in the services of the festivals and chiefly for the High Holidays differ from the modes. In these tunes we find Jewish and German-Gregorian elements fused and molded into forms which were current in the period of the Minnesong, from the eleventh to the fourteenth centuries. In some of these tunes, forms of the "Sequence" and "Jubilation" are traceable. Some of them show the *lais* form. They repeat two or three times, dividing the texts, though they are in prose, into two or three parts similar to stanzas. However, these parts being prose could not be symmetrical, so that shorter and longer divisions were inevitable, which had to be repeated according to the same tune. This procedure caused variations in the tunes. At times, some of the parts of the tunes repeated had to be sung without words because of shorter texts.

In the employment of the major scale for these tunes, German influence can be recognized. The preference for that scale started with the Minnesong. Indeed, the minor note still retains a considerable place in the tunes, while the Dorian (Greg. Phrygian) scale of the Pentateuch and *Tefilla* was gradually abandoned, being retained in only a few tunes. Neither was the *Ahavoh-Rabboh* mode or *Hedjaz* scale employed. Only later in the seventeenth century was this scale brought to Germany and Central Europe by the Eastern *chazzanim* (Chapter XI), who introduced variations into these tunes according to the scale of *Ahavoh-Rabboh*.

(A) The tunes for prose texts composed in the period of the eleventh to the fifteenth centuries are these (table XXIII):

1. *Olenu* (Adoration). The text was originally composed in the third century in Babylonia for *Musaf* (additional service) of the High Holidays. The singing of that text became cus-

TABLE XXIII
Ashkenazic tunes for individual prose texts

Ovos II   L. SÄNGER, 1840

Bo-ruch at-toh a-do-noy, elo-he-nu ve-lo - he   a - vo - se-nu,

e - lo-he av-ro -   - hom, e - lo-he yitz   chok

ve-lo - he ya -   a-kov ... le-ma-an   she-mo

be-a - ha- voh.

Ovos III   J. M. ABELOV, 1870 (?)

Boruch at-toh a-do-noy, e-lo-he - - - nu ve-lo-he ____

____ a-vo____ se-nu. e-lo - he - - - -

- - - - av-ro-hom - - -

e-lo-he - - - - - - - yız ____

____ chok ve-lo-he yaa-kov ..... êl

el - yon - - - - -

- - - - - go - mel cha-so-dim to-vim.

Fine

D.S.a F.

Kaddish I

JOSEPH GOLDSTEIN, 1791 (?)

Yıs-ga-dal ve-yıs-kad-dash she-me rab-boh

be-o-le-mohdi-ve-roh chir-u-se ve-ya-me lich mal-chu-se,

be-cha-ye-chon uv-yo-me-chon uv-cha-ye   de-chol bes yis-ro-el

ba-go-loh u-viz - man . . . . ko-riv . .

ve-i-me-ru o-men. yis-bo - rach ve-yish-

ta-bach ve-yis-po-ar ve-yis-ro-mam ve-yis-na - se,   ve-yis - -

ha-dor ve-yis-a - le ve-yis-ha-lol she - me   de kud-shoh be-rich hu.

Kaddish II

Yis _____ ga-dal   she-me ra-boh,   shme ra - boh,
v'yis - - ka dash

be-ol-moh di vroh chir-u - se   ve-yam-lich mal-chu - se,

be-cha-ye - chon   uv-yo - me-chon   uv-cha-ye dchol

bes yis-ro - el,   ba-a-go-loh u-viz-ma ko-riv   ve-im-ru o - men.

JOSEPH GOLDSTEIN, 1791(?)

Kol nidré I

A. BEER, 1765 (?)

Fine

noh, mi-yom kip-pu-rim   ze   ad yom kip-pu-

rim hab-boh o - le - nu   le - to - voh. kol - hon   i - cha-

rat-noh ve - hon,   kol - hon_____

ye-hon   sho-ron, she-vi - kin   she-vi - sin   be-te.

lin um-vu - to - lin,   lo she-ri - rin ve-lo ka - yo - min.

nid - ro - noh lo_____ nid - re

ve - le-so - ro - noh   lo e-so   - re.   ush-vu - o - so -

noh   lo_____ she-vu - os.

Akdomus

7

Ak-do-mus mil-lin v'sho-ro-yus shu-soh   av-loh sho-kil-noh har-mo-nur shu-soh.

8

Mi-cho-mo-choh   bo-e-lim a - do-noy, mi-ko-mo-choh ne'dor ba - ko-desh.

tomary apparently during the first period of the crusades, when Jews were forced to embrace Christianity. They preferred to be burned or killed, singing with exultation the sovereignty of the One Eternal Living God, expressed in the *Olenu*. It is related that "during the persecution of the Jews of Blois (France) in 1171, when many masters of the Law died as martyrs at the stake, an eye-witness wrote to Rabbi Jacob of Orleans that the death of the saints was accompanied by a weird song resounding through the stillness of the night, causing the Christians who heard it from afar to wonder at the melodious strains, the like of which they had never heard before. It was ascertained afterward that the martyred saints had made use of the *Olenu* as their dying song." [36]   The cantor Herz Treves of Frankfort (1470-1550) arranged some verses for the congregation to recite softly while the *chazzan* sang the *Olenu* on the High Holidays. [37]

We have the oldest MS. of the tune written down by Ahron Beer, *chazzan* in Berlin about 1765, which we give in table XXIII, 1, leaving out the embellishments obviously added by the writer. Since then the tune has been written down by several *chazzanim* of various localities in Europe with different variations, but all versions retained the essential motives to be found in the oldest example cited.

2. *Hammelech* (The King). The custom to sing this text in the morning service (*Shachris*) was established by Rabbi Meyer of Rothenburg (Worms, 1215-1293). [38]   However, in the communities in the Eastern districts like Regensburg, Nuremberg, etc., the usage was still unknown in 1300. [39]   Only the famous Rabbi and *chazzan* Jacob Mölin emphasized this custom. According to the description of his disciples he used to start in a low and soft voice, then gradually raise his voice with all force. [40]   A similar description is given by an author of

the sixteenth century.[41] In 1700 the tune was employed also
for Esther VI, 1, a custom which continued until lately.[42] The
reason given for singing the *Hammelech* was to remind the
people that God the King sat in judgment in that hour. The
tune in XXIII, 2 is taken from MS. L. Sänger (1781-1843).

3. *Ovos* (The Patriarchs, i.e., the first benediction of the
Amida, relating the merits of the fathers). Rabbi Meyer of
Rothenburg used to chant that text solo in an emphatic tune.[43]
In the seventeenth century the tune for this text was well
known and accounted traditional.[44] We possess a MS. of it
written in 1782 by A. Beer, which is given in XXIII, 3, I, with
omission of later embellishments. Beer's version contains elements which are to be found in L. Sänger's version XXIII, 3,
II, as well as in the Lithuanian version XXIII, 3, III, by
Jacob Moshe Abelov of Trocki (1846-1888). The latter contains even ancient motives (like 35) not to be found in the two
other settings. Besides, the Lithuanian shows Oriental influence in motive 33. It has likewise several modulations of
which we shall speak in Chapter XXIII.

4. *Kaddish* (Sanctification) had several musical settings, of
especial importance being one for Sabbaths and one for the
Three Festivals. On the High Holidays in Troyes (France)
and Mayence (Germany) *Kaddish* and *Borchu* were sung according to the tune of the Three Festivals, whereas M. Rothenburg changed that custom and ordered that on the High
Holidays *Kaddish* should be sung in the tune of Sabbath.[45]
In the seventeenth century the tune of *Kaddish* was like those
already named, known as awe-inspiring.[46] The text was considered very important and therefore it became the *chazzan's*
duty to prolong its singing in order to give the people time to
meditate while the tune was sung.[47] There were, besides, special tunes for the half-*Kaddish* and for the full-*Kaddish*, for
the *Kaddish* after the reading of the Pentateuch and for the

last *Kaddish* after the service. The most important of them, however, is the tune for the half-*Kaddish* before *Musaf* for the High Holidays and its variation for the Dew and Rain prayer. Originally one tune, it was later branched out into two variations. Already the MS. of the eighteenth century bears these two variations. Example XXIII, 4, I, by Joseph Gold-stein 1791 (omitting later embellishments) illustrates the version for the High Holidays, while XXIII, 4, II, gives the version for Dew and Rain prayer.

5. *Vehakohanim* in the *Avoda* (service of the High Priest at the Temple of Jerusalem) in the *Musaf* of the Day of Atonement was sung to commemorate the service at the Temple in Jerusalem.[48] The tune is given in XXIII, 5, I, from MS. Goldstein 1791. However, this tune, too, has various versions, as illustrated in XXIII, 5, II, from M. Kohn, 1839,[49] and XXIII, 5, III, from A. Beer.[50] The same tune used to be employed in the eighteenth century also for other texts of the *Avoda*,[51] and is still employed partly for the *Musaf Kedusha* on the High Holidays and on *Hoshanah Rabbah* as well as on the festal day on which the solemn character of the Day of Judgment is voiced. Because of its solemnity, the tune is used also for the poem *"Oz shesh meos"* on the Feast of Weeks (*Shavuoth*).[52]

6. *Kol Nidré* was recited in the eleventh century three times, beginning in a low and soft voice and gradually at each repetition increasing in volume.[53] The *chazzan* Meier ben Yitzchak of Worms, however, used to sing it twice only.[54] Rabbi Jacob Mölin used to sing the *Kol Nidré* text in various tunes, prolonging the singing until night, in order to enable the late comers to hear the content of the text. The Hebrew expression for singing given at that occasion indicates rather "improvisation" than the singing of a set tune.[55] Rabbi M. Jaffa of Prague was the first to mention a set melody tradi-

tional for *Kol Nidré,* known by the *chazzanim* of his time
(sixteenth century).[56]

The *Kol Nidré* tune is illustrated in XXIII, 6, I, according
to the setting of Ahron Beer, and it is the oldest version in
written form. It has the modulation to the sixth in major, instead of the parallel third in major, as is now customary and
as is illustrated in XXIII, 6, III (motives 6 and 49). The
Kol Nidré tune, too, has several versions in which other motives are inserted not found in Beer's setting. We give in
XXIII, 6, II and III, some of these insertions, of which II
is customary in Eastern Europe, while III is found in later
versions, especially in the settings of the nineteenth century, as
illustrated in 6, IV, in L. Lewandowski's version in his *"Kol
Rinnah,"* No. 107.

In example XXIII, 7, a mode for the *Kiddush* of the Three
Festivals is given, which is used also for the Aramaic poem
Akdomus for *Shavuoth.* This is a variation of the Psalm
mode given in table X, 9-12. Out of the same mode a rhythmical tune for *Shavuoth* was created for the text *Mi Chomochoh,* as illustrated in example XXIII, 8.

The singing of the "thirteen attributes" on fast days (Exod.
34: 6-7) while reading the portion of the Pentateuch was already customary in the eleventh century, and was sanctioned
by Rashi.[57]   The chant is identical to the mode of the Pentateuch for the High Holidays (Chapter III, table IX, 2), and
it has much in common with the Sephardic chant for the "thirteen attributes." [58]

The chant for *Hakkol Yoduchoh* at the beginning of *Yotzer*
was already known in the twelfth century.[59]   In Frankfort this
text was sung every Sabbath beginning with the "great Sabbath" before Passover, while in Mayence it was started six
weeks earlier (*Shekalim*) and was continued until the Sabbath
before *Rosh Hashanah.*[60]   The tune used to be rendered in re-

sponsive singing, in which form it is sung in Southern Germany up to the present day.[61]

Borchu, the *chazzan* Eliezer ben Meshullam "the Great" in Mayence (eleventh century) used to sing at the evening service of the outgoing Sabbath in a long tune.[62]   The custom became permanent for all services.[63]   For each occasion a special tune was invented.   The reason given was to give the people an opportunity to gather and to meditate for the service, while the *chazzan* opened the service with *Borchu.*   In XXII, 7, the tune of *Borchu* for the High Holidays is given, and in XXII, 8-9, its parallel tunes found in the old Gregorian and the Minnesong.

These tunes are the most outstanding ones set to prose texts mentioned in the medieval Hebrew literature of the Ashkenazic rabbis in the period of the eleventh to the fifteenth centuries, while the authors of the seventeenth century refer to the tunes as traditional, inherited from their forefathers.   The purpose of their creation was, as we have seen, a ritualistic and religious one, each individual tune having a specific reason.   But the general purpose of them was "to call forth in the hearts of the people awe and devotion, especially on the Day of Judgement."[64]   Thus it was then recognized that music had the power of inspiring the worshippers and calling forth in them sentiments and ideas for which the various festal days were supposed to stand.   Therefore, for joyous festivals joyous tunes were invented, while for the High Holidays tunes expressing solemnity and severity were demanded.[65]

In examining the musical elements of the tunes given in table XXIII, we find that these tunes are composed of fifty-two motives. Several of these motives repeat themselves within the same tunes and in various other tunes, while some of the motives occur only once. The motives 3, 5, 19, 24 occur seven times; 2, 37 five times; 11 six times; 6 eleven times; 7, 12, 21, 22 four times; 25, 27, 35, 38, 39,

45, 46, 52 three times; 1, 8, 9, 14, 26, 30, 31, 43, 47, 49, 51, 52 repeat themselves twice; whereas 4, 10, 13, 15, 16, 17, 18, 20, 28, 29, 32, 33, 34, 40, 42, 44, 48, 50 occur but once.

We mentioned above that these tunes were composed out of Biblical and German elements. This we see clearly when we classify the motives cited into (A) Biblical: 2, 3, 4, 5, 6, 13, 21, 24, 27, 35, 39, 51, 52; (B) German: 1, 7, 8, 9, 10, 11, 12, 14, 15, 16, 17, 18, 19, 20, 22, 23, 25, 26, 28, 29, 31, 32, 34, 36, 40, 41, 42, 43, 44, 45, 46, 47, 48, 49, 50; and (C) Slavic Oriental: 30, 33, 37, 38.

From this list we gather that thirteen motives are of Biblical origin, four of Slavic, and thirty-five motives are of German origin. In order to establish proof we give in XXIV a selection of motives of Gregorian and Minnesong of the period of the eleventh to the sixteenth centuries, and compare the motives of table XXIII to those in table XXIV as follows: 1-2 to 1-3; 3 to 7, 1; 4 to 16, 5; 11 to 6 (end); 6 to 4; 35 to 5; 37-38 to 9; 39 to 10; 36 to 10, 12; 41 to 10, 3; 44 to 8; 37 to 11. The Minnesong influenced even the Pentateuch mode, as becomes evident by comparison of 13 to 16, 4, and example 12 to 4 in table IV. On the other hand, the song of Heinrich Vrowenlop in XXIV, 13 (the last great Minnesinger, died in 1318) has decidedly Oriental character. This song has striking similarity to the *Selicha*-chant by Joshua Feinsinger, who lived in Eastern Europe five hundred fifty years later (example 14). Vrowenlop's tune reminds us further of the Arabic song in table I, 2.

From the list of motives given above we learn also that those most often repeated are, with exception of ii, of Biblical origin. Example ii is a popular concluding motive in the Minnesong and serves here, too, as such.

There is a type of motive which serves as links or as passages of instrumental character, and was inserted at a later time, most likely in the seventeenth century, influenced by the *ars nova*. These embellishments are found in abundant quantity in the tune in XXIII, 3, I (compare the motives 28, 29, 31, 42; 5, 9, 15, 45). Those motives which repeat themselves in the same melody or occur in various tunes may be considered

TABLE XXIV
Motives of the Gregorian and Minnesong

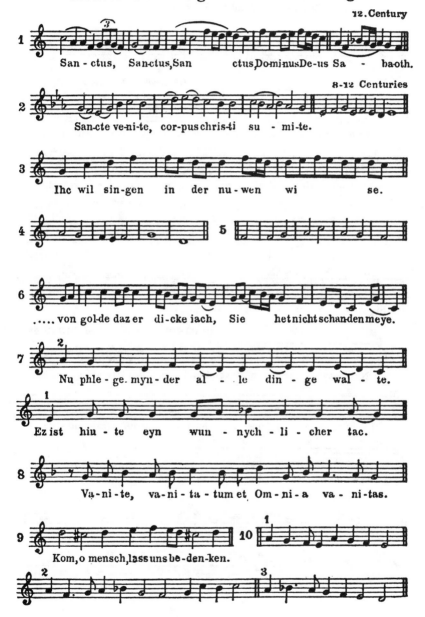

11 Ihr Chris-ten kombt hört was ich euch sag.

12

HEINRICH VROWENLOP, d.1318

13 Swa sich die tu-gent ir biv-tet. Da komt sie mit vur-mez-zen heit. Der

sel-den kleyt. Treit sie myt ir vil gar am vu-der-scheit.

JOSHUA FEINSINGER, 1838-1872

14 she-chu-loh a-chu-loh lo-moh

Siv-ki, lo-moh siv-ki

BERTHOLD von REGENSBURG, d.1272

15 Nun bit-ten wir den heil-gen Geist umb den rech-ten glau-ben

al-ler-meist, das er uns be-hü-te an un-serm en-de

wenn wir heim-farn aus die-sem e-len-de, Ky-ri-e e-lei-son.

16

the basic elements, the heart of the tunes. They resisted during the centuries all sorts of styles and yielded only to some reshaping. We meet them in the innumerable settings of the last two centuries, now in the *barock* style of the eighteenth century, now in the classical style of the first part of the nineteenth century, or in the Slavic-Oriental flavor of the Eastern *chazzanuth*. We find them shaped in the lyric-sentimental German *Lied* style of the romantic school in the middle of the nineteenth century, and a half-century later set in the elaborate form of the dramatic style for chorus and organ plus orchestra.

The other motives employed in these tunes are transmutable, or only of temporary value, in order to satisfy the taste of the age. Some of them, however, were retained, while others gave way to other motives in "fashion," as products of a new musical style.

The tunes of XXIII are highly regarded in the Orthodox Synagogue and are still sung with reverence in Central and Western as well as in Eastern Europe. They still bear the imprint of loose modal form, in which the predominance of the motive is apparent. In them the characteristic freedom of the modes is retained, for they offer free play to the singer for improvisation, in changing the motives or modifying them.

(B) Of the tunes with poetical texts from the same and later periods we give a selection in table XXV:

1. *Oschoh edrosh,* a poem based on the meter of four words to the line and four double lines to the stanza, by Simon bar Abbun (eleventh century). The tune and form of rendition are described in the fifteenth century.[66] The poem was repeatedly imitated in meter and form, and its tunes were adapted to these imitations.

2. *Emechoh nososi,* by Meshullam ben Kalonymos (tenth century). This "sweet and beautiful tune" was known already

TABLE XXV
Ashkenazic tunes for individual poetical texts

E-soh de - - i l'me-ro-chok she-on bos   me-ro-chok.

le-shod   ke-che-sef yim-chok, lo-cha-mi   le val yitz-chok

Tu-mas tzu-rom ve-chas - dom,   tiz-kor le -ni-ne   mo-lo-dom,

shiv-tom be-ge maf-chi-dom, she-fu-tim be-ro-a ma-a - bo-dom.

BENEDETTO MARCELLO, 1724

Adagio

Sho-fet kol ho- o - rets ve-o-soh ba-mishpot ya-a - mid.

no cha - yim vo -che - sed al am o - ni tatz -mid.

ve - es te'-fil-las ha-sha-char bim kom o - loh sa - mid,

ke - o-las hab - bo - ker a-sher le -o - las ha-to - mid.

9   E - li tzi-yon ve - o - re -hoh ke-mo i - shoh ve tzi-re-

hoh, ve-chiv-su-loh cha -gu-ras sok al - ba-al ne -u - re - hoh.

10   Mo-oz tzur ye - shu-o - si le-choh no - e le-sha-be - ach.

l'es to-chin mat - be - ach mi-tzor ham-na be - ach,

oz eg-mor be - shir miz-mor cha - nu-kas ha-miz - be - ach.

Addir hu

11   1644

Ad-dir hu yiv-ne be-so be -ko-rov bim-he-roh be -yo-me-

nu be-ko - rov, el be -ne, b'ne be-ne, b'ne bes-choh be-ko-rov.

in the fourteenth century.[67]   The tune was also adopted for
other poems, like *Osisi* by Simon bar Abbun, and *Yoreisi* by
Yekuthiel ben Moshe of Speyer (eleventh century).   It was
likewise used for the *Neila Kaddish* (concluding service on the
Day of Atonement) and for *Ochiloh loel*.   (Compare XXI,
6, b.)

3. *Aapid*, by Eleazar Kallir, three words to the line and
two double lines to the stanza.   The tune was famous in the
fourteenth century, and Jacob Mölin *Maharil* adopted it for
other poems of similar meter.   The tune is rendered in responsive form.   For the same text there are two tunes traditional in different congregations.   These tunes are employed
also for other poems (XXV, 2-3).   Both are identical in
rhythm (c), form (responsive) and length (eight bars).
They are alike based on minor and modulate to the parallel
major.

4. *Eder vohod*, four words to the line, by the above mentioned S. bar Abbun.   This tune too was adopted for several
poems.   It resembles the *Ledovid boruch* tune.[68]

5. This is a tune used for various poems.   The example is
taken from MS. Goldstein (1791).

6. *Esoh dei*, three words to the line, by Kallir.   The tune
consists of four parts, has no strict rhythm, and is used also
for other texts, such as *Boruch sheomar*.   In the Italian song
of the Synagogue the tune is used for another text.[69]

7. *Akeda* (dealing with the sacrifice of Isaac), three words
to the line and four lines to the stanza.   The tune was customary in the fourteenth century, and was referred to by
Maharil as the *Akeda* tune, because it was used for all the
poems with the same content and meter.   The author of the
poem in example 7 is Benjamin ben Yerach.[70]

8. This is of special interest inasmuch as it was known at
the beginning of the eighteenth century as traditional even

in the *Ashkenazic* congregation in Venice, and is one of the twelve Jewish tunes chosen by Benedetto Marcello as themes for his Psalms (Chapter X). The tune in example 8 was copied from Marcello's work *Esto poetico armonico*, No. 21.[71] This tune is also found in the German Protestant song in two forms, given in table XXVI, 3-4. Example 3 is similar to Marcello's version, while 4 is the version now used in the Synagogue, and is a composition by M. Vulpius of 1609.[72] The poem is by Solomon of France (eleventh century).

9. This is the elegy *Eli tziyon* sung on the Day of Destruction. The same tune is found in the German-Catholic Church as one of the "fast songs" printed in 1642, given in table XXVI, 5.[73] On the other hand, the tune is found as a Spanish Folksong of the seventeenth century, illustrated in XXVI, 6,[74] as well as a Czecho-Slovakian folk-song (XXVI, 7).[75] Thus this tune was popular simultaneously in Spain, Germany, and Bohemia. However, its character indicates that it originated in Spain, whence it was in all likelihood carried to Central and Eastern Europe by pilgrims; and was picked up by Jewish singers likewise. We find many such "travelling" melodies in the medieval age.[76]

10. *Mooz tzur* is the well-known *Chanukah* hymn. Its typical German characteristics are obvious, and we become more convinced of its German origin by comparing the tune with the themes in XXVI, 8, 9. No. 8 is the well-known chorale by Martin Luther *Nun freut Euch Ihr lieben Christen*, for which text he adopted the tune of an old German folksong: *So weiss ich eins was mich erfreut, das plumlein auff preyter heyde.*[77] From this chorale only the first four and the last two bars are to be found in the *Mooz tzur*, while the middle part (bars 5-8) has a reminiscence of the battle-song called the *Benzenauer* which was composed in 1504 and became very popular throughout Germany.[78] In XXVI, 9, the

TABLE XXVI
Motives and tunes of German religious and secular Folk-song

4. Lobt Gott den Herrn ihr Hei-den all, lobt Gott von Her - zen -
grun - de.　　dass er euch auch er - wäh - let hat
und mit ge-tei-let sei - ne Gnad　in Chris-to sei - nem Soh-ne.

5. Sa-lue mun-di sa lu - ta-re, Sa-lue sa--lue Je-su-cha-re, cru-ci tu - ae
me ap-ta-re　vel-lem ve-re tu scis qua-re, Da-mi-hi tu-i　co-pi-am.

Aiñhara

6. Gar-te tar - zu-nae ba - na-ra - bi-la, ai-ri-an aiñ-ha-ta be-za - la, Gay-ac e - re i gra-rai-ten di - tut e - gu-nae ba-li-ra be-za - la, o! mai-ti - a ni-bet-hi zu - ga - na.

7. Yes - li tě má mi-la hla-va bo - li nan-di si li - ste-ček ya-bo-ro - vy, li - ste-ček ya - bo - ra spa-del mně do Mo-ra, do Mo-ra, do Mo-ra, do Mo-ra - vy.

8. (1523) Nun freut euch lie-ben Chris-ten gmein und lasst uns fröh-lich sprin - gen. was Gott an uns ge - wen-det hat und sei-nen süs-se wun-der-tat, gar theu-er hat ers er - wor - ben.

9. (1504) Nun wend ir hö - ren sin - gen ie - tzund ein nüw ge - dicht. vil büch-sen und kar - tau - nen.

part of the song similar to *Mooz tzur* is given. The two German songs penetrated into the Ghetto, and were fused in the
mind of some Jewish singer into one tune and used for the
joyous theme of the victory of the Maccabees. It was first
sung at the home-service of the kindling the *Chanukah* lights,
and was later introduced into the Synagogue. The poem, however, was sung long before the invention of the present tune,
and it had another melody in 1450.[79] In 1606 we hear of an
imitation of this poem to be sung in the same melody,[80] while in
Venice the Ashkenazim sang the poem to another tune, which,
too, Marcello selected for his Psalms: No. 15.[81]

11. This is the well-known tune for *Addir hu* for the *Seder*
service on the first two nights of Passover, and it was, likewise,
carried over from the home into the Synagogue. This tune
underwent several variations until it received its present shape.
We have its oldest form printed in 1644 in the *Hagada* published by J. S. Rittangel (ii, I), a second form in 1677 by the
convert F. A. Christian in his *Hagada "Zevach Pesach"* (ii,
II), and a third version printed by another convert (Gottfried
Selig) in 1769 (ii, III). In the last-named, the Jewish-
German translation is added: "*Allmächtiger Gott, nun bau dein
Tempel, Schiera!* (Oh, praise!), *also schier* (a German word-
play on the Hebrew word meaning speedily) *und also bald, in
unsern Tagen, Schiera! Yau* (yea) *Schiera! Nun bau, nun
bau, deinen Tempel, Schiera.*" The song is called *Baugesang,*
i.e., the song of the rebuilding of the Temple.[82]

This tune found its way even to the Southern French Jews.
The Bavarian version (in MS.) by M. Kohn has still retained
the form of the seventeenth century (ii, IV). Its characteristics are decidedly German, though no identical German tune
has yet been found. There are many with some of its motives
and features, as for example "Maria's cradlesong" of 1544,
or the "Song of the Pilgrims" of 1537.[83]

Apart from the comparison of Jewish and German tunes offered, we give some more parallel tunes of the German-Catholic song in table XXVI, such as 1, which is similar to XXV, 4. The German melody was printed in 1619 and an older setting of it is known from 1582.[84] In like manner do we find for XXV, 7, a parallel in XXVI, 2.[85]

Jewish elements, we find only in example XXV, 5, in which the concluding motive is derived from the *sof-passuk* of the Prophetic mode, while 1 and 6 have the flavor of the Biblical modes. Thus, in the group of tunes for poetical texts we notice that the Jewish element is almost abandoned, that the rhythmical element became the basis, and that in most cases the tunes are either in toto or in their main features and elements adoptions from that period of German religious and secular folk-song.

The reasons for the stagnation of the musical creation of the Jews in Germany in the later period of the medieval era are manifold. Of first importance is the desperate social position into which the Jews were forced since the thirteenth century. German music was enriched through the Minnesinger, the Meistersinger, and, beginning with the sixteenth century, through the Protestant movement which strengthened German song and brought about the birth of German poetry and music. At the same time Jewish culture, the product of a small, oppressed, and disfranchised dwindling and scattered minority, declined, impoverished by reason of cruel persecutions and brutal expulsions from century-old settlements to Eastern Europe, to Italy, and the Balkan. The German neighbors, at first inferior culturally, became superior; and the Jews, crushed in body and spirit, were influenced by the song of their oppressors. The song of the Synagogue in Germany, beginning at least with the sixteenth century, became Germanized. All musical material that originated in that period has typical German characteristics with but little Jewish flavor.

This fact may give us a clue to the reason for the attitude of the spiritual leaders in Germany toward the tunes "newly" introduced into the Synagogue. With the beginning of the sixteenth century complaints were levelled against *chazzanim* for abandoning the old sanctified tunes inherited from the fathers, tunes which gave tonal expression to the religious thoughts. The above cited *chazzan* Herz Treves inveighs against the new *chazzanim* who neglected the traditional functions of the precentor and the study of Jewish lore, who centered their interest in displaying their singing and their art, employing tunes which had no relation to the prayer texts. They further embellished the poem with elaborate music, and did not pay attention to the prayers proper. The *chazzanim* chose to officiate only during the *Musaf* service because that service offered them the opportunity to display their art, and they considered the officiating at the *Mincha* service beneath their dignity. This change took place at the same time when in Central Europe the *ars nova* began its inroad from Italy into Germany.[86] On the other hand, the Protestant movement abolished the Gregorian chant about the same time and replaced it with the German folk-song.

The introduction of new songs into the Synagogue aroused opposition by reason of the innovation. But a more fundamental, if less obvious, cause for the antagonism was something in the very nature of the new tunes that was displeasing to the Jewish spirit, while in the old tunes there was something that spoke to the Jewish sentiment. Of that "something" we become aware on examining the two types of songs. The older elements explained in I, II and III (A) still bear Jewish Semitic features in that they consist, to a considerable part, of Jewish motives and retain to a certain degree the modal form;

while the "new" type, i.e., the tunes for the poetical texts treated in III (B), comprise adaptations and imitations of German folk-tunes. No wonder that in these melodies the people felt sentiments expressed which were not their own. And the Jew in medieval Germany certainly had sentiments different from those of his persecutors. Even the hopes which the Jews had placed in the liberal Protestants turned into disappointment, for the attitude of the latter toward Jews was by no means better than that of the Catholic Church.

For a long time the new tunes were tolerated by the rabbis. They remained secondary and inferior to the Biblical and prayer modes as well as to the *Missinai* tunes, namely, groups I, II and III (A). These groups of songs were adopted by all Ashkenazim and were retained also by the Ashkenazic settlers in the East; the "new" tunes in group III (B) remained mostly within the borders of Germany and did not survive in the East, in all likelihood on account of their German character.

In the Catholic Church an effort was made, beginning with Gregory I (d., 604) and continuing to the present time, to preserve the traditional song of the Church and to keep away vulgar secular tunes. In the Synagogue no laws or orders were issued to that end; the Jew being guided merely by his instinct. As long as his Jewish consciousness was strong, wherever he developed his spiritual culture and lived accordingly, his religious song was Jewish.

As stated at the opening of this chapter, at the period of the flourishing of Jewish culture in Germany, the rabbis paid much attention to the ritual of the Synagogue. The last prominent rabbi who rendered great service to the Synagogue song was *Jacob Levi Mölin*, called *Maharil* (born in Mayence c. 1356, and died in Worms in 1427). He found it his joy and considered it his high duty to be precentor on festivals, fast days,

and High Holidays.   By means of this office he could render
service to his people, elevate their spirits and arouse devotion
in them by his inspiring rendition of the prayers and songs.
He used to travel to many communities in Germany, and in
every place he officiated.   The *Maharil* was the greatest rabbinical authority of his time, at least in German countries; and
therefore his word was accepted as law all over the country.
His opinion was that the communities should hold fast to their
traditional customs and melodies.   When in the fourteenth
century the decay in the spiritual life of German Jewry began,
the *Maharil,* through his exalted personality, saved the integrity of the Synagogal ritual and music by sanctioning the old
tunes.   The following legendary incident told about him illustrates his attitude toward the sanctity of traditional melodies.
While officiating once on the High Holidays in Regensburg,
without being informed of the local customs, he changed a
tune and used a hymn not used there.   In the same year his
daughter died; and he considered the blow a punishment for
his violation of a local custom.   Many of his settings of poems
and prayers, as mentioned above, remain traditional to the
present day.

In spite of the care the *Maharil* exercised in Synagogue
song, the high spirit of the Ashkenazic service was affected during the atrocious persecutions of the fifteenth and sixteenth centuries, in which period many ancient communities were mo-
lested and partly expelled.   The German Jew, hated and en-
slaved during the week, wanted to be refreshed on Sabbath
and on the festivals by attractive popular songs which would
make him forget his dire position.   Hence, the less cultivated
people urged the *chazzanim* to satisfy their desires despite the
protest of the rabbis.   These people mingled all the week with
gentiles in business, and returning home to the Ghetto on
Sabbaths, they would demand that the *chazzan* sing the tunes

from the outside world for religious texts, to the greatest dismay of the more highly educated Jews.[87]

In many cases, ethics and morality declined in Jewish life in that period and lowered the standards also of religious life. More than once it happened that the service was interrupted by quarrels, and that the *chazzan* was attacked while officiating even on Rosh Hashanah and the Day of Atonement and was removed from the pulpit by police.[88] These same chaotic conditions were prevalent at the same time in the Catholic Church.[89]

The repeated expulsions of Jews naturally produced an unsettled community life, which resulted in many congregations not engaging permanent *chazzanim*. Consequently, the *chazzanim* used to wander from city to city giving concerts, guest-services, without finding a permanent engagement. This abnormal condition developed the type of the wandering *chazzan*, with all the bad habits of the wanderer. These, in addition to the artistic strain, gave the *chazzan* a minstrel-like character, resembling that of the wandering Italian musicians of that time who overran Central Europe.

Partly as a consequence of political and cultural circumstances and partly influenced by the above-mentioned wandering music-makers, the *chazzan*, as stated above, abandoned all functions connected with his office (Chapter VI), and confined himself to his music, constructing dazzling tunes in order to capture the attention of the mob. To put an end to this demoralization, at the request of the old community of Bamberg, Rabbi Moses Minz wrote detailed regulations for the *chazzan*: how he should behave in the synagogue while officiating, what garment he should wear while in the synagogue, how he should conduct himself with members of his congregation, and that he should always be concerned about the dignity of his sacred office.[90]

However, in those communities which were fortunate enough to escape the brutality of the raging Christian clergy and mob, the dignity and continuity of tradition were maintained. Consequently, their *"minhag"* (custom) became the standard for other communities which, after having been ruined by the "holy" crusades or other mob outrages, tried to re-establish their religious practices. Therefore, in places like Frankfort, Prague, Mayence, and Worms much stress was laid upon the dignity of the service and upon the quality of the *chazzanim*. And, indeed, we meet in those communities *chazzanim* of high rabbinic learning and ethical standard. Thus, an author of the seventeenth century, Joseph Hahn, states that his grandfather, Isaac Hahn, was appointed *chazzan* in Frankfort not because of his sweet voice but on account of his piety.[91]

From the evidence presented in this chapter, we conclude that the Synagogue song of the so-called Ashkenazim was well established at the end of the sixteenth or at the beginning of the seventeenth century, and that, with the exception of typical German tunes, the Ashkenazic song created in Southwestern Germany spread all over Central and Eastern Europe.

CHAPTER IX

THE SONG OF THE SYNAGOGUE IN EASTERN EUROPE TO
THE EIGHTEENTH CENTURY.

The thirteenth-century Hebrew poet Immanuel of Rome
gives in the fifteenth part of his work *Machbaroth* a very exact
description of a *chazzan*. He recounts that he was travelling
with a rich man and met several people, each bewailing his
condition. Among them was a *chazzan* who bitterly complained about his distress and poverty. In response to the
question whether he would agree to exchange his lot with that
of Immanuel's rich companion, the *chazzan* immediately
assented with joy; but when he was informed that he would
have to give also his voice for the voice of the rich man, he
grew indignant and spurned the bargain, because through his
voice he conquered the heart of the people. This characteristic
picture of the *chazzan* at the time of Immanuel in the thirteenth century would even better suit the *chazzan*-artist of the
seventeenth and eighteenth centuries in Eastern Europe where
the *chazzan* reached the highest degree as artist, casting from
himself all those tasks historically associated with his office
which drew him down to the station of beadle and servitor of
the community.

Only in Eastern Europe did conditions favor the *chazzan's*
making himself solely an artist. The Jewish population in
Eastern Europe, especially in Poland, Ukrainia, and Lithuania,
has increased during the past three centuries to a phenomenal
number. Living in concentrated masses in an environment of a

very low cultural standard, the Jews developed an original
spiritual life; and Judaism found a resting place safe from
every influence from without. Being of a people with pronounced musical abilities and inclinations, the Jew hungered
for music; and for lack of such performances as the gentile
world enjoyed, the Jew sought to satisfy his craving by his own
means. Inasmuch as Jewish life was concentrated in the Synagogue, and music meant only sacred music (that is concerned
with worship), it was a mere consequence that the *chazzan* was
urged to satisfy the longing for music, that he became the
artist, the supplier of tunes, and that the services came to be
viewed by the community as musical performances. Even in
small places where the *chazzan* was still burdened not only
with his traditional offices which had been transplanted from
Germany, but also with the work of *shechitah* (ritual slaughter-
ing), the demand was made of him to supply music. In the
big communities where the *chazzan* was released from all his
other offices and devoted himself to music only, he was honored with the title "city *chazzan*" (*Stadt-chazzan*). These
chazzanim created a special brand of Synagogue music which
the German Jews called *Polnisch*.

In the first place, let us note the component elements of
Eastern European Jewry. The earliest Jewish settlers in the
southeastern countries were Oriental Jews from Persia and the
Caucasus, were remainders of the Jewish Greek colonies around
the Black Sea or came from Crimea; were to a certain extent
also Tartaric Chazars who had become proselytes and who
after the fall of their empire were spread among and intermingled with the Jewish population. The language of the
Jewish settlers was either Tartaric or Slavic, which tongues
persisted till the fourteenth century. Only through the German immigrants from the fourteenth century on was the
spoken language changed into the German dialect of those

immigrants. This determining influence was due not to preponderant numbers, but to the immigrants' superiority by reason of the Jewish culture which they brought, and which made them teachers and spiritual leaders of the native Jews.

From the newcomers, the older inhabitants learned also the traditional songs. Now it is to be taken for granted, although no descriptions of examples remain, that, before the German immigration, the Eastern European Jews had a Synagogue song for their service, and that it was probably Oriental. While they neglected their tunes in favor of those of the newcomers, they retained the decidedly Oriental strain of their music, and *this* they introduced into the Ashkenazic Synagogue song. We saw in the previous chapter that in the preceding centuries the Ashkenazic Synagogue song had been Germanized to a degree that jeopardized not only its distinctive Jewishness but its very existence. In Eastern Europe, on the other hand, the ever-renewed Oriental sap penetrated also into the song. Hence, Eastern Europe Orientalized the Ashkenazic traditional Synagogue song, both in its elements and in its forms, by freeing it of the fixed mold of European melody, and developing again the unfettered improvisation of the modes. In this improvisation (in Yiddish, *Sogachts*), lay the chief power of the *chazzanim*. Through it, they developed an admirable and distinctive art which surpasses the improvisation of even the Oriental singers, for they created a unique coloratura with an unmatched elasticity and complexity of fine tonal groups and curves—a coloratura of dazzling intricacy and brilliance, of soaring fantasy, of sharp-witted finesse. That type of coloratura is to be found neither in the greatest Arabic and Turkish singers, whose coloratura is too sentimental and vapid, nor in the best coloratura work of Italian music, which is too artificial and rather of instrumental than vocal character. The coloratura in the Eastern European *chazzanuth* is like the soul in the body; without it, that *chazzanuth* loses its vitality, its charm, its fascination (Chapter II).

An attempt has been made to explain the coloratura and ornamentation in the Eastern European *chazzanuth* as the product of Talmudic *pilpul,* of the shrewd intricate dialectics which influenced sentiment as well as logic. But the opinion is a superficial one, for the period of identical *pilpulistic* character which flourished in Southwestern Germany in the earlier medieval times (the so-called period of the sages or Tossafists in Lorain) produced a *chazzanuth* which shows not the slightest similarity to the involved nature of that of the Eastern Europeans, but—quite to the contrary—is, as we saw, of a very simple style. On the other hand, the ornamental style which distinguished Eastern European *chazzanuth,* we find also in the Arabic and Turkish music, as well as in the Ukrainian folk-song and in the Gipsies' instrumental music. Yet these peoples have no Talmud.

In order intelligently to point out the originality of the Eastern European song of the Synagogue and the features distinguishing it from the Ukrainian folk-song prevailing in the South Russian districts from Volhynia through Ukrainia, Podolia, and Bessarabia down to the shores of the Black Sea, we shall have to analyze the characteristic elements of that song. In like manner, we shall proceed with the Roumanian folk-song, current also in Bessarabia and in parts of Hungary. With the aid of the painstaking investigations into and collections of these folk-songs that have been published in recent years, we are enabled to gain a clear insight into the matter.

The Ukrainian folk-song is composed of two types, the unrhythmical fluid recitative, which is supposed to be the older type, and the rhythmical tunes for dancing. The unrhythmical song is based entirely upon the scale: d^1—$e^{1/2}$—$f^{3/4}$—$g^{\#1/2}$—a^1—$b^{1/2}$—c, the fourth tone being an augmented second. The scale has seven tones only, i.e., a heptachord, and is, according to the Ukrainian Musicologist Philaret Kolessa, the (Gregorian) Dorian mode with the augmented fourth.[1] However, a group of songs ends on the second of that scale, namely on "e." In this case the scale is identical with the *Hedjaz* scale or scale IV (Chapter II). But Kolessa insists that nonetheless the scale remains the same Dorian.[2] Kolessa explains that this PECULIARITY is at home in the folk-song of the districts of Poltava and Charkov and is characteristic of the older elements of Ukrainian and Southern Slavic folk-songs.[3] The augmented step he considers as an Oriental influence. Furthermore, he states the fact that there is a tendency toward the neutral third, which at times impresses one as major, at times as minor.[4] We noticed a similar fact in the Semitic Oriental song (Chapter II, III). The Ukrainian folk-song is cultivated orally by the blind singers (*Kobsari*) who accompany themselves on string instruments. The song is improvisation on traditional motives, and Kolessa furnishes a multitude of variations on one and the same theme, improvised by various singers, or by one singer at different times. The accompaniment is usually applied as a short pre- and post-lude, which ends with a chord of tonic and fifth, the third being employed only in rare cases.

It is quite apparent that since the Ukrainian song is a mixture of Slavic-Tartaric and Semitic-Oriental elements (and Kolessa is of the same opinion),[5] it therefore has much in common with Jewish song. Yet in many basic features they differ. In the first place the main scale in the Ukrainian, the above-mentioned "Dorian," is not to be found in the TRADITIONAL song of the Synagogue. The Eastern European *chazzanim* apply it to a few prayers and call it the *Mi-sheb-erach* or *Av-horachamim-Steiger*. In table XXVII 1-2 we give Ukrainian and Jewish examples in this scale. Likewise, we furnish some examples of the Ukrainian song with the ending on the second XXVII 5-7.[6]

From these illustrations we gain an idea of the Ukrainian modal songs. They have mostly only one motive, varied and embellished. The examples 1, 3, 4, 5, 6, 7, are motives which serve as basis for many songs. We learn also the close relation between the type of song ending on the second and the *Ahavoh-Rabboh* mode explained in Chapter IV. Yet we see unmistakably the original features of

TABLE XXVII
a) Ukrainian Song

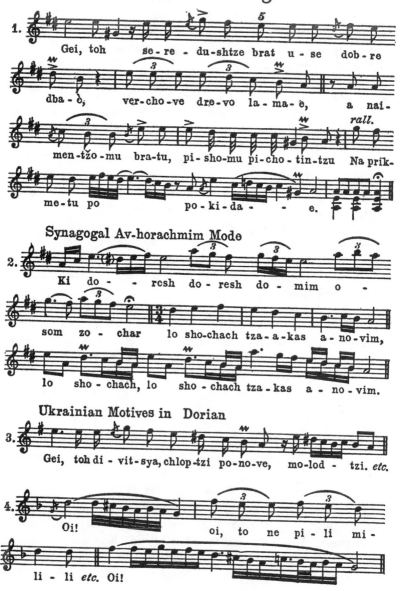

1. Gei, toh se - re - du-shtze brat u - se dob-re dba - è, ver-cho-ve dre-vo la-ma - è, a nai-men-tžo-mu bra-tu, pi-sho-mu pi-cho-tin-tzu Na prik-me-tu po po-ki-da - - e.

Synagogal Av-horachmim Mode

2. Ki do - - resh do - resh do - mim o - som zo - char lo sho-chach tza-a-kas a - no-vim, lo sho - chach, lo sho - chach tza - kas a - no - vim.

Ukrainian Motives in Dorian

3. Gei, toh di - vit-sya, chlop-tzi po-no-ve, mo-lod - tzi. etc.

4. Oi! oi, to ne pi - li mi - li - li etc. Oi!

Ukrainian Motives in Dorian, ending on the second

5. Gei, ge - gei, ge - gei, ge - gei, ge - gei!

6. Oi, si - ni mo - i, si - ni, Tri yak
yas - ni - i glas - ni - i so - ko - li!

7. Cho - tyab u vas vti - cho - mir stvi shtze po - si - di - la.

b) Roumanian Song

Poco rubato ♩= (132)

8. Oi, d'e mi ňe, un - ta - șu, oi d'e - ňe, un - ta - șu.

9. Ha - nc - ho - vim ve - ha - ne - i - mim
be - cha - ye - hem uv - mo - som
lo nif - ro - du.

10. Ki le - choh no - e a - do - noy e - lo - he ——
nu shir ush - vo - choh hal - lel ve - zim - roh.
bo - - - ruch a - toh a - do - noy   etc.

Roumanian

11.

Jewish

12.

Fine

D.C.

Jewish

13.

Ad-dir bim-lu-choh, bo-chur kah-lo-choh, gdu-dov yom-ru lo,

l'choh u - le-choh, l'choh ki le-choh, l'choh af le-choh,

l'choh ado-noy ha-mam-lo - choh, ki lo _no - e, ki lo yo - e.

14.

I II

(singers) (singers)

Roumanian

15.

16.

Jewish

17.
O - mar rab-bi el-o-zor, o - mar rab-bi el-o-zor

o - mar rab-bi cha-ni-noh tal-mi-de cha-cho-mim mar-bim

sho-lom, mar-bim sho-lom bo - o-lom, mar-bim sho-lom bo-o-

lom. shc - ne - e-mar: ve-chol bo-na-yich lim-mu-de a-do-noy ve-

rav shc-lom bo - no - yich al tik-ri bo-no-yich, e-loh bô-no-yich,

bô - no-yich. sho-lom rav le - o-ha-ve so-ro-se-choh, le-

o-ha-ve so-ro-se-choh v'en lo-mo mich - shol. ye-hi sho-

lom bc-che-lech shal ____ voh be - ar-m'no-so-yich.

each, through a comparison of illustrations given in table XV with those of table XXVII. Distinctive of the *Ahavoh-Rabboh* mode is its modulation-possibilities to several other modes and to the same mode on other scales, for which table XV, 3 furnishes an example. This characteristic is lacking in the Ukrainian Song. Also the melodic curves within the mode differ, for the dwelling upon the third, the gradual ascending of the melodic line, the predominance of the fourth and the seventh below the tonic are Jewish traits missing in the Ukrainian mode, the melodic structure of which is, according to Kolessa's statement, throughout of a descending character.[7] The Jewish mode is rather similar to the Arabic *Hedjaz*, as we have seen in Chapter II.

Roumanian folk-song has been investigated and published by Béla Bartók.[8] He is of the opinion that "the old Maramures style, the Hora lunga, was taken over from the Ukrainian."[9] We offer example 8 from his collection. The tune, in its scale and features, is similar to the Ukrainian examples in table XXVII. This type is called in the Roumanian Song "plaintive songs of the old people."[10] "These songs are here and there much embellished in parlando" style.

In addition to the already mentioned example 2 of *Av-horachamim*, we give another one of the same mode by Weintraub (No. 9) in MS. in the Ukrainian scale ending on the second. This example shows relationship to the examples 1, 3, and 4. However, the example presents only one phrase of the composition and should be considered only a modulation, for in the following development of the selection variations and modulation to other scales and modes lend it a rather minor and *Hedjaz* character.

There are those who maintain that the East European *chazzanuth* was influenced by the Gipsy's music. True, a certain similarity grows out of their common Oriental origins. Gipsy music is based chiefly on the so-called Gipsy scale which is similar to the *Ahavoh-Rabboh* mode, with the difference that this mode has the combination of the tetrachord e—f—g#—a and b—c—d—e, which means *Hedjaz* scale (Chapter II), while the Gipsy scale is the combination of two tetrachords with augmented steps, the second and the sixth step being augmented. This scale is used by Tartars and Turks and is called *Hedjaz-Kar*.[11] Gipsy music also is based upon the mode form and upon the principle of improvisation.

But a thorough analysis proves the difference between Gipsy and

Jewish music. These two types express two diametrically opposed worlds. Gipsy music voices nothing but primitive wild passions: the content of the Gipsy's life—quite remote from the doctrines and sentiments of Judaism. The great gentile musician Franz Liszt succeeded in penetrating into Israel's spirit, and in his remarkable work on the Gipsies and their music in Hungary, he draws a clear line of demarcation between the Jew and the Gipsy.[12] Example 10—a recitative by Dovidl Brod (Chapter XIV)—may serve as illustration of the way this Gipsy scale was employed in the Synagogue.[13] In the same scale we have example 14, a MS. from Amsterdam written about 1800. This tune was carried over by "Polish" chazzanim into Central and Western European Synagogues. In example 14 we notice also the part of the "singers" (i.e., the choir, assisting the cantor), which consists of the unison humming of a tone at the end of a phrase —a form taken over from the Ukrainian singers.[14] Despite the scale, the two examples have nothing in common with Gipsy tunes.

On the other hand, the relationship between the Roumanian song and the Jewish becomes evident through an examination of examples 11 and 12. The latter is also from Amsterdam. Both are in the Ukrainian Dorian. Of the same origin is No. 13, a song for the Seder meal on Passover evening. This tune found its way to Copenhagen, where A. P. Berggreen incorporated it in the tenth volume of his collection of folksongs.[15] The tune shows the typical Ukrainian and Roumanian manner of inconstant tonality, with the fourth (c) alternately sharp and natural; and the third alternately flat and natural.[16]

In the examples 15-16 a Roumanian style is given which has similarity to the Jewish style for meditation and study (Lern-steiger), illustrated in No. 17. In this case as in the previous examples, though we recognize the common Oriental basis in both types, we are aware that different aims and sentiments animate them. Here, too, the Jewish version is by far richer in motives, in range; is deeper in conception and expression as well as in modulation. Starting in minor on g (1) it makes a turn (in 2) to major on f, then (in 3) to Hedjaz on the fifth (d), which is followed by a modulation to the fourth (c) in major, from which it turns to the original scale in g minor. However, this manner can no longer be considered "folk-song," yet neither can it be taken as "art-song," at least not conscious art, for the executors, the *chazzanim*, did not know of any theory of music and modulation. Not even classic European theory suggests methods of modulation such as the one just analyzed. The Jewish song, however, developed original ways of modulation, which we shall treat in detail further on (Chapter XXIII).[17]

An essential consideration in East European *chazzanuth* is the *voice* of the *chazzan*. Like other Orientals, the Jew has preferred what he called a *sweet* voice, which meant to him a lyric tenor with nasal quality, rather than the powerful voice of a heroic tenor, baritone, or bass. At best, the heroic voice was designated as the "roar of the lion," whereas a lyric tenor usually had all the qualities required to move the heart of the Jew, by its natural sweetness and by its facile execution of the most ornamental coloratura, which art was called *Kelim* (instruments, implements). This lyric quality the Jew loved in instruments, the violin becoming his favorite. *Singing* he termed *han-im* (to sweeten), and King David he called *něim zemiroth*, he who sweetened the songs (compare the Greek *melos*). As a matter of fact, the great *chazzanim*, with the exception of very few, were tenors; or, if baritones, they "tenorized" their voices.

As we already explained, the *chazzan* had to satisfy the popular desire for music—for a music which should express the sentiments of the Jew, interpret his ideals, his wishes, and his hopes as a Jew, give tonal expression to his pains and sorrows, release him from the weight of his heavy burden as an oppressed and disfranchised human being, and interpret that glorious past from the Exodus from Egypt to the Fall of the Temple. The Jew demanded that the *chazzan*, through his music, make him forget his actual life, and that he elevate him on the wings of his tunes into a fantastic paradisaical world, affording him a foretaste of the Messianic time in the heavenly Jerusalem. The *chazzan* chose those texts, the contents of which indicate all the above-mentioned sentiments. This choice led to a marked differentiation between the Eastern European *chazzanuth* and the German Ashkenazic. In the latter, as we have seen in Chapter VIII, only those texts were intoned which, for one or the other *Hallachic* or Cabbalistic reason, called forth Rabbinic demands for musical settings. But the Eastern European *chazzanim*, in their choice of texts, were guided only by the contents of the lines, which were of a religious, national, and ethical nature. Thanks to this attitude, the *chazzanim* revived many wonderful poems which had been entirely forgotten during the sixteenth and seventeenth centuries by the Italianized *chazzanim* in Central Europe, who, influenced by Italian art and German folk-song, had preferred texts of laudation and exultation for their musical settings. It is remarkable to notice that while the Berlin *chazzan* Beer (Chapter XI) wrote some sixty compositions for *Lechoh dodi* and *Mìchomochoh,* he has not a single tune for texts like *Avhorachamim, Hashkivenu, Umipne Chatoenu,* for each of which the Eastern European *chazzanim,* and especially Kashtan (Chapter XIII), left a multitude of settings. Of course, in order to intone the above-explained types of texts, the *chazzan* had to understand them, to feel the vibrations of the Jew's heart in reciting them; he had to be saturated with their spirit, life, and history. He had to be brought up in the same atmosphere in which these texts had grown. He not only had to be a talented singer and musician with a feeling heart, but also necessarily had to be steeped in Jewish tradition and folk-song. In reality, the majority of the famous *chazzanim* in Eastern Europe, like those in Germany in the earlier medieval centuries, were of this type.

Up to the eighteenth century there is available but scanty information of conditions of the Synagogue song in Eastern Europe. Occasionally we hear about restrictions as to the number of tunes a *chazzan* was permitted to sing at services, restrictions either growing out of a consistent effort to prevent waste of time, or due to temporary mourning over renewed persecutions.[18]   At times we find in the responsa of the rabbis decisions regarding the conduct, income, etc., of *chazzanim*. However, nothing has been preserved depicting the essence of the song itself.   For the first time, a record of the Chmelnitzki pogroms in 1648 describes a *chazzan* Hirsch of Ziviotov, who, through his emotional chanting of the memorial prayer *El Mole Rachamim*, moved the Tartars to save three thousand Jews from the hands of the raging Cossacks.[19]   At the end of the seventeenth century, Rabbi Selig Margolis of Kalisch describes that quality in the Eastern *chazzanuth* which tended to stir the people and move them to tears.[20]   He claims that the Eastern *chazzanim* were capable of inspiring the people with their singing much more than the rabbis by their preaching; that it frequently happened that people who did not cry even when their parents died and had no desire to pray, were moved to tears and to repentance through the touching song of the *chazzan* Baruch of Kalisch.   "Such ability," says Margolis, "is possessed by the *chazzanim* in OUR country [i.e., Poland] only, whereas in other countries they [the *chazzanim*] have neither melody nor emotion."

Eastern European *chazzanuth* has been accused of having a melancholy character, of being a lamentation, a weeping. We have already explained (Chapter II) that the main basis of Semitic and Jewish music is the minor scale which, at a very late date (beginning of the nineteenth century), came to be considered of a melancholy character by the Anglo-Saxons only.   Of far deeper significance is the truth that genuine music is the offspring of profound emotion: of exaltation, pain, or joy.   Music produced out of a situation between these poles of the human heart is of banal character, bloodless, watery.

A music to be understood and to be intelligently analyzed must be approached in the spirit and from the point of view of the people of whom it was born.   For genuine music is the tonal expression of the life and struggle of a people or of a group which has created ideals of its own, an outlook of life of its own, as the result of its life, its convictions, its faith. "The musician," says J. G. Frazer,[21] "has done his part as well as the prophet and the thinker in the making of religion. Every faith has its appropriate music, and the difference between the creeds might almost be expressed in musical notation. The interval, for example, which divides the wild revels of Cybele from the stately ritual of the Catholic Church is measured by the gulf which severs the dissonant clash of cymbals and tambourines from the grave harmonies of Palestrina and Handel.   A different spirit breathes in the difference of the music."

After the Chmelnitzki pogroms which caused the dispersion of hosts of Jews, the *chazzanim* who emigrated to Central and Western Europe transplanted their Eastern *chazzanuth* and fused it with the traditional German-Ashkenazic song.   We shall treat this influence in more detail in Chapter XI.

CHAPTER X

THE INTRODUCTION OF HARMONY AND POLYPHONY INTO
THE SYNAGOGUE IN ITALY BY SALOMON ROSSI.

Influenced by the Renaissance, the Jews in Italy began to
enter musical life, and to contribute toward general European
musical creation. Although they were excluded from social
circles and were without human rights, some Jewish musicians,
nevertheless, were privileged at the court of the art-loving
Dukes in Mantua (Guglielmo, 1555-1587, Vicenzo I, 1562-
1612, and Ferdinando, d. 1626) in the second half of the sixteenth and the first quarter of the seventeenth centuries.[1]
Among these Jewish musicians, singers, and performers were
such as: Abramo dall' Arpa Ebreo, who was employed at the
court as singer and actor in 1542-1566; his sister's son
Abramino dall' Arpa in 1566-1587, who was the favorite
musician of Duke Guglielmo; Isacchino or Jacchino Massarano,
who played the lute, sang soprano, and was instructor in acting
and dancing in 1583-1599, whose house the Duke and his
court used to visit; Davit da Civita Hebreo, composer, who
dedicated his seventeen madrigals for three voices to Duke
Ferdinando in 1616; [2] Allegro Porto Hebreo, composer. The
last named dedicated a collection of songs called *Nuove
Musiche*, to Signora Conte Alfonso da Porzia (Venice 1619),
and two collections of *Madrigali à Cinque Voci* he dedicated
(Venice 1625) to Emperor Ferdinando II of Austria.[3]

The most gifted and famous Jewish musician at the court
of Mantua was Salomon (or Salomone) Rossi. He was a
descendant of a prominent family, whose pedigree went back to

the captives of Jerusalem whom Titus brought to Rome. For over forty years (1587-1628) he was composer, singer, and violinist at the ducal court. His sister, Madama Europa, was famous there as a singer and actress; and also his nephew Anselmi Rossi was employed as musician at the court.

Salomon Rossi was prolific. He became one of the greatest composers of canzonets and madrigals, "but his most important works were instrumental, being contained in four books, called *Sinfonie e Cagliarde* and *Sonate*." [4] H. Riemann considers Rossi "doubtless to be the most important representative of the new style in the instrumental field." [5] "He certainly was one of the first cultivators of the 'Trisonata'; and the manner of his conception remained for a long time a model for the simple form of it. His way of writing the Sonata as well as the simple, small *Sinfonia* (he cultivated) is homophonous throughout, and his inclination to the Florentine reform is obvious. . . . He prefers simple forms of the 'Songtype' (*Liedform*) . . . ; for longer selections he employs the Variation form, in thematic unity." [6]

Rossi's first publication (1589) was a collection of nineteen canzonets for three voices, dedicated to Duke Vincenzo I. During the forty years of his activity he published about thirteen works of various types, his last publication (1628), containing "twenty-five *Madrigaletti a due voci, per cantar a doi Soprani, overo Tenori . . . Opera tergadecima*." [7] He was likewise the composer of one number inserted in a religious (Christian) opera "Maddalena." [8]

Rossi was highly regarded by his contemporaries and was invited by princes to present concerts at their courts. He enjoyed such high favor with two successive Dukes that he was privileged to dispense (in 1606) with the yellow badge that all Jews were ordered to wear at that time. [9]

But what interests us in particular is the fact that Rossi de-

voted his talent also to the Synagogue. It was toward the end
of the sixteenth century that the communities in Venice, Mantua, Ferrara, Padua, and Casale Monferrato, inspired by the
Renaissance music, wanted to introduce some modernization
into the Service. The greatest protagonist of the idea was the
encyclopedic Jewish scholar Leon of Modena. According to
his own statement he had a good voice, was a trained musician,
and even taught music.[10] In 1605 he organized in the Italian
synagogue in Ferrara a choir of six or eight voices, conducted
according to "musical science," i.e., harmony.[11] But to this
innovation there soon arose a strong opposition, which argued
that "joy and song in the Synagogue have been prohibited
since the destruction of the Temple.[12] L. Modena submitted
the case to the rabbinical assembly in Venice, and the latter
decided in favor of his enterprise. One member of the Assembly, Rabbi Benzion Zarfati, stated that in his youth, when
he was studying in Padua, he used to join in singing in the
choir in the synagogue.[13]

Rossi manifested his Jewish religious piety in composing
Psalms and prayers for the Synagogue. It became his aim, as
he relates in his Hebrew dedication, "to glorify and beautify
the songs of King David according to the rules of music."
These compositions gradually grew into a collection of thirty-
three, for choir and soli, for three, four, five, six, seven, and
eight parts. They were set to Psalms, Hymns, and prayers
for Sabbaths and Festivals, and were performed before they
were printed. His friends, and especially Mose Sullam—a
rich and prominent man in Mantua—persuaded him to publish
this collection of Synagogue songs. M. Sullam and his parents
had been Rossi's supporters, who had helped him in his education until his attainment of his high position. Accordingly
Rossi published that collection; and, in a preface written in
Hebrew, dedicated it to Mose Sullam.[14] Leon of Modena

undertook the proofreading of the music and he, too, wrote a preface, or rather an apology, in Hebrew, with the aim of winning over the rabbis, most of whom had opposed the innovation. The collection was printed in Venice in October 1622 and was called *Hashirim Asher Lishlomo*—the Songs of Solomon, a play on the first verse of the Song of Songs. Only the PARTS were printed (not the complete score) with the text in Hebrew letters running from right to left, while the music runs from left to right. In 1877 Samuel Naumbourg, cantor in Paris (Chapter XIII), re-edited Rossi's collection in score and in modern musical transcription, adding a biographical sketch of Rossi, and an evaluation of his creative work. To the Synagogue songs, a collection of Rossi's secular madrigals was added, edited by Vincent d'Indy.[15]

The compositions of Rossi for the Synagogue have not the slightest sound of Jewishness. They are entirely in the Italian Renaissance style, and they have the same spirit as his secular compositions. Naumbourg entertained the opinion that Rossi introduced a cadence in minor in which the Jewish music distinguishes itself from the sacred (Christian) music of his contemporaries.[16] In fact, about twenty numbers out of the thirty-three have minor character, being based either on a minor or "Dorian" (Gregorian) scale; but they finish either in unison on the tonic or in a major chord on the tonic, as was the custom during the sixteenth century and afterwards throughout the classic period.

Technically, his Synagogal music is much simpler than his secular music. This difference may have been made intentionally, because he was aware that his compositions would be rendered by Jewish laymen, or it may have been due to the then general tendency toward the simplification of Church music.

On the other hand, no traditional modes or motives are to

FACSIMILE 5.
Salomon Rossi. Pub. Venice, 1622; pg. 1 (Tenore).
H. U. C. Library.

be found in Rossi's music. Neither did he utilize any traditional melodic line as theme or *cantus firmus,* as was then customary in Church music.

We do not know exactly how long Rossi's music was sung in the Italian synagogues. At any rate it could not have lasted long, because a few years later, in 1630, when Mantua was swept over by war and was captured by Emperor Ferdinando II, 1,800 Jews were expelled from the city. The glorious era—an era which illumined their darkness for a short while—ceased for the Jews in Northern Italy with the Austrian régime, and with it all desire for the *ars nova* was killed in the Jew. He abandoned his ambition to become a co-worker in the Renaissance and the few attempts made toward the introduction of European achievements in music were deserted. Soon Rossi's music was forgotten, and the Italian Synagogue went back to the old traditional song with more zeal than ever. Indeed, when in the same synagogue in Ferrara, in which already one hundred and forty years earlier a choir had sung "new music," someone dared to change the musical setting of the priestly benediction from the tradition, he was excommunicated by the Rabbinate in Ferrara.[17]

Apart from the Jewish musicians thus far discussed, we hear of *chazzanim* in Italy trained in music, such as Abraham Sagri and his disciple Jacob Finzi, both Ashkenazim officiating in the Ashkenazic congregation in Casale Monferrato. The first compiled a collection of Synagogue tunes according to the Ashkenazic tradition for his disciple Finzi.[18] The latter, born about 1581, was also scholastically trained, was a fine Hebrew writer, and compiled a Hebrew grammar in verse, in 1605.[19]

Some Jewish scholars of that period occupied themselves with musical science. Noteworthy were Jehuda Moscato and Abraham Porteleone. The latter was a physician and wrote a great deal on Biblical instruments.[20] A certain Jehuda ben

Jischac made an attempt to translate or rework a theory of
music from Italian into Hebrew. The theory is based upon
that of Marchettus of Padua, who lived in the early part of the
fourteenth century.[21]

At the beginning of the eighteenth century we hear from a
Jewish traveller, Abraham Levy of Amsterdam,[22] that in the
great (Levantine) synagogue in Venice a very fine song was
cultivated. Though he gives no description of the nature of
that song, his comment affords us a clue to the reason why the
Italian composer Benedetto Marcello took about a dozen traditional tunes from the Sephardic and the Ashkenazic synagogues
in Venice and used them as themes in his fifty Psalms which
he published in 1724-27.[23] The synagogue must have had a
reputation among the Christian musicians in Venice. However, with the exception of *Shofet kol hooretz* (Chapter VIII),
the tunes chosen by Marcello have no bearing on Jewish tradition, but seem to be ADOPTED tunes, even the above-named
exception being (as we have seen in Chapter VIII, table XXV,
8 and XXVI, 3-4) of German origin.

As stated above, no trace was left of Rossi's attempt to introduce polyphonic song, according to the *ars nova*, into the Synagogue song. As proof of the Italian Synagogue's adherence to
tradition, we have: *Libro dei canti d'Israele, Antichi Canti
Liturgici del Rito degli Ebrei Spagnoli*, collected and published by Federigo Consolo, a renowed Jewish violinist (born
in Ancona 1841, died in Florence 1906). He devoted himself
to the study of the Synagogue song of the Jews in Livorno.
These were descendants of the Spanish fugitives that had settled there after 1492. Though he claimed that the song he
presented in his collection was the Sephardic tradition, it is in
reality the Northern Italian tradition. The song shows Levantine as well as Ashkenazic influence (Chapter VIII); and
several of the tunes are imitations or adoptions from the

Italian song of the seventeenth or eighteenth centuries. However, a considerable part of the tunes is common among the Sephardim in the Orient as well as in Europe, as it was pointed out in Chapters III, IV, and VII.

The material presented by Consolo contains neither harmony nor polyphony. It has partly the unrhythmical, partly the rhythmical, form; is partly for solo and partly for solo with congregational response, or unison, with a strong Oriental flavor.

Thus we see that Rossi's songs vanished entirely from the Italian Synagogue. But they did exert an influence, by arousing interest in elaborate music in another country, Germany. Indirectly, Rossi's efforts influenced the communities in Central Europe through the introduction of the Italian style, choral singing in parts or in octaves, and even instrumental music into the Synagogue in the seventeenth and eighteenth centuries.

CHAPTER XI

At the beginning of the sixteenth century a new spirit penetrated into the GHETTO, and aroused the artistic temperament
of the *chazzanim*. It seems that the new flame of life—the
Renaissance coming from Italy and spreading northward—cast
its sparks into the dark corners of the Ghetto (Chapter VIII).
We find an echo of the movement of that time in the Cabbalistic
rabbi and cantor in Frankfurt am Main, Rabbi Herz Treves,
1470-1550, who bitterly complains against the new movement
and the strange attitude that the *chazzanim* took toward their
holy function: "They have ceased to be writers of *Torah*,
Tefillin, Megilloth; nor do they care for the correct grammatical reading nor for the meaning of the prayers—only for
their songs, without regard for the real sense of the words.
They neglect the traditional tunes of their ancestors." [1]   Gradually there arose the interesting phenomenon that the *chazzanim* devoted themselves more and more to music, and began
to consider all other communal functions as burdens.   Hence
their effort to free themselves from these tasks!   From Italy
travelling singers and musicians overran Northern Europe,
spreading their new art.   Italian music came to be the synonym
for music in general. [2]   Under the spell of these minstrels, the
chazzanim, too, abandoned all their other functions, devoted
themselves to music, and started travelling from community
to community to perform their concert-services.   The *meshorer*
or chorister is the product of and largely the creation of those

Renaissance *chazzanim*. In Germany, despite all the orthodox attitude, we find that the opposition to that Renaissance influence on the Synagogue music was much less pronounced; and some communities were even more favorably disposed toward it than those in Italy itself. While Italy saw the fight between Leon of Modena and the majority of the rabbis over the introduction of "music" into the Synagogue, Prague equipped its new synagogue (built in 1594 by Mordecai Meisel) with an organ and a special orchestra organized to play and to accompany different songs including *Lechoh dodi* on Friday evening, which number was elaborated into a concert of more than an hour's length.[3] The same concerts were held in almost all the nine synagogues of Prague, including the *"Alt-Neu-Schul"* in which a new portable organ, built by a Jewish organ builder, Rabbi Maier Mahler, was installed in 1716.[4] There is a report of instrumental music in the synagogues around the beginning of the eighteenth century in the communities of Nikolsburg, Offenbach, Fürth, etc.[5]

The somewhat strange phenomenon of employing elaborate instrumental music in the Synagogue for the Friday-evening service had two reasons. The one was called forth by the Cabbalistic movement which started with Isaac Luria (1534-1572). He laid much stress upon receiving the Sabbath with music for which purpose he inspired his disciples to compose special songs.[6] Soon that custom spread all over Europe, so that with the beginning of the seventeenth century the custom was established. "The Sabbath is received with great joy and with pleasant songs and hymns; and in several communities, choral singing with string and wind instruments is employed. The reason for it is that the Sabbath should be received with joy; and the divine Shekinah dwells among us only when we are joyous."[7] The other cause was the influence from without. At that time it became customary in the Protestant Church in

Germany to play instrumental selections, or to render choral singing with instrumental accompaniment on Sundays before the service. This performance was called religious Concert or "Cantata," and it is continued to the present time.[8]

Indeed, the employing of instrumental music at religious celebrations, as the dedication of a Synagogue or a Scroll and at weddings was customary throughout the medieval time. Jacob Segal Mölin "Maharil" already used instrumental music for the procession of the wedding ceremony in Mayence.[9] The instrumentalists were Jews. In almost every community there were Jewish musicians who, united into a band, used to travel throughout the country playing music before the gentiles at various occasions. For their trade they needed special permission from the governmental authorities, for which privilege they had to pay heavy taxes.[10] The rabbis gave them permission to mingle with the Christians and to play even at Christian festivities, considering their performances professional labor only.[11] The Jewish musicians were naturally acquainted with German and Church music [12] and would play that music occasionally in the Ghetto, and even at religious celebrations. On the other hand, they used to compose music of their own.[13] We hear of the Jewish musician *Woelflin von Locham* who wrote thirty-six songs, the text and music in polyphonic style c. 1450, for his wife Barbara to whom he dedicated that collection in Hebrew lines.[14] The MS. is considered one of the most important sources of old German music. Some of the Jewish musical productions of the sixteenth century, especially the "Jewish dance music," was retained. However, they are rather caricatures of Jewish music.[15] (More in Chapter XX.)

The Jewish musicians volunteered to play every Friday evening for about an hour in several congregations throughout the seventeenth and eighteenth centuries. In Prague the custom continued in all the nine synagogues until 1793, when the custom was abolished because the musicians used to continue their music even after sunset. Likewise, instrumental music was prohibited at wedding ceremonies in the Synagogue. Even in Livorno in Italy instrumental music before Friday evening service was introduced in the eighteenth century, and its performance was restricted to Jewish musicians.[16]

It is quite natural that the *chazzanim* learned from the Jewish musicians the reading of music and the playing of instruments. In Prague there were at the same time musically trained *chazzanim*, like Lipman Katz Popper (d. 1649 or 1655) "who was a master on several instruments and a brilliant improvisor," according to the poem-eulogy of him, written in Judeo-German.[17] We hear of Jewish instrumentalists and secular singers who were related to *chazzanim*, such as Süsskind of Offenbach, the son-in-law of the *chazzan* Salman in Frankfort. Süsskind used to travel with his cast concertizing at the beginning of the eighteenth century (1714). His son was the tragically famous "Jud Süss Oppenheimer."[18]

Despite the antagonism toward the *ars nova* introduced by the *chazzanim* in the sixteenth and seventeenth centuries and the opposition to the choir which it created and required, the latter innovation became an established organization in almost every congregation or community. At the beginning of the eighteenth century, we find from Prague to Amsterdam "community or *kahal* singers" consisting of a bass and a "discant" or "singer," that is, a soprano or falsetto. These men were sustained by the congregations, and together with the *chazzanim* received the nickname *keleichomos* (instruments of robbery)— an abbreviation of *chazzan, meshorer,* singer.[19] In Amsterdam choir singing was introduced in 1700, and at the same time also in Hamburg.[20] In Frankfort,[21] about 1714, the institution of a choir was considered a long established one. In Prague, every synagogue had its choral society of volunteers,[22] aside from the employed singers. Among the first institutions of the newly established community in Berlin (1671), we find that of community singers, for whose admission the Jewish community had to obtain special residence permits from the government in 1697. It seems that a permit for the bass alone was procurable, so that the other singers' residence in Berlin was illegal.[23] Even in small communities the people were enthusiastic over having a choir. One such example is Prosnitz,[24] Moravia, which became a center for Jewish singers and song in the first half of the eighteenth century and from which prominent Jewish composers came forth, as we shall see later. A similar attitude we find in Hildesheim[25] in Western Germany, which like Prosnitz served as the cradle for a considerable number of Jewish musicians. In other communities that innovation was barely tolerated, so that any severe calamity, in the form of persecutions or restrictions, brought among the first orders for repentance laid upon the community by the spiritual leaders, the prohibition of "Synagogue singing" which meant the *ars nova* of the *chazzanim*. We meet such orders of repentance in different countries at the same time, as for example in Selz and Brisk, both in Lithuania (Chapter IX), and in Worms[26] and Hamburg.[27] Even in Eastern Europe, in Podolia and Galicia, the institution of choristers was established at the time of Israel Baal Shem-tob.[28]

Concerning the origins, uses, and abuses of the new style of song introduced by the *chazzanim*, we have two sources of information: on the one hand, the caricature drawn by rabbis of the seventeenth and eighteenth centuries; on the other hand, the music manuscripts of the *chazzanim* themselves. "The custom of the *chazzanim* in our generation is to invent tunes, and to transfer tunes from the secular to the sacred. They know not how to read the *Torah*, because the congregations prefer to have *chazzanim* show off with sweet voices and fine singing. Every Saturday the number of new tunes increases —tunes which we knew not before." [29] In the same vein write the two *chazzanim:* Yehudah Leb ben Moses [30] in his pamphlet "Shire Yehudah," and Solomon Lifshitz,[31] cantor in Metz. Both testify that the *chazzanim* used to take tunes from the theatre or the dance hall and use them for the service. Other *chazzanim* were accused of taking tunes from the Catholic Church. Peculiarly enough, to the question of borrowed melodies Rabbi Joel Sirkas responded [32] that there was no objection whatever so long as the tunes had not been used for the Christian service, by which judgment he pronounced non-Jewish tunes permissible. Menahem de Lonzano [33] was of the same opinion, while Rabbi Joseph Hahn opposed strongly.[34] A serious complaint was that the *chazzanim* introduced their own or borrowed compositions for those prayers which had never before been sung, and that they neglected both the traditional tunes and the principal parts of the ritual. "The *chazzanim* run through the main prayers with such rapidity that even the swiftest horse could not follow them; while on the *Kaddish* or Psalm tunes they spend so much effort and time that the annoyed congregants begin to converse." [35]

Considering the fact that some of the traditional tunes as those for *Kol Nidré, Olenu,* or *Borchu,* were also very long drawn out, and that nevertheless no protests were uttered against these by the rabbis, we must conclude that the reason for the complaints was not only the prolongation of the service, but the introduction of new tunes for prayers, the especial emphasis of which was not sanctioned by the necessities of the ritual. While they did not hesitate to spend over an hour in singing *Boruch Sheomar,*[36] since to that usage they ascribed a cabbalistic or mystic connotation, they violently opposed the new tunes of the *chazzanim,* which had no other purpose than a musical one.

The invasion of the *ars nova* into the Synagogue and the custom of adopting or imitating secular music were paralleled by the same procedure in the Church. In 1700 a clergyman, Erdman Neumeister of Weissenfels, published Cantatas for the Church in the form and style of the secular Cantatas with Arias in the style of the Italian opera. The texts to these he did not take from the Bible and prayers, but he wrote them himself. In his preface he stated that there is no difference between the style of the Cantata for religious purposes and the operatic style. "Neumeister's innovation caused the last barrier between the secular and sacred to be abolished." [37] Since that attempt was made, every Cantor and Church musician considered it his task to compose or compile a collection of sacred songs for the entire cycle of the year, based upon the operatic Aria style. Hence, the Church melody lost its original characteristics, and resembled the operatic melody. [38]

This innovation aroused a strong antagonism, especially on the part of the "Pietists," as Butstedt (1717) and Joachim Meyer (1726). [39] Not only in the Protestant Church, but in the Catholic Church, likewise, secular music penetrated, and even to a larger extent than into the Protestant. [40] Tunes were introduced with coloratura, vulgar in spirit, arias and minuets, which belong to the theatre. Notably, the collection *Tochter Zion* (1741) was considered detrimental to tradition with regard to both text and music. [41]

This condition continued throughout the eighteenth century. In a collection of 1778 we read that "the artistic singers in their ambition to show their art and to entertain the public with new tunes, forget the difference between the sacred place and the profane. Therefore, we hear in the sanctuary concerts, symphonies, and arias which belong in the dance hall and in the theatre. They call forth in the heart of the congregation profane sentiments instead of religious." [42] On the other hand, complaints were heard that "the old traditional Church-song is dull, heavy and sad, and has a plaintive character, and does not appeal to the 'modern' listener who is accustomed to exciting symphonies." [48]

The borrowing of secular folk-tunes for the Church was an old custom. But in the earlier times the secular folk-song was in its spirit and its musical elements closer to the Gregorian Song. According to W. Bäumker, there was hardly any difference between a secular and a Church tune,[44] whereas in the later period, especially in the seventeenth and eighteenth centuries, the folk-song and the secular music took another course and influenced the Church song to the extent that it departed from the traditional chorale style, and adopted the secular style.[45]

Thus, we see that the Church lived through the same struggle as did the Synagogue. To the Church, however, the innovation meant a secularization only of its sacred spirit, while to the Jew it meant much more. It not only secularized Jewish worship, but in addition it Europeanized and Germanized the Jewish song and, simultaneously, also the Jewish sentiments. The European music in the seventeenth century was completely emancipated from the remnants of Orientalism and antiquity, dropping all those scales and melodic forms borrowed from Asia and Greece, and was confined to Major and Minor, founded on harmony. Harmony, a pure European expression of music, created a new type of melodic line, a "harmonic melody," i.e., a melody developed out of harmonic principles, with tonic third, fifth, and octave as predominant tones, and the modulation to dominant and subdominant as the scope of the melodic curve. These harmonic principles were applied even for old preharmonic melodies, accordingly remodeled, i.e., modernized. The same procedure we see also regarding the modernization of the Synagogue songs in the eighteenth cen-

tury, as far as the material retained serves. All the tunes and
selections composed at that time are influenced by harmonic
principles and by the Italian-German style. We look in vain
for some Jewish features. With the exception of those pieces
adopted from the East, called "Polish," which, as mentioned
above, were introduced by Eastern European *chazzanim* and
were based upon the minor or the *Ahavoh-Rabboh* mode, no
distinction can be discovered between those "Jewish" compositions and German or Italian instrumental or vocal selections
for secular or even "sacred" purposes prevalent in the
eighteenth century.

Chazzanuth in Central Europe seems to have gone through
the same development in the seventeenth and eighteenth centuries as did the Synagogue song in the Orient in the eleventh
and twelfth centuries—in that period when the *piyyut* was at
its height. Here, as well as there, we see the inclination of the
chazzanim to neglect traditional folk-song and to elevate the
Synagogue music to the realm of art; and here, as well as there,
the result was either a reaction or a complete failure. First, the
artistic flavor caused the people to cease to understand the song,
although they favored it as a novelty and as art; and secondly,
inasmuch as the art demanded professional singers to devote
themselves to it, it excluded laymen entirely. Hence, the
traditional occupancy of the position of precentor by rabbis and
prominent men was, by reason of the new art, impossible.
Therefore, precentorship gradually became a matter of sweet
voices rather than of religious spirits. The best account in
caricature has been preserved in a pamphlet of the beginning
of the seventeenth century.[46]

If until the seventeenth century Germany had supplied
Eastern Europe with rabbis and *chazzanim*, the one trans-
planting thither Ashkenazic Jewish learning, and the other
Ashkenazic traditional songs and customs, that rôle was no

longer hers after the massacres of Chmelnitzki (1648-60), which caused the Polish and Ukrainian Jews to leave their dwelling place and to migrate westward. In the course of a very short time, the Polish influx colored the character of many a Central European congregation; or, in some instances, separate Polish congregations were established. Toward the end of the seventeenth century, Rabbi Selig Margolis of Kalish complains against those rabbis, religious teachers, and *chazzanim* who, for the sake of material returns, left their native places and migrated to the wealthy German communities. Not approving of such actions, he travelled instead to the Holy Land.[47] In fact, we find around the same time in Germany, Holland, and even Italy, many rabbis and cantors of Polish origin. Especially a famous *chazzan* Jokele of Rzeszow of Poland made a furor through his tremendous voice and wonderful singing. We find him now in Prague [48] as *chazzan,* and later (in 1715) in Metz, where, while he was officiating on the feast of Shabuoth, a terrible calamity occurred at the Synagogue, fatal to many worshippers.[49] A great many of the Ashkenazic *chazzanim* in Amsterdam were from Poland, as for example Michael ben Nathan of Lublin, who was the first to introduce choral singing of bass and "singer" into the Amsterdam synagogue (officiated 1700-1712), causing heated contention in the synagogue over this innovation.[50] We find similar examples in many other communities such as Fürth.[51] Those East European *chazzanim* introduced the Polish style of singing into Central European synagogues, until their type of song became so much a part of *chazzanuth* that even the German *chazzanim* were obliged to give it to their congregations.

The eighteenth-century manuscripts of Synagogue song betray a striking monotony of style and texts. The Jewish singers adopted that peculiar *barock* style which flourished so widely in the seventeenth and eighteenth centuries. Altogether neglecting the fluid Oriental recitative chanting, they developed the rhythmical melodic form, utilizing the *minuetto, andante, allegretto, aria, rondo, polonaise, preludio, adagio, Siciliano,* and *Waldhorn.* The texts selected to be intoned were of hymn or laudatory character, such as *Lechoh dodi,* Psalm 95, *Mi chomocho, Kaddish, El hahodo-os, El odon, Kedushah, Ashre, Hodu, Ono, Hallel;* on the High Festivals much stress was laid upon *Mechalkel chayim, Hayom haras olom,* etc. And we never find an attempt of one of the composers to choose for his musical creation a text other than those habitually sung. Because of this dull conformity to routine, we find in the manuscripts innumerable tunes for one and the same text.

In form and character, the tunes were rather instrumental than vocal—and this for two reasons. In the first place, the Jewish singers had no opportunity to listen to vocal music since they had no access to Christian society functions or Church programs and services, while they did hear the instrumental music played mostly in the open air by travelling musicians or military bands. In the second place, the vivacious Jewish spirit preferred the more sprightly music, especially of string and wind instruments. Although the tunes are written for the cantor and the two singers (bass and discant), yet we never find harmony in the manuscripts, that is the three voices do not carry three individual parts sung simultaneously, and thus provide opportunity to achieve harmonic combinations; but the manuscripts are throughout of one melodic line, separated alternately for the various voices. We do not know whether this is an abbreviated method of indicating only the melodic line, while the accompaniments were primitively extemporized; or whether the music was sung merely in one part or in unison. Only in the later manuscripts of the end of the eighteenth and the beginning of the nineteenth century do we meet with the at-

tempt to write three different voices simultaneously in harmony
—naturally, in poor harmony.

The education of the *chazzan* both in Jewish knowledge and
in music was the same three hundred years ago as it still is in
Eastern Europe. The before-mentioned Solomon Lifshitz
leaves us a description of his own education in the second half
of the seventeenth century. He studied at the *Yeshivah* of
David Oppenheim in Nikolsburg, where he learned *shechitah*.
Chazzanuth he acquired from his father, Moses Lifshitz, *chazzan* in Fürth (1652-1731). He became *chazzan* and *shochet*
and religious teacher in a little place. Gradually advancing, he
secured a better position where he abandoned *shechitah* and
teaching, and devoted himself to his *chazzanuth*. In about
1709, he became the official community cantor in Prague. This
position he could not retain. He resigned and went to Frankfort. In 1715, he became the cantor in Metz, where he died
in 1758. He had been fortunate in having a father a *chazzan*
with whom he could study, for usually the singers had to serve
chazzanim from their childhood, travelling and suffering with
them from place to place, without the possibility of having any
general education. In the *chazzanuth-brief*, the agreement
between the community of Hildesheim and the *chazzan* Yosef
of Bicksheim, of 1780, paragraph eight provides that the
chazzan must keep one "singer" at his own expense, and that
in case the *chazzan* has another singer called "bass," the community would pay the bass one-half of his salary, that is one-
half *taler* a week, and the various households would supply
him with food.[52] This type of condition continued at least in
Eastern Europe till late in the nineteenth century. In his
memoirs, Elkan Cohen (born in Hungary 1806), son of
Lipman Bass, writes that in his twelfth year he was stolen by a
chazzan and brought to the *chazzan* Yisroel in Prosnitz, who
travelled over Moravia, Bohemia, Galicia, and Prussia. On

his travels he came to Budapest, where the famous *chazzan* of that time, Dovidl Brod (Chapter XIV), who had been newly appointed, accepted him as a "singer" under these conditions: "I know that you are a *drong* (a special *chazzanic* term meaning LOG, applied to those with an unmusical, wooden voice); but if one wants to sing, he should not be frightened. You can remain with me. I will supply you with DAYS (the privilege of eating regularly with specified families—one for each of the seven days of the week—throughout the year). Wages, I do not give; but at weddings and festal meals you can have a collection plate, the proceeds of which you will have to divide with the discant (falsetto singer). On *Chanukah* and *Purim* you may go from house to house with the bass, and share with him what you thus gather. *Erev Yom Kippur*, when it is customary for the *meshorerim* to be posted in the Schul, you will receive many donations." [53] The essential requirement for a "singer" was not only a good voice, but also a good memory, since the *chazzanim* for the most part could not read music, or, if they could, then only with great difficulty. Hence, they were dependent upon the memory of the singers for the retaining of their tunes or the obtaining of new ones. For this reason, a "singer" with a great repertoire in his head was very desirable and much sought after. And for the same reason, a "singer" could not remain long with the same cantor, because after handing over the entire treasury of tunes obtained from some other *chazzan*, he was a useless and empty shell, and was compelled to go further and start anew with the dissemination of his treasures. With the growth of musical knowledge, it rested with the "singers" to compose or to copy tunes and to present them to the *chazzanim*. We possess many manuscripts of those singers, some of them inscribed with dedications to *chazzanim*. Toward the end of the eighteenth century, we find even "singers" who supplied *chazzanim* with compositions for remuneration. After a long period of travelling from one community to the other, "singers" (*meshorerim*) might succeed in obtaining the position of *chazzan*. Their title was usually *Hamshorer Hagodol*—the great "singer." Some of them always retained the title *bass*; while many of them, never succeeding in obtaining a cantorship, remained "singers" all their lives. The previously quoted Solomon Lifshitz traces the musical knowledge of the cantors in Prague in the seventeenth century from some of their epitaphs, e.g., 1668, Jacob the son of Peretz "in the wisdom of music he was the chief of all singers"; Lipman Poppers (died 1656) was "a virtuoso on all string and wind instruments" (on him there was a poem written in Yiddish; it was printed by Wagenseil in his book *Sota*, 1674, p. 3; see Chapter XX); David, son of Jacob Futralmacher, 1724, "who could play on different instruments, was a singer, and one of the music scholars."

The following are some of the composers and singers of the Synagogue in the eighteenth century.

Ahron Beer was born in Bamberg, Bavaria, in 1738. He became *chazzan* for a short while in Paderborn, and was appointed *chazzan* in Berlin in 1765. Through his fine tenor voice and attractive singing he gained fame in Berlin; and his picture is still preserved in the art museum there. He was one of the first *chazzanim* who obtained some musical knowledge. As a result, he was able to write music and even to compose.

During the long period of his activity (died 1821) he gathered compositions of all his contemporaries in a large collection of over twelve hundred numbers, marked with the dates of the compositions and, in most cases, with the names of the composers. He included also traditional songs. Of chief interest in the volume we find the oldest form of *Kol Nidré* dated 1720, and another variation of it marked 1783; *Ovos* for the High Festivals; *Olenu, Omnom Ken, Al horishonim,*

Hodu for Succoth; *Kaddish* for *Neila,* and *Vechach hoyoh omer* using the tune of *Vehakohanim.* Since these traditional songs show no difference from their present form, we may assume that the traditional songs were already fixed in the seventeenth century. There is a *Kaddish* for *Neila* and for the last day of *Pessach* by Rabbi Michael Chosid, who was rabbi in Berlin 1714-1728 (Chapter VIII).

Ahron Beer prepared a collection of songs in 16/0 size probably for his own use at services. It is in his own hand, neatly written, and bound in leather, with an illuminated title page in Hebrew. Written in 1791, it includes 447 numbers, arranged for the entire cycle of the year, for fifty-three Sabbaths, for each day of the festivals and semi-festivals. On the title page Beer wrote a preface significant for the conditions of the Synagogue song of the eighteenth century. There he states, for instance, that the reason for his arrangement of special songs for every Saturday and feast day of the year was to prevent the members of the congregation from grasping the tunes, and thus to make it impossible for them to sing with the cantor. His intention was that a tune be sung once a year only, for "if a person hear a tune but once a year, it will be impossible for him to sing with the cantor during the service, and therefore he will not be able to confuse the *chazzan.* It has become a plague to the *chazzanim* to have the members of the congregation join the song." The tunes throughout the book are all for single voice, sometimes marked "singer" or "bass." The names of the prayers are given above the tunes, but there is no indication of apportionment of the text to the phrases and notes of the melody.

The texts used are for Saturday: *Lechoh dodi, Hisorari, Veahavas'cho, Malchus'cho, Mechalkel chayim, Kaddish, El hahodoos;* for holidays: *Hamelech hamromom, Tisborach tzurenu, Hodu, Ono, Al zos shibchu, Berach dodi* for Passover, *Akdomus* for *Shabuoth, Or ponecho*

for Sabbath *Shekalim,* a *Shir Hashirim Kaddish,* and a Ruth *Kaddish.*
Some traditional tunes are utilized as, e.g., *Akdomus, Sefira Lechoh
dodi,*[54] *Kinos Lechoh dodi* for Friday evening before *Tisha be-av* and
in the same tune *Av harachamim* for the Saturday before *Tisha be-av.*
For *Rosh Hashanah* there are *Melech elyon, Ovinu malkenu, Eder
vohod, Siluk Kedushah, Ase lema-an shmecho, Veye-esoyu, Heye im
pifiyos, Hayom haras olom,* Psalm 150, *Hayom teamezenu;* for *Yom
Kippur: Yaaleh, Vidui, Ki onu Amecho, Veal chatoim, More chatoim,
Imru lelohim, Amitze Shechokim, Eso dei, Veoviso sehilo, Ho-oches,
Vechach hoyo omer, Vechach hoyo moneh, Ashre ayin.* This constitutes the complete list of texts for which so large a variety (447 numbers) of tunes was composed. The songs are for cantor and singer,
and include no recitatives and only a few traditional tunes.

As mentioned above, this collection incorporates material of many
other composers whose music was either well known or found special
grace in the eyes of Beer. Due to this use by Beer, some names of
Jewish composers with their creations were preserved. Thus, we make
the acquaintance of a certain MOSHE PAN to whom Beer always gives
the title RABBI, and from whom he incorporated 144 selections in the
last named collection. Pan's compositions show considerable musical
talent and originality; and it seems that many other composers (also
Beer himself) imitated him. Up to the present time, it has been virtually impossible to identify this Pan with any degree of certainty.
However, by tracing his daughter (who was married to the *chazzan*
Meier Coblentz in Offenbach near Frankfort) who died in 1814 and
on whose tombstone the father is named *Hameshorer Hagodol Rabbi
Moshe Pan* without the addition of the usual *zal* (for departed per-
sons) we can assume that he was still alive at that time. The name of
Pan is the Jewish pronunciation of the place Peine near Hildesheim.
In the archive of Hildesheim several Moshe Peines are named as
citizens.

Ten numbers are marked *Mi-haschaz be-Berlin,* probably referring
to the predecessor of Beer, Leb *Chazzan* (1736-1758). One number
is by Yitzchok, *chazzan* in Glogow, who was the teacher of Israel
Lovy (v. below). Fifty numbers are marked *M Sch B* and *R Y Ch,*
both abbreviations which probably mean *Mishër-besori* (relative of
mine) and Rabbi Yitzchok *Chazzan* in Glogow, the same just mentioned.

Twelve numbers are marked LEON SINGER, the composer of the famous "Leoni" *Yigdal*. His real name was Meier Leon. In 1766 he was appointed singer in the newly rebuilt Duke's Place Synagogue in London on an annual salary of £40 sterling. His sweet voice and wonderful singing attracted a great attendance of even gentiles. James Piccioto says in his "Sketches": [55] "Meier Leon the humble chorister rose to be Leoni the opera singer. He possessed a tuneful head, and he composed light and sacred melody. He adapted some Synagogue airs to Church hymns, but he preserved strictly his religion, declining to appear on the stage on Friday nights and Festivals." Nevertheless the Board of the synagogue did not hesitate in 1772 to reduce his salary to £32 sterling. Hence, he left the synagogue and became a stage singer. "But his appearance on the Boards was a failure merely because he had not the slightest conception of the histrionic art." After a time, he turned back to the Synagogue choir. There he composed tunes especially for the High Festivals which "used to be sung in the English Synagogue until the advent of the foreign *chazzanim* in 1814-1815." "The writer of the hymn which is sung to the tune 'Leoni' was Thomas Olivers, a Welshman who was born in 1725 . . . became a Wesleyan minister in 1753, and died in 1799. One day . . . Oliver went to the synagogue where he heard a *tune* which so completely enraptured him that he resolved to have it sung in Christian congregations; and he therefore wrote for this purpose an hymn 'The God of Abraham, Praise.' It was published in 1772 and became so popular that eight editions had to be published in less than two years, and it had reached the thirtieth edition in 1799. A writer on hymnology relates how the son of an old minister once said: 'I remember my father told me, during a conference in Wesley's time, Thomas Olivers, one of the preachers, came down to him, and unfolding a manuscript, said: "Look at this.

I have rendered it from the Hebrew, giving it as far as I could a Christian character, and I have called on LEONI THE JEW, WHO HAS GIVEN ME A SYNAGOGUE MELODY TO SUIT IT; HERE IS THE TUNE, AND IT IS TO BE CALLED 'LEONI.' " I read the composition and it was that now well-known grand imitation of Israel's ancient hymns—"The God of Abraham, Praise." ' " [56] When in 1787 the Ashkenazic congregation in Kingston, Jamaica, built a new synagogue and asked the Ashkenazic congregation in London to recommend to it a reader, Leon took that position and settled in Kingston, where he died in 1800.

The *Yigdal* tune can be considered a compilation of an old folk-motive which is prevalent both in Jewish, Spanish-Basque as well as in Slavic song, as proved in Table XXVIII. We find the same melodic line in 1, a Spanish *cancion;* [57] 2, in the Jewish-Spanish prayer for Dew; 3, in a Polish Song; [58] 7-8, in the folk-song of the Basques; [59] 9, in the symphony Moravia by Smetana; 4, in the Zionist hymn *Hatikva* and 5, in the Zionist song (in German) *Dort wo die Zeder.*

YEKEL SINGER of Prague, called also "Yekel Bass" or J. Lehman, lived at the end of the eighteenth century. He was a productive composer, and much of his work remains to us in manuscript form. His songs became popular with the *chazzanim* in Germany. He seems to have had little knowledge of Hebrew. His orthography is faulty to the point of the comic.

MS. No. 28 A: 1 and 2 is inscribed with the following dedication written in Hebrew letters: "*Meinen herzlichen Gruss an Hameshorer hagodol Rabbi Meir Schaz. Ich werde bald das Vergnügen haben, persönlich aufzuwarten. Dann von allem, so viel Sie wollen. Dieses nur in Eil. Ihr Freund, Yekel.*" MS. No. 28 C: 1 and 2 he dedicates: "*Meinem Freund Abele Wachenheimer gewidmet mit der Bitte nicht weiter zu geben. Yekel Singer.*" This was the way that the "singers" used to

TABLE XXVIII
Table of Folk-songs
Compared with the Yigdal tune

1.
Spanish cancio
Pedrell II 186

Vir-gen de la Cue-va   qien-te vi-noa

2.
Jewish Sephardic
for Tal

Leh le-ša-lom ge-šem u - vo le-ša-lom

3.
Polish, Collection
Noskowski p. 218

Pod   Kra - ko-wem   na   blo -

4.
Zionist Hymn
Hatikva

Kol   od bal - le-vav   pe - ni -

5.
Dort wo die Zeder

Dort,   wo die Ze-der   schlank die Wol-ke

6.
Yigdal

Yig-dal e - lo-him chay we-yish-ta-bach, nim-

7.
Basque

8.
Basque

9.
Smetana

1. ver El cho choy el Ri‑toy el fla ‑ re Fe ‑ rrer

2. tal a ‑ šir ši ‑ ra ‑ ti we ‑ a‑sim div‑ra ‑ ti w'ag‑

3. niu. A ‑ ha ‑ ha wij ‑ wi‑jal ja‑sio

4. ja od lo av ‑ da tiq‑wa ‑ te ‑ nu

5. fliesst, dort, wo die A ‑ sche mei‑ner Vä‑ter ruht, das

6. yi ‑ chu ‑ do ne' ‑ lom we gam en sof ‑ le‑

7.

8.

1. el fill de Mi - que - lay - el del tra - mu - ser

2. bi - ra se - fa - ti le - tsur ye - šu - a - ti

3. na - ko - niu

4. la - šuv le - e - rez a - vo - te - nu ir ba - da - wid ha - na

5. Feld ge - tränkt hat Mak - ka - bä - er Blut, die - ses schö - ne Land am
   etc.

6. ach - du - so.

7. etc.

8. etc.

introduce themselves to the *chazzanim*, presenting them with
their compositions to show their ability.

ABRAHAM SINGER of Prosnitz, father of the famous John
Braham. (The latter's name was formed by dropping the "A"
of Abraham. This son was co-editor with Nathan of the collection of Hebrew melodies under their joint names, 1815).
Singer lived in London, where he died about 1780.

Another manuscript, No. 196, by L. M. MAYER, *chazzan* in
Aarhus Denmark, written around 1825, has a tune for *Kol
Nidré* (No. 25) which is entirely different from the usual *Kol
Nidré*, being based on the mode of the Psalm recitative accord-
ing to Ashkenazic tradition.

One of the outstanding Synagogue singers toward the end
of the eighteenth and the beginning of the nineteenth century
was ISRAEL LOVY—born in Schottland near Danzig (1773).
His parents came from Poland. While he was still in his childhood, his parents settled in Glogow, where he became *meshorer*
to Yitzchok Glogow, whose compositions are included in Ahron
Beer's MS.—(v. above). Equipped with unusual quality of
voice and musical talent as well as intelligence, the young
Israel Lovy became very popular. In accord with the custom
of that time, he organized a group of singers, with which he
started a tour throughout Central Europe, giving Synagogal
concerts.

In 1798 he came, in the course of his tour, to Fürth in which
community the post of *chazzan* was vacant. He made a deep
impression with his singing, and was elected *chazzan* there.
(His predecessor was Isaac of Prosnitz, 1782-1795.) In the
eighteenth century that community was one of the most pros-
perous in Germany, and very fond of music. Already in the
beginning of that century it had maintained a choir of four
singers; and, on special occasions, had increased it to ten.[60] Because of their pleasure in being entertained with music, the

Jews of Fürth secured residence permits for a troup of Jewish musicians, making them legal "community officials." *Chanukah* and *Purim* were celebrated with great pomp. Indeed, the head of the community found it necessary to issue a prohibition against the engaging of more than three musicians for entertainments. In Fürth, the first Jewish Songster with musical scores was published under the name of *Simchas Hannefesh* by Rabbi Elchonon Henle Kirchhain, containing thirteen songs in Yiddish for Sabbath and festal days (Chapter XVIII). It was printed by a Jewish press. In Fürth, Lovy continued his education and studied with eagerness piano, violin, and violoncello, as well as the classic music of Mozart and Haydn. At the same time he attained facility in the Italian and French languages, the latter of which became and remained his vernacular to the end of his days. Here he began to call himself Lowy. He achieved a mastery of Hebrew literature. However, his outstanding strength was his phenomenal voice. He soon became a concert singer, especially of Haydn's and Mozart's compositions; and was invited by the Duke (later king) of Bavaria, Maximilian Joseph, to sing the tenor part in Haydn's "Creation" at a court concert. Lowy also received special permission, for the first time in the history of Germany, to give public concerts in Nürnberg, a place where a Jew was not allowed to stay over night and was permitted to enter only when accompanied by a Christian woman.[61] In 1799 Lowy, accompanied by two singers, gave a concert in Nürnberg, after which the local paper *Friedens-und-Kriegs Courier*, No. 67, March 20, 1799, carried the announcement: "The three singers, especially Mr. Lowy, who gave the 'musical academy' on the seventeenth, in the Bitterholz, thank the public for the great applause and kindly reception; and herewith make acknowledgment of the courtesy extended them." The concert he repeated annually for six years, until he left

Fürth in 1806. Among the *chazzanim*, he became famous as
ISRAEL GLOGOW and later as REB YISROEL FÜRTH. The
Hebrew Union College Library possesses in MS., No. 65, a
collection of fifty-six items by Lowy from his Fürth period.
In those tunes he shows no originality, but walks rather in the
path of his colleagues, in the style of the eighteenth century.
Although he was accounted well acquainted with the vocal
music of Haydn and Mozart, this knowledge had no influence
upon his *chazzanic* creations. They are, throughout, instrumental in character, and require considerable technique not
only for a singer but even for ar instrumentalist.

In 1806 Lowy left Fürth with the intention of going to the
metropolis of the Europe of that time—to Paris. However,
since he progressed by the old method of concert-touring, he
was kept in Mayence as *chazzan* for three years, and in Strassburg for eight. Finally in 1818 he succeeded in reaching the
goal of his travel, Paris, where he gave concerts of secular
music, and where he soon became famous in musical circles as
a great singer. Attempts were made to inveigle him into stage
appearances. We do not know what it was, but something
held him back from that step. At that time the Jewish community in Paris, which had received official recognition in 1791,
attempted to complete its organization; to that end, planned
the building of a great Synagogue, and introduced some reforms in the service. Therefore in 1818, the community engaged Lowy as cantor and regenerator of the Synagogue service. In 1822 the synagogue on Rue Notre Dame de Naza-
rite was dedicated. There Lowy organized a choir in four
parts, for which he composed a service for the entire year.
Thus he was really the first to have introduced a modern four
part choir.

Lowy here became Lovy, in conformity with French pronunciation.

Lovy's voice was baritone-bass from lower F, while in the high range it had tenor timbre and reached the highest notes. He died in 1832. After his death, all his reform endeavors melted away. However, many of his tunes became popular not only in Paris but also as far as Poland; and one of them was adopted by Goldfaden in his opera *Shulamith* (Chapter XX). Some of them were published by Naumbourg in his Synagogal work; and a selection of them, with his biography, was printed by his family under the name *Chants Religieux*, Paris, 1862. To the *chazzanim* in Germany he was known as Israel Glogow, Israel Fürth, Israel Mayence, and Israel Strassburg; and they used to sing his songs written in those cities—all of which were composed in the old style of the eighteenth century. But after he had settled in Paris, he disappeared from the *chazzanic* world. His reform attempts made no impression on the *chazzanim*, as they left no trace upon the course of modernization of the Synagogue Song in the beginning of the nineteenth century. Although he was endowed with all the gifts required for a reformer, this rôle was accorded not to him but to Sulzer in Vienna, to Naumbourg in Paris, and to Lewandowski in Berlin. The explanation may be found in the fact that Lovy was an extremist, as we see from his compositions, whose effort was to break with the past and tradition and to introduce entirely new tunes—an effort in line with the general attempt to do away with the old Jewish life and create an entirely new Jew and Judaism.

Another prominent *chazzan* belongs to the eighteenth century, although his activity lasted to the middle of the nineteenth century. He is SHOLOM FRIEDE, *chazzan* in Amsterdam, born in that city in 1783. He officiated for some time in Utrecht. In 1809 he was appointed first *chazzan* in Amsterdam. Concerning the pompous ceremony of his installation (interesting because indicative of the important position that

the *chazzan* occupied at that time), the archive of the Ashkenazic community there provides a detailed description. He had
a fine taste for music. His numerous collections are retained
in the Hebrew Union College library (in MSS., Nos. 17, 34,
35, 39, 40, 42, 69,—) containing in all about two hundred
numbers, in the style of the eighteenth century. He had a
love for the Polish-Jewish songs; and due to that fact, we are
in possession of the early Polish *chazzanuth* and of tunes in
Chassidic style. He died in Amsterdam in 1854.

JOSEPH S. GOLDSTEIN—BASS of Oberlauringen bei Schwein-
furth am Main—wrote a collection of Synagogal songs (probably toward the end of the eighteenth century), consisting of
tunes in the usual style; and, in addition, several recitatives
for the High Festivals in the traditional modes. This is the
first and only written music of that particular style, and it demonstrates that the recitative of the eighteenth century is in no
way different from the recitative of East European *chazzanuth*, for Goldstein, by his own testimony, was of German
origin. In 1813 he became the bass of Moshe Raff, *chazzan*
in Jebenhausen in Bavaria, to whom he presented his collection
and whom "he taught the tunes by playing them on the violin," according to the statement of the son of Raff (providing
us with another sidelight on the relationship of Bass, "singer,"
and *chazzan* of those days).

From a glance over the entire field, one should not infer
that the *chazzanim* entirely abolished the traditional tunes and
recitatives. Quite to the contrary, parallel to the new and free
Synagogue compositions, the traditional modes were preserved
—and usually very carefully, as we see in the traditional
chazzanuth of Southern Germany, copied by S. Naumbourg
in 1840, according to the singing of the *chazzan* of München,
Loew Sänger (1781-1843) (Chapter XIII). Those recita-

tives, inasmuch as they had certainly been in tradition for many generations, give us a grasp of the state of the recitative of the earlier centuries. They have not the elaborate *chazzanic* flavor of the recitatives of the above-mentioned Goldstein, for they are much simpler. The *chazzanim* of the eighteenth century, with the exception of Israel Lovy, did not make any effort to reform the recitative. Their only innovation was the introduction of measured melodies—tunes in the style of the eighteenth century, through the use of which they contributed toward the Europeanization of the Synagogue song.

CHAPTER XII

One of the best proofs that ideas and ideals influence music, creating new melodic lines, as well as changing the taste for music, is the reform movement in Jewry at the end of the eighteenth and at the beginning of the nineteenth century. As long as the Jews lived in the belief that their stay in the Diaspora was compulsory *Golus*-"exile," that they belonged to and would return to Palestine, they instinctively preserved the Semitic-Oriental element in themselves and in their cultural creations.

So also in their music! Even the attempts of the *chazzanim* in the eighteenth century to introduce "European" music into the Synagogue were without any intention to abolish the Semitic-Oriental element of the Synagogue song, and without any desire to supplant it by European music in order to Europeanize the Jewish taste. Their activity was but the attempt to satisfy the hunger for music of both singers and public; and to achieve their goal they were compelled not to be selective in the choice of musical material. Despite the opposition of the spiritual leaders and spirited Jews, they gave to the masses what they liked, namely, the music heard in the Christian environment.

But the *Golus*-viewpoint of the Jew sustained a shock by the flare of the new spirit aroused in Europe at the end of the eighteenth century by the Revolution in Paris and by the philo-

232

sophical schools in Germany. Free-thinking, irreligiosity, enthusiastic belief in humanity, made some Europeanized and
free-thinking Jews here and there in Central Europe believe
that the source of their misery as Jews lay in their seclusion
from general modern European culture and in their adherence
to an ancient Asiatic religion, a religious culture the human-
ism of which those neo-humanists could not see. A bitter
hatred arose in their hearts against Judaism and Jewish customs. The same ritual which, a half-century before, had had
the power to inspire their ancestors became obnoxious to them.
Those extremely modernized Jews who with Heine considered
Judaism "a calamity," which had no justification for existence,
deserted their faith and their people and went over to the
Christian Church, thinking thus to become complete human
beings and full-blooded citizens of their country, Germany or
France. Others, whose Jewish consciousness was stronger,
could not take this step; and therefore came upon the idea to
reform their Judaism, by which they meant to cut away exotic,
Semitic-Oriental parts, and retain only that part of Judaism
which was of a general religious and ethical nature.[1] The idea
was so to remodel Judaism that it should not be a stumbling
block by reason of its Orientalism and Medievalism, that it
should be as easy to observe as is Christianity, that, furthermore, the modern Jew should not be offended by its strangeness and should be attracted by its European exterior.

It is significant to notice that this first "practical" reform attempt was made not by rabbis but by laymen. Against it the
rabbis conducted a fight for many years; and not until a generation later did some rabbis of prominence become reformers.

The Jewish movement for reform was called forth by the
general struggle in Europe for social emancipation and justice
and for freedom of thought. Who more than the Jew was
deprived of social, yea, human, rights? Who more than he

suffered from medieval prejudices and barbarism? And who more than he was craving for light and enlightenment, for the abolition of customs and practices founded on inhuman conceptions? The amount of cruelty and injustice, abuse and degradation, slavery and brutality, he experienced from his Christian environment in that long dark period of eighteen centuries accumulated in his heart until it burst forth at the touch of that explosive element which spread all over Europe, and shattered all "traditional" institutions, social and individual, religious and secular. Indeed, religion received the brunt of the attack. Religious practices, and especially the ritual, became subject to criticism and reform. In the Church, there had arisen opposition against the dead Latin language, unknown to the people, and an effort was made to substitute instead the vernacular of the respective countries. That change caused fights in the Church. There were cases where the priests were progressive and intoned the prayers in German, while the public, being conservative, responded in Latin, and vice versa.

The same fight raged regarding the music, as told in Chapter XI. The progressives claimed that the old traditional song did not appeal to them any longer, while the conservative elements denounced the reformers in that "they started to intone the Mass in the brilliant style of the opera in order to cover the emptiness in their hearts, caused by lack of religiosity, and that they started using all kinds of effects to stimulate the senses." [2] The antagonism resulted at times in a tumultuous and bloody riot, such as the sad incident in the Church of Ruedesheim in 1787. When the new German songs were introduced into the service, against the opposition of the public, the Archduke sent soldiers and guns into the Church, causing the death of thirty people.[3]

Quietly building behind the chaos of the crude public fight were the two spirits—Henry Purcell (1658-1695) in England

and Johann Sebastian Bach (1685-1750) in Germany—who created the new forms which became the foundation of Protestant Church music in both countries.

A similar striving toward the reform of Synagogue worship started in Jewry. The first to make an attempt toward reform were, as mentioned above, laymen. They, as practical men, facing the problems of life, felt the severity of the social problems of the Jew more intensely than the rabbis, who in that time generally lived apart from social life, secluded in the realm of study. The first reforms were chiefly directed toward social and practical aspects of religion. The first protagonist of reform was David Friedländer in Berlin, a wealthy merchant and an intellectual. He made the attempt to translate the prayerbook from the Hebrew into German (1787). But being such an extremist as even to propose an affiliation with Christianity minus the belief in Jesus (see note 1), he found no following.

The first successful reformer of the Synagogue ritual was Israel Jacobson (1768-1828), a rich and influential merchant who, with the aid of the French government in Westphalia, made it his aim to reform the ritual as well as to reorganize the religious education of the Jews in Germany. In Seesen (Westphalia) he established in 1801 a boys' school for elementary knowledge and trade; and he repeated the venture in Cassel in 1808. There he arranged a children's service into which he introduced hymns, the tunes of which he took from the Protestant chorales. To these tunes he set Hebrew texts, and printed a collection of chorales with the notes running from right to left (Cassel, 1810).[4] In Seesen, in 1810, he erected on the grounds of the boys' school the first Reform Temple in Europe, in which he installed an organ and for which he arranged the ritual as well as the music. He provided the Temple with a bell which, according to Christian custom, should announce the time of prayer. Jacobson's program for the service was this: Alongside of the Hebrew texts of the prayers, which at the beginning he did not touch, he introduced German hymns to the tunes of Christian chorales. He abolished the chanting of the Pentateuch and Prophets according to traditional modes as well as the unrhythmical prayer modes, and together with these he discarded the *chazzan*. He himself *read* the service without any chant, according to the manner of reading the Bible text and prayers in the Protestant Church. He introduced the sermon in pure German—he himself preaching in his Temple. He brought to his Temple the gown of the Church. He also introduced the confirmation of boys and girls (1811).

In 1815 he settled in Berlin, where he opened a Temple in his private home, which was of short duration, for it was closed by the Prussian government in the same year on the ground that according to the law only one house of Jewish worship was permitted in Berlin.

However, utilizing the occasion of the renovation of the Synagogue in Berlin, Jacob Herz Beer, the father of the composer Meyerbeer, opened a Temple in his private home, according to Jacobson's program. The music was arranged by his son, who, as he himself stated, opposed the using of an organ in the Jewish service.[5] In order to attract a greater audience, to whom a service without a *chazzan* was unthinkable, Beer was constrained to engage a *chazzan*. Whether or not from intent, he chose a *chazzan* without a voice but with some modern culture, Asher Lion (1776-1863), who later became the successor of Ahron Beer (Chapter XI). In Beer's Temple the first Jewish preachers officiated, such as Zunz, the promoter of the "Science of Judaism," and Israel Eduard Kley.

After the completion of the renovation of the old Synagogue, built in 1714, Beer was forced by the government to

I.

2. סָבִיב תְּחוּיָנָה עֵינַיִם ‏ — יצוּרֶךָ ‏ 3. מִי יָצַו לָרוּחַ וְיֹשׁוֵב ‏ — יֹאמַר
שִׁמְךָ יְפָאֵרוּ.‏ — יִפְעַת וְטֹהַר הַשָּׁמַיִם ‏ — הִרְעִיפוּ שְׁחָקִים?‏ — מִי מֹצִיאָ, נַפְשֵׁנוּ
הֲדַר עוּזְךָ יְסַפֵּרוּ;‏ — מִי שָׁם הַשֶּׁמֶשׁ לְשׁוֹבֵב, — מֵחֵק אֶרֶץ לְחַם חֲקִים?‏ —
לָצַהַר? — מִי הַלְבִּישָׁה חוֹד נֵס זֹהַר? אַתָּה' אֲדֹנָי עֹשֵׂה אֵלֶּה! — יָדְךָ לֹא
— לְמִי כּוֹכְבֵי אוֹר יַזְמָרוּ? תִּקְצָר' וְלֹא תֵלֶא — אֲמִתְּךָ עַד
עוֹלָם תָּקוּם!

FACSIMILE 6.
Israel Jacobson Hymnal. Pub. Cassel, 1810. No. 1.

close his Temple and thus the reform attempts in Berlin were suppressed until 1842, when the Reform Society was founded which built the Temple existing to the present day.

But even in Jacobson's Temple in Seesen its leaders had to yield to the demand of the public and engaged the *chazzan* Hirsch Goldberg (1807-1893) in 1833. He served there until 1842 and was then appointed *chazzan* in Brunswick. Together with Julius Freudenthal (Brunswick 1805-1874), Dukal musician, he modernized the Synagogue song and published in 1843 a collection of songs for solo and small choir in two parts.[6] To this songster Freudenthal contributed several tunes and, especially his famous tune for *En Kelohenu*, which he had composed in 1841.[7] This tune has the typical German melodic line, and in its first part resembles a German melody of 1774 (No. 1) (see table XXIX), which was reworked in 1819 and in 1844 (No. 3) and published in 1844.[8]

It is of interest to state the fact that the School in Seesen educated its own musical director who also became the organist of the Temple, the first Jewish organist in the first Reform Temple. This was Gerson Rosenstein (1790-1851). In 1849 he published a collection of 106 "chorales," melodies to the song-texts in use at the school. These "chorales" have the genuine German chorale style. He compiled also a collection of traditional tunes for the Temple service (Hamburg, 1852) for solo and unison singing. The songster contains sixty-three numbers, twenty-seven of Ashkenazic and fourteen of Sephardic origin. The reason for the inclusion of the latter we shall explain later. The other tunes are new compositions.[9]

Jacobson's program was accepted as a foundation by the "Tempel Verein," founded in Hamburg in 1817 through the initiative of I. E. Kley. The latter brought along a collection of hymns used in Beer's Temple in Berlin, and introduced them in Hamburg. Kley published *Religious songs for Israel-*

TABLE XXIX
En Kelohenu

1. 1774

Gros-ser Gott wir lo-ben dich, Herr wir prei-sen dei-ne stär-ke

2. 1819

3. 1844

4. 1843

En ke-lo he-nu, en ka-do-ne-nu,

1. Wie du warst vor al-ler Zeit, So bleibst du in E-wig-keit.

2.

3.

4.

en kmal-ke-nu, en ke-mo-shi-e-nu.

Etz Chayim

5. Etz cha-yim hi la-ma-ch'zi-kim boh ve-som-che-hoh m'u-

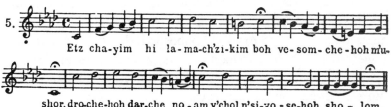

shor, dro-che-hoh dar-che no-am v'chol n'si-vo-se-hoh sho-lom.

ites in German, in 1818, which became the nucleus for the "Hamburg Hymnal" published in 1845.[10]

The suppliers of music for the Temple were mostly Christian musicians: Bethuel, who was the first organist at the Temple (1818-1828), contributed nineteen chorales; I. H. G. Stoewing; A. G. Methfessel; J. A. G. Heinroth; Lütgert; F. J. Groenland; Demuth; Schinck; Schwenke, and others. Ferdinand Hiller, a Jewish convert to Christianity, contributed some chorales. Likewise Jewish laymen like M. Levy and the chairman of the Temple, Isaak Seckl Frankel, contributed thirteen tunes to German texts. The latter was also a member of the committee to compose a new prayerbook for the Reform congregation, which was published in 1819 and dedicated with high esteem and appreciation to Israel Jacobson. The organ was a gift of Salomon Heine, the uncle of the poet Heine. A boys' choir in two parts was trained. Following the intention to abolish all "ugliness of medievalism," although originally it was planned not to employ a *chazzan* at all,[11] a Portuguese, David Meldola (born in Amsterdam in 1780; died in Hamburg in 1861), was engaged. He had very little musical ability, but was preferred on account of his Portuguese pronunciation of the Hebrew which was regarded by Kley nearest to the scientific.[12]

D. Meldola introduced Portuguese tunes into the Temple. In doing so, the Ashkenazic *chazzanuth* was naturally done away with. The Bible was read without chanting. Only in 1879 did the then appointed Cantor of the Temple, M. Henle (1850-1925), reintroduce the chanting according to the Biblical modes, and in 1909 he reintroduced the Ashkenazic pronunciation.[13] In 1846 Kley published the melodies to the *Israelitish Songbook*, containing ninety-nine tunes to German texts. In style and character these tunes are similar to the tunes published by G. Rosenstein.

On special occasions a mixed choir of volunteers would sing German music in four parts. In the preface to his collection, Kley promised to publish those songs, but did not carry out his intention. A collection of these songs was compiled in 1827 by Methfessel and M. Haarbleicher, in which the *Etz Chayim* melody is contained (table XXIX). This melody seems to be a rearrangement of the Portuguese *Tal* tune (table XXVIII[2]). The same melody was printed later by Goldberg and Rosenstein in their above-mentioned collections. In 1833 another collection in part-singing was arranged by I. F. Schwenke, the organist of the Temple. Both remained in MS. All these "chorales" were lately abolished by the present cantor L. Kornitzer; and, according to his statement, "Jewish" music was introduced instead.[14]

Following Jacobson's reform, several other German "chorale" books for Israelites were compiled, such as the *Songster for Israelites* in Wuertemberg in 1836, in four parts, arranged for all the Sabbaths and festivals of the year (397 numbers). In each hymn the contents of the weekly portion of the Pentateuch, or the underlying idea of the Festival, is expressed. The music is entirely Christian. Another collection was published by Joseph Johlson in Frankfort for the Jewish educational institution "Philantropin." This *Israelitish Songbook*, published in 1840 (second edition in 1842), contains among its 102 melodies many popular Protestant chorales, such as No. 16a, introduced by I. Jacobson in his songbook printed in 1810. This "chorale" J. S. Bach, for example, utilized four times in his St. Matthew (Nos. 23, 53, 63, 72), in his Christmas Oratorio, Nos. 5, 64, etc. The tune was composed by Hans Leo Hassler in 1601.[15]

Likewise No. 9b and No. 41, found in Jacobson's Songbook, is the famous Protestant chorale utilized by Bach in St. Matthew, No. 31; in his Christmas Oratorio, Nos. 12, 60. This melody is of Christian origin with Latin text dating back to 1539.[16]

In the matter of adoption from Christian sources Kley was more careful, for he did not adopt popular Christian melodies, but had, according to his statement in the preface, seventy out of ninety-nine tunes especially composed for the texts he submitted to the musicians.

The radical reform introduced by Jacobson and carried out in the Hamburg Temple called forth a stormy opposition throughout Central European Jewry. Many prominent rabbis of that time announced their disapproval of the German prayers and hymns, of the changing of the traditional texts, of the abolition of the traditional *Missinay* modes of the Bible, of the introduction of the organ, and of the singing of mixed choirs.[17] That fight continued for many years, and in 1845 at the rabbinical conference in Frankfort, after a long debate, the young reform rabbis, such as Holdheim, Abraham Geiger, Salomon, Samuel Adler, etc., adopted the resolution that the employment of the organ in the Synagogue even on Sabbaths and holy days is not only permissible but also advisable, and that making music by playing instruments on Sabbaths and holidays in homes should be recommended from a spiritual-religious standpoint.[18] Geiger was of those who considered the chant of the Bible of no validity, since it was, to his opinion, a later, post-Biblical innovation.[19]

The Reformers, notably the rabbis, apart from their endeavor to emancipate the Jew and make him a modern European human being by stripping off all the medieval and Oriental elements still clinging to him, were deeply interested in retaining the youth which started to drift away from their people and culture and to become absorbed by the Christian environment. In their honest effort, they wanted to reconstruct Judaism and to beautify it according to the model they had before them. The Jewish youth found delight in Christian forms of worship and religion. Hence, the Reform leaders adopted all those forms and customs of the Church which seemed to them to be in harmony with what they considered to be PROPHETIC Judaism, completely neglecting all post-Biblical culture, ignoring the result of over two thousand years of Jewish spiritual and social life and creation and the sentiments developed from them. The craving for assimilation roused a dislike for old music, which nevertheless in some places retained its pristine beauty. Around that time an English Christian traveller, speaking of the characteristic old Synagogue song, says: "It has often excited our wonder that in the principal capitals of Europe, wherever there is a Synagogue we have generally found a vocal performer or two who sang in the Italian manner and in exquisite taste . . . so it was in Paris, Amsterdam, Milan, Venice, Rome, Naples, and we have had instances at home of exquisite Hebrew singing in our own country (England)."[20]

At first, the radical reformers found but a few adherents in Germany: a group in Leipzig which organized, in 1820, a service similar to that of Hamburg, a group in Frankfort, and later, in 1842, one in Berlin. The bulk of German Jews at that time was still saturated with Jewish tradition and consciousness, so that the few ultra-reformers in every community could arouse interest only in some minor modernization of the ritual and the music. Soon, in almost every community, a battle began between the radical elements and the Orthodox—a fight which led to a division of the communities into Progressive and Conservative congregations. But even the Progressive group did not go so far as did the Temple in Hamburg. The Progressive congregations adopted from Hamburg the singing of German chorales in Protestant style, the mixed choir, and the organ; while, on principle, they retained the *chazzan* and the traditional tunes. Throughout Europe not a single congregation became entirely Reform according to the program of Jacobson. Every community in Central Europe, notably in Germany, is still divided into Orthodox and Progressive or "Organ" congregations.

Almost all the composers for those Progressive synagogues in the first part of the nineteenth century were Christians. Their musical creations are naturally German music in the Church style. Even in arranging Jewish traditional tunes, they employed European structure and German modulation (Chapter XXIII). The solo part of the *chazzan*, the unrhythmical chant, did not receive any attention; it remained in its eighteenth-century form and frequently became stale and lifeless. This remainder of the old Semitic-Oriental song was tolerated only for the sake of those members who still belonged to the older generation and who, through education and habit, considered a service without *chazzanuth* as unJewish. The opinion of the young progressive element was that, inasmuch as they were good Germans, this type of non-German song had no place in their worship, and should be abolished sooner or later.[21]

From the history of European music we know that through the gigantic classic creations of the eighteenth and the first quarter of the nineteenth centuries the style of and the taste for music were entirely changed. This change, of course, influenced the Jews also. Without radical reform attempts, the Synagogue would have felt the change of taste and would have immediately produced songs in the classic style, but also in accord with the Jewish traditional genius of Synagogue song. This would have fused Jewish elements with classical to new musical forms. But, with the abolition of the entire Jewish song, the Jewish spirit was simultaneously forced out.

As we survey the musical creations of the ultra-reform

movement of the first half of the nineteenth century, we see that its leaders failed to sense the truth so well expressed by J. G. Frazer in his above-quoted statement (Chapter IX): "Every faith has its appropriate music, and the difference between the creeds might almost be expressed in musical notation. . . . For we cannot doubt that this, the most ultimate and affecting of all the arts, has done much to create as well as to express the religious emotions, thus modifying more or less deeply the fabric of belief to which at first it seems only to minister."

Even more applicable is this statement to the Jews, as a religious, historical and racial group with pronounced original spiritual and intellectual features. They cannot but have a musical expression of their own! Verily, Jacobson and his adherents in Europe and America did not realize this truth.

From the historical point of view it should be recorded that JOSEPH PERL was the first to establish a modern service in Austria, and, like Israel Jacobson in Seesen, he erected a House of Worship in Tarnopol (Galicia) at his own expense in 1819 with choir, called "*Tempel für geregelten Gottesdienst.*"

CHAPTER XIII

THE INFLUENCE OF MODERATE REFORM UPON SYNA-
GOGUE SONG DURING THE NINETEENTH CENTURY IN CEN-
TRAL AND WESTERN EUROPE.

I. Salomon Sulzer (1804-1890)

Judaism in Germany was too strong, too deep-rooted, Jewish
sentiment too full of vitality and of desires for life, the Semitic-
Oriental elements in the Jew still too virile to succumb to the
ultra-reform movement, to submit to the Europeanization
and Germanization of the Jewish soul. Therefore, Ultra-
Reform had no direct success. But indirectly it aroused the
desire for modernization, for the purification of the vessels of
the sanctuary from the rust of ages. It drew the attention of
Israel's intellectual spirits to the need of a thorough investigation of the inherited treasures, in order to learn their nature
and their manner of development in the past, and to determine
which of their elements are essential to Judaism and should be
retained and which had value only for the past and should be
relegated to the sacred archives. That scientific and philosophical movement embraced all the intellectual spirits in
Israel regardless of their practical attitude toward tradition,
and it directly influenced the Synagogue song.

Around the beginning of the nineteenth century, some members of the newly established Jewish community in Vienna (organized in 1790) sought the introduction of the Reform Service of the Hamburg Temple, to which end they elected one
of the prominent leaders of the Reform movement, Isaac Noah
Mannheimer, as principal of the religious school and preacher

246

and erected a Temple in 1826. The old *chazzan* who had also
been religious teacher and minister, Koppel Markbreiter [1] (in
Vienna from 1792), was found incompetent to undertake a
modernization of the music; and, therefore, Christian musicians were employed from 1812—among them also the Jew
Ignaz Moscheles, who composed for the Vienna synagogue's
celebration of 1814, but who later embraced Christianity. [2]   In
this connection, because it is significant for the attitude of the
Reform Jews in their relation to Christianity, we digress a
moment to note that the Hamburg Temple invited the Chris-
tianized Felix Mendelssohn in 1844 to compose for the
twenty-fifth anniversary of the Temple, which invitation he at
first accepted but later declined. Likewise, Beethoven was
asked by the Vienna community to compose a cantata on the
occasion of the dedication of the new temple in 1826. [3] Mannheimer was the son of a well-known *chazzan*, Noah Mannheimer. [4] The son inherited from his father some musical and
chazzanic appreciation and understanding. He therefore considered the old Markbreiter incapable. In truth, he would
have preferred to abolish the office entirely, as his general attitude toward reform was a radical one, and his aim was to introduce the Jacobson-Hamburg program (see further in Sulzer's statement). Yet the majority of the congregation in
Vienna, rooted still in the tradition of the past, for most of
them were from the Hungarian and Slavic countries of the
Austrian Monarchy, opposed him. Probably the conservative
Catholic atmosphere of Vienna, in contradistinction to the liberal Protestant atmosphere in Northern Germany, may have
contributed to the conservatism of the Jews. Consequently
Mannheimer, despite his personal views, was constrained to
make far-reaching compromises with conservatism, as he himself admitted in his letters. Among his compromises was the
engagement of a *chazzan*.

And here it happened that the *chazzan* whom the Vienna community engaged was a genius—SALOMON SULZER. Had he been a mediocrity, the result would have been—as in so many other communities—that Christian composers would have provided chorales and German music, while the *chazzan* continued his stale recitative. Sulzer was in every aspect quite unique in the *chazzanic* caste. The son of a rich and intelligent family of manufacturers, he was through accidental circumstances directed to the service of the Synagogue. In the recklessness of early boyhood, he had fallen into the river, and was thought drowned. His mother, frantically summoning all possible aid, vowed to devote him to a sacred career if he would be saved. His instructor in *chazzanuth* was the *chazzan* in his native place, Hohenems: Salomon Eichberg (1786-1880). Eichberg had been a "singer" under Israel Lovy in Fürth (Chapter XI), and probably instructed his disciple Sulzer in the traditional song of Southern Germany as well as in the compositions of Israel Lovy. Aside from this, Sulzer had a modern general and musical education. He was gifted with a phenomenal voice, a Baritone-Tenor, and a fiery temperament. No wonder that his appearance in Vienna at the newly built Temple caused a sensation.

The policy of the leaders of the Vienna community—and in this Mannheimer concurred—was to maintain the unity of its members, and therefore to avoid every extreme reform which might cause a split such as had occurred in Germany. The young Sulzer instinctively felt "in the first place, it behooves us to fight the opinion that the regeneration of the service can be materialized only by an entire break with the past, by abolishing all traditional and inherited, historically-evolved liturgy. To limit the entire service to a German hymn before and after the sermon, to give a certificate of divorce to tradition, was the intention of those who instigated the ill-fated reform in Hamburg and Berlin. . . . But to me it appeared that the confusion of the Synagogue service resulted from the need of only a RESTORATION which should remain on historical ground; and that we might find out the original noble forms to which we should anchor, developing them in artistic style.   The old generation should recognize the familiar and endeared element, while the young generation should be educated to the appreciation of it.   Jewish liturgy must satisfy the musical demands while remaining Jewish; and it should not be necessary to sacrifice the Jewish characteristics to artistic forms.   The principle was 'to unite the heart of the fathers with that of the children, and to win ambitious youth for the sentiments of the old generation. . . .' Among the most beautiful memories of my life, I count that moment in which the truth of my conviction completely captured the great and noble nature of the preacher MANN-HEIMER, whose ideal for a long time had been that radical reform of Hamburg and Berlin; and in which he frankly confessed that the way which I had opened was the one and only possible avenue to the goal."   This is the program which Sulzer worked out, as presented in his own words in his *Denkschrift*, Vienna, 1876.

In order to give the complete program of Sulzer, we have to add another statement of his which will throw much light on his real attitude.   He says: "The old tunes and singing modes which became national should be improved, selected, and adjusted to the rules of art.   But also new musical creations should not be avoided; and for that purpose, great heroes of music stood helpfully at my side, such as SEYFRIED, SCHUBERT, FISCHHOF, and others (all Christians).[5]   The traditional part of the music they left entirely to me, but their contribution was very essential to the beautifying of the Synagogue song; and therefore part of the success which the Vienna

ritual earned is to be accredited to them." In his preface to
Schir Zion, I, written in 1838, he says: "I set it as my duty
. . . to consider, as far as possible, the traditional tunes bequeathed to us, to cleanse the ancient and dignified type from
the later accretions of tasteless embellishments, to bring them
back to the original (?) * purity, and to reconstruct them in accordance with the text and with the rules of harmony. For
obvious reasons, this could be more easily achieved with the
songs of the festivals—especially with those of the High Holidays—than with the Sabbath service, because for the latter
(particularly for the Friday evening service) there were frequently employed profane tunes which desecrated the holiness of the service . . . whereas the songs of the High Festivals have an inwardness and depth, a gripping and moving
power, which they have preserved through the centuries."

Worthy of note is Sulzer's attitude toward the traditional
modes of the Friday evening and Sabbath services. His habit
of disavowing these modes he shared with most of the *chazzanim*, who—as a result—adopted all foreign types of music
in preference to their own. The fact is that for Friday evening and Sabbath there are dignified traditional modes of no
less value than those for the holidays (Chapter VIII). The
reason for the neglect lies probably in the circumstance that
the traditional Sabbath tunes are not rhythmical but are MODES
only, and could easily have been misjudged by those lacking
appreciation of non-rhythmical music.

After weighing these quotations of Sulzer's, expressing his
underlying ideals and principles in regard to the reformation
of the Synagogue song, let us analyze the result of his work
given in his *Schir Zion*,[6] and estimate his achievements. Although his purpose was the artistic re-creation of the traditional

---

* It is doubtful just what Sulzer could have meant by "original" and by what
standards he could have judged. Hence I add the question mark.

songs, the two volumes of his services prove to be not this RE-CREATION but only a RE-SHAPING. Traditional tunes remained to him a product of the past, to be retained for the sake of the sanctity associated with them through the generations, and not as a living body pregnant with new artistic forms, a treasury of musical atoms sentient with the power of new life. He did not recognize the Jewish musical inheritance as an echo of the living Jewish soul. To him it was merely a body of song that had somehow become national and as such was sacred to the Jew. This same attitude he showed in regard to the Hebrew language. To him it was not the question of HIS desire and sentiments but those of the PEOPLE's. He thought himself to have outgrown such sentiment. His moderateness in reform was, therefore, not the result of his innermost feeling but the consequence of conditions. Thus he says in the preface of the *Schir Zion*, II, written in 1865: "Especial attention did I pay to the old tunes of the Nestor 'Maharil' (Chapter VIII) which I repeatedly took as a basis for my compositions, in that I excluded everything which could detract from the musical dignity. . . . Likewise, I considered those congregations which had introduced the organ as the musical basis for their services, so that the work (*Schir Zion*), starting from existing conditions, linking with the old, and proceeding by the evolution of creation, moves toward the new. It performs a mediatory mission between the past and the future."

From this statement we may conclude that Sulzer did not consider moderate reform as a goal in itself, but only as a bridge from the old to the new. Hence, we can understand his apparent shifting of position when, after fifty years of struggle for moderation, he pleaded (in his above-mentioned *Denkschrift*) for the introduction of the organ in his Temple, for the diminution of the Hebrew text in the prayers, and for the inclusion of hymns in the vernacular, "even though," he says, "I appreciate and venerate the sacred sounds of the holy tongue in which our ancestors expressed their joy and pain." He further urged the abolition of the chanting of the Pentateuch, the adoption of the three-year cycle of Torah-reading, and the introduction of the modern declamation—a plea which he laid before the Synods of Leipzig and Augsburg in 1869-70. And lastly he made a strong appeal against allowing *chazzanim* to improvise, insisting that everything that the *chazzan* sings should be fixed. Finally, he strongly opposed participation in the functions of the service by the congregation in unison or by the individual members of it. We see here that, in reality, Sulzer had in mind the program of the Hamburg Temple; but for practical purposes he preferred to start slowly —very slowly in his reform attempts.

It is most interesting to notice in the movements of Judaism that, while on the one hand the extreme Hamburg reform, having gone too far away, started moving back, gradually reintroducing Hebrew prayers, until finally in 1879 it again adopted the chanting of the Pentateuch (Chapter XII), on the other hand those who moved gradually, still hold as their goal and still strive toward that which the extremists discovered to be suicidal. We see this process now in Europe: reform and assimilative elements turning back after becoming aware of a dangerous abyss before them, while the orthodox elements—unwarned by the experience of the others—are still blindly driving with full power toward the fatal extremity. There appears to be the same pendular movement in America. Indeed, it seems that the entire history of Judaism is of this character.

Sulzer's attitude toward music must be viewed in the light of the almost universal misconception of music's source. The notion tenaciously persists that music is an art obtained and developed APART from daily life, that the musical creative power is a "gift of the heavens" and not an outgrowth of the earthy soil of environment, a product of the struggle of life, of history. It refuses to recognize music as an aggregation of the echoes, of the breathings, of the troubled or of the over-joyed hearts of a long line of generations, as accumulated tones inherited from ancestors, and buried and hidden in the hearts of the children—sounds which cannot be comprehended by hearts which are unattuned. So long as men blind themselves to the true roots of song, any understanding of music will remain unattainable. Until we realize that MUSIC as such, without a nourishing soil, does not and cannot spring to life, until we see that MUSICIANS in the abstract, without concrete derivation, do not and cannot exist, all our efforts to appreciate music—and especially Jewish music—will be in vain.

Sulzer's preparation in Jewishness and his impressions of Jewish life were very meagre. He did not drink from the deep and rich wells of Jewish traditional life, because his native community was small and far removed from Jewish centers. The spirit there was the usual spirit of decay to the point of caricature, a drifting away from Judaism toward European culture. How then can we expect Jewish music to be an instinctive, natural, living power in his heart—a part of his soul? And yet he was surely inspired, full of enthusiasm for Jewish ideas—at least, the Prophetic ideas. A sacred fire burned in his heart, the light and warmth of which inflamed all his hearers. Of him, the great musician and creator, Franz Liszt, in his famous work "The Gipsies" [7] says: "Only once we witnessed what a real Judaic art could be if the Israelites would have poured out their suppressed passions and senti-ments and revealed the glow of their fire in the art forms of their Asiatic genius, in its full pomp and fantasy and dreams—that hot fire which they kept so carefully hidden and they

covered with ashes that it should appear cold. In Vienna we
knew the famous tenor Sulzer, who served in capacity of precentor in the synagogue, and whose reputation is so outstanding. For moments we could penetrate into his real soul and
recognize the secret doctrines of the fathers. . . . We went to
his synagogue in order to hear him. Seldom were we so deeply
stirred by emotion as on that evening, so shaken that our soul
was entirely given to meditation and to participation in the
service." This quoted thought of the gentile was the standard opinion of all the gentiles who heard Sulzer. To them,
his song and singing were something foreign, un-German, and
even un-European. The same opinion was shared even by assimilated Jews whose Jewish sentiments had dwindled to a
minimum, while Jews from the Ghetto—untouched by foreign
influence—were overwhelmed by his powerful and sweet voice
and inspiring rendition, but were unaffected by the Jewishness
of Sulzer. To them, he was a wonderful singer only. They
considered his music *galchish* (Church style) and by no means
Jewish.

Sulzer's music affords but another proof of the general phenomenon which we may observe in regard to the identifying of
the music of a foreign people. Music, the originality of which
has so dwindled that it would not be recognized as their own
even by its own people, is yet by another people considered
foreign. Not by its faithfulness to its own tradition is a national music judged by a stranger, but by its unlikeness to that
to which he is accustomed. For example, the Oriental pieces
by Rimsky-Korsakor, the Oriental parts in *Aïda* by Verdi
or in *Samson and Delilah* by Saint-Saëns, would hardly be
recognized by Orientals as their own music. The Oriental
flavor of them is as thin as a drop of wine in a cask of water.

Sulzer did not KNOW what Jewish music was, but he did
instinctively feel or he deduced the fact from the general

character of Jewish traditional tunes that the manner of Jewish musical expression was a different one from that of the German. Therefore we find a very peculiar phenomenon, at least in his *Schir Zion*, that somehow there are avoided the specifically German melodic lines and curves, not only in HIS creations but even in the creations of all his German collaborators. We know that at least a third of *Schir Zion*, I (most of the choral numbers) is the work of Germans.[8] Many of these numbers became famous and popular. The Jew does not recognize their German character, although he does sense something foreign if not specifically German. All the choral part of *Schir Zion* is rooted in the classical Church music, especially the choral responsa that have the typical Catholic character, e.g.: 28, 66, 67, 75, 99, 222, 272, 478, 545, 548. The specifically Catholic marks have been consistently avoided. And yet the Jew considered this creation non-Jewish, while the Christians felt it foreign to them, and therefore counted it Jewish. It has the character of a careful attempt to express something original, something different from Germanism and the Church. We cannot credit Sulzer with making this attempt consciously, for in his GERMAN songs for Jews he is quite a good German (see *Dudaim*, II, pp. 27-32), while only in his compositions for *Hebrew* texts does he avoid these German characteristics.

Sulzer's positive contributions may be chiefly outlined under the following divisions: (1) His form of expression distinguishes itself by a brevity and conciseness similar to the ancient Hebrew style. (2) No lyrical melodies of playful character occur, his melodic line always being serious and dignified. (3) He was the first to base the Synagogue song on classical harmony and style. (4) He further introduced the regular four part singing, consisting of boys (soprano and alto) and men (tenor and bass). In this innovation, however, the above-mentioned Israel Lovy preceded him by inaugurating four part singing in the newly built Temple in Paris in 1822. Until that time, the Synagogue choir ("singers" or *meshorerim*) consisted of a soprano or an alto and a bass, who together with the *chazzan* made a trio (Chapter XI). (5) He overemphasized the phase of exultation and holiness in the Synagogue song, neglecting the no less important emotional strain, the sentimental note in Jewish song, an important feature in Semitic-Oriental music. Due to the lack of that element Sulzer's music and style makes an exalted but cold impression upon the pious orthodox Jew, though in a few pieces he touches the deepest Jewish emotions, as in No. 236 *Veseerav*, or No. 381 *Meloch*. However, these themes he adopted from Polish *chazzanim* and gave them an artistic touch.

His opinion was that "harmony is a cheerful art" (preface to *Schir Zion*, II), and that sadness cuts off the wings of the spirit, and Israel's martyrdom, to his mind, prevented the creation of a musical art (l.c.).

It seems that Sulzer's caution against the introduction of Germanism greatly aided his popularity. His new music was not so *goyish* as the typical German chorales of the Hamburg Temple. But this alone would not have been sufficient to make him so popular, and so firmly to establish him as an authority all over the world. There was a more striking power in him; and this was his great, almost unique, talent as singer. It was not so much the MUSIC which convinced the people, as the manner and the marvelous beauty of rendition which fascinated and bewitched them. A mania spread among the *chazzanim* to sing *à la Sulzer*, to dress *à la Sulzer*, to wear their hair *à la Sulzer*, to cough *à la Sulzer*. For the first time in Jewish history in the Exile did a cantor become so famous, so honored by kings and princes, by artists and musicians, by magnates of wealth, and by academies of art. For a half century he not only reigned over the entire caste of *chazzanim*, but held the veneration of the entire modern rabbinic and scholarly world, esteemed by it as the authority and genius of Israel's song. Hundreds and hundreds of *chazzanim* were his pupils. They sang in his choir or received some instruction from him or were his attentive auditors. From 1835 till 1876 practically every modern Synagogue in Central Europe as well as in Eastern Europe reorganized its music according to Sulzer's service.

Judging from Sulzer's own statement quoted above, that his aim was to retain the traditional tunes, giving them artistic forms, and to introduce new creations, we should be led to believe that in his music we should find traditional tunes preserved and new creations based upon and in the spirit of those traditional tunes, thus building a continued creation of Jewish music in new forms. But such belief is dissipated as soon as we peruse his *Schir Zion*. Indeed, he did preserve the traditional tunes; and though he abolished all their *chazzanic* flavor and abbreviated them, he at the same time also improved them artistically. We do find, indeed, recitatives based on the traditional modes, as the following numbers will prove: (The numbers are according to the second Edition.)   39, 42, 44, 63-69, 80, 82, 85-92, 109, 135-141, 143-147, 154, 158-161, 165-169, 294, 373.   He was the first to pay attention to the value of the Biblical modes: of the Pentateuch (29-30, 108, 340, 341), Esther (511-529), Lamentations (549-566). Similarly based upon the traditional modes are the recitatives, or solos, with choruses in the form of responses, or vocal accompaniment: 43, 110, 157, 163, 236, 238, 245-253, 254-257, 271, 277-279, 296, 300, 336, 344, 347, 348, 350-357, 361, 365, 366-367, 381, 384, 387, 388, 390, 391, 447, 450, 458, 545-567, 572, 574. Sulzer composed short choruses in minor with Jewish flavor: 162, 179, 205-211, 214, 221, 289-291, 295, 385, 396, 397, 413, 462, 479-481, 563, 567, 575-578; yet they have rather the character of responses than compositions complete in themselves. Not a single tune that he created anew has a genuine Jewish character. In none of his compositions is there to be found a Jewish motive employed and evolved. While the modal structure and loose recitative character of Jewish song presented some difficulties for modern compositions, nevertheless Jewish musicians many centuries before Sulzer had succeeded in utilizing motives of these modes for new creations (Chapter VIII); the Jews of Eastern Europe developed their folksong from these modes (Chapters XVIII-XIX); and the Eastern European *chazzanim* built most of their tunes from the same material (Chapter XIV). Most of Sulzer's compositions in MAJOR are not to be distinguished by any special Jewish flavor from those of his Christian collaborators. He was praised for introducing the recitative of the oratorio, that is, a musical reading more nearly approaching speaking than singing. But also herein he was more imitator than creator. The recitative style in its oratorio form is the original Jewish Psalmodic recitative with the elimination of the *melisma* at the end of every sentence.[9] Here as in many other cases, Sulzer's complete ignorance of the elements, types, and forms of Jewish music led him to imitate imitations instead of drawing directly from the source. He did not know that the recitative form is traditional among the Oriental Jews as well as among the Portuguese. He did not understand the Semitic-Oriental character of the Jew—despite the conviction of gentiles that he was the embodiment and symbol of the ancient Hebrews—an opinion which was strengthened by his typical Semitic complexion and features. He did not feel the Eastern European *chazzanuth*, in spite of the fact that he tried to learn it in order to satisfy his hearers, and that he tried even to imitate it in several recitatives incorporated in his *Schir Zion*.[10] In his above-mentioned preface to his *Schir Zion*, II, he says: "I paid attention to even the Polish song,

i.e., the traditional modes of the Jews in Eastern Europe, in
so far as it presented real individual characteristics, seeking to
utilize it in its original features, and to set it in musical forms."
But he could not sufficiently digest and assimilate that *chazzanuth* to be able to think and feel in its language; and it always remained apart from his spirit. His nature, like that of
most of the Central European partially assimilated Jews, retained a German-Catholic attitude, with a gloomy subconscious
leaning toward the ideals and inheritance that they called
JUDAISM.

But one improvement of far-reaching significance Sulzer
brought into the Synagogue, which contribution alone would
have made his name unforgettable in history; and this is
DIGNITY—dignity of the SONG and dignity of the SINGER.
Toward the end of the eighteenth century, the song had become decadent to the point of caricature; it was an imitation of
every low type of vapid secular music, and it had in consequence lost all power to inspire any devotion and to elevate
the spirit. It had taken on the character of provincial entertainments, while the singers had degenerated to the level of
minstrels. In his casting aside all the musical products of the
eighteenth century and in his introduction of the pseudo-
Church and classical style with powerful harmony, Sulzer restored to Synagogue music its tone of dignity. He himself
became the symbol of a *chazzan* of high artistic and social
standing. He urged his pupils to equip themselves with elementary education, thus to raise their standard and lend them
dignity. He even demanded that the *chazzan*, or "Cantor"
as Sulzer chose to be called,[11] be acknowledged the equal of the
rabbi. In this attempt, of course, he never succeeded. Indeed, his insistent demand for the same degree of credit for
himself as that paid to Rabbi Mannheimer by A. Jellinek,
called down upon him the rebuff of the president of the Vienna

Community; and he was officially suspended from his office for three months. Only his tremendous popularity among the members of the community protected him from severe consequences.[12]

II. MAIER KOHN (1802-1875); SAMUEL NAUMBOURG (1815-1880)

The old stock of German Jewry, deep-rooted in South and Southwestern German countries from the days of Charlemagne, survived in Bavaria, Württemberg, Hessen, and Baden, despite terrible persecutions lasting through a period of eight hundred years. Those Jews retained their distinctive Jewish tradition—a tradition imprinted with blood and fire. Their conservatism, in the course of time, had taken on the color of Catholic Germanism. They remained almost untouched by the winds of Reform. Yet in the capital of Bavaria, Munich, a new community was formed at the beginning of the nineteenth century, after an interval of almost four hundred years from the time that the old Munich community had been partly killed, partly driven out. That new community had some members who had somehow been slightly brushed by the breeze of Reform coming from afar. They demanded therefore some modernization in the service of the Synagogue newly built in 1826. But since the appointed *chazzan*, Loew Sänger (1781-1843), was of the old type of the German *chazzanim* of the eighteenth century, the Board of the Congregation decided to appoint a special music committee with the purpose of organizing a choir and introducing some innovations in the Synagogue song. In 1832, such a choral society was formed. It consisted of music lovers from among the members of the congregation, and also of boys; and it was placed under the leadership of Maier Kohn.

Kohn was a teacher of religion, who had charge of a boarding school and who claimed to have a musical strain. In reality his knowledge of music was equivalent to nothing, consisting only of the ability to read a simple melody with the aid of a violin. He lacked the knowledge of even the simplest rudiments of music. He seemed to have only one virtue, and this was a strong ambition to work for the benefit of the Synagogue. He knew traditional *chazzanuth* by inheritance; and he was very eager to become choir leader and SECOND cantor—second, because he had no voice. It must be noted that his co-laborers were not greater musical geniuses than he. There was David Hessel, the son of the Rabbi in Munich, who contributed a few melodies from an obscure source, one of which, "*Yigdal*," became famous and reached Sulzer in Vienna. Even as far as Berlin and in many communities in Bavaria, it is sung to the present day. Another associate in the work was Wimmelbacher, who later became cantor and choir master in Aix la Chapelle, and in about 1842 assumed a similar post in Bernburg in Anhalt. One by the name of Neuburger and still others contributed tunes for Kohn's choir. Among the choristers was SAMUEL NAUMBOURG, who also gave one number.

At that time the custom became general to follow the plan, first introduced by Israel Jacobson in the Seesen Temple in 1810 and standardized in the Hamburg Temple, of employing gentile musicians to supply music for the Synagogue. For this procedure there were two reasons: in the first place, the Jewish musicians had no modern musical training and did not know a thing about harmony; and in the second place, the aim was to replace the Jewish Asiatic tunes with German European melodies which alone were considered capable of arousing devotion. Matters went so far that Synagogue music was considered good music, if it had the approval of a gentile musician. In every synagogue the song was composed of two

elements, of the "musical" part, that is, compositions by gentiles or, if by Jews, at least true imitations of gentile music;
and of *chazzanuth*—the insinuation being that *chazzanuth* was
not included in MUSIC.   That opinion still persists in certain
groups all over the world, whether in Central or Eastern
Europe, whether in America or Palestine.   Maier Kohn, becoming aware that he could not get along without gentile help,
engaged a few German musicians in Munich, who harmonized
Jewish tunes and added compositions of their own.

All the material that he collected was arranged and set in
order by a certain musician, Ett, and published in Munich in
1839, a year before Sulzer published his *Schir Zion*, I.   In comparison with the musical value of the *Schir Zion*, the music of
Maier Kohn's publication is very poor.   But in the *chazzanic*
numbers, he presented very important material from the Southern German traditional tunes of the Jews.   Moreover, Kohn
promised a second collection containing only *chazzanuth* without any MUSIC for the entire cycle of the year.   And he really
prepared the manuscript for it; but unfortunately he never
succeeded in interesting anyone to publish it, likely because it
was *chazzanuth* and not MUSIC.   His work, as the first attempt
at a moderate-reform service, met with favorable reception in
Germany, and answered a need at least until another work of
similar intention superseded it—a work of much higher musical
and artistic value and of more extensive *chazzanic* elements—
the work of SAMUEL NAUMBOURG.

Naumbourg was a descendant of a three-century-old *chazzanic* family in Germany, saturated with Southern Ashkenazic
chazzanuth and gifted with musical talent and with intelligence.   In Munich he received a musical training, and after
being choir-master in Strassburg with a then famous *chazzan*
LOEWE, he came to Paris warmly recommended to Jacques
Fromental Halévy, in 1843.   Halévy was the son of a

Parisian *chazzan* and teacher, originating in Fürth in Bavaria.[18] He took interest in the Jewish communal life and was a member of the Consistoire Israelite. After the death of Israel Lovy (1832), the Paris community remained without a *chazzan*, probably for lack of interest in religious life. The reforms that Lovy had introduced vanished, and confusion came into its own again. Naumbourg bent his efforts toward becoming first *chazzan* and reorganizer of the service. The reactionary atmosphere in Paris at that time helped him a great deal to achieve his goal. Religious officers were then considered governmental officers; and the French government started paying much attention to the religious life of the denominations. So Naumbourg presented to the government a memorandum in which he explained the state of the Jewish worship and the necessity of its reorganization; and since his program bore the endorsement of Halévy, it found ready ears in the Departments of Cults and Education. Naumbourg received the order to work out a Jewish musical service; and, thus favored by the government and Halévy, he procured the appointment to the post of first *chazzan* in 1845.

In an astonishingly short time, considering the hugeness of the task, he fulfilled the governmental order; and by 1847 he succeeded in compiling and publishing his great work in two big volumes, under the name ZEMIROTH YISRAEL, containing the complete service for the entire cycle of the year, arranged for *chazzan* and choir, and partly provided with organ accompaniment. In Naumbourg's work, we find for the first time a musical task of high artistic rank, achieved by Jewish musicians only. Aside from his own compositions, he incorporated several tunes by his predecessor Israel Lovy. Furthermore, he succeeded in interesting Halévy in composing some items, one of which, *Min Hametzar* (Ps. 118), became very famous. He included also some compositions of other

Jewish composers. He even received permission from Meyerbeer to adapt a Christmas Carol composed by him, for *Uv'nucho
Yomar*.[14] But the most striking part in Naumbourg's work is
his adherence to South German *chazzanuth* of which he embodied a considerable quantity. Although, as already said, he
himself knew that *chazzanuth* to perfection, he nevertheless
for some reason or other preferred to follow the version of it
he had written while in Munich from the singing of the above-
mentioned Loew Sänger.[15] Another important feature in
Naumbourg's work is that among his compositions we find,
for the first time in modern services, creations of new Jewish
tunes based upon old material. Although these are few in
number, they yet give expression to Naumbourg's noteworthy
attitude and sentiment toward Jewish music. The traditional
elements occupy about half of Naumbourg's work. Though
his talent was inferior to that of Sulzer, his harmony conservative and at times dull, he succeeded in creating some im-
pressive pieces, such as No. 179 *Veseerav,* No. 233 *Berosh
Hashonoh,* No. 269 *Onnoh tovo.*

In regard to Naumbourg's style in his un-Jewish creations
for the Synagogue, a word should be said. He was influenced
by the art music then current in Paris. From the time of the
Revolution, Paris increasingly became the metropolis of civi-
lized Europe—in music as well as in other things. Especially
was it the center of Grand Opera. Everyone with musical
talent from Italy and Germany went to Paris. Italian, German and French music were accumulated and amalgamated in
that center. Different styles intermingled, but Grand Opera
predominated. Every branch of music, even sacred song, was
influenced by that operatic style. MUSIC became synonymous
with OPERA. Hence the operatic flavor in Naumbourg's compositions! And hence also the Parisian music-style mixture in
his melodies—that style-mixture which, by reason of its limit-

less possibilities and his skillful utilization of it, had made Meyerbeer so victorious over all other composers, so successful and great in HIS time—that Parisian mixture against which Wagner as well as Liszt battled.[16]   This style gave to Naumbourg's work some international features, and helped it to become widely known, much liked and used.[17]

Aside from his activity as regenerator, he made historical investigations in Jewish music, on which subject he published a long essay as an introduction to his collection of popularized Synagogal tunes which he called *Agudath Schirim* (1874).[18] It was the first attempt made to present, along historical lines, the features of Jewish traditional song, and hence it still has the historical value of an initial attempt.   In the *Agudath Schirim* he brought together Ashkenazic traditional tunes as well as Portuguese, and added the cantillation of the Pentateuch according to those traditions.

Finally, we must treat his edition of the collection of Synagogue compositions of SALOMON ROSSI, originally published in Venice, 1622—those compositions which Salomon Rossi had written for the modernized service in Italy and which, in spite of all the efforts of Leon of Modena, met with no success.   The original publication was of separate parts only, and not in score. Baron de Rothschild collected the scattered parts and entrusted them to Naumbourg for publication.   In 1877 Naumbourg brought out the work under the name *Schir Haschirim Asher Lischlomo*.   Despite all the book's blunders, due probably to Naumbourg's ignorance of the history of music and his inability to read old musical prints, or due—according to Birnbaum's opinion—to lack of accuracy, we nevertheless have to be thankful for his publication of Rossi's songs, for if they have no practical value for Jewish music, they have historical value as music BY a Jew.   The distinguished scholar, HEYMAN STEINTHAL, made this importance clear when, in his essay on Jewish music, he said: "Let our descendants, the future generation, know all that our ancestors sang, be it even of foreign origin. Let the future generations know the participation of our ancestors in general culture and its influence upon them." [19] Naumbourg, through this publication of Rossi's songs, awakened the interest of *chazzanim* in historical research in a deeper understanding of the tradition. He called their attention back to the past, and caused them to broaden their horizon and to see the truth that Synagogue song did not begin with *Sulzer*, all before him having been *tohu vavohu*, but that Jewish musical activity dated back centuries, perhaps thousands of years.

III. HIRSCH WEINTRAUB (1811-1882)

Already in the seventeenth and the beginning of the eighteenth centuries, famous Eastern *chazzanim* are cited in literature. But nothing of their products has survived. The first *chazzan* whose compositions were written down and preserved is *Salomon Kashtan* (born in 1781 in old Constantine, and died in 1829). His was the greatest voice of his time. His coloratura, according to the testimony of his contemporaries, was inimitable even by instruments. He was, at the same time, a man of profound religious devotion and piety, and of a great knowledge of Hebrew literature. Although officially *chazzan* in the famous community of Dubno, he used to travel from city to city throughout Lithuania, Poland, Hungary, and Prussia, all the year round; and his function as city *chazzan* of Dubno he fulfilled only three days of the year—*Rosh Hashanah* and *Yom Kippur*. His art of performance was overwhelming, and nobody could resist being moved to tears when he intoned those tunes which express pain. He could, on a simple *Shabbos*, create the atmosphere of *Yom Kippur*, and in the following moment rouse the whole congregation from deep melancholy to the mood of dance. As composer, he established a school, an original style in Eastern *chazzanuth* which may rightly be designated as the finest. The cradle of the earlier Eastern *chazzanuth* was Volhynia, whence came two styles: one was the style of Kashtan, which found its recognition in the Northwestern communities; and the other which turned to the South, and was developed and spread by the famous *chazzan* Bezalel in Odessa and by his pupils. Although both have the same elements and forms and are mostly based on the *Ahavoh-Rabboh* Steiger, Kashtan's style has more depth of thought and dignity, while Bezalel's is more lyric and sweet and ingratiating. Of the innumerable pupils of Kashtan, we shall name the two most prominent: his brother Nochum Leb, *chazzan* in Berditchev, who—although not possessing Kashtan's heroic voice—had, as composer and Talmudist, the same qualifications; and it is rather impossible to know which of the compositions belong to the one brother and which to the other, because the two men had the same style. Both died in the same month, in November 1829.[20]

The second pupil was Kashtan's son HIRSCH WEINTRAUB, who became his successor in Dubno, but left his native country while still young, and—as his father before him—traveled throughout Austria and Prussia giving service-concerts. He had not the vocal qualities of his father, but he inherited his coloratura and his creative talent. His meeting with Sulzer, the first model of a Europeanized *chazzan*, and the influence of the European classic music with which he gained acquaintance through his artistic playing on the violin, made him decide to abandon his native country and to establish his permanent home in Germany, where he became *chazzan* in Königsberg. After a deep and thorough study of the theory of music and the classics, he reworked his father's compositions in order to give them a more European form. At the same time, he composed services in the modern style which had been created by Sulzer. Indisputably dignified and genuine as are these compositions from the general musical point of view, they have nothing Jewish in them, and they clearly indicate that this style had been merely adopted by Weintraub in order that he might become MODERN, a quality which to him apparently meant un-Jewish. The compositions, therefore, lack the warmth of life; they have no soul. When the composer creates, he intones the emotions of his heart; and, in embodying these echoes in tonal creations, he breathes into them the warmth of his life. But when a composer seeks to imitate creations born of another spirit, he can only shape figures but never endow them with living souls. He cannot acquire another's soul. This truth we see in Weintraub's compositions. While his un-Jewish creations are soulless, and were, therefore, scarcely ever used in any congregation, his Jewish compositions—whether his own or reworkings of his father's—found an enthusiastic reception, and were sung and imitated by numberless *chazzanim* throughout the nineteenth century. And this, despite Weintraub's comment in the preface to his work wherein he says, with reference to his father's compositions: "They should be considered rather as antiquities. I have transcribed them for those Jewish precentors who are trained in and are familiar with the ancient spirit . . . with coloratura and embellishment, as they are especially tolerated and demanded in Oriental song." Indeed, Weintraub combined a deep Jewish feeling and enthusiasm for the high ideals of Judaism, in the light of a genuine Jewish tradition and education, with European culture. Therefore he succeeded in creating a style in Eastern *chazzanuth* that had high musical value. He created a special form for the formless fantastic improvisation. He utilized classic harmony for the Orientalized Eastern *chazzanuth*, which achievement appeared to be impossible till his time. He showed his great genius in intoning one and the same text in different settings. He composed about forty tunes for the text *Hashkivenu* (evening prayer) and the same number for *Av Horachamim* (a supplication), thirty-seven for *Veshomru* (Exod. 31: 16-17), ten for *Yehi Rotzon* (the benediction for the new moon), about the same number for *Umip'ne Chatoenu*, etc. In 1859, he published a collection of his Synagogue compositions—the greater number in un-Jewish style which were ignored entirely—the minor part, Jewish, which made him popular and saved his work from oblivion. But the greater part of his compositions, hundreds of numbers of Jewish character which he neglected, evidently considering them not modern enough, and in which are buried wonderful musical jewels, remained in manuscript, and are in the possession of the Hebrew Union College Library. In his effort to employ classic harmony to Jewish modes, he created an original system of harmonization, which we call Jewish harmony. We shall treat this subject in detail in Chapter XXIII.

IV. Louis Lewandowski (1821-1894)

Lewandowski originally came from the province of Posen, that Polish district which, although taken by Frederick II as the Prussian part in the division of Poland at the end of the eighteenth century, nevertheless remained Polish in its character. Its Jews, too, remained Polish Jews in life, tradition, and custom. Lewandowski, a villager from the little settlement Wreschen, son of poor parents, entered the city of Berlin at the age of thirteen. After bitter struggles, he became a *singerl* under the *chazzan* Asher Lion (Chapter XII), who continued the *chazzanuth* of the eighteenth century. The young Lewandowski's desire for musical training opened his way to a member of the Mendelssohn family, who, although no longer a Jew, still preserved sympathy for poor Jewish youths longing for light and education. Mendelssohn, who himself was musically inclined and who was proud of having the famous Felix Mendelssohn as his cousin, became the boy's patron and supporter. In this way Lewandowski received a thorough musical education, and dreamed of becoming a second Mendelssohn. His first attempt at composition received a prize at the Sing-Akademie in Berlin. Thus the lad of sixteen faced a great future in general music, and might have shared the lot of many other Jewish musicians, of drifting away from their Judaism and Jewishness and drowning in the general stream of European culture. But a serious nervous disorder made an end to all his dreams. For a few years he was unable to continue his musical studies at all. He had to relinquish his scholarship at the Academy, and for a while it seemed that he would be forced to abandon his entire musical career. However, the urgent necessity of sustaining himself compelled him, after a partial recovery, to start upon some musical activity. Although his strength was insufficient to recommence work along the lines of general music, he counted it sufficient for participation in the work of Synagogue music.

The Jewish Community of Berlin, the cradle of Reform, was swept by the spirit of reaction after the government forcibly closed the Beer Temple in 1817 (Chapter XII). Asher Lion, the *chazzan* of the Reform Temple, upon his appointment as *chazzan* of the Community Synagogue, became a reactionary, reintroducing the old eighteenth-century *chazzanuth* with SINGERL and bass, which style he continued until 1836. In general, the eighteenth-century style lasted in many communities till about the middle of the nineteenth century. Thus, for instance, in Dessau, the birthplace of Mendelssohn, the service was conducted in the same way as in the centuries preceding. The same situation obtained in different communities of central

and northern Germany. In 1838 the young and talented
Hirsch Weintraub came to Berlin on his Synagogue concert
tour. He had started from Dubno, as mentioned above, and
with his quartet gave a few service concerts in private homes.
These aroused such enthusiasm in the city that he was invited
to officiate at the Community Synagogue. Lewandowski describes in the most attractive manner that event which caused
the reformation of the service in Berlin.[21] Thus Weintraub
was the cause of the first enduring musical reform in the Berlin
synagogue; and he opened the door to the new possibilities of
Lewandowski. Weintraub's quartet was wonderfully trained.
As Prelude and Introduction, he played violin solos. Then
his choir SANG instrumental quartets by Mozart and Haydn
with an exactness and perfection that called forth the pro-
foundest appreciation of gentile musicians. Thereafter he recited the prayers with responsive accompaniment of his quartet
in a perfect harmonic style and with deep Jewish feeling. The
profound Jewish music voiced in Weintraub's recitatives, he
inherited from his father, Salomon Kashtan, and expressed in
fine musical style. Weintraub's appearance in Berlin was like
a sudden illumination in the darkness. He convinced both the
ultra-reform elements and the ultra-orthodox elements of
the possibility of having music modern in form and really
traditional in character. And a general demand arose among
the members to have the same kind of service. But the greatest
influence—a sort of hypnotic power—Weintraub exerted upon
the young Lewandowski. It was the first time that Lewandowski, as he himself stated, heard real Jewish music molded
in rich-sounding classic harmonic form. And it was the first
time that he heard Synagogue singers performing European
music in a most satisfactory manner. This influence struck
deep root in Lewandowski's spirit, slumbering on in his heart

until one day it brought forth musical blossoms which later delighted hundreds of congregations.

In the meanwhile, the *chazzan* Asher Lion faced the demand of the Berlin community to reorganize his Synagogue song. Lion was rooted in the *rococo* style. His musical ability extended as far as the deciphering of the tones of a tune on a piano (this with great difficulty and with but one finger); but they were insufficient for the distinguishing of the rhythm of the melody. He was placed in a very critical situation. However, his greatest strength lay in his cleverness. He determined to act in accord with the custom of the *chazzanim* of the *rococo* age, that is, to capture Weintraub's quartet, believing that in enticing Weintraub's singers, he would *eo ipso* come into possession of Weintraub's music. He did, indeed, succeed in winning the tenor Mirkin, who later became cantor in Copenhagen. But, alas, the tenor knew his part only, without having any idea of the leading melody of the soprano, nor any notion of the cantor solos or the bass part. Thus, the problem remained as unsolved as before. The only information that Lion could obtain from the tenor was that Weintraub utilized Sulzer's music which was still at that time unpublished, and that Weintraub had obtained from Sulzer his service in manuscript. Lion now demanded of his committee the procuring of Sulzer's music, trusting that that aim was an unattainable one, so that his problem, if not solved, would thus be removed, and he would be allowed to return to his good old *rococo*. But soon the old man had to experience the worst. After the short space of TWO years, a copy of Sulzer's manuscript arrived in Berlin. Lion was faced with Hamlet's problem: TO BE OR NOT TO BE. Sulzer's scores were written in the unheard-of system of the four clefs: Soprano, Alto, Tenor, Bass, while for poor Lion, with the exception of the treble, clefs were nonexistent. However, he relied upon his cleverness; and started training singers, reading all parts as if in the treble clef. Aside from this dilemma, he had his difficulty with the community bass, the seventy-year-old Kasper, who never in his life had seen music notes, but who had inherited his art of singing bass from his predecessors of many generations, which art consisted of certain instrumental intervals or passages of an imitation of the melody in the octave or of the producing of a single sound in his deep register, just "in order to bring forth a sentiment of devotion in the congregation, that the members may HEAR and FEAR." Lion's singers could not find any taste, either melodic or harmonic, in what Lion extracted from Sulzer's score; and the tenor, enticed by Weintraub, who boasted that he was a great musician, entered into discussion with Lion as to the exactness of his reading. After a considerable time wasted in hard struggle, without any results, while the entire community waited impatiently for the new music, Lion decided to turn in his distress to his former SINGERL who, as he was told, had studied MUSIC. In a most confidential interview, he asked his SINGERL to help him with that most peculiar musical manuscript, and probably promised to reward him— even financially. Young Lewandowski, sickly and without employment as he was, took over the job willingly. His first task was to transfer the parts from their distinctive clefs to the treble, in order that Lion might read them; his second, to help Lion drill the choir. The singers, who conducted themselves most impudently toward Lion, were overwhelmed by the young Lewandowski's stupendous musical knowledge, seeing that he read the parts without any assistance from an instrument. Even the intractable rococo bass was deeply impressed by the musical superiority of the SINGERL. Thus Lewandowski became master of the situation; and wisely enough left old Lion as titular choir-master. Things went along smoothly, and soon the choir was sufficiently trained to present its first performance at a Friday evening service. This was in 1840. The rendition met with the approval of the members of the Board and of the Congregation. In connection with the first performance of one of the selections of the new music, Lewandowski tells this amusing episode, indicative of the musical education of the higher class of Jews in Berlin at that time. Lewandowski had trained the choir in a selection of Sulzer's, written in fugue or canon form. After the service, a member of the Board, a rich *Kommerzienrath*, most ambitious to exhibit his musical knowledge, gave his criticism of the rendition of the music by saying that, while on the whole the performance was good, in the one item just mentioned, the singers lost themselves and could not keep together; whereupon Lewandowski, realizing the futility of explanation, answered: "Oh, yes, you are right; but I trust that they will improve in the course of time."

Lion, seeing that without Lewandowski he would be lost, graciously permitted Lewandowski to train the choir; and in most confidential manner, granted Lewandowski the honor of teaching him some of those solos of Sulzer's which were combined with choral work. Lewandowski, although still very young, was intelligent enough to perceive that a new world of activity was opening before him. The Berlin community was in the process of rapid growth, and it was obvious that it was soon to become the leading Jewish community in Prussia. In the same year (1840), Lewandowski was appointed singing teacher at the Jewish Free School, and he made up his mind to devote himself to the development of music in the Jewish institutions in Berlin, in which position he remained for over fifty years, climbing slowly higher and higher from step to step, until he conquered not only the German synagogues, but also those beyond Germany's boundaries.

In view of the difference in the circumstances of their labors, we may account Lewandowski's personal accomplishment greater than Sulzer's. The latter started his career with complete power, as first cantor and official reorganizer of the Synagogue service. His influence and authority were established from the very beginning, created by his position and strengthened by his great talent as singing artist; while Lewandowski started with practically no position, with no office, with no fame, and with no attracting art—merely as a poor young musical aspirant. He was just the *chazzan's* assistant—his indispensable right hand, while to the community he still remained the poor SINGERL. No wonder, therefore, that for many years he was not noticed at all.

Indeed, his position was an entirely new one in the history of the Synagogue, for there had never been such an office as that of a choir-master. The leader had been the *chazzan*—had to be the *chazzan* even if he had no voice. So we had voiceless, silent *chazzanim*, the latest of whom was NISSI BELZER (Chapter XIV).

Fortune did not seem to favor Lewandowski in his young years. In 1845, he succeeded in publishing a song (always a great event in the life of a young composer); but because the text expressed political ideas too free for the reactionary Prussian government, the publication was confiscated, and Lewandowski was placed in a dangerous situation. For fully thirty years Lewandowski remained unnoticed, hidden, of no importance—a choral leader and singing teacher. He published a few little songsters for the Public School, written in the routine German Lied-style; and a few numbers for piano and voice which remained unnoticed. For many years his repertoire at the Synagogue consisted of Sulzer's music, he himself not daring to compose anything. In 1845, the community in Berlin, tired of its voiceless *chazzan* Lion, appointed Abraham Jacob LICHTENSTEIN, then *chazzan* in Stettin.

Lichtenstein (1806-1880) was gifted with a most wonderful dramatic tenor voice of phenomenal power and brilliancy, with a bewitching art of performance, and with an Italian temperament. He was a pious and warm-hearted Jew, and master of traditional *chazzanuth*. In comparison with his contemporary *chazzanim*, he was accounted musically trained. He played the violin in the symphony orchestra, and used to sing tenor parts in oratorio, under the leadership of Karl Loewe. It was he who called the attention of Max Bruch to Jewish traditional tunes, as a result of which interest, Bruch—according to his own statement—composed his *Kol Nidré*.[22]

At that time every *chazzan* of importance had his own style of service and his own melodies. So with Lichtenstein! But he lacked knowledge of one important essential—harmony! Since there was established a four part choir in Berlin, it was necessary to arrange his *chazzanuth* for four part choir—a task which Lewandowski undertook.

With that work began Lewandowski's real activity. Lichtenstein's *chazzanuth* became to Lewandowski the model and symbol of *chazzanuth*. He studied it; he arranged it; he re-modelled it in the course of years, until his spirit was saturated with it. It became so much a part of him that he considered Lichtenstein's *chazzanuth* as his own. For twenty-five years Lewandowski worked on Lichtenstein's *chazzanuth*, until the material acquired a new form—the form bestowed by Lewandowski's genius. And in publishing that *chazzanuth* in his work *Kol Rinnah Utefillah*, Lewandowski did not mention even the name of Lichtenstein, apparently believing that this music was or had become HIS. Only by means of Lichtenstein's own manuscripts do we recognize the origin. Lewandowski had no fund of traditional song nor of Synagogue song—Polish or Southern German. Aside from Lichtenstein's *chazzanuth*, Lewandowski used to obtain Eastern European *chazzanuth* from innumerable *chazzanim* passing through Berlin. He had the inclination, the love, and the instinct for Eastern European *chazzanuth,* as he himself states, which was bequeathed to him by his birthplace.

The most outstanding talent in Lewandowski was his tasteful and skillful re-shaping in modern forms of old material. His recitatives and solos for the Synagogue song have the wonderful quality of being suitable for and easily rendered by any voice of fair quality. His recitatives and solos, even the traditional tunes, are not merely well preserved, as in the manner of Sulzer, but they are creations molten anew. His greatest strength in that branch is the cantabile, in the region between tune and recitative, in the free-flowing Jewish solo-singing, in minor. He created and developed a noble warm-breathing style of Jewish melody, purged of the tangled fungous growth of sentimentality. As examples, we have all those numbers in minor or in the *Ahavoh-Rabboh* mode, found in quantity in his above-mentioned *Kol Rinnah* and in his principal work *Todah Wesimrah.* No sadness is expressed in them, but a sweet lyric strain inspiring hope and life—that distinguishing characteristic of the real Jewish minor melody. And not only in his solos but also in his choir pieces, Lewandowski created real Jewish selections which will remain marvelous jewels in the treasury of Jewish song. We name such choruses as *Hallelujah* (*Todah Wesimrah,* II, No. 202), *L'Dovid Boruch* (o.c., I, No. 91), *Zocharti Loch* (o.c., II, No. 198). In his style and harmony, Lewandowski was entirely under Mendelssohn's influence. His solo as well as choral style follow the path of Mendelssohn's oratorio. He was saturated with Mendelssohn's art to the extent that he unconsciously utilized some of his master's themes, as, for example, *Enosh K'chotzir Yomov* (o.c., II, No. 34), from the first duet in Elijah, "Zion spreads her hands." Greatly amazed must we ever be by the fact that at the same time we find in Lewandowski's music a real German element, a slavish imitation of the German folk-song and Lied form. Lewandowski, the Polish Jew, was so far Germanized as not to be able to distinguish between conscious and instinctive imitation. Those texts which had no traditional tunes or did not express a plea or sorrow but were rather of hymnal or laudatory character were open to GENERAL interpretation. The conception was and still is current among certain Jewish musicians that JEWISH means the expression of pain and sorrow, and that Jewish tonal expression cannot be used for joyous texts. These must be intoned by the music of the joyous nations; that is, it must be German or English. To Lewandowski it was German. All his *Lechoh Dodi* tunes, his Psalm tunes, especially No. 92, his music for the removal and replacing of the Torah, all his laudations, are based either on German folk-song or on oratorio. There is one thing which Lewandowski carefully avoided, and this is CHURCH style. There is no taint in his music of either the Catholic or the Protestant Church. We do not find any hymn or chorale that tastes of the Protestant Church. With the exception of one number, No. 196 (*Seu Sheorim*), which he adopted from a Christian composer, from the new service in Dresden in 1840,[23] and which he published in his *Todah Wesimrah*, II, No. 196, we know of no non-Jewish composition in Lewandowski's Synagogue works. As proof of Lewandowski's fine talent and skill in reshaping and developing high type music out of old primitive themes, his composition *Weye'esoyu* (ibid., II, No. 193) may serve. He utilized two themes of two tunes composed for that text by Ahron Beer (Chapter XI). Those two tunes probably used to be sung by Beer's successor, Lion, and Lewandowski as his SINGERL, undoubtedly sang them for many years until their themes were engraven in his memory.

All his achievements in the realm of Synagogue song were the fruit of the last two decades of his life, for, as already said, his early activity was that of interpreter of Sulzer's music. In 1855, after fifteen years of activity, Lewandowski, together with Lichtenstein, then about thirty years in office, was sent to Sulzer to be instructed and advised. So powerful and authoritative was Sulzer even in Berlin! It is understandable that under such circumstances Lewandowski had no chance to introduce any of his own compositions. Indeed, he says in his preface to *Todah Wesimrah* that his compositions were hidden in his desk for many years before they were performed. It required great self-restraint to suppress his ambitions to have his own works heard, rare equanimity to await a propitious time, and never-flagging alertness to grasp the opportunity to introduce them. That opportunity came to him in 1864 with the building of the new Oranienburgerstrasse Temple, which was equipped with an organ and for which a modified service was arranged by Geiger and Joel. As long as he had acted as choir-master in the old orthodox community synagogue on Heidereuterstrasse, two obstacles had prevented the presenting of his own compositions: the first was Sulzer's music; the second, Lichtenstein's *chazzanuth*. The new Temple offered him the opportunity of creating an entire service with organ accompaniment—a task until then never undertaken. Sulzer's music was unsuited, since it was arranged for the orthodox prayerbook and was without organ accompaniment. Therefore, Lewandowski's creative activity really begins with 1864. It is interesting to note how little he was valued at that time for his true significance in Jewish life. In 1865, at the celebration of his twenty-fifth anniversary as music teacher in the Jewish Free School and the Jewish Teachers' Seminary, Zunz, upon whom as principal of the

Seminary fell the obligation of delivering the address of the celebration, could find no other merit to praise in Lewandowski than that of faithfulness to his office and his family.[24]

In the meanwhile the Berlin community not only grew in membership but became a European center for Jewish culture and education in general as well as for music. Numerous young Jewish musicians pilgrimed to Berlin to study—many of them with the object of becoming cantors. They turned to Lewandowski for instruction and help. Thus gradually Lewandowski became a trainer and advisor of *chazzanim*. It was for the aid of these pupils that the already described solos were created.

How unshakable Sulzer's authority was we may see from the fact that Lewandowski did not dare to begin his publication with his four part compositions; but he started with a new branch— not cultivated by Sulzer [25]—that of popular easily executed Synagogue music written in solos and duets, especially designed for those small congregations which were not in position to employ a trained four part choir. His aim was to provide a complete service for the entire year, its recitative part for the cantor, popularized choral parts, and congregational songs. None of these three classes of Synagogue song had at that time been cultivated. The recitative was still either overgrown with tangled flourishes of Eastern *chazzanuth*, as we find it in the third part of Weintraub's work, or it was of the style that Sulzer had introduced in his first volume. And even Naumbourg, who at times gave a Jewish recitative natural and simple and at the same time artistically purified, had not provided for the entire service. It was therefore Lewandowski who first fully understood the importance of the recitative in the modern Jewish service, and supplied the ritual of the entire year with a natural singable recitative based mostly on traditional Jewish modes.

He was first to recognize how the entirely foreign form of the Catholic Church song, introduced by Sulzer, froze the warmth of Jewish sentiment, and silenced the congregation, precluding its participation in the singing. But, although well-intentioned, he failed to solve this latter problem; for he introduced, instead, the German folk-song for congregational singing, which, while well received in Northern German communities, had a decidedly assimilative influence in that it Germanized the sentiments of the Jews. Lewandowski's blunder here, as we already mentioned, grew out of the prevalent opinion that choral parts could be created by non-Jews out of non-Jewish material—an opinion which Lewandowski expressed in his preface to *Kol Rinnah*. Furthermore, despite all his opposition to the Church style of Sulzer, he was so far influenced by Sulzer that he imitated his responsive style—a style which has remained standard in our modern services of both ultra-reform and moderate-reform. Lewandowski's statement, in his above-mentioned preface, that there was no congregational singing, is true only with respect to Eastern European and Northern German communities, for the old Southern and Western congregations had always had responsive congregational singing which dated far back to the earlier medieval times, and was the continuation of the Oriental, Italian, and Spanish-Portuguese service. This group participation was one of the principal features of Jewish worship since Bible times. Lewandowski, not knowing the history of Jewish worship, and being acquainted with the Eastern European service only, considered this contribution of congregational song his innovation.

The appearance of his *Kol Rinnah* in 1871 caused a sensation in the *chazzanic* circle. It was the first time that a complete service for Sabbath and festivals, with detailed recitatives for the entire text of the prayers, had appeared—a work which enabled every young man of fair musical ability and voice to master the liturgical and traditional *Chazzanuth* in a modern form. The *Kol Rinnah* became the most popular reference book for the average *chazzan*. It developed a certain type of cantors who were called *Kol Rinnah* cantors. The appeal of the book to what we called the second grade *chazzanim*, casts no aspersions on the work, but is accounted for by the fact that *chazzanim* with attractive voices and fine power of musical execution preferred the intricate flourishes of Weintraub and his like and the high, sounding phrases of Sulzer, which afforded opportunity for the demonstration of their artistic gifts and powers. Because of its provision for congregational responsa and congregational choir singing, the *Kol Rinnah* maintained its position even after the publication of Moritz Deutsch's *Vorbeterschule*, which, in respect to its recitatives, was of a higher quality, and even after the publication of Abraham Baer's *Baal Tefillah*, which gave a very rich variety of traditional and *chazzanic* recitatives of the Polish as well as of the Ashkenazic rite. The *Kol Rinnah* brought Lewandowski popularity; while his *Todah Wesimrah* (two volumes, Berlin, 1876-1882) for four part choir and cantor solos with congregational singing, established his fame as Synagogue composer. Most of the tunes of that latter publication had been utilized in the *Kol Rinnah* in the simple form already described. The singability and the freshness as well as the elaborate musical form of the choir parts, and last but not least the German *lied* style, made them so beloved by the Jewish congregations in Germany. Lewandowski developed the choral part in the Synagogue song to a greater degree than did Sulzer. He gave to the organ a specific rôle. Soon Sulzer was dispossessed, and Lewandowski became dominant. Not only in the synagogues with organ did he hold sway, but also in those without, for with the intention of serving the synagogues without organs, Lewandowski had composed the choral parts for a cappella rendition, without put-

ting into the organ any artistic part of the composition. As he
himself states in his preface to the work, the organ was simply
a support to the voices of the choir. With the publication of
Todah Wesimrah, Lewandowski climbed to the summit of his
path. He attained the pinnacle. He became the recognized
genius of Synagogue song; he was honored by the Jewish communities in Germany as well as by the German government,
which rewarded him with medals and titles. He was elected
honorary president of the Cantors' Association. He was made
chief choral master of all the synagogues of Berlin, in which
only his music was to be heard. It is not pleasant to reflect
on the tyranny with which he ruled over the dominion thus
finally acquired, the harshness with which he crushed or the
shrewdness with which he excluded possible rising rivals. The
long struggle which would have softened a greater soul,
profiting such as came for his protection, his guidance and assistance, left him only the determination to hold fast to the hard-
won glory. By a system of rotation of *chazzanim* in the Berlin
temples, he prevented any one from gaining sufficient popularity to detract from his own supreme position. Men with
voices of too promising a quality, he found means of sending to
other cities. The sceptre had long eluded him. He wielded
it now with despotism.

Among Lewandowski's *German* compositions, his Eighteen
Psalms for chorus and soli gained wide use even in the Protestant Churches in Germany. They are in the genuine oratorio
and *Lied* form, but have not the slightest sound of Jewishness.
On the other hand, his arrangement of traditional themes for
organ, piano, and violin may be accounted a pleasing contribution toward the popularization of Jewish song.

Lewandowski was the youngest of the line of those who may
be termed moderate or temperate regenerators of the Synagogue song; and he was the most capable as composer, and the

nearest to Eastern European Jewish song. He, more than the others of Western Europe, gave proof of the possibility of the re-creation of Synagogue song, and of its adjustability to modern musical forms.

V. Israel Meyer Japhet (1818-1892)

Though Japhet was connected with the ultra-orthodox tendency of Rabbi S. R. Hirsch in Frankfort, for whose service he wrote his music, nevertheless, as a Synagogue composer, he belongs to the moderate-reform. Indeed, when we look into his music, we may even come to the conclusion that his style was similar to that of the ultra-reform of Germany. In his preface to collection I, Japhet emphasizes the great value of traditional tunes, and emphatically opposes the Reform endeavor to introduce Catholic Church music. But the fact is that with the exception of nine (9) numbers (i.e., 5, 9, 15, 29, 30, 37, 40, 57, 58)—a few selections in which he utilizes traditional tunes—his composition is based on the secular German *Lied* style and even on the Protestant hymn. He, like the Christian Protestant and the Jewish Reform composer, cultivated the laudatory part of the service. For example, he offers for *Lechoh Dodi* twelve different settings—these constituting one-fourth of his entire work. Likewise, does he provide Psalm 92 and the removing and the returning of the Scrolls, with various tunes. And therefore does this statement in his preface sound ridiculous: "The author tried to give the traditional tunes as well as his own compositions the impress of *chazzanuth*, the character of which is entirely different from that of the Church song, for the aim of the latter is to develop solemnity and esthetic sentiments in the minds of the hearers, and to lift them to a higher region where they may be forgetful of the earth beneath, whereas the Synagogue song comes from within, filled with emotion and inwardness, with yearning after and joy in the presence of God, thus combining heaven and earth." Yet he offers not a single song of petition and supplication expressive of either the joy of the Jewish spirit or the depths of its yearnings. He further says that he paid attention to the *chazzan's* part of the service; but he did not provide a single recitative in any of the traditional modes, his solos for *chazzan* being rhythmical numbers in modern form. We look in vain for settings for some of those wonderful texts of the traditional prayers. It is true that he was handicapped by the ultra-orthodox restriction against the insertion of music into the service (*Tefillah*) proper because of "distraction of the mind." For that reason, according to his own statement, he did not compose music for *Kedushah, Shema Yisroel, Veshomru, Borchu, Mi Chomocho,* etc. He had opportunity for music in only the introductory and concluding parts of the service. But the restriction could not have prevented his composing these permitted parts in genuine Jewish style. All in all, from the musical point of view, Japhet was as German as any composer of the German Reform temples, though—it must be stated— he did avoid the Catholic style. In this connection, it is interesting to note that, in his recommendation of the second collection of Japhet, the before-mentioned I. Moscheles says that he gives preference to the *traditional* material of the collection rather than to the NEW compositions.

These works, despite their earnest intention to preserve tradition, to modify and modernize it, yea, even to attempt to create new tunes out of the old material, did in reality cultivate only a part of the traditional modes—chiefly the so-called *Mogen-Ovos* and *Ahavoh-Rabboh* modes, neglecting all the others. Especially the *Adonoy-Moloch* mode, which constitutes a considerable part of Synagogue song, was (since Sulzer) transferred to major. Only Weintraub paid attention to it in its original form, in so far as he gave at least his father's composition in that mode, which Weintraub mistakenly designated "mixolydian." It is really a pity that that lyrical and delightful mode was either ignored or assimilated with the European major, simply as a result of ignorance, and in spite of the emphatic warning given by men like Lachmann and Friedmann in their works mentioned below. In like manner the Biblical modes were neglected in their original form; and, in modern forms, no one except Emanuel Kirschner [26] attempted to utilize them.

Moderate-reform song developed the rhythmical music, and made it predominant in the Synagogue service. The modal form of recitative chanting, on the other hand, was gradually reduced, in some places to a minimum; but it was not entirely abolished. This trend was not determined by the use of the organ. We find the same conditions in the Synagogues with, and in those without, organs. The moderate-reform Synagogue did not completely cast aside that Jewish Oriental form of singing, as did the ultra-reform.

The music—from the point of view of its Jewishness—shows no difference by reason of the presence or absence of organ obligato. There is no more Jewishness in the service by Mombach and Hast in England, though they are without organ, nor even in the service of the ultra-orthodox of Frankfort by Japhet than there is in those of Lewandowski and especially of Kirschner, though in these the organ work forms an integral part of the music.

Moderate-reform can hardly be viewed as a unit, since its manifold shadings range from a leaning toward conservatism to a drifting toward the opposite extreme. Even so, the song —from Weintraub's father or Boruch Schorr to Japhet and Mombach—runs a far reach in the scale of Jewishness. Yet one thing is common to all—one thing unites them; and this is the positive conviction that the essentials in traditional songs should be preserved, not merely, as in Sulzer's opinion, as a BRIDGE, but for their distinctive and eternal values to the Jew.

BIBLIOGRAPHY

A century has passed since the dedication of the Temples in Vienna and Munich, wherein was inaugurated the tendency toward moderate-reform—a tendency which exerted a decided influence upon the Synagogue song. The effort was to modernize and to Europeanize the music, while at the same time retaining the traditional material. To execute that program, a considerable number of talented and cultured musicians labored. Their work was along two lines: first (1), the modernizing and beautifying of Synagogue song for practical use; and second (2), the collecting of traditional tunes and the investigating of their origins and history. Worthy of mention are:

Group I:

IsRAEL Lovy (Schottland, near Danzig, 1773—Paris, 1832). (Cantor in Fürth, 1799-1806; Mayence, 1807-1810; Strassburg, 1810-1818; Paris, 1818-1832.)

Chants Religieux, Paris, 1862, with biography by his grandson, Eugene Manuel.

SALOMON SULZER (Hohenems, Tyrol, 1804—Vienna, 1890). (Cantor in Hohenems, 1820-1825; Vienna, 1826-1881.)

Schir Zion, I, Vienna, 1838-1840; *Schir Zion*, II, 1866.

Dudaim, Kleines liturgisches Gesangbuch für Schulen, kleinere Gemeinden und die häusliche Andacht., I and II, Vienna, 1860.

Schir Zion, I and II, second edition, published by Joseph Sulzer, 1905.

MAIER KOHN (Schwabach, 1802—Munich, 1875).

Münchener Synagogengesänge, I-III, Munich, 1839.

SAMUEL NAUMBOURG (Dennelohe near Ansbach, 1815—Paris, 1880). (Cantor in Paris, 1845-1880.)

Zemiroth Yisrael, I-II, Paris, 1847; Vol. III, 1857; *Schiré Kodesch, chants religieux*, Paris, 1864; *Agudath Schirim, Recueil de chants religieux et populaires des Israelites des Temps les plus reculés jusqu'à nos jours . . . Précédées d'une étude Historique sur la musique des Hebreux*, Paris, 1874.

HIRSCH (ALTER) WEINTRAUB (Dubno, 1811—Königsberg i/P., 1882). (Cantor in Dubno, 1830-1835; Königsberg, 1838-1880.)

Schire Beth Adonai—Tempelgesänge, I-II, Leipzig, 1859; III, *Schire Sch'lomo*, Leipzig, 1859.

LOUIS (ELIEZER) LEWANDOWSKI (Wreschen, 1821—Berlin, 1894). (Choir Leader and Music Teacher in Berlin, 1840-1894.)

Kol Rinnah Utefillah, Berlin, 1871; *Todah Wesimrah*, I, Berlin, 1876; II, 1882.

ISRAEL LAZARUS MOMBACH (Pfungstadt, 1813—London, 1880). (Choir Leader in London, 1841-1880.)

Ne'im Zemiroth Israel—The Sacred Musical Compositions of Mombach, London, 1881.

MORITZ DEUTSCH (Nikolsburg, 1818—Breslau, 1894). (Disciple of Sulzer, 2nd Cantor with Sulzer in Vienna, 1842-1844; in Breslau, 1844-1894.)

Breslauer Synagogengesänge, Breslau, 1880; *Vorbeterschule*, Breslau, 1871; *Anhang zu Vorbeterschule*, 1890, including *Nachwort: Der Ritualgesang der Synagoge*.

MAX G. LÖWENSTAMM (Trebitsch, 1814—Munich, 1881). (Disciple of Sulzer, Cantor in Pest, 1842-1844; in Munich, 1847-1881.)
S'miroth l'El Chaj—Synagogengesänge, I-IV, Munich, 1882.

ISRAEL MEYER JAPHET (Cassel, 1818—Frankfort, 1892). (Choir Leader and Teacher at the Orthodox Congregation in Frankfort, 1853-1892.)
Schire Jeschurun, I, Frankfort, 1856; II, 1864.

ANTON (AHRON WOLF) BERLIYN (Amsterdam, 1817-1870). (Composer and conductor.)
Schire Beth Elohim.
Schire Beth Ahron.
Schire Chag Wetoda.
Drei hebreeuwsche Gezangen, for 3 children's voices.
Vier hebreeuwsche Gezangen voor Kinderstemmen.
All published in Amsterdam.

HIRSCH GOLDBERG (Wollstein, Posen, 1807—Braunschweig, 1893). (Cantor in Holzminden and Seesen, 1829-1842; in Braunschweig, 1842-1893.)
Gesänge für Synagogen, Braunschweig, 1843.

(JOSHUA) OSIAS ABRASS (called "Pitzsche"—Pitzele in Yiddish, the "little one," because of his fame as singer while still a child. Berditschev, 1820—Odessa, 1896.) (Disciple of Bezalel Schulsinger, Cantor in Tarnopol, 1840-1842; Lemberg, 1842-1858; Odessa, 1858-1884.)
Simrath Yah, Vienna, 1874.

CHAIM WASSERZUG (Schiradz, Poland, 1822—Brighton, 1882). (Cantor in Konin, 1840; Novy Dvor, 1841-1854; Lomza, 1854-1859; Wilna, 1859-1867; London, 1868-1882.)
Sefer Schire Mikdash, London, 1878.

Boruch Schorr (Lemberg, 1823-1904). (Cantor in Lemberg.)

N'ginoth Boruch Schorr, New York, 1906; published by his son, Israel Schorr, Cantor in Brooklyn.

Samuel David (Paris, 1836-1895). Musical director at the Jewish Temple in Paris, 1872-1895; composer of operas and symphonies, etc. *Poal Chayé Adam: Musique Religieuse Ancienne et Moderne en usage dans les Temples consistoriaux Israelites de Paris*, Paris, 1895. Publication of the Consistoire de Paris.

Jacob Leopold (Leib) Weiss (Neutra, Hungary, 1825—Warsaw, 1889). (Disciple of Sulzer, Cantor in Agram, 1850-1; Botschowitz, 1853-9; Warsaw, 1859-1873; Wilna, 1873-1876.)

Ozar Schire Jeschurun, Vienna, 1874; II Ed., 1881.

Josef Goldstein (Kecskemet, Hungary, 1837—Vienna, 1899). (Cantor in Neutra, 1850, as successor of his father; Neusatz, 1852-4; in Vienna, 1855-1899.)

Schire Jeschurun, Vienna, 1862.

Emile Jonas (Paris, 1827—St. Germain, 1905). (Composer of Operettas and Professor at the Conservatoire in Paris.)

Schiroth Israél—Recueil des Chants Hebraiques anciens et modernes exécutés au Temple du rite portugais des Paris, 1854.

Jacob Bachmann (Berditschev, 1846—Budapest, 1905). (Cantor in Lemberg, 1868-1884; Odessa, 1884-5; Budapest, 1885-1905.)

Schirath Jacob, Petersburg and Moscow, 1884.

David Rubin (Gebitsch, 1837—Baden near Vienna, 1922). (Choir Leader in Prague, 1860-1912.)

Schire Hechal, Prague, 1860, etc.

Adolf Grünzweig (Choir Leader in Arad, Hungary, 1829-1905).

Sabbath Songs—Mayence, 1863.

Matte Ahron—Mayence, 1893.

Marcus Hast (Praga, Warsaw, 1840—London, 1911). (Cantor in London, 1871-1911.)

Abodath Hakodesh, I-IV, London, 1910.

Simon Waley (London, 1827-1875). Pianist and composer. He composed hymns for Sabbaths and festivals, of which his tune for *Adon Olam* became popular.

Emanuel Kirschner (Rokinitz, Silesia, 1857—living in Munich,   ). Cantor in Berlin, 1880-1; in Munich, 1881-1928.)

Tehilloth Le'el Elyon—*Synagogengesänge*, I-IV, 1897-1926.

Josef Heller (Szatmar, Hungary, 1864—Brünn). Cantor in Kaposvár, 1884-1859; Brünn, 1889-   .)

Kol T'hilloh, I-II, Brünn, 1905-14.

Francis Lyon Cohen (Aldershot, 1862; Rabbi in Sydney, Australia) and

B. L. Mosely, in 1889, compiled *The Handbook of Synagogue Music*, re-edited and re-arranged by F. L. Cohen and D. M. Davis as *The Voice of Prayer and Praise* . . . for the Choir Committee of the Council of the United Synagogue with the Sanction of the Chief Rabbi, London, 1899; 2nd edition, 1914. This hymnal for choir and congregational singing contains 310 numbers for Synagogue, religious school and home, for the Sabbath, the festivals and for special occasions, according to the Orthodox ritual. The musical material is drawn from traditional sources and from Synagogue composers, such as Sulzer and Naumbourg, but mostly from Mombach, Wasserzug, Hast and Davis. A few tunes are adopted from Beethoven and Mendelssohn.

M. Cohen-Linaru (Born in Adrianople—.) (Choir Leader at the Sephardic Temple in Bucharest.)

Thehilloth Israel, I-II, Bucharest, 1910.

Moritz Henle (Laupheim, 1850—Hamburg, 1925). Cantor in Thalheim, 1868; Laupheim, 1867-1873; Ulm, a/D., 1873-1879; Hamburg [Tempelverein], 1879-1913.)

Many compositions and essays, especially *Der Gottesdienstliche Gesang im Hamburger Tempel*, 1918; in *Festschrift*, etc., Hamburg, 1918.

Group II:

Josef Singer (Illinik, Hungary, 1841—Vienna, 1911).

Die Tonarten des trad. Synagogengesange, 1886; many essays in various periodicals in German.

Isaak Lachmann (Dubno, 1838—Hürben, Bavaria, 1900).

Abodath Israel, I, 1899; many essays in German periodicals.

Samuel Naumbourg (See Group I).

Cantiques de Salomon Rossi with introduction, Paris, 1876; *Agudath Schirim*, l.c., Group I.

Moritz Deutsch (See Group I).

Vorbeterschule. Breslau, 1871; Appendix, 1890.

Abraham Baer (Filehne, 1834—Gothenburg, 1894). (Cantor in Pakosch, Gothenburg, 1857-1894.)

Baal T'fillah, Leipzig, 1877.

N. H. Katz (Cantor in Brilon) and L. Talbott (Cantor in Oberlustsadt).

Die traditionellen Synagogen-Gesänge, I-II, Emmerich, 1868.

David de Sola (Portuguese Rabbi, Amsterdam, 1796—Shadwell, near London, 1860) and Emanuel Abraham Aguilar (London, 1824-1904). (Composer and pianist.)

The Ancient Melodies of the Spanish and Portuguese Jews, London, 1857; Historical Introduction by David de Sola. Music by Aguilar.

Federico Consolo (Jehiel Nahmani Sefardi) (Ancona, 1840—Florence, 1906). (Composer and violin virtuoso.)

Sefer Shire Yisrael—Libro dei Canti d'Israelle, antichi canti liturgici, Rito degli Ebrei Spagnoli, Firenze, 1891; *Cenni sull'origine e sul progresso della musica liturgica, con appendice intorno all 'origine dell 'organo,* Firenze, 1897.

Jules Salomon Crémieu and Mardochee Crémieu.

Chants Hébraïques suivant le rite des communautés Israelites de l'ancien Comtat Venaissin, Aix, 1885.

Aron Friedmann (Schaki, Lithuania, 1855—living in Berlin,   ). (Cantor in Berlin, 1882-1923.)

Schir Lishlaumau, 1901 (Chasonus); *Der Synagogale Gesang, eine Studie,* Berlin, 1904; 2nd edition, 1908; *Lebensbilder berühmter Cantoren,* Vols. I-III, Berlin, 1918-1921-1927.

Eduard (Asher Ensel) Birnbaum (Cracow, 1855—Königsberg, i/P., 1920). (Cantor in Magdeburg, 1872-74; Beuthen, 1874-1879; Königsberg, 1879-1920.)

Jüdische Musiker am Hofe von Mantua von 1542-1628, Vienna, 1893; many essays in various periodicals; collector of musical and historical material.

Francis Lyon Cohen. Author of most of the articles on Jewish music in the Jewish Encyclopedia; several essays in English.

Pinchos Minkowsky (Biela Tzerkow, 1859—Boston,

1924). (Cantor in Kischenew, 1878; Cherson, 1880-84; Odessa, 1884; New York, 1884-89; Odessa, 1889-1920.)

Reshumoth, I, II, III, IV. *Hashiloah,* Odessa, 1899; *Die Entwickelung der synag. Liturgie,* Odessa, 1902; *Der Sulzerismus,* Vienna, 1905.

Many articles in Hebrew, German, Yiddish, and Russian (in the Jewish-Russian Encyclopedia).

ABRAHAM BER BIRNBAUM (Poltusk, 1865—Tschenstichov, 1922). (Cantor in Tschenstichov.)

Omonus Hachazonus—The Art of Chazzanuth, Tschenstichov, 1908; *Theory of Music,* 1902; *A Monthly for Chazzanim* (4 numbers 1897). Several essays in Hebrew and Yiddish.

ARON ACKERMANN (1867-1912). (Rabbi in Brandenburg.)

"Der Synag. Gesang in seiner historischen Entwickelung," in Winter and Wünsche, *Die jüd. Literatur,* Vol. III, pp. 477-529.

HERMANN EHRLICH (1815-1879). (Cantor in Berkach, near Meiningen.)

Founder and Editor of the magazine *Liturgische Zeitschrift,* I-IV (1852-55), including essays, historical research, and the publication of traditional songs, etc.

ABRAHAM BLAUSTEIN (Riga, 1836—Bromberg, 1914). (Cantor in Gnesen, Bromberg, 1874-1914.)

Founder of the Cantor-Association in Middle Europe in 1879, and founder and editor of the weekly *Der Jüdische Cantor,* 1879-1899.

JACOB BAUER (Gr. Pristerst near Czenits, Hungary, 1852—Vienna, 1926). (Cantor in Szigetwor, 1875-78; Gratz, 1878-81; at the Turkish Temple in Vienna, 1881-1926.)

Modernizer of the Sephardic Service at the Turkish Temple in Vienna. Friday Evening Service published in cooperation with I. Löwit, Vienna, 1889. Editor of the weekly *Die Oesterreich-Ungarische Cantoren-Zeitung*, 1881-1898, and from 1899 on, under the name *Wahrheit*.

The second group we shall treat in Chapter XVI. In this chapter we devoted our attention to the practical workers.

Though most of the men listed in Group I certainly made important contributions toward the furtherance of Moderate-Reform, yet they were rather followers of the real pathfinders and pioneers: Sulzer, Maier Kohn, Naumbourg, Weintraub, and Lewandowski, who merit the individual and detailed treatment accorded them in this chapter.

CHAPTER XIV

"CHAZZANIM" AND "CHAZZANUTH" IN EASTERN EUROPE IN THE NINETEENTH CENTURY.

While in Central Europe the fight between reform and orthodoxy was in progress in the beginning of the nineteenth century, menacing the very existence of traditional Synagogue music, in Eastern Europe Jewish song unfolded a remarkable creative power, both in Synagogue and folk-song. A long line of inspired *chazzanim* and talented singers and composers arose in Galicia, Poland, and Lithuania in the course of the nineteenth and the beginning of the twentieth century, until the World War and the subsequent disasters caused the ruin and misery of the present-day East European Jewry.

The Eastern *chazzanim* of the first half of the nineteenth century can be classified in two groups: (1) those who possessed fine voices combined with marvelous talent of performance, and were at the same time gifted composers, and (2) gifted composers and choir-leaders who had poor or no vocal ability. They were compelled to function as *chazzanim*, because there was no other post for a musician created in the Synagogue, as we saw in Chapter XIII with regard to Lewandowski.

The *chazzanim* of the first group created schools of their own not only by their original music but also by their original method of performance. There were those of them who created selections in fixed forms, in tunes; but for the most part they founded their strength upon their free spontaneous song, improvised while conducting the service. As a result of the latter practice, in the course of time, certain motives and

melodic curves, modulations and coloratura passages and embellishments within given modes became distinctive of their chant.
And thus an individual style was created, crystallized during a
lifelong improvisatory singing. The style of an individual
used to be copied by his "singers" and admirers and used to
be called *motzoh*—style of expression. The same procedure is
still customary among the Oriental singers as well as among
the Ukrainian *Kobsari* (Chapter IX).

The reason for that procedure is to be found in the fact that
the reading and writing of music had been unknown accom-
plishments to the greatest number of Eastern *chazzanim* during the first half of the nineteenth century. They had held
their compositions in mind, and had trained their "singers" accordingly. It had rested with the singers to remember the
compositions improvised by the *chazzanim* while officiating.

Of type (1), apart from the already mentioned Salomon
Kashtan (Chapter XIII), we shall name:

1. DOVIDL BROD STRELISKER (born in Brody, 1783; died
in Budapest, 1848). · He distinguished himself from childhood on with his sweet singing; and, while still a young boy,
he was privileged to officiate in the synagogue of his native
town. He never received any musical training, neither was he
meshorer with any *chazzan.* Destined originally for the vo-
cation of rabbi, he finally became an accountant and later a
merchant. Traveling to various business centers, he volunteered his singing talent in the service of the Synagogue wherever he happened to be.[1]

Through adverse circumstances he lost his fortune and was
compelled in 1822 to accept the post of *chazzan* in Alt-Ofen,
to which post he was recommended by his friend Salomon
Kashtan. In 1830 he was called to Pest, in which synagogue
he officiated until his death in 1848.

Though no authentic compositions of his have been retained,

since he could neither write nor read music, his influence upon
the *chazzanim* in Galicia and Hungary was enormous. He was
of those *chazzanim* who, in the course of their activity, created
an original style of *chazzanuth*. His many choristers carried
his style with them. This style, as explained in Chapter IX,
was mainly based upon the *Ahavoh-Rabboh* mode and on the
Ukrainian-Gipsy scale. In his later years Dovidl Brod made
an attempt to acquire the rudiments of music, but he finally
realized that it was too late. Dovidl Brod was highly regarded
by Sulzer.[2]

2. BEZALEL SHULSINGER, called Bezalel Odessaer. The
place and date of his birth are not known. He was born some-
time around 1790 in Galicia or Podolia. In 1826 he was already a renowned *chazzan*. Soon thereafter he became city
chazzan in Odessa, where he stayed until 1860, when he left
for Jerusalem. He died in the Holy City shortly thereafter.

Bezalel, too, was an autodidact and established a style distinguished by simplicity, inwardness, and grace. Almost all
the famous *chazzanim* of the first half of the nineteenth century were his "singers." Though without any musical knowledge, he composed; and his creations became popular and were
written down by his pupils who acquired technical knowledge
of music. Due to this circumstance, no claim to authenticity
can be made for the manuscripts, though the various writings
in circulation show but minor variations.

3. SENDER POLATSHIK, called "Sender Minsker." He was
born in Gombin, Poland, in 1786, and he was singer with
Nochum Leb Kashtan (brother of Salomon) in Berditschev.
He became *chazzan* in Mir; and, in 1822, in Minsk, where he
remained until his death in 1869. Sender had a powerful
bass-baritone voice, and was likewise without any musical
knowledge. His manner of composing was later described by
one of his singers.[3] At moments of inspiration he would

gather his choristers who were always at his command and would work out his compositions, weaving the theme through the different voices in variations, repeating from the beginning, and with each repetition adding some new phrase, until the piece was completed. Thus, in the course of its creation, the composition was simultaneously rehearsed. It was now the choristers' task to preserve the new selection in their memory; and woe to a chorister if he forgot his part!

Sender opposed the style of Bezalel, the so-called Volhynian *chazzanuth*, distinguished by its ingratiating motives and its tendency toward embellishments. He created a style noteworthy for its depth and lack of embellishment, if we may judge from the few pieces accredited to him.

4. JOSEPH ALTSHUL, called "Yoshe Slonimer," was born in Wilna in 1840. He received some instruction from Chayim Wasserzug (Chapter XIII); he became "singer" with Yeruchom Hakoton in 1861-3; later he was *chazzan* in some villages in Lithuania; then in Slonim and finally in Horodna, where he died in 1908. He had a powerful bass voice and acquired the rudiments of music, so that he was able to read and write music. He was a prolific composer in the folk-tune style, and a great number of his tunes for solo and choir are circulating in MS., some of which became popular among the Eastern *chazzanim*.

5. We shall select but one more *chazzan* from the great number belonging to type 1, and this is YOEL DOVID LEVINSOHN, called "Wilnaer Baalhabessil." His father, Hirsch Bochur Levi (1786-1830), was *city-chazzan* in Wilna (1822-1830), and died young, leaving Yoel Dovid a boy of thirteen (born in 1816 in Libau, Latvia, where his father was then *chazzan*). Already as a little boy of ten and eleven, he was famous as a wonderful singer; and his father was urged by the public to let the lad officiate in the big synagogue on Saturday services.

After the sudden death of the father, the boy was selected as his successor.[4] Soon a rich member of the congregation took him as a son-in-law, and granted him an allowance for his entire life.[5] So the young Yoel Dovid, who till now had been called *Der Yingele* (the little lad), now that he was married and affluent, received the pet name *Der Baal-habessil* (the little member of the community). It was probably the first time in the history of the Synagogue that a talented *chazzan* was financially independent. The young lad, endowed with genius and fortune, was beloved and venerated by his people to a degree of idolatry. From all over Lithuania lovers of *chazzanuth* streamed to Wilna in order to hear and see the little *Baal-habessil*. Apart from his fascinating voice and singing (he had a lyric tenor with a brilliant coloratura), he was also a talented composer. His compositions were of an original charm, of genuine Jewish-oriental sentimentality and in the Jewish folk-tune style, and therefore they became popular. At the age of twenty-three, already ten years in office, Yoel Dovid started studying music with the Polish musician Stanislaus Moniuszko, who in 1839 established himself in Wilna as teacher and organist.[6] The *Baal-habessil*, who up to that time lived in the fantastic realm of self-glorification, now became acquainted with European music and musical geniuses of his time. Gradually his *chazzanuth* became distasteful to him, and his environment too narrow. Upon Moniuszko's suggestion he decided to leave his position and go to Warsaw, at that time a center of music. In Warsaw he was enthusiastically received by the Jews. At the recommendation of Moniuszko, he was invited to give concerts before the Polish public, in which a Polish woman-singer participated. A web of legends is woven about this event. It is said that he was attracted by the gentile woman-singer and was plunged into a gloomy melancholy from which he never recovered. From Warsaw he went to Vienna, where he was cordially received by Sulzer, but this meeting proved to be the cause of another terrible shock to him. He had considered himself the greatest *chazzan* of his time. Suddenly this fantasy was shattered as he listened to the powerful, artistic and overwhelming singing of Sulzer. He felt that his own voice and singing were only those of a child in comparison with those of a hero. At the same time, the passion for the Polish singer unconsciously grew in his heart, until he became aware that it was love—love of a married orthodox Jew for a gentile woman! In his mental derangement which followed he abandoned his musical career and became a penitent.

Hence, he left Vienna, and started on his penitential way, according to the old Jewish fashion, walking from community to community, without speaking to anyone, occupying himself with the study of Talmud only, like the old type of *Porush* (recluse). Finally his family got hold of him and placed him in the insane asylum in Warsaw, where he died in 1850.

Once, while in Dubno, he was by accident recognized and was persuaded to officiate on a Sabbath. We have a description of that service by Isaak Lachmann, who was present at that service.[7] He says:[8] "Never again in my life did I hear such a voice, such a performance, such a holy spirit expressed in worship. I never again in my life heard such a coloratura which seemed living garlands of pearls coming from his mouth and flying in the air of the synagogue. His voice was a lyric tenor—rather weak, for he was greatly worn, and more spirit than body. It was a year before his death. He seemed to stand before the pulpit entranced, oblivious of his environment, swaying in the higher spheres. His singing was without effort. He hardly moved his lips even. It was more an exhalation of soul than a sounding of voice."

He left no pupils nor any school. Only half a dozen of his

compositions have been retained. Report has it that the manuscripts were burned by his wife when she had heard of his attraction to the Polish woman-singer.[9]

Of the second type of *chazzanim* we shall mention only a few of the most outstanding, such as:

6. BORUCH KARLINER, a disciple of "Sender Minsker." He was *chazzan* in Karlin, later in Pinsk; and he died in Brisk in 1879 on his way back to Bialistok, where he had been appointed *chazzan*. He was original both as an untamed individual and as a composer. With but little voice and without any musical knowledge, like his master Sender, he would compose when "the spirit came upon him," be that on the street or in the synagogue during the service. He would drill his choir on certain pieces for the services, but suddenly during the service "the spirit" would come upon him, so that he would abandon the tune prepared and start creating a new composition for the text. His choristers were trained to his ways of improvisation, so that they would immediately catch up the theme just invented by Boruch and continue developing it according to his "style," thus creating a new composition to the greatest delight of his congregants, who, knowing their *chazzan's* ways, immediately felt the new inspiration. Some of his singers were greatly devoted to him, and knowing how to write music, retained several of his compositions. The creations are remarkable for their power and their bold modulations. His chief singer, Nehemia Bass, had the privilege of adding a *shtel*—a vocal prelude without words, to his master's compositions. Such a privilege was usually accorded the chief singers by their *chazzanim*.[10]

7. YERUCHOM BLINDMAN, called "Yeruchom Hakoton" (the little one). He was born in Bessarabia or in Galicia c. 1798. In 1834 he was already a well-known wandering *chazzan*. Until 1860 he was *chazzan* in Kishenev, and in 1861-

1877 in Berditschev in the old synagogue. Though in his agreement with the later congregation he had pledged to refrain from touring the country and remain at that post all his life, he nonetheless broke his contract and became *chazzan* in Tarnopol from 1877 to 1886. He died at the age of ninety-three. Yeruchom seems to have been a "singer" of Bezalel Odessaer. He acquired later some knowledge of music, even in elementary harmony. His compositions show attempts at harmonic arrangements in four parts. He had in his younger years a high lyric tenor with a limitless falsetto. Many of his compositions are still circulating among the *chazzanim*. Some of them, especially those in minor, breathe warm Jewish sentiments. They are new creations of the old material of *Mogen-Ovos* or *Selicha modes*. In them Yeruchom created new melodic turns through which the Eastern Jewish folk tune is echoed. His compositions in major are imitations of military music.

8. NISSON SPIVAK, called "Nissi Belzer." This most gifted composer for the Eastern Synagogue of the old school was born in 1824 in a little village in Lithuania. As a boy, he sang with Boruch Karliner. Then he wandered south to Yeruchom, whose niece he married, in Bessarabia. Through an accident he lost his voice. Nevertheless, he became *chazzan* by merit of his remarkable talent as composer and choir-leader. He occupied the post of *chazzan* in Belz (hence his name Belzer), Yelissavetgrad, Kishinev (1864-1877), and from 1877 on in Berditschev as successor of his uncle Yeruchom (with whom he had been on bad terms), where he remained until his death in 1906. He died in Sadegora, while on a concert tour to the famous chassidic rabbi of that town.

It is remarkable that in Eastern Europe, where so much emphasis was laid upon a beautiful voice, we find *chazzanim* of great fame who were voiceless. Under West European conditions, these men would have probably been Synagogue composers and choir-leaders; but in Eastern Europe until a half-century ago such a position was still unknown. Therefore, they had to be *chazzanim*. Strangely enough, the public seemed to be willing to listen to such voiceless singers. The unpleasantness of the performance is easily imaginable, but the public felt repaid by the wonderful tunes that those *chazzanim* composed and rendered by the fine voices of the choir. This phenomenon caused two changes of considerable importance in the Synagogue song: First, taking into consideration their inability to sing solo, these *chazzanim* limited their solo parts to a minimum. And secondly, in order to cover their vocal deficiencies, they tried to select fine voices for their choirs. Thus, while the *chazzan* with the beautiful voice often made the prayers merely a tool of his solos, using the choir as a mere accompanying body, these voiceless *chazzanim*, through sheer emergency, were forced to express the Synagogue song through the choir primarily. The singers, partly as soloists and partly as an ensemble, carried practically the entire service. And the remarkable aspect of this arrangement was that the public seemed never to miss the *chazzan*. Of Nissi Belzer it is told that after his and his choir's performance of his best compositions before the chassidic rabbi Dovidl of Talno, the rabbi asked him how much his choir cost him, whereupon he answered, "Fifteen hundred rubles per annum!" "Oh, Nissi," responded the rabbi, "you are too economical! Why do you not spend another couple of hundred rubles and engage also a good *chazzan*?" [11]

Out of the school of this voiceless *chazzan* there arose a great number of *chazzanim*. Nissi's *meshorer* was no longer only a helper to the heroic *chazzan*; but he became, even while still a chorister, an important factor in the service. This was another significant step in the development of Synagogue song.

Compelled by the circumstances described above, Nissi created a new genre in the Synagogue song, a style which though based upon the principle of chorus, nonetheless gave ample solo-work of the *chazzanic* type, i.e., the modal form, the execution of which he divided among the choristers. For solo only or for solo with choir accompaniment he never wrote. His pieces are mostly choruses with interspersed solos of considerable length. In Nissi the harmonic sense is much more developed than in Yeruchom. At times he attempted a small canon or fughetta and dared modulations with the boldness of his first teacher, Boruch Karliner.

The reason for his lengthy compositions lies in the fact that he did not write for the average service but for concert-services, for he, being a *city-chazzan*, had the task of supplying the large Jewish community of Kishinev or Berditschev with "music." As a *city-chazzan*, he used to officiate on special Sabbaths or feasts and fast days only. These services were regarded as religious concerts which members of different Jewish congregations used to attend usually after they had finished the regular service in their own synagogues. The *city-chazzan* would prepare a musical program, the texts of which were selections from the ritual, though the setting was hardly adaptable to the service, inasmuch as some of these compositions would consume a half hour or more.

Nissi's themes are striking in their genuineness, and his creative power in variations of his themes is refreshing and rich. Strongly influenced by military music, he shows also what seems to be the influence of the opera. In his compositions based upon the *Ahavoh-Rabboh* mode he strikes the soul of the Jew to its very depth. To a considerable extent he is also influenced by the Ukrainian scale. But what a difference of conception! None of the Ukrainian tunes in folk style could match some of Nissi's creations. Nissi's music shows his striv-

ing after form; but being without any training in the art of
form, he gropes in darkness. At times, he repeats the first
theme at the end, but usually, influenced by instrumental military music, he repeats the sections of the compositions in a manner imitative of the rondo. Furthermore, his selection of texts,
formless from the musical point of view, and his faithful adherence to their content which he tried to voice, were in themselves barriers to form in his musical settings. In addition, he
lacked the sense of economy; he produced a rich treasury of
wonderful themes which he lavishly spent without developing
them.

We may count Nissi Belzer as the greatest musical genius
of Synagogue song that Eastern Europe produced. He stands
wholly on Jewish-Oriental ground, gazing at the EXTERIOR of
the European palace of music.

His numerous compositions are still in manuscript form,
scattered among the Eastern *chazzanim* in Europe and America. They constitute an integral part of the music of the Orthodox Synagogue.

In the second half of the nineteenth century Eastern Europe
was more and more opened to Western European culture; and
the large communities started building the modern Synagogue
called *Chor-Schul*, according to the model of the Vienna Temple of Sulzer—of course, without the organ. It was a thorough imitation of Sulzer, even to the dress and long hair of
the *chazzan*. The *chor-chazzanim* in the first place elimi-
nated the whole East European Synagogue song, and replaced it with Sulzer's service. They tried to abolish embellishments and ornaments because Sulzer did thus, but they
lacked Sulzer's tremendous voice and his wonderful execution.
Deeper inland in Russia, where the Jews never saw Sulzer or
his pupils, but heard and saw only the Eastern European imi-

tation of him, they found a great similarity between the pseudo-Sulzers and the Russian Greek Catholic priests, who were in their neighborhood and whom they could easily imitate. Hence, the *chor-chazzanim* received the HONORABLE name of *galochim* and their song was called *galochish*, i.e., dressed as priests, and singing in long-extended tones without ornaments, similar to those of the song of that Church. Needless to say, these modern *chor-chazzanim* could not gain the sympathy of the Jewish public; and the well-built modern synagogues were more visited by gentiles, mostly military officers and their wives, than by the Jews, who preferred the old-fashioned *chazzan* and even the simple *baal-tefillah*. A few exceptions there were among these *chor-chazzanim*, who were equipped with Jewish knowledge and feeling. And they, out of consideration for the taste of the Jewish people, retained in the service some tunes which had real Jewish character.

1. NISSON BLUMENTHAL was the first modernized *chazzan* in Russia in the first *Chor-Schul* in Odessa, founded in 1840, and called "Brody-Synagogue" because it was organized by the Jewish settlers from Brody. Blumenthal was born in Berditschev in 1805 and was raised in Jassy, Roumania. He was an autodidact in music and in German classic literature; he was a man of fine spirit and taste. He endeavored to raise the musical standard of the Synagogue song by means of a well-trained choir (men and boys) singing in four parts. He likewise tried to simplify the modal chant of the *chazzan*, giving it more inwardness rather than acrobatics of vocal technique. Not having any creative ability himself, he used to adapt for Hebrew texts selections of oratorios and sacred music by Handel, Haydn, Cherubini, and Mendelssohn. He had a fine lyric tenor voice, and presented an inspiring interpretation of the Synagogue modes. During the long period of his activity (1841-1892, he died in 1903 at the age of ninety-

eight) he exerted a good influence upon his congregation and upon young Jewish musicians by developing in them a finer musical understanding. Especially fortunate was his success in obtaining as choir-leader a man of considerable musical talent and a marvelous choir trainer, and this was:

2. DAVID NOWAKOWSKY. He was born in 1848 in a small village (Malin) in the government of Kiev. From the age of eight he was chorister for ten years in the new *Chor-Schul* in Berditschev.[12] In 1870 or 1871 he was appointed choir-leader in the "Brody-Synagogue," at which post he remained for a half-century until his death in 1921.

Nowakowsky is the most Europeanized Synagogue composer in the East. He made a thorough study of harmony and counterpoint, and acquired the technique of the forms of the classic vocal music for choir, notably the oratorio style. His themes he often takes from the traditional modes or tunes; and he displays a fine talent for variation and development. His compositions are mostly of great length and suited rather for religious concerts than for an average service, a manner of composition which, as already explained, is to be found in the Eastern *chazzanic* creations. This manner of writing was a far cry to Sulzer's music distinguished by its brevity of form and created with the aim of suiting the regular service. Nowakow-sky's harmony is likewise of great interest, but we shall treat that in Chaper XXIII.

During his life he published a service for Friday evening and one for the concluding service (*Neila*) of the Day of Atonement. The greatest part of his creations remained in manuscript form.

3. WOLF SHESTAPOL, called "Welwele Chersoner," the son of Samuel, *chazzan* in Odessa, was born c. 1832. He sang with his father and with Bezalel, and became *chazzan* in Cherson. His congregation sent him to Vienna to be instructed

by Sulzer. Shestapol was a prolific composer of sweet and
ingratiating tunes of but little originality. He was influenced
by the Italian opera in Odessa to the extent of adopting themes
and snatches of arias. Thus he adopted a part of an aria from
La Traviata, No. 6 for *Adonoy Zechoronu* (Ps. 115: 12-18,
beginning with the word *hashomayim*). From there A. Goldfaden took the tune over into his musical play *Shulamith*
(Chapter XX).

Shestapol's choral harmony is poor and of instrumental
character. On account of their sweetness and folk-character,
his compositions, notably his tunes in minor, became very popular, though they were never printed. He died in 1872, not
reaching even the age of forty.

4. BORUCH SCHORR. The second *chazzan* of fame that Galicia produced was born in Lemberg in 1823 of a prominent
chassidic family. At the age of nine he became a *singerl* with
Bezalel in Odessa; at eleven he sang with Yeruchom; and at
thirteen he already conducted services. After officiating in
various congregations in Podolia and Roumania, he was appointed *chazzan* in the great synagogue in Lemberg in 1859.
Though very pious, Schorr was nonetheless touched by European culture. In 1890 he composed an operetta, *Samson,*
which was performed in the Jewish theatre in Lemberg. At
the call of the audience Schorr appeared on the stage led by
the prima donna. Such conduct was regarded by the orthodox
element as undignified for an orthodox *chazzan,* and Schorr
was suspended from his office for one month. Hurt by this
rebuke, Schorr went to New York, where he remained for five
years. But the Lemberg community was lonesome for its
popular *chazzan* and recalled him to his post which he occupied until the end of his days. He died while officiating on the
last day of Passover in 1904.

Schorr's Synagogue compositions for the High Holidays are

notable for their genuine Jewish motives and melodic structure,
for their simplicity and singability. Schorr gave the traditional tunes a pleasant shape, without taking away their unique
originality, without trying to Europeanize them. In his responsa he imitates Sulzer, likewise in his use of brief forms,
especially in those compositions for the High Holidays published in New York in 1906 by his son Israel Schorr. In this
collection many pieces are the work of the latter. Apparently
also the son has to a great extent doctored his father's harmony.[13] Schorr's compositions are almost entirely either in
minor or in the *Ahavoh-Rabboh* mode (in major there are
only two, Nos. 142 and 143). He raised six sons as *chazzanim*.
These are officiating in various communities in the Old and the
New World.

5. ELIESER GEROVITSCH is one of the first *chazzanim* who
received a musical education in the conservatory of music in
Petersburg. He was born in a village in the government of
Kiev in 1844, sang in choirs in Berditschev and Odessa, went
later to Petersburg to study music and voice, and occupied the
post of *chazzan* in Rostov on the Don for about twenty-five
years. He died in 1913. In 1890 he published a collection
of songs for Sabbath, the Three Festivals, and the High Holidays, called *Schiré Tefillah*. Gerovitsch is a master of counterpoint and of the Church-style which he acquired in the
above-mentioned institute. He applied the method of the
classic composers to the utilization of traditional tunes as "cantus firmus," around which he created artistic forms. He mas-
tered all the traditional modes of the Synagogue, even the
most neglected *Adonoy-Moloch* mode (in his work, Nos. 2-3)
and created out of that mode choral items. He introduced a
Persian scale, called Suz-Nak,[14] into the Synagogue (No. 22),
probably influenced by Persian or Tartaric song frequently

heard in the environment of Rostov. In 1904 Gerovitsch published another collection, called *Schiré Zimra*.

Gerovitsch, like Nowakowsky, created music which may be designated "Jewish art music," utilizing European technique for Jewish elements.

Southeastern Europe brought forth infinitely more creative Jewish musicians than did the Northern part, apparently because of the inspiration drawn from the Near East which borders the Southeastern districts. Volhynia, Ukraine, Podolia, and Bessarabia were the cradle of the great Jewish singers and composers. Weintraub and his father, Kashtan, too, originated from the South, though the former spent the greatest part of his life in the North (in Koenigsberg—Prussia). From the biographies of *chazzanim* given in this chapter we notice that the *chazzanim* of the North (Lithuania) were trained in the South. By almost all the *chazzanim*, with the exception of Sender Minsker, the South was considered the cradle of *chazzanuth*. Nonetheless, due to Weintraub's influence, several of his disciples became prominent *chazzanim* in the Northern districts, in Prussia, Lithuania, and in the Baltic provinces, where they transplanted Weintraub's style and art. The most prominent of these was:

6. Boruch Leib Rosowsky, for almost a half-century *chazzan* in Riga (Latvia). Born in a village near Wilna in 1841, he went in 1867 to the then newly established conservatory in Petersburg (founded in 1863 by Anton Rubinstein). In that institute Rosowsky studied for three years. There Tschaikowsky is reported to have been his classmate in composition.[16] In 1870 he went to Weintraub, and in a short time he absorbed Weintraub's *chazzanuth* to such an extent that, according to the master's own statement, he rendered it in a more accomplished manner than Weintraub himself. And

truly, Rosowsky was a wonderful interpreter of Weintraub's art to which he remained faithful all his life. Rosowsky had a well-trained choir; and during his activity in Riga, from 1871 until his death in 1919, he trained many *chazzanim* and a number of Jewish singers who became prominent on the stage, such as Joseph Schwarz and Jadlowker. In his compositions Rosowsky adhered to the Jewish folk-character. Judging from a collection of his compositions published by his son, Solomon Rosowsky (Chapter XIX) in 1923, he lacked originality and depth.

At the end of the nineteenth century, the spirit of Russian revolutionary endeavors with its concomitant breakdown of the religious traditions and life in the Jewish Ghetto, resulting from the Russian pseudo-European education, robbed *chazzanuth* of the soil from which it had drawn its nourishment, and reduced it to a virtuosity consisting of powerful voices without any depth of feeling or purpose. The *chazzanim* of the last generation in Eastern Europe were mostly without any Jewish training, without religious spirit and sentiment. They conducted themselves as professional artists, as religious actors on the stage of the Synagogue whose only purpose was to captivate the mob. They used cheap means, especially dazzling tricks of coloratura combined with powerful tones, and sought to appeal to the sentiment of the Jew through motives which drew tears. It would seem that East European *chazzanuth* has already reached its end, and belongs to history. After surveying it, we must pay it credit, for—at its best—it was in a sense a new creation and an addition to Synagogue song. Besides the many wonderful and genuinely Jewish tunes that were born of it, its main value and achievement were its bringing back to Jewish song the elements lost in Central European *chazzanuth*—the Jewish-Oriental strain, in European form. Even on the *Missinai* melodies and on the traditional modes it had its influence, casting out German additions of the Middle Ages and replacing them with Eastern material.

The World War caused the destruction of the Jewish center in Eastern Europe. The spiritual life therein was crushed by brutal force, the survivors of the intellectual group mostly dispersed throughout the Old and the New World. All the spiritual values created in that center in the last two or three centuries, including the Synagogue song, were brought to a standstill. Yet here and there some of those musical refugees try to revive the art they carried with them from the East, and transplant it in the new environment.

7. SAMUEL ALMAN, choir leader in the Duke's Place Synagogue in London, is one of these promoters of the Eastern song of the Synagogue. In 1925 he published *Synagogue Compositions* for Sabbaths and weekdays "in the spirit of Nissi Belzer and Bezalel of Odessa," as he states in his preface. He aims "not to furnish his compositions with foreign forms as the Western *chazzanim* did . . . not to corrupt the Jewish tunes, but to set them to modern harmony."

Alman was born in 1877 in Podolia. He studied in the conservatory in Odessa and served in the Russian army band. After the pogrom in his home city, Kishinev, he went to London, where he continued his study in the Royal College. There he took to composing operas, but finally returned to the Synagogue song.

Despite his effort to free himself from the style of the Western *chazzanuth*, he could not escape Sulzer, whose style is deeply impressed in his settings of *Lechoh dodi* (Nos. 1-4), of *Kiddush* (Nos. 17-19), and of the removing and replacing the Torah (Nos. 28-29, 37-38). Even in the *Kedushoh* (No. 142) and *Mi-sheberach* (No. 30) he is decidedly a follower of Sulzer's forms and models. The reason is that these forms of Sulzer had been accepted in the East since the establishment of the *Chor-Schul* in the middle of the nineteenth century, and were gradually adopted also by the orthodox *chazzanim*. Alman, indeed, followed the *chazzanuth* of Nissi and Yeruchom (not Bezalel), but without analyzing which elements were Jewish and which foreign. Especially in his compositions in *Ahavoh-Rabboh* mode, in the Ukrainian "Dorian," and in minor, he follows the folk steps of the two *chazzanim* mentioned above. He utilizes intricate modern harmony with an abundance of augmented and diminished intervals and chromatic steps and plentiful operatic effects, without considering the appropriateness of these elements for Jewish religious music, or whether they are in keeping with the spirit of Jewish music. Since his music is destined for the English Synagogue and for the conservative ritual, he writes a cappella, substituting at times for the organ the sustained humming chords by the choir, a device originally borrowed from the Ukrainian folk song, as pointed out in Chapter IX.

It remains to be seen what impression this Southeastern Orientalized style will make upon the Occidentalized Synagogue in Western Europe in general and upon the Anglo-Saxonized Synagogue in England in particular, where for almost a century Occidental song has been cultivated and a tradition established by SIMON ASHER (1841-1870), L. MOMBACH (1840-1880), and MARCUS HAST (1871-1911). Asher came from Holland, Mombach from Germany, while Hast was born in Praga, near Warsaw. Hast, the most prominent of the three, received a thorough training in Hebrew literature and in Synagogue song as well as in classic music. In London he became Occidentalized, as shown from his voluminous creative works for Synagogue (Chapter XIII). He composed, also, several oratorios on Biblical and post-Biblical subjects: "Bostanai," "Azariah," "The Death of Moses," "The Fall of Jerusalem," in the style of Handel. He showed skill and ability in these works, but no originality, and but slight suggestions of Jewishness. Asher introduced the German-Dutch *chazzanuth*. However, none of his tunes were published. Mombach's music, with the exception of a few selections which are in Jewish traditional modes, is a fusion of the German and English popular song style. It became the standard music of the English Synagogue. A collection of his *Sacred Musical Compositions* was published in 1881 (see Chapter XIII).

CHAPTER XV

The Jewish settlement in the United States is comparatively very young—all in all somewhat more than two centuries. During that period the settlers struggled hard to acclimatize themselves and adapt themselves to the new environment. This adjustment caused them to drop a great part of their inherited conceptions and to abandon manners to which they had been accustomed in their old dwelling places. Such a period of struggle immigrants and new settlers usually have to endure in the first few generations, until they root themselves in the soil of their adopted country. Thus, during the period of acclimatization and adjustment there was no possibility for spiritual creation. Yet, following that period of struggle, forecasts of creations of a new Jewish—we may say American Jewish —type are noticeable. It is from this point of view that the achievements in the field of Synagogue song in America have to be considered. And it is, therefore, not a history of achievements that we can offer here, but rather an insight into its first steps.

Though the first Jewish settlers in the middle of the eighteenth century were of Portuguese stock, nevertheless, as in Europe, that group remained a very small minority, and is now gradually dwindling away. The bulk of the first Jewish settlers in the beginning of the nineteenth century came from Central Europe, especially from the German countries. Medieval prejudice, which weighed heavily upon their shoulders as Jews and which brought about their social and economic handicaps, urged them to leave their homes and emigrate to

316

the land of freedom, a land, then, without tradition. Upon their arrival in this country, though engaged in the driving struggle for their existence, they nevertheless found the need and the time to care for their Judaism. And thus, under the greatest handicaps and with the poorest means at their disposal, they tried to organize Jewish religious institutions as best they could. True, their first attempts were modeled after the traditional forms of the religious institutions in which they had been born and raised in the Old World. Thus, the Portuguese Jews established institutions according to the model of Amsterdam and London, and the German Jews according to the model of their respective homes in different parts of Germany; whereas the Bohemians and the Hungarians copied their home institutions with all their medievalisms and their antiquated religious forms which had no cause for existence in this new environment.

The Synagogue song, too, as all other spiritual values, was transplanted into these homes of worship newly sprung up on American soil. That song, as a tonal expression of the long history and martyrdom of Israel during the Dark Ages and as an exalted expression of its high and eternal ideals, had made a deep impression upon the worshippers when properly rendered by the traditional interpreter, the *chazzan*, if he had devotion and understanding, a sweet voice and the power of presentation. But in the new country there were neither properly prepared spiritual leaders, rabbis, nor well-trained *chazzanim*. The qualified men preferred rather to stay in their old homes than go out into the New World and do pioneer work. The result was that the newly established synagogues in America were led by unqualified leaders, and the song was vulgarized by untrained and unfit *chazzanim*. These circumstances brought about a lower standard of Jewish public worship.[1]

But even with qualified ministers, the traditional service and song were doomed to but a short life, for new conditions soon robbed the old ritual of its appeal. True to the principle that the song is the tonal expression of ideas and sentiments, of modes of life and the combats of life, the Synagogue song had to undergo changes in order to become once more a genuine expression of that group of Jews which was being remolded under new conditions. So too the Jewish congregations could no longer remain mere continuations of those in the Ghettos of the Old World, for the adjustment and acclimatization of the Jews to their new environment caused a change in their attitude toward life and in their sentiments. The long dark period of oppression was over. In this country of freedom and equality they no longer felt themselves inferior, outlawed strangers, a nation within a nation, in a condition of exile, but full citizens of the country which they began to consider their real home. In addition, they prospered economically, so that for the first time after a period of about two thousand years, the Jew began to regard himself a free man and a citizen, having a home.

If socially and economically the change was fundamental and somewhat sudden, the spiritual change grew and developed gradually in the successive generations born and raised in the atmosphere of Anglo-Saxon culture and American ideas and standards; so that a deep psychological change in the second and third generations was noticeable. Consequently, a part of the Jewish inheritance lost its significance. Numerous religious laws which had been considered for many centuries as fundamental to Judaism on account of the conditions in which the Jews lived—as all ordinances connected with the underlying idea of Israel being in exile and its dwelling place in exile being of only a temporary nature, or laws which had the aim of separating the Jewish people from the hostile environment —were no longer of vital value to the free Americanized Jew.

This change manifested itself in various attitudes toward the old religious code.   First of all, to many people who were pious by nature that part of the code became burdensome.   Secondly, other people, iconoclasts by nature, rejected that burden altogether; and some who were indifferent by nature neglected it.   And finally, a fourth group, either not conscious of any change in these new conditions or in spite of that change, insisted that not an iota of the religious laws be changed, that every minute injunction must be observed.   These people did not realize that, while they believed themselves strictly observant, the undercurrent of American life was stronger than they, and that it was against their own will causing a fundamental change in their attitude.   At any rate, the psychological transformation from the second generation on was practically the same in all groups.

And more than in any other cultural sphere that psychological change manifested itself in the Synagogue song, song being a genuine expression of emotions and sentiments.   Fundamental changes could be expected here.   A handful of men at first—three thousand being the entire population of Jews at the time of the War for Independence—their numbers grew to fifty thousand toward the middle of the nineteenth century. Scattered in small groups throughout the vast country of predominant Anglo-Saxon *milieu*, imbued by its culture, educated in its schools, carried along by its train of thought, the heart of the young generation from its infancy on vibrated to the sound of Anglo-Saxon song.   The Germanized Synagogue song which the Ashkenazic immigrants had brought with them to this country, was thus more and more Occidentalized, and the Oriental-Jewish elements gradually deteriorated to a meaningless exotic chant.

Yet, out of the above-mentioned groups some came forward, unwilling to await the tardy process of circumstance, environ-

ment, and accident, anxious to adjust their religion to the new
condition by abandoning elements which had become obsolete
and by reshaping that part which to their mind was fundamental and would meet the needs of the new life—these men
came forward and set about to turn their ideas into deeds.
The first attempt was made in Charleston in 1824 in the organization of a "Reform Society of Israelites" with the aim
"not to overthrow but rebuild, not to destroy but to reform."
As a model, that Society took the Hamburg Reform Temple,
organized but a few years earlier (Chapter XII). But it was
not until 1843 that the entire congregation in Charleston was
drawn over to Reform and accepted the organ and prayers
and hymns in English texts. Many hymns and tunes, as stated
by the editors in the preface of the first prayer-book in English
published in 1830, were taken over from the Christian Church.
Later, several chorales from the Hamburg chorale-book were
translated into English. A native Charlestonian, the poetess
Penina Moise (1797-1880), was the first Jewish woman after
many centuries to contribute toward the Synagogue ritual
(Chapters VI, VIII). She wrote a number of religious hymns
for Jewish schools which have become popular in the Reform
service.

At the same time (1842), a Reform congregation in Baltimore ("Har Sinai") was organized and adopted the Hamburg
Temple Prayer-book for its service. In 1845 the "Emanuel"
congregation in New York was founded. Within the following two decades several Reform congregations throughout the
country were called into being, or Orthodox congregations were
transformed into Reform.[2] The Reform service, with its abbreviated Hebrew texts, its introduction of prayers and hymns
in English, and its use of the organ, caused a great technical
difficulty in the musical rendition of the service. The historical
interpreter of the Synagogue song, the *chazzan*, could not suf-

fice. First, most of the cantors were not trained in modern music and in singing with organ accompaniment. Secondly, the song of the *chazzan* itself, the traditional chant in unrhythmical modes, no longer appealed to the Occidentalized American Reform congregations. And finally, there was no possibility of having a Synagogue choir of Jewish men and boys, since the historical "Singer-guild" (*meshorerim*) did not obtain in the New World, and the American Reform congregations, like those in Germany, preferred a mixed choir, after the model of the Protestant Church. Thus, other—non-Jewish— services had to be utilized to supply music for the Temple. First, the Church organist who was available in all places was engaged in the Temple. Jewish organists did not exist at all then, and if there had existed any, there might have arisen the disturbing old problem of a Jew playing an instrument on Sabbaths and holidays. Since only in rare cases could Jewish singers and especially female singers be obtained, the organists were commissioned to engage the Church choristers for the Temple. But the greatest difficulty was brought about by the music itself. Tunes for hymns were adopted from the Church, or, following the procedure of the Hamburg Temple, composed by Christian musicians in the Church style. Anthems and solos, a new item introduced into the Reform service, according to the model of the Protestant Church, were also taken from the Christian sacred music.

This arrangement still did not solve the problem of music for the prayers proper. In the first years of the existence of the Reform congregation there was no other modernized music for the Synagogue on the market but Sulzer's *Schir Zion*, I, and Naumbourg's *Zemiroth Israel*. Both these works were based on the Orthodox ritual with Hebrew texts only and without organ accompaniment (Chapter XIII); both were published in large unhandy volumes. All these obstacles made it impossible for gentile organists and singers to make extensive use of them. In addition to musical skill, familiarity with the traditional song was essential to adjust it to the new requirements. And in this familiarity the gentile musicians were naturally lacking. The general attitude of the Reform movement was: "Whatever makes us ridiculous before the world as it now is, may be and should be abolished," and, "Whatever tends to the elevation of the divine service, to inspire the heart of the worshipper and to attract him, should be done without any unnecessary delay." [3] Besides, the train of thought and sentiment of the Americanized generation was Occidentalized. It was, therefore, quite natural that the organists set the Jewish prayers to Christian music, without meeting with any objections. Though the transformed congregations retained the *chazzan* for some time, he, instead of influencing the music, had to yield to the new song-style introduced and conducted by the gentile organists, who now became the creators and shapers of the Synagogue song in the Reform Temples. The rabbi again became the only central figure in the Synagogue. As in olden days, but in Occidentalized form, he became both preacher and precentor. This custom was retained in the Sephardic and Portuguese Synagogues throughout the ages.

There were, however, also a few Jewish musicians who contributed to the upbuilding of the modernized and reformed service in the United States, and mention should be made of the following:

JACOB FRAENKEL (1808-1887), the brother of Carl, who was the brother-in-law of Sulzer (his choir-leader and bass), was appointed *chazzan* in the congregation *Rodeph Sholom* in Philadelphia in 1848. He served there for nearly forty years, until his death in 1887. Of Sulzer's school there was also ALOIS KAISER (born in Hungary in 1840 and died in 1908), who occupied the position of *chazzan* in *Ohev-Sholom*,

Baltimore, from 1866 to 1908. SAMUEL WELSH, born in Prague in 1835, became *chazzan* in *Ahavath Chesed*, New York, in 1865, but in 1880 he returned to Prague, where he died in 1901. There was also MORRIZ GOLDSTEIN, born in Hungary in 1840. His father was the well-known *chazzan* Shmelke, a "singer" with Dovidl Brod (Chapter XIV), who died young in 1849, leaving behind ten little children. The oldest boy, Joseph, who was eleven at his father's death, became the successor to his father. Later he gained fame as *chazzan* in Vienna from 1858 to 1899. Morriz Goldstein sang under Sulzer and studied music in Vienna. In 1868 he came to New York to accept the position as cantor in the Norko Synagogue. In 1881 he was appointed cantor in the *Benei Israel* Temple in Cincinnati, which position he held until his death in 1906.

The last three of these *chazzanim*, realizing the need of new music for the American Synagogue, compiled a collection of songs for choir and solo with organ accompaniment, for prayers and Psalms in Hebrew, English, and German. This collection, named *Zimrath Yah*, was published (New York, 1871-1886) in four volumes, for Sabbath, the festivals, and other occasions. The music was written partly by the three editors and partly by gentile musicians, or was adapted from different sources. The style is intricate, of operatic character, though at times the intention to adopt the oratorio style is apparent. A striving after virtuosity and effect runs through the organ accompaniment. German in melody and character, the collection contains but few traditional elements. M. Goldstein independently compiled "services" for the Sabbath, the three festivals, and the High Holidays in three volumes (1895), arranged according to the Union Prayer-book. He borrowed compositions from Sulzer, Löwenstamm, Naumbourg, and others, without mentioning their names. Likewise he inserted several items by the French musician Amres and others. His music lacks originality and Jewishness, and is in part too theatrical. He also published a collection of hymns, *Kol Zimra*, with English texts, in 1885.

Of Kaiser's activities, we mention his editing for the Conference of American Rabbis the music of the *Union Hymnal* which was published in 1897. To this collection, consisting of about one hundred forty-nine items, he contributed about forty tunes. Sixteen tunes of this collection are marked "traditional," though some of them (Nos. 110, 118) are not traditional at all. The remainder are modernized to the extent of being robbed of their original flavor. With the exception of two tunes by Sulzer, two by Lewandowski, and one by Kirschner, the bulk of the tunes (C. 88) are adaptations from German, English, and French Christian composers. Of far greater value is Kaiser's cooperation in *A Collection of the Principal Melodies of the Synagogue from the Earliest to the Present*, which he, together with William Sparger (cantor of Temple Emanuel, New York), compiled as a "Souvenir of the Jewish Women's Congress held under the auspices of the World's Parliament of Religions," Chicago, 1893. In their preface the compilers gave a survey of Jewish Song, summarizing the state of research done until that date. They conclude with a warm appeal "to preserve carefully its inherited characteristics and originality, and plant it again in the Synagogue and home of our people in the only form in which this can be achieved now, namely, *in the form of hymns*." Probably the compilers were convinced that the unrhythmical modal form in Jewish Song was a matter of the past, and had no longer any place in the Occidentalized Synagogue.—The volume has two parts. Part I contains fifty traditional melodies with accompaniment and English texts; Part II has sixteen modern compositions partly based upon traditional themes and partly original compositions. The selection of traditional tunes is well chosen, and some of the original compositions are of significance.

In both collections there is a noticeable tendency to reduce the minor melody to a minimum and to emphasize the major note, the German melodic line.

SIGMUND SCHLESINGER is the only Jewish musician whose music gained wide popularity in the Reform Synagogue in America. He was born in Uhlen (Württemberg), Germany, on March 1, 1835, and received his musical education in Munich. In 1860 he came to America and settled in Mobile, Alabama, in 1863, where he served as organist and choir-leader of congregation *Shaarei Shomayim* for forty years. He died April 14, 1906. "His funeral received the nature of a public demonstration in Mobile." [4] Schlesinger was one of the first to recognize the need of a musical setting for the Union Prayerbook. He composed six complete services: three for Sabbath evening and morning, one for the three festivals and two for the High Holidays.

Schlesinger's popularity, especially with the non-Jewish choirs and organists of the Reform temples, lies in the fact that his music is entirely Occidental. He omitted all Oriental and medieval Jewish characteristics from the Synagogue Song, such as the modal chant, the minor note. From the treasury of traditional tunes he left only two (*Ovos* and *Kol Nidré*) for the High Holidays, and he utilized a few motives for the same occasion. His is the German Protestant style plus operatic flavor. He also adapted several tunes from the Italian opera, the sources of which he sometimes mentions. Whenever he wishes a minor setting, he turns to the eighteenth-century Italian Opera or Church music. His melody is German, vigorous, usually major with dramatic strength, but at times sentimental—Italian. His harmony is simple, frequently shallow; his accompaniment is rather a support for the voices, often without individuality or depth.

Quite different is the music of EDWARD STARK (1863-1918). His father, Joseph Stark, was *chazzan* in Hohenems and Ichenhausen, and later in New York. From his father, Edward Stark inherited the understanding and knowledge of *chazzanuth* in Sulzer's style. He was gifted with considerable creative talent, with power and depth of Jewish expression. In 1893 he became cantor of Temple Emanuel in San Francisco, where he served for about twenty years. He composed services for Friday evening, one for Sabbath morning, one for New Year, and one for the Day of Atonement (1909-1913, New York), and arranged them according to the Union Prayer-book.

His music shows a strong influence of the classic oratorio. He likewise acquired the style of modern harmonization and organ accompaniment. His music for Sabbath contains very few Jewish elements, but his services for the High Holidays are provided with cantor solos in the old modal form and choruses based upon traditional themes. He also provided organ pre- and interludes, utilizing traditional motives. As a whole, his High Holiday service shows unity of style and spirit, in addition to a considerable amount of Jewish-Oriental flavor. Since his services contain a large number of cantor solos with choir, the cantor or, at least, a soloist to assume the cantor part becomes indispensable. This requirement often presents an impediment in rendering Stark's music in temples which employ a quartet only. A still greater difficulty in using Stark's music lies in the lack of singers capable of rendering the cantor parts with understanding. In Stark's music for the Memorial service we again perceive the depth of the Jewish soul, with its Semitic sensitiveness, with its Jewish clinging to life and to faith. His chief merit consists in reintroducing traditional Jewish musical elements into the Reform Synagogue.

Stark arranged the *Kol Nidré* for a small orchestra; and in some of the selections of his service he uses violin, cello, cornet, trombone, or harp obbligatos, with skill.

FRANZ WALD, born in Hungary, sang bass in the choir of Zion Temple in Chicago, and became organist in Bethel congregation. In 1908 he published a Sabbath evening service, and compiled a selection of traditional songs for the High Holidays with (poor) organ accompaniment (in MS.).

M. GRAUMANN, cantor of the West End Synagogue, New York, composed a Friday evening service, in Sulzer's style, with a few genuine Jewish cantor solos in the *Mogen-ovos* mode with organ accompaniment.

Apart from these Jewish musicians, a great number of Christians, as a rule organists, composed services for the Reform temples in America, mostly for the Sabbath. Out of the vast publications we furnish here a list of the works which became known.

1. M. SPICKER and W. SPARGER: Sabbath evening and morning, New York, G. Schirmer, 1901. (With contributions by H. Zoelner, W. Mackfarlane, Ottenhofer, Frank van-der-Stucken. *Seu Sheorim* adapted from Gounod's *Faust*.)

2. FRED E. KITZINGER, organist in Judah Turo Temple in New Orleans. He published four volumes *Shiré Yehuda* for choir with organ accompaniment according to the old and the new ritual: Vol. I, Sabbath evening and morning, 1888; Vol. II, 1891; Vol. III, Sabbath evening and morning for a small choir; Vol. IV he "dedicated to the promoter and lover of song," Dr. I. M. Wise, 1899.

3. FRANK T. FISK, organist in Kansas City. He published a Sabbath evening service in 1899.

4. JAMES H. ROGERS, organist in Euclid Temple, Cleve-

land, published a Sabbath evening and morning service, G. Schirmer, New York, 1912. Rogers uses Jewish traditional tunes as themes for some items; he uses the tune of *Berosh Hashonoh* of the High Holidays for *Veshomru,* and employs the Traditional High Holiday *Adon Olam* tune.

5. ABRAM RAY TYLOR, organist in Detroit in Temple Beth-El, published a Sabbath morning service, Bloch, New York, 1914.

6. W. G. OWST, organist in Baltimore, published a Sabbath morning service, Oliver Ditson Co., Boston.

7. A. J. DAVIS, organist in Temple Emanuel, New York, published a Sabbath evening service, Oliver Ditson Co., Boston, 1898.

8. W. H. NEIDLINGER, organist in Chicago, published a Sabbath evening service, Oliver Ditson Co., Boston.

9. CARL GRIMM, organist in the Reading Road Temple, later Plum Street Temple, Cincinnati, published a Sabbath morning service, Church Co., Cincinnati, 1916.

10. HOWARD THATCHER, organist in the *Ohev Sholom* Temple, Baltimore, published a Sabbath morning service, Bloch, New York, 1911; Sabbath evening, ibid., 1913.

11. EDMOND SERENO ENDEL, organist Eoff Street Temple, Wheeling: *Sabbath Morning,* "Short and of moderate difficulty," Bloch, New York, 1908.

12. T. L. KREBS: *Sabbath Evening,* Bloch, New York, 1906.

13. ARTHUR FOOT, *Ozi vesimrath Yah,* Boston, 1902.

14. MARX HELFERE, *Synagogue Songs,* New York, 1897.

15. ARTHUR DUNHAM, organist "Sinai Temple," Chicago, published a *Sunday Service,* Chicago.

In the last few years new attempts have been made in the field of song for the Reform Temple with the aim of introducing ultra-modern harmony and style into the Synagogue.

We mention here two services composed by American Jews. The one is of special interest for the mere fact that this is the first attempt made by a Jewess to write music for the Synagogue.

Rosalie Hausman: *Sabbath Morning Service,* Bloch, New York, 1924; and

Heniot Levy, composer in Chicago: *Synagogue Hymns and Responses for Sabbath Evening and Morning,* Bloch, New York, 1926.

Hymnals

The singing of hymns in English (at first also in German) became an integral part of the Reform service in America. Hence, several collections of hymns were compiled, partly translated from the German *Hamburg Songbook,* partly original compositions by Jewish and Christian writers. But Hebrew poems of the medieval Synagogal *piyyut* were also paraphrased in English hymn forms. The musical settings, however, were generally done by Christian musicians or were adopted from German and English hymnal music. The first successful composer of hymns was the non-Jewish organist of Zion Temple, Chicago, Otto Lob. In 1876 he published his *Israelitische Tempel-Gesänge,* consisting of forty hymns for the Sabbath and Holidays. Many of his hymns became popular in the Reform Temples and in the religious schools. Rev. Simon Hecht, Evansville, Indiana, compiled a collection of *Jewish Hymns for Sabbath Schools and Families* in 1878. This hymnal contains forty-three hymns in English and nine in German. The music is partly arranged for one voice, partly for two and three voices. Twelve tunes are original compositions of S. Hecht, while the remainder were partly composed especially for that songster by local musicians in Evansville (M. Z. Tinker, P. Esser, Chr. Mathias, C. C.

Genung), partly adapted from the German classic music of
Mozart, Gluck, Mendelssohn. The two traditional tunes for
Chanukah and *Pesach* are likewise given.

The most popular hymnal thus far was compiled by RABBI
ISAAC S. MOSES of the Central Synagogue, New York (Posen,
1847—New York, 1926), in 1894. In 1920 the fourteenth
enlarged edition was put out. In addition to about two hundred fifty hymns in English, four Hebrew hymns are given
(*Adon Olam, Yigdal, En Kelohenu,* and *El Nora*). There
are likewise responses in Hebrew and English for Sabbath's
and High Holiday's services for School and small congregations as well as some solos and traditional tunes with accompaniment. There are furthermore seven services for children, a
Sabbath service for the home, a Flower service, a National
service, a Harvest service, and a *Chanukah* and *Purim* service.
The hymns are classified as: Songs of Praise and Prayer, Songs
of the Sabbath Day, the Word of God, Festivals and Seasons,
Patriotic Songs, and Songs of Duty. In the preface to his
sixth edition the editor makes the following statement: "The
improvement of this book will be found not only in the larger
number of hymns but chiefly in its 'Jewishness.' It is emi-
nently proper that hymn-books intended for Jewish worship
should be Jewish in character, and that the hymns of prayer
should be the products of Jewish authors. An exception to
this rule may be made to hymns that are versifications of
Psalms or of other portions of the Hebrew Bible. A collection of fine poems and melodies culled from the hymnals of
the different Churches has no place in the Synagogue. Has
the Jewish genius produced nothing of value that we must
needs go begging at the doors of every denomination?" The
editor was aware of the value of Jewish music for Jewish education and service, and he, therefore, did not fail to insert
this element. "Many traditional melodies," says he, "have

been utilized for hymn purposes for the first time." In this work Theodor Guinsburg, for over forty years cantor in the same temple (1844, Suvalk, Poland—1923, New York), contributed a considerable number of hymns and solos based upon traditional tunes. Likewise, Gideon Froelich, organist in that temple, furnished the Hymnal with an abundant number of tunes. But according to I. S. Moses "he (Froelich) has caught the spirit of Jewish melody, and the character of Jewish worship," though his tunes do not certify that statement, for they have the regular German melodic line. The editor, likewise, inserted original compositions by P. C. Lutkin, A. J. Davis, S. Sabel, as well as many tunes adapted from Mozart, Schumann, Beethoven, Mendelssohn, Rossini, Spohr, H. W. Hawkes, Weber, Schubert, etc. He also borrowed several hymns from Otto Lob's Hymnal. The general impression of the music is decidedly German, though a few Jewish modes and tunes were inserted.

Mention should be here made of a Hymn for Confirmation, No. 101, composed by a Jewess, Mrs. S. E. Munn, of Newark, New Jersey. The text was written by Felix Adler, the founder of the Ethical Society in New York. This song became very popular in the Reform Synagogue.

HENRY GIDEON, the Jewish organist in Temple Israel, Boston, published in cooperation with L. WEINSTEIN (a *chazzan*) a hymnal for modern congregations, both Reform and Conservative (Bloch, New York, 1919). The compiler follows the usual Church hymn style and typical Church hymns such as No. 30 are inserted. A considerable selection of traditional tunes was added. Furthermore, various compositions in simplified form by Sulzer and Naumbourg, etc., are given, thus furnishing musical settings, in part at least, for the services of Sabbaths and the festivals.

A new and enlarged edition of the *Union Hymnal*, treated

above, was published in 1914. It was edited by a committee
of rabbis, under the chairmanship of Rabbi Harry H. Mayer,
Kansas City. The material of the first edition was retained
only in part. Many new hymns were added, bringing the total
to 226 numbers. Eleven of these numbers cover two tunes:
"first" and "second." On the other hand about 12 tunes are
repeated. The authors of the new texts are Jews and gentiles.
About 140 tunes are of non-Jewish origin—several of them
adopted from Church Hymnals. Some melodies are popular
in all Churches, such as No. 97, which was first introduced
into the Reform Temple by Jacobson (Chapter XII). Forty
tunes are marked "traditional," of which only 16 really are so
(Nos. 1, 8, 41, 55, 68, 100, 103, 136, 138, 162, 164, 171,
178, 186, 189, 217), the others being unknown tunes of recent
date and have German features. Four of the 16 tunes (Nos.
100, 103, 138 and 186) are taken from the Jewish-Portuguese
song, the rest are of Ashkenazic-German origin. Some of these
melodies, as given in the Hymnal, are extremely modernized
and partly corrupted, such as No. 68, the old form of which
is given in *Baal-Tefillah*, No. 1321, 1; No. 171, which is to
be found in table XXII, 7; No. 178, see table XXV, 4;
No. 162, for the original form of which see *Baal-Tefillah*, No.
1306; No. 217, compare *Baal-Tefillah*, No. 1467. The
Hymnal contains over 50 tunes by Jewish composers, of which
two have Jewish flavor (Nos. 7 and 77). No. 77, the *Yigdal*-
tune by "Leoni," is given in the form as it occurs in the Christian Hymnals (Chapter XI), not in its JEWISH version (see
table XXVII, 6; L. Mombach's work cited in Chapter XIII,
p. 76). Two hundred and fourteen tunes are in major and 12
in minor. In addition there are 22 Hebrew hymns and responses (No. 227-248), five children's services for week-days,
one for Sabbath (without music), one for the Three Festivals,
which utilizes none of the traditional tunes of these holidays,

and one for Chanukah and Purim. The music supplied in the
"Responses" and "Services" is restricted to such texts as
Borchu, Shema, Mi chomochoh, Kedushoh, which since the
eighteenth century have been those habitually used for responses in the German Synagogue. Neither traditional modes
nor motives of Jewish folk song have been utilized. The style
of the hymns is that of the Protestant Hymn, both in its melodic line and in its harmonization in four-part choruses. This
procedure adopted also by the other Hymnals is detrimental
for congregational unison singing as well as for an appropriate
instrumental accompaniment. It leaves a dull and choppy
impression.

Almost all the congregations founded by Jewish settlers of
Germany and Bohemia became Reform; whereas the Hungarian Jews and, especially, the great influx of Polish and Russian Jews in the last two decades of the nineteenth century
increased the number of Orthodox congregations. "However,
even many of these immigrants, often living in the country
for some time, affiliate themselves with Reform congregations.
The free spirit of American institutions is impatient of the re-
straints of rabbinical legislation as embodied in the *Shulchan
Aruch.* The descendants of the immigrants, even in the first
generation, are so affected by the free school, the free state, and
the free atmosphere in which they live and move and have
their being that they can impossibly entertain the religious views
of their Orthodox forebearers. Frequently, they swing to the
opposite extreme and become outspokenly irreligious and
atheistic." [5] This statement of over twenty years ago holds
true to the present day. Many of the so-called Orthodox congregations are so by name or in theory only, for in practical
life very few of the members are strict observers of the Orthodox teachings and laws. The observance of Orthodoxy is for

the most part restricted to the Synagogal service only, to the retaining of its traditional customs and ritual. Traditional music is retained; likewise the *chazzan* with the *meshorerim* in the old primitive style of bass and "singer" or in a modernized form of men and boys in four-part singing, as introduced by Sulzer and practiced in Eastern Europe. The *chazzan* is still the leader in the service, the central figure of the Synagogue and his *chazzanuth;* his musical art constitutes the chief purpose and attraction. As a rule, the existence and prosperity of an Orthodox synagogue depends upon the musical ability of the *chazzan* and upon his vocal artistry.

Frequently there are *chazzanim* with fine vocal ability and with marvelous *chazzanic* talent. They were all born and trained in Eastern Europe, in the "schools" of the prominent *chazzanim* of whom an account is given in Chapter XIV. Thus far no *chazzan* of note is American born. Moreover, the musically gifted sons of immigrant *chazzanim* choose to enter a secular musical career.

Several *chazzanim* gained a reputation of popularity, such as JOSEPH ROSENBLATT (born 1880 in Bielozerkov, Southern Russia), MORDECAI HERSHMAN (1886 (?) in Volhynia), ZAVEL KVARTIN (born 1874 in a village in the government Cherson), and others. These gained their reputation and popularity not only because of their achievements in the Synagogue, but also because of their vocal performances in the concert house, and notably because of their phonograph records. By the latter means, they have popularized (and at times also vulgarized) the Synagogue song. Their strength lies in their rendition of the Synagogue modes in unrhythmical improvised form, with accompaniment likewise improvised, on piano or string-instrument. With respect to improvisation, these Orthodox *chazzanim* are in this country the only protagonists of the traditional Jewish-Oriental song. However, none of them have thus far created music of any originality. They continue to sing in the style of the Eastern European *chazzanuth*, and some of them, in order to attract the public, do not hesitate to sing arias of operas and musical selections of dubious sources set to prayers, as was customary among the *chazzanim* in the seventeenth and eighteenth centuries.

Apart from the groups thus far treated, there was organized about fifty years ago a third group, called "Conservative." Realizing, on the one hand, the impossibility of the retention of the Orthodox form of Judaism, but on the other hand, considering sudden fundamental changes dangerous, this group chose a slow and gradual process of reform. However, no platform nor unity of policy in achieving this aim has been observed. The Conservative congregations differ in their reforms. Some consider the organ, mixed choir, English prayers and sermon, and an abbreviated ritual within the frame of Conservatism; others, however, restrict their reforms to the English sermon and to the abolition of some medieval poems. Indeed, all Conservative congregations have thus far retained Hebrew prayers containing the idea of Resurrection, of the restoration of the Temple with its sacrificial cult in Jerusalem, and of a personal Messiah. Almost all the Conservative congregations insist, likewise, upon covering the head during worship and upon the retention of the *chazzan*. The music in the Conservative Synagogue is based on Sulzer's principle (Chapter XIII), though some *chazzanim* still use Eastern European *chazzanuth*, while others do not hesitate to employ arias and selections from operas as well as items from the Reform music. No original features were thus far brought forth in the Synagogue music by this group.

Of the few attempts made by musicians belonging to this group we cite:

SOLOMON BAUM, Friday evening and Sabbath morning service for cantor and choir with organ accompaniment, in which the *Mogen-ovos* and *Ahavoh-Rabboh* modes are employed for choral numbers.

M. HALPERN, *Z'miroth Ut'filoth Yisroel*, a Synagogal Hymnal for Sabbath and Festivals, The Boston Music Co., 1915, consisting of cantor solos and choruses (with exception of Nos. 106, 110, 121, 123, 129, 130) without accompaniment. Several items are in the traditional modes and tunes. Many cantor solos have the unrhythmical modal form with embellishments. The material is partly Halpern's own compositions based on traditional modes, partly imitations of and adoptions from prominent Synagogue composers. The term "traditional" he uses so broadly as to cover even tunes which are apparently his own compositions. His collection supplies songs for the services of all Jewish festivals. In the section of hymns and songs the compiler threw together Christian hymns, such as "Oh, Paradise," with Jewish folk-songs, such as *Cheder Koton* (—*Afn Pripitshok*).

LOUIS M. ISAACS and MATHILDE S. SCHECHTER edited a *Hebrew Hymnal for School and Home* (—*Kol Rinnah*) London, 1910, containing 24 numbers arranged for four-part choir, in Hebrew with English translation. The material taken from Sulzer, Naumbourg, Lewandowski, Mombach and *Adon Olom* of Salomon Rossi (Chapter X), as well as from *The Voice of Prayer and Praise* (Chapter XIII), is often badly corrupted.

ISRAEL and SAMUEL E. GOLDFARB are engaged in compiling songsters for the Hebrew Schools in America. The largest of their compilations is the *Jewish Songster* (*Hamnaggen*), Brooklyn, 1925. It contains religious and secular songs for Sabbaths, the festivals and for various occasions. The musical material is partly their own, partly adopted from popular folk tunes, or from Jewish composers. The texts are mostly in Hebrew, and some in Yiddish and English.

CHAPTER XVI

COLLECTIONS OF AND LITERATURE ON SYNAGOGUE SONG.

I. Collections

The compositions for the Synagogue service of the eighteenth and nineteenth centuries were mostly the creations of individual Jewish musicians, even when the works were constructed out of traditional material. Hence the ambition of the musicians to publish their products or, at least, to write them down! The effort to preserve works of unknown men, or merely traditional tunes, is not early met with. Indeed, we are informed that at the end of the sixteenth century the *chazzan* Abraham Sagri in Casale Monferrato in Italy prepared a collection of traditional tunes for Bible, prayers, and *piyyutim,* according to the Ashkenazic ritual for his pupil Jacob Finzi;[1] but since only one page—that of the Psalm mode—remained of his manuscript, we cannot judge the nature of that collection; we cannot know whether it was of strictly traditional tunes throughout, or whether it was a mixture of his own compositions and reworked tradition (Chapter X). In the manuscripts of Ahron Beer and of the Bass Joseph Goldstein, at the end of the eighteenth century (Chapter XI), there are some traditional tunes which seem to be genuine, that is, without individual modifications. But from among all of his recorded compositions, these numbers are few. The first collection known which can be considered an objective copy of traditional tunes without personal additions is that of the Southern German *chazzanuth* which S. Naumbourg (Chapter XIII) wrote down according to the singing of L. Sänger (1781-1843), Cantor in Munich, in 1839-40. For

a long time no stress was laid upon the exactness of traditional
tunes. It was counted permissible for every singer and *chazzan*
to modify the traditional tunes in innumerable variations according to the taste and voice of each, as we so clearly see in
all the published and unpublished works of the eighteenth and
nineteenth centuries. While in the beginning, the Reform
Movement regarded tradition as a valueless old burden from
which it sought to release itself, Moderate Reform, little by
little, came to exhibit the same degree of enthusiasm in retaining the old traditional tunes and chants as it had previously
shown eagerness to forget them, for it is the nature of men to
begin appreciating things after they are removed from them.
Already in the first years of the appearance of the *Allgemeine
Zeitung des Judenthums* (published from the year 1837) traditional tunes were occasionally printed. An earnest attempt at
collection was made by a magazine called *Liturgische Zeitschrift*, which was devoted to liturgy and Synagogue song,
started by the teacher and cantor HERMANN EHRLICH in the
fifties of the nineteenth century in Berkach, Meiningen, and
continued for about four years. In that magazine there was
gathered a considerable number of traditional tunes and of
their different variations. Prior to that attempt, a collection of
Hebrew tunes had been published (London 1815) by I.
NATHAN 1792-1864, and JOHN BRAHAM, 1774-1856, the son
of Abraham Singer (Chapter XI), who was the most celebrated
tenor in England in his time. The compilers harmonized and
arranged the tunes for choir, and provided piano accompaniment. But the tunes, with the exception of those for *Chanukah*
and *Pesach*, were not traditional at all. They were melodies
created or adopted by various *chazzanim*. Of greater value is a
collection of Portuguese tunes published by DE SOLA and
AGUILAR in London, 1857. These are mostly adopted tunes
of Dutch origin from the seventeenth and eighteenth centuries,

only less than half of them being traceable back to Spain.² Of still greater value than the music of the last-named book is its introduction of which we shall speak later.

In 1868 a collection of Southern German traditional tunes was published by Katz and Talbott.³ This volume was really the first of its type, an objective rendition of traditional tunes as they lived in the Synagogue from the Middle Ages on; and it may be considered a trustworthy source-book of the Synagogue song in Southern Germany, even though some numbers invite suspicion as being the compositions of individuals. In 1871, the *chazzan* MORITZ DEUTSCH published in Breslau his *Vorbeterschule,* a collection of traditional chants, modes, and solo tunes for the entire cycle of the year, as a guide and reference book for young *chazzanim*. That collection is based upon the Eastern German tradition, which embraces Moravia, Austria, Bohemia, and Silesia. Deutsch's purpose was to offer a refined form of the traditional tunes of the Synagogue. Hence, he did not care always to give the tradition in its originality where it failed to satisfy modern European taste. As he pointed out in his introduction to the collection, he did not regard the Synagogue song as original. Deutsch's volume does not provide traditional tunes for week day services.

The greatest and most complete collection is that published in 1877 by ABRAHAM BAER, *chazzan* in Gothenburg, Sweden; it is called the *Baal Tefillah.* Baer utilized not only the above-mentioned collections but also the works of Sulzer, Weintraub, Naumbourg, and Lewandowski, as well as the already mentioned collections of De Sola-Aguilar and Katz-Talbott. He, too, sought to prepare a guide for young *chazzanim;* but he likewise provided the simple reader in small congregations with every possible tune for all those texts of the prayer-book for the entire year, which were customarily sung. It was not his aim to give strictly traditional tunes, but rather to offer a great number of variations for every text, be the tunes modern or traditional compositions. He also gave the EASTERN EUROPEAN (called by him POLISH) rite and the German rite, as well as the OLD TRADITION and the NEW STYLE. He selected some Portuguese tunes [4] and inserted them into his collection. The volume contains about fourteen hundred numbers, and for this quantity alone it is very remarkable. Yet, for historic investigation, Baer's collection is of minor value, because he never indicates what is real tradition and what is innovation. From the practical point of view, his book filled a great need. It became so popular that in the course of twenty-five years it reached its fourth edition.

Under the influence of Baer, many other collections were published which were arranged according to his method. They are either of Southern Germany or Austria or even Eastern Europe. Especially noteworthy is *Schir Lisch'laumau* by ARON FRIEDMANN, in that it gives the scale of the mode in which the traditional numbers are written. He presents the Lithuanian tradition with German modifications.

Of far more scientific value, however, than the just-mentioned works are two collections which present with certainty their tradition and without individual additions. The one is *Zemiroth Yisrael, Chants Hébraïques*, Marseilles 1885, J. and M. CREMIEU containing the traditional tunes of the entire year of the Southern French Jews, the so-called *Minhag Carpentras* (Chapters VII, XIII).[5] These Jews were partly of those descended from the ancient communities in Provence who remained in France after the expulsion of 1394 because they were protected by the Pope in Avignon, and only a few of them were of the offspring of the refugees from Spain in 1492 and 1496.[6] They did not mingle with German Jews; they even strongly opposed extending full rights to the German Jews in Paris in 1791-1810.[7] Their traditional tunes differ to a great extent from those of all other Jewish communities. They contain elements of original Jewish modes intermingled with French chants of the Middle Ages.[8] Peculiarly enough, these Jews accepted the German Ashkenazic *Pessach* tune of *Addir Hu* (o.c., p. 197). The collection contains three compositions for four-part choir, three solos, and one piece in three parts— all with the accompaniment of organ, harp, and flute. The other collection contains traditional tunes of the Italian Jews or rather of the Italianized *Spanish* Jews, as explained in the preface by the author, the violinist and composer, FEDERICO CONSOLO (Chapter XIII), who says that he gathered the tunes in Leghorn, where the Spanish tradition was best retained. He himself claims to be a descendant of those Spanish refugees, and signs himself "Yehiel Nahmani Sefardi." His collection, called *Sefer Shire Yisrael, Libro de Canti D'Israele,* printed in Firenze, 1891, gives all traditional tunes as well as the beginnings of chants and modes. Most of them are similar to the Portuguese tunes in Europe and the Sephardic tunes in the Orient, and offer a valid proof of the antiquity of the song of the Spanish Jews who, though scattered over both hemispheres for more than four centuries, yet preserved the traditional tunes as they had them while still living in Spain. In a separate volume, Consolo published traditional tunes arranged either in four parts or in solo, with piano or organ accompaniment.

In the prayer-book "Order of Service according to the custom of the Spanish and Portuguese Jews of London," *Shaar Hashamayim,* edited by M. Gaster, London, 1904 (five volumes), the traditional tunes for the entire cycle of the year were added by JESSURUM, choir leader at the Portuguese Synagogue in London. With slight variations, several of these are the same tunes as those in the collection of De Sola and Aguilar. But Jessurum rendered a valuable service in giving psalms, prayers, and poems in their entirety as rendered responsively in the service by reader, choir, and congregation. Through this presentation, we gain a clear idea of the character of these ancient modes.

Of similar character is the publication of *M. A. de Villers* (published in Paris, 1872), *Recueil des chants trad. et liturgique composent les offices hébraïques du rite oriental.*

Concerning the musical illustrations in the *Jewish Encyclopedia*, we must say that, despite the blunders and many fallacies, the work must be highly regarded as a laudible first attempt. On the one hand, the editors recognized the existence of and gave due space to traditional song. On the other hand, the author, though handicapped by his lack of information and material, succeeded in many articles in giving some valuable data.

There are the following collections of the Eastern European tradition: *Hammithpallel* by A. A. NEZWIZSHKI, who was cantor in Ruzshani in the government of Grodno. This collection is printed in MS. form by lithography, Wilna, 1903. It contains recitatives and traditional modes for the High Holidays, etc.

M. WODAK follows the same method in his collection *Ham'natzeach—Schule des isr. Cantors, praktische und bewährte Methode zur gründlichen Erlernung aller Sing- und Vortragsweisen der gesammten Synagogen-liturgie mit besonderer Berücksichtigung des Recitativ . . . etc.*, Vienna, 1901. He presents the Eastern European, especially, the Hungarian tradition.

An ambitious attempt to offer something "scientific" was that of ABRAHAM EISENSTADT, week-day cantor in Berlin, who published a collection called *alt-israelitische Gesänge I and II* in Berlin, 1897. In his preface he claims that this material was traditional in his family for many generations, and that many members of his family functioned as *chazzanim* in different cities in Poland. He further claims that his ancestors, coming from Jerusalem, settled in Worms before the destruction of the Second Temple. He makes the statement that the Jews settled on the banks of the Volga in the eighth century; and, establishing there a Jewish empire called Chazzarian Kingdom, they maintained in it their traditional song which subsequently spread throughout Eastern Europe. From this direct line his progenitors received the tradition. Eisenstadt succeeded in convincing of his contention a scholar like Oskar Fleischer and a musician like Joseph Joachim, both of whom recommended his collection. In spite of these important patrons, his material is nothing but a compilation of low-class *chazzanic* improvisation of the type current among the *chazzanim* in the small Lithuanian villages. The book is important only as a colossal monument to ignorance.

The writer of the present book published, in Leipzig in 1914, the first volume of his *Thesaurus of Hebrew-Oriental Melodies* (German edition: *Hebraisch-Orientalischer Melodienschatz;* Hebrew edition: *Otzar Neginoth Yisrael*) entitled *Songs of the Yemenite Jews (Gesänge der jemenitischen Juden)*. It contains a collection of the traditional songs of the Yemenite Jews, with an introduction explaining the characteristics of the music; and it presents comparisons with the traditional song of other Jewish communities of the Diaspora. With several additions, the same volume was published in Berlin in 1923 in Hebrew, and it was translated into English in 1925 (Benjamin Harz Verlag, Berlin). Volume two, *Songs of the Babylonian Jews (Gesänge der babylonischen Juden)*, was published in Hebrew, German, and English in 1922-1923. Volume three, *Songs of the Persian, Bokharian, and Daghestan Jews (Gesänge der persischen, bucharischen und daghestanischen Juden)*, was published in 1922 in Hebrew and German. Volume four, *Songs of the Oriental Sephardim* (*Gesänge orientalischen Sefardim*), was published in Hebrew and German in 1923. The Hebrew edition has more folkloristic material, while the volumes in German and English present more musical research studies. Volume five, *Songs of the Moroccan Jews* (Hebrew edition), was published in 1928, and volume six, *Songs of the Ashkenazim* (German edition), is still in press. The entire collection is compiled by the method of recording traditional tunes phonographically, transcribing the music from the plates, comparing the phonographical records with the performance by various people of one and the same tune, in order to ascertain those characteristics of each tune common to all traditions. A synopsis of this work was published by the Vienna Academy of Sciences in 1917 in its proceedings, volume 171: *Phonographierte Gesänge und Aussprachsproben des Hebräischen der jemenitischen, persischen und syrischen Juden.*

From the Christian side, attempts were made to collect and transcribe Synagogal songs: e.g., VILLOTEAU in *Dissertation sur la musique des ancien Egyptians, in Description del "Egypt,"* Vol. I, p. 337 ff.; DOM J. PARISOT in *Rapport sur une Mission scientifique en Turquie D'Asie*, Paris, 1899, p. 245, who collected in Jerusalem three Ashkenazic tunes: one for *Kaddish* for *Musaph* on the High Holidays, one for *Hammelech*, and a third for a *Kinoh* (Lamentation), the last named being a composition of Sender, cantor in Minsk (Chapter XIV). A fourth tune is for the hymn *Bar Yochay* which is used as a dancing song at the celebration for "Simeon the Righteous" on the thirty-third day of the *Omer*, and this tune is of Turkish origin. It is quite evident that these four tunes do not represent Jewish traditional song; and it may be readily understood why Dom Parisot himself did not consider them representative. His ignorance of Jewish ritual and tradition deprived him of the means of selecting and collecting the genuine material.

Aside from the published works thus far named, several collections remained in manuscript form, such as the above-mentioned Naumbourg-Sänger volume, and that work of Maier Kohn which, although announced in his publication of 1839, was really finished thirty years later (1870). The latter contains Southern German *chazzanuth* with several insertions of modern tunes (Chapter XIII). A collection which follows Baer's *Baal Tefillah* in giving GERMAN and POLISH traditions is that of ISAAK LACHMANN, *Avodath Yisrael*, a small part (weekdays' service) of which was published in 1899. Lachmann tries to give tradition as truly as possible, according to his knowledge of it. Although a man of information, he blindly regarded the Eastern European tradition of the environs of Dubno, where he was born, and the Southern German tradition of the neighborhood of Hürben-Bavaria, where he spent half of his life, as the only standards.[9]

We see that a number of the collections mentioned above cannot, from the scientific point of view, be considered authentic sources for the traditional song. It was this fact that induced EDUARD BIRNBAUM to start collecting material free of all emendations and personal modifications. And, indeed, he succeeded in amassing a remarkable quantity, especially of German and Eastern European traditional songs. He was the first among the workers in the field of Synagogue song who perceived the necessity of possessing *all* sources, if the research was to be scientific.[10]

We should expect records of traditions of cantillation, because of the special stress always laid upon the chanting of the Pentateuch and the other books of the Bible. Already the punctuator and vocalizer, Ben Asher in Tiberias, of the ninth century tried to explain the tunes of the Bible in words (Chapter III). Since then many grammarians, such as Jehudah Hayyuj, Kalonymos (in Abraham de Balmes' Grammar, *Mikne*

Abram, printed in Venice in 1523), Simon Duran (in his *Magen Avoth,* Livorno, 1780, F. 55), and especially the physician Abraham ben David Portoleone in Italy (in his work *Shilte Haggiborim,* printed in 1612, see Chapter X) followed along the same path of explaining in words the tonality of the Biblical modes. In this, of course, they did not succeed. The first who tried to set the Pentateuch tune, at least according to the tradition of the Ashkenazim, in music notes was the priest Johann Böschenstein,[11] who prepared the writing for the Hebrew Grammar of Johannes Reuchlin which was printed in Hagenau in 1518. Böschenstein, a Catholic priest and scholar, was very much attached to Jews, and he mingled with them. Since his time, different attempts have been made, mostly by gentiles, to consign to score from the Jewish Biblical modes. Such a publication was that of ATHANASIUS KIRCHER entitled *Musurgia Universalis* (Paris, c. 1660), which gives the Sephardic tradition of the Pentateuch chant. There was also JULIUS BARTOLOCCI's *Bibliotica Rabbinica* (*Kiriath Sefer*) (Rome c. 1675-93), Vol. IV, pp. 429-40, *Neginoth* Ashken. for Pent. and Sephard. and Ital. for Pent. and *Haftara* in music notes. Of special interest, however, because the writer of the music was a Portuguese Jew, the physician David Pinna of Amsterdam, is his transcription of the Pentateuch and Prophet modes according to the tradition of the Amsterdam Portuguese Jews, printed in the preface to the Bible edited by JABLONSKI, Berlin, 1699. The most complete presentations of the modes of the Bible according to the Ashkenazic tradition are given in the *Baal Tefillah* of Baer and in the Jewish Encyclopedia, sub-verbum "Cantillation," in both of which the examples of Portuguese and Moroccan traditions are copied from Naumbourg's *Agudath Schirim* (Paris, 1874). The readings for Bagdad, the Orient, and Egypt in the Jewish Encyclopedia, s.v. "Cantillation," are all incorrect.

II. Literature

The Jewish sages did not write theories of music like those of the Greek philosophers; they did not leave us descriptions of the nature and characteristics of ancient Jewish song. This statement does not mean to ignore the occasional comment on music, or the detailed descriptions of the song and musical instruments of the Temple in Jerusalem, or the many traditions of the manner of performance of the songs which have been preserved among the sayings of the sages in the Mishnaic, Midrashic, and Talmudic literature, as well as in the works of Josephus. Although in most cases exaggerations, these statements are, nevertheless, based upon some historical facts. They are scattered through all ancient Jewish literature, not only in the just-mentioned post-Biblical works but also in the Bible itself. Through an exhaustive search for and careful compilation of these references, we can accumulate material sufficient to reconstruct the musical conditions of the time of the Second Temple [12] (Chapter XV).

Of a different type, however, is the description and interpretation of Israel's ancient music in the Medieval literatures, both in Hebrew and in the Vernaculars, for—under influence of mysticism—music, like other subjects, was removed from the sphere of reality into the realm of fantasy. Further damage was caused by astrology, for it attributed musical inspiration to the movements of the stars and planets. Material of great value for the history of Synagogue song and singers of the Middle Ages is to be found in the Responsa of the Gaonim and Rabbis in which records of actual problems in the form of decisions concerning definite issues give us a key to the understanding of conditions of the music of the Synagogue from the eighth to the nineteenth centuries.[13] On the other hand, all the references to music in medieval philosophic literature are without any historical significance, because they are nothing more than a mere continuation of the philosophized interpretation of music of the Greek philosophers, exaggerated by the Sophistic and Scholastic fantasy of the medieval dreamers.[14]

Similarly valueless is the Christian literature on Jewish music and musical instruments. At the beginning of the nineteenth century, some Christian theologians still tried to ascribe musical value to the Hebrew vowels, and thus reconstruct an ancient Hebrew scale.[15] Forkel in his history of music (1788-1801) was the first to try to describe in a somewhat natural way the ancient Hebrew music, but his treatment is a construction in accord with his logic, rather than a reconstruction from authentic sources.

The first attempt to explain the musical instruments of the Bible in a manner approximating fact was made by Moses Mendelssohn and his collaborators in translating the Bible, at the end of the eighteenth century.[16]

The literature worthy of consideration started around the middle of the nineteenth century. In the above-mentioned magazine *Liturgische Zeitung* there was published some good material, such as contributions bearing upon the history of the *chazzan*, by Hecht. Furthermore, there are Weintraub's introduction to his work *Schire Beth Adonai* (Chapter XIII); Deutsch's introduction to his *Vorbeterschule* (1871); De Sola and Aguilar's introduction to the Portuguese songs (London, 1857); Naumbourg's introduction to his *Agudath Schirim* (1874); and Baer's introduction to his *Baal Tefillah* (1877). In 1879, there was organized a cantor association of Central Europe which started the publication of a weekly under the name of *Der Jüdische Cantor*, printed in Bromberg. This continued for twenty years. Soon after its beginning, another organ, *Die Oesterreichisch-Ungarische Cantoren-Zeitung*, was founded (1881) which, likewise, continued till about 1898, and which was later incorporated into the weekly *Die Wahrheit*, in Vienna. In those two organs there was accumulated rich material: research work, historical data, biographies, liturgies, music, general facts, and so on. For a long time both organs carried musical supplements. Both discussed many questions concerning Jewish music in general and *chazzanuth* in particular. Both included contributions from all the prominent *chazzanim* and investigators of that time. They reflect the life of the Synagogue of the last quarter of the nineteenth century. Another Jewish weekly, *Das Hamburger Familienblatt*, likewise offered a special supplement devoted to the interests of the *chazzan* from the beginning of the twentieth century. Likewise, *Der Lehrer und Cantor*, a monthly supplement to the *Juedische Presse*, Berlin; *Ost und West*, an illustrated monthly, Berlin, 1901-1922; *Ungarische isr. Kultus-Beamtenzeitung*, Budapest, 1883-1892; *Isr. Wochenschrift und freie Lehrer-und Cantorzeitung*, Berlin, contain valuable material. In 1886, Josef Singer (Illinik, 1841—Vienna, 1911), the *chazzan* of Vienna, published a pamphlet on the scales of the traditional tunes of the Synagogue, which was a first attempt to force a path into the labyrinth of Synagogue song. His pamphlet aroused vigorous discussion in the press. In his book *Cenni Sull'origine e Sul Progresso della Musica Liturgica con appendice Intorno, all'origine dell'organo* (Firenze, 1897), Federico Consolo tries to give some historical and scientific surveys.

ERNEST DAVID (Nancy, 1824—Paris, 1886), noted composer and author, wrote *La Musique chez les Juifs, essai de critique et d'histoire*, Paris, 1873. The first part of this book is devoted to an explanation of the Biblical instruments, the author merely repeating the hypotheses of others. The last part of his essay he devotes to the post-Biblical tunes of the

Synagogue. He admits his inability to approach this problem properly, due to the lack of an authentic collection of traditional material.

In 1877, S. NAUMBOURG edited the Synagogue compositions of SALOMON ROSSI, including the Hebrew and Italian letters of Rossi and Leon of Modena, as well as an introduction in French (Chapters X, XIII).

G. S. ENSEL, minister of Congregation *Yeshurun* in Paducah, Kentucky, made an attempt to explain the *Ancient Liturgical Music* in a "comparative and historical essay on the origin and development of sacred music of the Synagogue, Church, and Mosque," Paducah, 1881, lithographed.

EMIL BRESLAUR (Kotbus, 1836—Berlin, 1899), musical director of the Reform Temple of Berlin, and noted musician, published an essay *Sind originale Synagogen- und Volksmelodien bei den Juden geschichtlich nachweisbar?* Leipzig, 1898, wherein he declares that music is only that which is rhythmical, and that the unrhythmical chant, therefore, does not belong to music. He further tries to deny to the Synagogue Song any originality.

EDUARD BIRNBAUM wrote many essays and articles in the above-mentioned papers, some of which are reprinted, e.g., *Juedische Musiker am Hofe von Mantua von 1542 bis 1628,* Vienna, 1893 (Chapter X).

In the *Souvenir Volume,* a collection of traditional tunes with accompaniments, published by the National Council of Jewish Women, Chicago, 1893, the editors, ALOIS KAISER (1840-1908) and WILLIAM SPARGER, cantor at Temple Emanuel, New York, provided an introduction comprising a compilation of statements previously made by others (Chapter XV).

ARON FRIEDMAN published a collection of biographies of prominent cantors *Lebensbilder berühmter Cantoren,* Vols. I-III, Berlin, 1918-1927, and a collection of essays on Jewish music in memoriam of Eduard Birnbaum, Berlin, 1922, which works contain valuable data and studies.

The number of pamphlets, lectures, and essays on the subject of Jewish music increased toward the beginning of the twentieth century. In English, FRANCIS L. COHEN published a pamphlet on *The Rise and Development of Jewish Music* (printed in London, 1888). He also wrote many articles on this subject in the Jewish Encyclopedia. More complete is the book by Aron Friedman (Berlin, 1904) *Der Synagogale Gesang —Eine Studie.* A. ACKERMANN, Rabbi in Brandenburg, likewise published a survey of Jewish music in WINTER UND WÜNSCHE's *Historic Anthology: Hebrew Literature,* Vol. III, 1896. AMBROS, in his *History of Music,* Vol. I, third edition, 1887, p. 404, gives a survey of ancient Hebrew music, without adding much to the before-mentioned chapter in Forkel's history. The general and the Biblical encyclopedias deal with ancient Hebrew music in the Temple, but they entirely ignore the post-Biblical times. Some brief surveys are to be found in the Judeo-Russian and the Hebrew encyclopedias, the author of the articles in both being PINCHOS MINKOWSKY, late *chazzan* in Odessa, who unfortunately wrote from an exceedingly subjective point of view, without considering the researches of others. Popular and in journalistic style are the writings of Minkowsky in Hebrew, German, and Yiddish in various magazines and pamphlets. An attempt was made in Russia by ABRAHAM B. BIRNBAUM, *chazzan* in Chenztochow, to publish a magazine on Jewish music in Hebrew under the name *Yarchon Lechazzanim,* of which only four numbers appeared. The articles of A. B. Birnbaum in the Hebrew weekly *Haolam* [17] and in some other Hebrew magazines provided much information, especially in regard to the characteristics and conditions of chassidic song. Aside from these, there are innumerable articles scattered in the Jewish and general press, the detailed mention of which is impossible. And finally there is the popular presentation of Jewish music, in the form of illustrated lectures, written in English by A. IRMA COHON, and published by the National Council of Jewish Women, 1923. The two-fold significance of this publication lies first of all in its attractive style—its writing breathing a love for the subject and inspiring the larger public; and secondly in the fact that it is the first attempt to cast the material into a popular form.

The "Jewish Ministers Cantors Association of America" (New York) published in 1924 the history of *chazzanuth* in Yiddish, *Die Geschichte von Chazzanuth,* issued on the thirtieth anniversary of the Association. It contains popular and folkloristic material, also biographical notes on contemporary cantors as well as on some East-European *chazzanim* of the last generation. The publication is bountifully provided with photographic illustrations.

Much information on the life of the *chazzan* and of the conditions of Synagogue song in the seventeenth and eighteenth centuries is to be found in the booklet *Teudath Shlomo,* Offenbach, 1718, by SHLOMO LIFSCHÜTZ, *chazzan* in Prague and Metz (1675-1758) (Chapter XI). We note also the apologetic booklet *Reach Nechoach,* published in Fürth, 1724, by JOEL, *chazzan* in Leipa. It is written in rhymes in Hebrew and Yiddish.

JEHUDA LEB, *chazzan* of Zellichov, Poland, published a booklet *Shire Yehuda,* Amsterdam, 1697, in which very interesting details are given (Chapter XI).

In the book *Noheg Katzon Yosef* by JOSEPH HAHN NORDLINGEN, published in Hanau, 1718, there appear several valuable notes on the Synagogue song of Southern Germany and on those in Frankfort in particular. Later, a complete description of the Synagogue Song in Frankfort was given by SALOMON

GEIGER, brother of the famous Rabbi Abraham Geiger, in his Hebrew work *Divre Kehilloth*, Frankfort, 1862.

There are also books by non-Jews containing either descriptions of or research into Synagogue Song:

FRANZ LISZT: *Die Zigeuner und ihre Musik in Ungarn*, Leipzig, 1883, pp. 20-68.

FRANZ LEITNER: *Der Gottesdienstliche Volksgesang im Jüd. und Christl. Altertum*, Freiburg i/B, 1906.

OSKAR FLEISCHER: *Neumenstudien*, II, Berlin, 1897, Chapters I-II.

PETER WAGNER: *Einführung in die gregorianischen Melodien*, I, Leipzig, 1910, Chapter I, Vol. III, Leipzig, 1921, pp. 240, 367.

ROBERT LACH: *Studien zur Entwicklungsgeschichte der Ornamentalen Melopoie*, Leipzig, 1913, pp. 16ff., 133-138, 145, 150, 197.

HEINRICH BERL: *Das Judentum in der Musik*, Berlin und Leipzig, 1926.

Besides the above-mentioned works, the writer of this book published a history of Jewish music in Hebrew: Vol. I, Dvir, Berlin-Tel Aviv, 1924; Vols. II and III in press. He likewise published *Parallelen zwischen dem Synagogengesang und den gregorianischen Melodien* in *Die Zeitschrift der deutschen Musikgesellschaft*, 1922; *Der Missinaj Gesang der deutschen Synagoge*, ibid., 1926; also several essays in Hebrew, in the periodicals *Hashiloah, Haolam, Jerushalaim, Reshumoth, Hatoren*, etc.; in German, in the *Monatschrift für die Wissenschaft des Judentums, Archiv für Musikwissenschaft, Ost und West*, etc.; in English, in the Journal of the Palestine Oriental Society, Proceedings of the Music Teachers National Association, Hebrew Union College Jubilee Volume, etc.

PART II

FOLK-SONG

CHAPTER XVII

THE FOLK-SONG OF THE ORIENTAL JEWS.

Every nation that possesses its own soil, that has made a history for itself and that has created an individual atmosphere must, according to the established premises in musical science, have its own folk-song. Inversely, a folk-song must spring from a nation. But are the Jewish people a nation? For two thousand years, they have been rent from the physical homeland that cradled their youth; they have been scattered over the entire earth; they have been influenced by almost every climate, culture, and nation, constituting a small minority in each country. On the basis of these determining factors, the Jews may hardly, in the commonly accepted sense, be adjudged a nation. And yet through circumstances peculiar to them— circumstances that know no parallel in history—the Jews have never been divorced from the land where they developed from nomadic tribes into a nation. The topography, the atmosphere, the very soil of Palestine, was molded into their faith, their thought, their spiritual culture, and folklore. Through these intangible, yet very real, roots, they never ceased to draw nourishment from the vale of Sharon, and to drink inspiration from the dews of Hermon. Of vastly deeper significance, however, is that power by which a nation survives: the power of the spiritual ideal incorporated, in the case of the Jew, into his spiritual culture—into Judaism. Wherever a Jew settled, whether in the North or in the South, in the desert of Arabia or in the plains of Siberia, in North America or in North Africa, he carried his spiritual home in his heart—the home of the Kingdom of God, of the optimistic belief in the final victory of righteousness and purity, of the staunch faith in the good and the true, and of the firm conviction that his ideal will become the ideal of mankind. Indeed, such a spiritual nationality—unique as it is among the races of man—has proved itself potent in the case of the Jew. Its power springs from a religion which means the sanctification of life, and in the light of which life means religion. Thus, life as the Jew visualized it, has no room for what is commonly denominated "secular."

This spiritual nationality brought forth a folk-song as distinctive as the people itself. Just as to the Jew religion meant life and life religion, so to him sacred song has been folk-song, and folk-song, sacred song. In the folk-songs current among the Jewish people there are included tunes for Bible texts or tunes based upon Biblical themes, for prayers, for religious poetry, melodies for meditation, for the elevation of the soul to its Creator, for rousing the spirit to ecstasy, for joy in the moment in which the spirit becomes aware of the majesty and love of God, and, finally, melodies which express the innumerable struggles and pains the Jew has suffered. There are songs for the family table on Sabbaths and holidays —songs which give those various holy days tonal expression and which aim to spiritualize the meals. Even those types of songs common to all peoples, which are designated as "secular," such as cradle and love songs, humorous songs and ballads, received in Jewish folk-song a different complexion; they received an impress of the religious life-concept that flowed in the blood of the Jew. And because of this conception, vulgar songs that sought to insinuate themselves never did become rooted in Jewish folk-song. If by folk-song we understand words and tunes of war and drink, of carnality and frivolity, then the Jews have no folk-songs. Jewish folk-song, like Jewish life in the last two thousand years, nestles in the shadow of religion and ethics.

Indeed, in ancient Israel a "secular" folk-song flourished—a folk-song of war and carnality and lust inspired by wine and women—a folk-song against which the prophets and the sages carried on a battle for centuries. Still in his day BEN SIRACH, in Chapters XXX and XLIX, praises song at a wine-banquet and compares it with a diamond in a gold setting, or he likens it to a honey-cake. He warns the people, however, against associating with female singers (ibid., Chapter IX). Occasionally we hear echoes of the fight against secular song in the beginning of the Common Era through comments such as that of Elisha ben Abuya (see Chapters I, V), who relates that at a celebration the sages sang religious hymns, while the other guests intoned secular songs. We have already seen that this fight continued for a long period thereafter, as several references in Midrash and Talmud testify; and only through gradual religio-ethical education did the spiritual leaders check the secular folk-song and substitute songs with religious content. On the other hand, the "Destruction" and the "Exile" and the social and political misery in which the Jew lived for so many centuries tended to tear him away from the secular joy of life. "Rejoice not, O Israel, unto exultation, like the peoples" (Hosea 9: 1) became the motto of the spiritual leaders after the Destruction; and they were on their guard to prevent the people from singing secular songs at joyous occasions (Chapter V). All folk-songs of a secular nature were suppressed. The Biblical Song of Songs, the secularity of which is so apparent, and which, inasmuch as it is a part of the Bible, could not be suppressed,[1] was classified as "sacred" by ascribing to it an allegorical interpretation: the love between God and Israel.[2] The sages tried to suppress the opinion that the Song of Songs was secular, and sought to prevent its use as a mere love-poem.[3] The authorship of the Song of Songs was accredited to King Solomon, who was supposed to have written by holy inspiration.⁴

Thus, Jewish folk-song received more and more a religio-ethical character, interwoven with motives expressing national trouble and hopes, until it became a mirror of the spirit dominating Diaspora-Judaism. Abraham Ibn Ezra, the distinguished poet and scholar, writing eight hundred years ago, recognized the ethnological truth that every people fashions its song to suit its spirit, and reflects in its chant its inner mood and characteristics. Thus, he says in one of his Hebrew epigrams:

> The Arabs sing of love and lust,
> The Christians of war and revenge,
> The Greeks of wisdom and cunning,
> The Hindus of proverbs and riddles,
> But Israel's song is to the Lord of Hosts.

Indeed, the efforts of the spiritual leaders were not always and in all countries successful in preventing the people from singing secular songs, as we shall see later on.

No post-Biblical texts of folk-songs were retained from before the *paytanic* period. From that time on, some songs created in Babylonia and Palestine as early as the tenth century spread throughout the Diaspora and became the standard songs of the Jewish home. They are all in Hebrew; most of them are in the form of alphabetic acrostics, and some are built in stanzas with a recurring refrain. Their contents is religio-nationalistic. The same ideas and hopes found expression in many songs. Thus, there are Elijah-songs, dealing with that prophet who became the legendary guard of Israel and who was expected to be the messenger of the Messianic era (Mal. 3: 23-24). Already in the eleventh century there were songs of Elijah sung by all Jewish communities on the outgoing of Sabbath.⁵ The oldest part of this group is the refrain "Elijah, the prophet, Elijah, the Tishbite, Elijah, the Gileadite, may he speedily come to us with the Messiah, the son of David." Another group has as its subject matter, "Sabbath, the bride, the queen." In the third century it was customary to receive the Sabbath with the refrain: "Come, let us go forth to receive the Sabbath the queen" and "Come, O bride!" [6] Beginning with Dunash ben Labrat (tenth century), many poets wrote poems glorifying the Sabbath which became popular as home-songs, called *Zemiroth*, which were sung at the meals on Friday evening, Sabbath noon, Sabbath afternoon, and on the night of that holy day. Both groups were later inserted into the *Siddur*, the prayer-book. This became not only a book for the Synagogue but also the Songster of the Jewish people for its daily life. A third group of popular songs is for the celebration of the *Seder* on the first two nights of the Passover Festival. Its oldest part, the *Hallel* (Ps. 113-8), used to be sung in Jerusalem in every home before the Destruction. From the tenth century on, there were composed several songs in folk-character, such as *Ki lo noé, Addir hu, Echod mi yodea,* the latest (from the fifteenth century) being *Chad gadyoh.*

Apart from these groups, there were likewise composed songs for the Three Festivals, for *Chanukah* and *Purim,* for Circumcision and wedding ceremonies. All these popular folk-songs sprang forth in the East, in Palestine and Babylonia, and were carried over to the European and North African communities, where they were imitated in style and form, while they also served as a stimulus for further original creations. Only in rare cases were the tables turned—that is, European creations being adopted by the Oriental Jew. Oriental Jewry continued to influence Occidental Jewry in folk-song up to the seventeenth century. The last folk-singers, whose products were accepted throughout the Diaspora, were SOLOMON ALKABETZ (c. 1505, Salonica—1580, Safed), the author of the famous Sabbath

hymn *Lechoh dodi*, Isaac Luria (1544, Jerusalem—1572,
Safed), who wrote the famous cabbalistic songs in Aramaic:
Azammer Bishvachin, Athkinu Seudathah, Benei Hechalah,
which became popular among the chassidim (Chapter XIX),
and Israel Najara (Safed, 1550—Gaza, 1620), the author of
the popular Sabbath song *Yah Ribbon alam*.[7]   The Oriental
poems remained the standard songs of all Jewish communities,
and they are retained to the present day, although in the course
of time local poets arose in various countries: Northern Africa,
Italy, Spain, France, Germany, and Yemen—whose poetical
productions overshadowed the Babylonian-Palestinian creations.

The interest in folk-song of the religio-national character
increased in the Oriental communities, stimulated partly by
inner religiosity, partly by the Arabic enthusiasm for popular
song.   The love for song called forth many folk poets in almost every community.   Not only rabbis, but also laymen, well
versed in Hebrew lore, composed songs and hymns in the
adopted style for the above-mentioned ideas and occasions.
Most of these poems did not spread beyond the immediate community; others gained more popularity and were adopted by
other communities of the same country, at times even crossing
the boundary of the country and becoming the favorite songs
of Jewish settlements in foreign lands.   Congregations used to
collect, in Arabic manner, songs which had gained popularity
among their members, and published these in DIWANS which at
times would be favored also by other congregations.   But also
individuals, popular poets, or singers would publish diwans of
their own compositions, and some of these gained wide popularity.   This diwan production—thus compiling community-
songsters or songsters of individuals—continued in the Orient
till lately, and became an industry, especially since the establishment of printing-houses in various cities in Asia and Africa.
In 1587, Israel Najara published the first edition of his diwan

Zemiroth Israel in the newly founded Hebrew press in Safed. This was the first songster published in the Orient. In 1599-1600, he published in Venice a second and enlarged edition of the same diwan, which soon became the most popular song-book among all the communities in the Orient. A great number of the three hundred forty-six poems which the collection contains was adopted into other diwans and reprinted innumerable times. The success of Najara's songs lies, first of all, in their contents. Najara struck the Oriental-Jewish romantic note in a fascinating folk-manner, such as had not been done since Jehuda Halevi. The success is due, secondly, to the popular ingratiating style, which at times has a strong Oriental sensuous strain. This latter feature aroused the dismay of some rabbis.[8] Thirdly, Najara's success should be ascribed to the music, for Najara had likewise musical ability and a sweet voice and was well versed in the popular songs of his day. He knew a great number of Arabic, Greek, Turkish, and Spanish songs, to the tunes and according to the rhythm of which he wrote his Hebrew lyrics, imitating even the sounds of the syllables of foreign texts. As he explained in the preface to his diwan, his imitation was consciously executed, with the intention of preventing the mob from singing profane and vulgar folk-songs in the above-named languages, and with the aim of winning over the people through the deceit of giving them their favorite tunes and even the sounds of the words they liked.[9] For the same reason, Najara arranged his diwan according to the plan customary in the Arabic diwans, that is, the grouping of the songs according to the musical *Makams* (Chapters II, VII). This manner which Najara introduced into the Hebrew songsters was imitated by subsequent poets and editors of diwans in the Near East and in the Balkans. Najara's tunes, except for six for which he claims authorship, were all adopted. But long before him, non-Jewish melodies of the neighboring peo-

ples had been borrowed either by the poets themselves or by
the performers, as we have seen in Chapter VII. Hence, no
claim to originality can be made in the case of the music of
the Jewish Oriental folk-song. The tunes, being of Oriental
origin, satisfied the musical taste of the Oriental Jew; and
only in the SELECTION of the musical material was Jewish taste
manifested. As we glance over the vast number of tunes
adopted for the Jewish-Oriental folk-song, we notice a preference for melodies based upon the *Makams* that were related
to the modes of the Synagogue, such as *Bayati* and *Nawa,* corresponding to the Prophetic, *Mogen-Ovos,* and Lamentations
modes; for *Siga* and *Irak,* which correspond to the Pentateuch,
Ruth, and *Tefilla* modes; for *Hedjaz,* which corresponds to
the *Ahavoh-Rabboh* mode; and for *Rehaw,* which resembles
the Job mode.

Of all the Jewish communities in the Orient, that of Yemen
accomplished most in the creation of folk-poetry, some of the
compositions reaching the rank of art. In the sixteenth century the poetic pulse of this severed member of the shattered
body of Israel was quickened. A number of highly gifted and
talented poets arose who enriched Jewish poetry with new artistic forms. This period reached its zenith in the ingenious
poet SHOLEM SHABZI of the seventeenth century, who composed several hundred poems in various forms and of diversi-
fied contents.

What was it that moved the Jews of Yemen at that time to
new life and increased activity, after they had been exposed
to inhuman persecutions and oppressions for almost a thousand
years following their complete subjection by Mohammed? Of
a certainty it was not redemption from their social misery, for
at that time the hatred of their Arabian oppressors vented itself in as bestial a manner as ever before. It seems that the
spiritual fermentation of the cabbalists, who in the sixteenth

century established a center in Northern Palestine (Safed) and aroused the dormant susceptibilities of the Orient, penetrated also into Yemen and had the effect of a messianic message to the languishing souls longing for redemption.

This cabbalistic-mystic movement called to new life by Isaac Luria, finding enthusiastic adherents in the Spanish refugees in the Orient, reaching its highest development in the pseudo-messiah Shabbatai Zevi and through him finally carried to the grave—this fantastic movement gripped all Jewry in the Orient, as well as in the Occident. It called forth many dreamers and visionaries, each one of whom attempted to reproduce his feelings and illusions in verse and rhyme, probably after the manner of the saintly Isaac Luria, who himself, as mentioned above, had composed numerous poems.

Thus, at that time a new era dawned for Jewish poetry in the Orient. Indeed, after a close examination of the contents of Yemenite poetry, it becomes evident that it is saturated with the mystic spirit of that cabbalistic school.

The overwhelming majority of these poems consists of wedding songs, intended for the various ceremonies of the wedding and the daily festivities of the first week after the wedding. But these are not wedding songs in the ordinary sense. In them, the wedding is SYMBOLIZED. The poet speaks, indeed, of bride and bridegroom. But thereby he in no sense signifies the young human pair, but rather, true to cabbalistic implication, he intends the bridegroom to be God while the bride is the personified people Israel, an allegorical interpretation of old which was applied already to the Song of Songs, as pointed out at the beginning of this chapter. Almost all wedding songs deal with the same subject: on the one hand, with the tribulations and lamentations of the bride, Israel, and on the other, with the promises, the forgiveness, and yearning of the bridegroom, God.

In addition, a third figure plays an important part in these songs, namely, Palestine or rather Jerusalem concentrated in the Temple. The train of thoughts is as follows: The pair, designated now as engaged and now as married, quarrels and separates. It goes without saying that in this conflict the bride, i.e., wife, is the guilty party. The result is that the bridegroom, i.e., husband, banishes his beloved from his house— Palestine, especially the Temple. But now he feels unhappy to be alone in the house, and he, too, abandons his home, which thereupon remains desolate. However, as soon as the reconciliation between the angered husband and his beloved will take place, the pair will return to its old home. For the poetical expression of these fancies several forms were employed. Thus songs in which the longing and complaints of the bride are pictured, received the form *Neshid;* the love songs of the bridegroom were couched in the form *Shira;* the march toward reconciliation was treated in the form *Zafát;* and the joyful effusion after the reconciliation in the form *Chidduyoth,* while the *Haleloth* served as an interlude, overture, or postlude.

1. *Haleloth.* These songs have folk-character. Some of them are compilations of Psalm-verses; some have rhyme but no meter. They always begin with the word *Wehaleluyoh*— "praise the Lord"; and they are rendered in unison in the Psalm mode.

2. *Zafát.* This Arabic word signifies "wedding." The songs of this class are sung as the bridegroom goes in procession to the house of the bride. They commence either with "Come, O bridegroom, in peace," or "Be blessed at thy going out." All of them express the hope that through the reconciliation of the beloved, the Messiah will come to Zion.

3. *Chidduyoth.* The Yemenites explain this name to be derived from the Hebrew stem *chada*—songs of joy. These songs are sung immediately after the nuptial ceremony. They

usually start with "I shall sing to the beloved one" or with "The beloved coming from the myrrh-hill"—meaning God descending on Mount Sinai.

The three classes of this poetry thus far explained are really nothing more than a preparation for the wedding celebration, an introduction to the festal song. Hence, the poems are few in number, for no great importance was attached to these songs which used to be sung on no other occasion than at the dressing of the bridegroom or during his passage (procession) from his home to the neighboring house of the bride. Poor in quality as are these classes, just so rich in the number of songs and melodies are the other groups which constitute the wedding-songs proper.

4. *Neshid.* The wedding dinner is ushered in through the singing of *Neshid* songs. This class of songs has almost invariably the form of the *Kasida,* i.e., two-lined strophes. The number of the *Neshid* songs may be estimated to be two hundred, and of these only a few consist of four- or five-line stanzas.

Neshid, plural *Nashwad,* signifies in Arabic "folk-song"; *Anshada* is the term for measured song, in contrast to *Tartil,* which stands for recitative.[10] In the Yemenite interpretation, *Neshid* signifies "song of request." Hence, the bride chooses this type of song in which to address to her bridegroom her plea for his grace and love.

5. *Shiroth.* This class of poetry is the greatest achievement of the Yemenite muse. It is distinguished from the other poetical types, first, by its content. In it, with exultation and emotion, the bridegroom sings to the bride his extravagant praise and fiery love. But the *Shirah* is especially distinguished by its form. The greatest number of these songs is composed in the so-called girdle form, in Arabic *taushich.* With the Yemenites, *Shirah* poetry is identical with artistic

poetry. The girdle form is considered by Arabic singers as
the acme of poetical achievement, wherefore it is styled MAS-
CULINE, inasmuch as the girdle serves as a symbol of masculine bravery.

The girdle form takes its name from a variant meter introduced in the middle of the stanza. The *Shirah* stanza consists of three parts: (a) the chief part, which is usually a
quatrain; (b) the GIRDLE consisting of three lines, all shorter
than those of the presiding selection; and (c) the conclusion
composed of two lines of the same meter and number of feet
as part (a). The shortened lines give the reader the impression that part (b) girdles the body of the stanza. There are
girdles of four or five lines, and sometimes two or three girdles in one stanza.

Apart from the wedding-songs, which, as stated above, constitute the greatest part of the Yemenite folk-songs, there are
songs for Sabbath, likewise called *Shiroth*. While the festivals, too, are provided with songs, the Sabbath, having acquired
a special sanctity, is far more richly adorned. The cabbalistic
school gave the Sabbath a mystic interpretation. But to every
Jew, oppressed as he was, tortured physically and morally, the
Queen Sabbath became the divine dispenser of rest, bringing
peace and bliss to his soul. On at least ONE day of the week
the Jew could conjure up a Messianic era where he breathed
freely and happily. This romanticism is voiced in the Sabbath
songs of the Jews throughout the Diaspora, and so also in those
of the Yemenite Jews. Many of the texts of the Yemenite
Sabbath songs are taken from the Jewish-Spanish classics or
are imitations of them.

The Yemenite poems for the festivals and for the ceremony
of circumcision have no fixed melodies, but are sung to the
tunes customary for Sabbath songs, and they resemble the latter also in their forms.

While the Synagogue song of the Yemenite Jews consists of the modal chants only (Chapter VII), their folk-song for the most part has strict rhythm and melodic form. It is true that the *Haleloth* and the Sabbath songs are based upon the Synagogue modes and are generally without any rhythm. The reason for this exception lies in the fact that these lyrics are not accompanied by dance—the propelling force of rhythm. The other songs are, as a rule, sung to dancing and hand-clapping, and, consequently, they acquired fixed rhythmical melodies.

The Yemenite Jews entertain the opinion that the tunes of their folk-songs are their original creations and have no connection with the Arabic songs. However, this claim holds true in part only, for, according to their own statement, it is the tunes of townspeople only, principally of those in the capital San'a that are original; while the folk-song of the village Jews, who live in close contact with the Arabs, is strongly influenced by Arabic music. In some instances, entire melodies were borrowed. Hence, all melodies which are of doubtful and non-Jewish origin the Jews in San'a call "village melodies." In San'a the Jews have been separated from the Mohammedan population for the last three hundred years, and closed up in a Ghetto apart from the main town. This seclusion has caused the development of specific Jewish folk-tunes which differ from all current Arabic melodies that are accessible.

Unlike its poetry, the music of the Near East retained its folk-character, artistic endeavors being confined to embellishment and subtle modulations from one *Makam* to the other. The other form of "art" consists in the PERFORMANCE. The various types of the Yemenite poetry are, with the exception of *Haleloth,* sung in responsive and antiphonal forms, and are executed by a minimum of four singers divided into two groups, in one of which the chief singer functions as soloist and director. The partner of the director is called "colleague," or sec-

ond singer; and the two in the second group are the third and
fourth singers. Only the first line of the song is intoned by
the first singer solo, whereupon his "colleague" joins the singing of the first stanza. The second group, i.e., the third and
fourth singers, respond with the second stanza. The song usually ends in a coda without text, which is sung in unison by
both groups, the singers carrying the melody either on the last
syllable of the last word or with "ah." Assembled guests
participate by clapping their hands to mark the rhythm. In
rare cases, however, is the little drum *duf* or *darbaka* employed.

During the singing of *Neshid* and *Shirah*, dancing is obligatory. The dance is executed by one pair, sometimes two pairs,
of men only; and it has the Arabic character. The dance starts
with a slow tempo, but the more the excitement rises the
quicker becomes the tempo, until finally it becomes a whirling
prestissimo. There are among the Yemenite Jews very skillful and graceful dancers. Aged and worn-out men dance with
an astonishing celerity and agility. Women are excluded from
dancing; the festivities take place among groups of men alone.

In the chant each stanza is repeated. After the antiphonal
response, the first singer is at liberty to introduce another melody for the subsequent stanza for the sake of variety. This
process is known as "reversing." Skillful singers make several "reverses" in one and the same poem, in case it consists
of many stanzas. Among the Yemenite singers "reversing"
is considered the highest "art."

In addition to those in Hebrew, several songs were written
in Aramaic, though more than a thousand years ago Aramaic
ceased to be a spoken language. Through the influence of the
cabbala, this tongue revived as a medium of expressing mystic-
poetical sentiments. The above-mentioned poem of I. Luria
as well as *Yah ribbon alam* by Najara are written in Aramaic.

The Arabic language, which became the vernacular of the Oriental Jews, was, next to Hebrew, the chief vehicle of Yemenite poetry. Some lyrics peculiarly employ Hebrew and Arabic in alternating stanzas, or even within one and the same stanza; nay, even in one and the same line Hebrew and Arabic words are used promiscuously. Approximately one-fifth of the Yemenite poems is purely Arabic, and about half of them are Hebrew-Arabic. There are also trilingual poems, Hebrew-Arabic-Aramaic, similar to the combination found occasionally in the poetry of Halevi, Alcharizi, and other Spanish-Jewish poets.

Table XXX illustrates the folk-songs of the Oriental Jews. Group A indicates songs in Hebrew, the texts of which are of a religio-national character. Numbers 1-6 are of Babylonian origin. Example 1 is a *seder* song for the beginning of the ceremony. Its text is a mere list of the subdivisions of the service. The tune is in the Pentateuch mode. No. 2 is an Elijah song sung at the outgoing of the Sabbath. The tune is in *Bayati-Huseni,* which resembles the *Mogen-Ovos* mode. No. 3 celebrates the famous revered saint Rabbi Simon bar Yochai, and it is sung on the thirty-third day of the *Omer*. The tune is in *Bayati-Sabba,* and it has the tetrachordal form in minor. While singing this song the people work themselves into an ecstasy which results in a whirling dance. No. 4 is a plea for redemption from the exile of Ishmael (Arabs). The tune is in *Hedjaz*. In the same *Makam* we have also No. 5, used for "Rejoicing with the Torah" (*Simchath Torah*). Both songs are stimulating dancing numbers. No. 6 is associated with the outgoing of the Sabbath. Its text, known throughout the Diaspora, originated in Babylonia.

The second group, Nos. 7-10 comprises songs of Sephardic-Syrian origin. No. 7 has the same text as No. 6. Its tune, which is in *Bayati,* is known also in Italy.[11] No. 8 is a responsive song for the return to Zion, its tune being in *Makam Nawa*. No. 9 is a plea for the restoration of Galilee (North Palestine), most likely dating from the time when, under Joseph Nasi (sixteenth century), an attempt was made to establish a Jewish settlement in Tiberias.[12] Its tune is in *Hedjaz*. No. 10, in the same scale, is used for the "Rejoicing with

TABLE XXX
Folk-songs of the Oriental Jews
a) Hebrew songs

Babylonian

1. Kad-desh u - re-chats, ka - re-pas ya-chats ma - ror, ko-rech, shul-chan o - rech, tsa -fon ba-rech, hal-lel, nir-tsa.

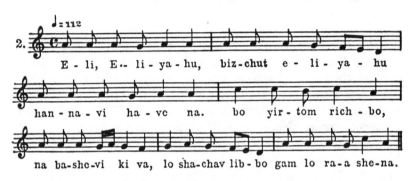

2. E - li, E - li - ya - hu, biz-chut e - li - ya - hu han - na - vi ha - ve na. bo yir-tom rich - bo, na ba-she-vi ki va, lo sha-chav lib-bo gam lo ra-a she-na.

3. Wa - a-mar-tem ko le-chai rab-bi shim-on bar yo-chai.

D.C. a Fine

4. Shad-dai, êl, ma ro-ra ye kab-bets e-chem bim-he-ra, e-lê tziy-yon be - kol zim-ra mig-ga-lut yish-ma-el.

5. Sim-chu na, sim-chu na be -sim-chat hat-to-ra.

D.C. a Fine

6.

Ham-mav-dil ben ko-desh le-chol chat-to-te-nu

hu yim-chol, zar-e-nu we-chas-pe-nu yar-be cha-chol we-

cha-ko-cha-vim bal-lay-la, cha-bib al-la, e-

li-ya-hu, a-ziz al-la, e-li-ya-hu.

Sephardic-Syrian
Andante
mf

7.

Ham-mav-dil ben ko-desh le-chol chat-to-te-nu

hu yim-chol, zar-e-nu we-chas-pe-nu yar-

be cha-chol we-cha-ko-cha-vim bal-lay-la.

Moderato
mf **Solo**

8.

A-ro-mim-cha li-che-vod shim-cha, yit-ba-rach we-yit-ro-mam,

unison

le-ir tziy-yon har ko-de-she-cha sham ni-se-mach we-na-a-le.

12. A-ha-vath ha da-soh al le-bo-bi le-bo-bi. ta-a-wath le-bo-bo-m la-a-so-th to-b go-be-roh. ya-a-lu le-ga-n e-den we-cha-yim no-ha-rim.

13. a) Singer 1.-2. A-ha-vath ra-a-yoh re-so-ni. Singer 3.-4. yish-a-loh ma-re-pe le-os-bi.

b) e-le-choh de-rech me-sil-loh ha-ze-hi-rim ba-te-fil-loh. Singer 1.-2. es-me-choh an-she ye-go-ni, ye-go-ni.

Singer 3.-4. esh-ke-choh ul-li we-o-le-bi.

c) I-III IV Tutti gam we-yis-chok rab pe-cho-dim ah!

the Torah," the text being based on *Hoshanah*. It starts largo, but in the last part it changes to Allegro-vivace.

The third group, Nos. 11-13, consists of Yemenite songs. No. 11 belongs to the type *Zafat*. This poem praises the beauty of the bride in terms taken from the Song of Songs, such as "Thy temples are like a pomegranate split open; Thy height is like the height of the palace. . . . O gazelle, her eyes captured my eyes." The tune is Hypo-Phrygian, which resembles the Prophetic mode; the melodic line has a tetrachordal curve and consists of four-bar periods with a coda of two bars. No. 12 is a *Neshid* song. The tune is composed of three themes: the first of six bars repeated several times; the second and third of eight-bar periods. The tune is based upon the *Makam Nawa*. No. 13 illustrates a "girdle song"—*Shirah*. The poem has the abbreviated *Ramal* meter (Chapter VII). The tune has three parts: (a) intones the first part of the stanza in six bars, (b) gives the girdle which consists of four bars, and (c) intones the concluding part of the stanza with an additional coda of four bars sung in unison. The scale is the Hypo-Phrygian in a tetrachordal melodic line.

JUDEO-SPANISH (LADINO) SONGS

While still in Spain the Jewish people used to sing Spanish *canciones* and romances in the old Castilian dialect. These songs the Jews carried with them in their exile in 1492 and continued to sing in their new settlements in Northern Africa, in the Balkans and, until lately, in Turkey.[18] The Oriental environment and the new conditions caused the creation of specific Jewish folk-songs in the Spanish vernacular which the Jewish refugees retained as their idiom. Already in Spain the Jews incorporated into their familiar dialect many Hebrew terms employed for religious subjects, until these words became an integral part of their Spanish idiom. Now in Greek, Turkish, and Arabic environment many idiomatic expressions of these languages crept into the Spanish, thus molding that language into a peculiar medium of expression of the Jewish population of Spanish extraction. This Spanish-Yiddish became known as

b) Judeo-Spanish   (Ladino) Songs

Moderato

14. La ro-sa in - flo-re - se en el mez de mars i mi al - ma se - cu-re - se de-es-tar en es - te mal es - te-mal.

15. Pur la tu puer - ta yo pa - si la tu-pi in-se-ra - da, la ya vi-du-ra yo bi-zi cu-mo bi-zar tus ca - ras, zar tus ca - ras.

Adagio

16. Ma-ma si yo mi-mue-ro, ma-ma si yo mi - mue-ro, ma-ma si yo mi - mue-ro cha-za-nim no que-ro yo. yo.

Moderato

17. Seš me-zes es - tu vin Vie-na u - na no-che non dor-mi. Ma-til-da en los iš-pi-ta-les nis o žos en Se-la-nik.

Ladino (corrupted from "Latin"). Religion and race as well as their superior culture separated them from their Oriental neighbors and caused the creation of their own cultural values. Thus, in the course of four hundred years, they developed a popular literature in *Ladino*, in which the folk-poetry occupies a prominent place. This folk-song is partly of a religious and partly of a secular character.[14] The tunes have an Oriental color and are either adoptions or imitations of Greek-Turkish melodies.

Examples 14-17 in table XXX furnish some love-songs in *Ladino*. No. 14 speaks of the rose blooming, of the moon shining, while in the heart of the lover there is darkness. The tune starts in minor and ends in the fifth in *Hedjaz*. No. 15 says, "I passed thy door and found it locked; so I kissed the lock. It was as sweet as if I had kissed thy cheek." The tune is in minor. No. 16 expresses the last will of a girl, sick unto death, whose heart was broken by love. She importunes her mother, "When I die, I do not want *chazzanim* (to officiate at my funeral), but I want twelve boys led by my sweetheart to walk in procession." The tune is in the Dorian scale, and seems to be of Greek origin. No. 17 is obviously of the last century. In that song the sweetheart or young husband complains, "You have already been six months in Vienna, during which time I did not sleep a single night; for Mathilda is in the hospital (in Vienna) while my eyes are in Salonica." The tune starts in minor and modulates to *Hedjaz* on the same scale, a peculiarity frequently to be found in the Synagogue as well as in the Yiddish folk-song in Eastern Europe, as we shall see in the following chapters.

CHAPTER XVIII

THE FOLK-SONG OF THE ASHKENAZIM.

(a) The folk-song of the Ashkenazim in Germany.

As their brethren in the Orient, the Jews in France and Germany cultivated a home-song, in Hebrew as well as in the vernaculars, French and German. The content of the Hebrew songs was of a religious nature. The texts of these were carried over from the Orient or written by local poets. The early songs of the vernacular were translations from the Hebrew songs, and, consequently, they had religious themes. No specifically Jewish secular songs are traceable in the early medieval centuries. As long as the Jews in Western Europe lived and mingled among the gentiles, they spoke the language of the nations and sang their secular folk-songs, so that there was no need for particular Jewish secular folk-songs. The cause of the creation of Jewish folk-songs of a secular nature was the expatriation of the Jews and their separation from the people in whose midst they dwelt. This exclusion from the life of their environment brought about peculiar modes of life for the Jew which found tonal expression in Jewish folk-songs. Thus, with the erection of the Ghetto walls, we perceive the first sounds of original Jewish secular folk-songs in the vernacular. Beginning with the sixteenth century and down throughout the Ghetto period, Jewish folk-song was cultivated; and it discontinued with the readmittance of the Jew to the society of his neighbors, because his separate social life ceased then to exist. In Western and Central Europe Jewish secular folk-song vanished about the beginning of the nineteenth century, while in the East European countries it continued until lately, and in some places it still lives.

But little is known of the Judeo-French folk-song. In 1874 M. Sabatier of Nîmes published *Chansons Hebraico-Provençals des Juifs Comtadins*,[1] containing three songs: (1) a translation of *Chad Gadya* (*Un Cabri*) for the *Seder* celebration of the Passover evening, which dates back to the sixteenth century; (2) the story of Abraham and Sarah; and (3) a Purim song. The tunes to these songs were taken from old French and Provençal folk-songs,[2] as tunes for Synagogue hymns were often borrowed.

The oldest collection of texts of secular folk-songs in Judeo-German thus far known was compiled by Eisik Walich of Worms in 1595-1605.[3] It contains fifty-four poems, forty-two of which are of German origin, mostly popular love, dance, and humorous songs. The compiler changed in these songs all references to Christian beliefs and religious customs, substituting Jewish names and symbols. Many of these can be identified in collections of old German songs. Twelve texts in this collection are of Jewish origin, written by Jews on various Jewish subjects. In the last stanzas some of these authors mention their names. In addition to the compiler, there are "The Joyous Jew" SCHLOME OF PRAGUE, who apparently was a *badchan* (a merry-maker, see Chapter XX), and JOSEPH THE SON OF BENJAMIN. The texts of the Jewish songs are peppered with Hebrew words and phrases, and are either of a didactic or of a humorous character. Some of the latter were widely known, and their tunes were used also for other lyrics. One such favorite was:

> "Jüdischer stamm, von echten art,
> Ich will euch singen von einem, der
> hat einen gruen bart.

> Eisak Stilingain ist er genant,
> er wont im Schweizerland. . . ."

This song is a satire on Jewish community life in Germany. Its tune was very much liked, and several texts were set to this melody.

The GERMAN verses of the collection, in most instances where the melody is named or can be traced, were sung to the German tunes. Similarly were German tunes adopted for the JEWISH texts. The source of the tune is sometimes indicated, as in the case of a bridal-song which is marked: *beniggun*—(in the tune of) *"Es ist uf erden kein schwerer leiden."* This German song was really the prototype of the Jewish song in form and meter. We give here the first stanzas of both songs:

JEWISH:

> "Es ist kein grösser freud uf erden
> als wen zwei lieb zusammen geben werden;
> Zu dieser freud sol sich jederman sein bereit,
> knecht und maid,
> Choson und kalloh zu eren." [4]

GERMAN:

> "Es ist auf erd kein schwerer leiden
> (als) wen sich zwei herzlieb mussen scheiden.
> Ja bitter tot, mit deiner not
> und ganzen rat:
> dir kan ich nichts vergleichen." [5]

We illustrate the Jewish version with the prescribed German tune in table XXXI, 19. This melody was well known at the end of the sixteenth century.[6]

In the verses of this collection there is no sadness nor lamentation over Jewish troubles. Later, in the seventeenth century, persecutions and massacres, conflagrations and expulsions of whole communities, or the misfortune of individuals became the themes of the Jewish popular and didactic songs. This collection, however, gives but a partial picture; for the greatest part of Judeo-German songs of its date, and the tunes before and after, were of a religious nature, and comprised translations or paraphrases in verse of Hebrew poetry or prose. Almost the entire Bible was translated. Of these endeavors, the "Book of Samuel" ranks highest in standard of poetry.[7]

To all the poems and translations there were melodies adopted, which contributed much to the popularity of the texts. Tunes greatly favored by the public were sometimes employed also for other texts, in order that the popular melody might carry the text. Some of the tunes retained their popularity for a long time. Thus, for example, the melody of the above-mentioned Book of Samuel continued to be attractive to the people for over a century and a half, from the time of the publication of that book (Augsburg, 1544) up to the end of the seventeenth century. Likewise, the tune of the *Bovo-book* survived from 1507, when that fascinating story appeared, up to the seventeenth century; and still in 1654 a eulogy on the death of Emperor Ferdinand was published in Prague to be sung to the tune of the *Bovo-book*.[8]

The poetical forms and meters used in the Judeo-German folk-songs were German. Some of the German texts were Judaized by making the subject matter Jewish. The tunes used for the songs up to the eighteenth century were forgotten, for they were not written down in musical notation by the Jewish singers. Only through the original names of the songs, the tunes of which were adopted, do we obtain a clue of their origin. From that source we learn that the tunes were taken partly from the Synagogue and partly from the German folk-song. Synagogue tunes are marked by the name of a prayer or a hymn, as, for example: *beniggun Ani hu hashoel, Eftechoh pi, Akeda, Eil mole rachamim, Adir oyom venoroh, Schochnei botei chomer,* and so forth. German sources are such as *Hoch rief der Waechter, Dietrich von Bern, Halb schwarz halb weiss, Das Pavierlied, Das Schloss in Oesterreich, Vom jungen Grafen,* etc. Besides these there are tunes mentioned the origin of which cannot be identified, such as the tune of *Rabbi Simon of Prague, Gut Shabbos, Jüdischer Stamm, Wie in der Tora steht geschrieben,* or the tune of Haman of the Ahashverosh play.[9] Occasionally "special" tunes are mentioned, but there is no way of finding out whether these tunes were especially composed or especially adopted. In the adoption and selection of tunes in Germany, no other features than sweetness and popularity were considered, regardless of origin. This attitude was the cause of so many rebukes and complaints expressed by the rabbis on the use of Christian tunes for home-songs. Even the "Marseilleuse" was adopted for a satiric song which Amsterdam Jews wrote on the leaders of their community.[10]

The first collection with music was printed in Fürth in 1727.[11] It is named *Simchath Hannefesh*—the delight of the soul—and it contains thirteen songs in Judeo-German written by Elchonon-Henle Kirchhain, who adopted tunes for his poems. The tunes were written down by a professional and expert musician, the author assures us. The songs have a religio-ethical content and are written for the following occasions: (1) Friday evening, (2) Sabbath morning, (3) Sabbath evening, (4) New Moon, (5) The High Holidays, (6) Tabernacles, (7) *Chanukah,* (8) *Purim,* (9) Passover, (10) *Shavuoth,* (11) Circumcision, (12) Bridal songs, and (13) Daily songs. The texts lack poetical spirit. They are didactic, describing the ritualistic regulations of the holy days and the religious duties. They were written with the intent to prevent the people from singing secular and vulgar German songs, an effort made throughout the Middle Age by both Synagogue and Church. Thus, these songs have little or no claim to the title FOLK-SONGS; and were probably rarely used. The adopted or imitated tunes have the German melodic line of the seventeenth century. They are in the *barock* style which flourished at that time. We give these tunes in table XXXI as an illustration of the type of melodies used for the Judeo-German songs. Nos. 7 and 12 have a strong resemblance to the tune of the German song *Der Tod als Schnitter*, which became popular after 1637 (XXXI, 14).[12] Some of them, as Nos. 1, 5, 6, have folk character, whereas Nos. 3, 7, 8, 9, 12 and 13 have alterations which presuppose artistic influence. No. 8 has peculiar chromatic steps, which apparently are supposed to express a state of intoxication, because it is a *Purim* song, at which celebration banqueting was permissible (Chapter XX).

We can identify some of the tunes of the seventeenth century used by German Jews for their *Zemiroth* (Sabbath songs). For example, the tune of the *Zemirah Kol mekaddesh shevii* is designated as adopted for the song *Mensch, gedenk*. This tune resembles *Bruder Veit's* tune (XXXI, 15 a-16).[13] The latter tune was very popular in Germany in the sixteenth and seventeenth centuries, and it appealed to the Jews because it had similarity to the *Mogen-Ovos* mode, (Chapter IV). In Eastern Europe the *Kol Mekaddesh* song is recited in the *Adonoy-Moloch* mode, as illustrated in table XXXI, 15 b. In the *Mogen-Ovos* mode there was chanted another *Zemirah, Sholom Aleichem* (Peace unto you, O angels of peace!), which, too, as mentioned above, resembles Veit's tune (XXXI, 17).[14]

Another Sabbath song, *Ma Yofis*, became popular in Germany and Poland in the seventeenth and eighteenth centuries. To the Polish "Pans" this song was the symbol of Jewish song, and they used to delight themselves urging their Jews to sing it accompanied by dances and comical gestures. In the middle of the nineteenth century the tune of *Ma Yofis* was adopted for a German Sabbath song, written by Rabbi Leopold Stein of Frankfort. In table XXXI, 18, we give the *Ma Yofis* song according to M. Kohn's version in his MS. from 1870 (Chapters XIII, XVI). The tune is decidedly German.[15]

The songs of the German Ashkenazim thus far analyzed can by no means be considered "folk-songs" either in style or in content of the texts, for they bear the marks of artistic endeavors of individuals. Neither do the melodies show any Jewishness, for they are as a rule adopted from the German popular songs. Indeed, the home-song was Germanized long before this was done with the Synagogue song. Rich Jews used to engage Christian music-teachers to teach their daughters German vocal and instrumental music. Already in the seventeenth century the above-mentioned Joseph Hahn complains against this custom current among the wealthy families in Frankfort.[16] At social gatherings and joyous occasions they would sing German folk and popular songs of vulgar contents, called *Huren lieder*, to the greatest chagrin of the rabbis.[17] Thus, we see that the German Jews continued to be strongly influenced by German music, despite Ghetto walls and social separation.

(b) The folk-song of the Ashkenazim in Eastern Europe.

The folk-song of the Jews in the East-European countries took another course of development from that of the Jews in Central Europe. It is distinguished by its genuine folk-character. Created out of the people, it remained anonymous.

TABLE XXXI
Tunes of Ashkenazic songs in Judeo-German of the 17th Century

Der Tod als Schnitter

14.

15.

Kol me-ka-desh she-vi-i ko-ro-uy lo, kol sho-mer shab-bos ka-

dos me-cha-le-lo,   sho-ro har-be me-od al pi fo-o-lo,

ish   al mach-ne-hu   ve-ish   al dig-lo.

Bruder Veits Ton

16.

17.

Sho - lom a - le -chem mal - a - che ha - sho - reis, mal - a -
che el - yon, mi - me - lech mal - che ha - me - lo - chim ha - ko - dosh bo - ruch hu.

Moderato

18.

Ma yo - fis, ma yo - fis u - ma no - amt ah - voh be - sa - nu -
gim, at shab - bos me - sos nu - gim, le - choh bo - sor ve -
gam do - gim, ncho - nim mi - b'od yom, ncho - nim mi - b'od yom.

19.

Es ist kein grös - ser freud auf erd'n als wen zwei lieb zu -
sam - men ge ben werd'n; zu die - ser freud sol sich je - der - man sein be - reit,
knecht und maid, cho - son und kal - loh zu e - ren.

Neither can the time of the songs' creation be determined. They are simple and short in form and content, voicing the sentiments of the life of the people at large. The Eastern song consists not only of religio-ethical folk-songs in Hebrew and Judeo-German, but to a great extent also of secular songs of various types, as love, cradle, humorous, and satiric jingles, usually composed in the Judeo-German dialect which developed in the Eastern countries into a Jewish idiom, called "Yiddish," from the German *Jüdisch*.

In this song we again find the spirit of the Jewish people, of the masses, expressing itself. In the Eastern folk-song the life of the PEOPLE as a whole is reflected, but nonetheless are the sentiments of the individual voiced. Moreover, the Jewish woman, as a loving girl, as a married woman, and as a mother, found in it a channel for the outpouring of her heart. This song is no longer entirely governed and directed by the Synagogue and religious principles and doctrines, though in many folk-songs we find the influence of the Synagogue in both text and melody. At times we sense a heavy cloud of melancholy settling upon the spirit, as a result of century-long suffering under the pressure of the *Golus*. On the other hand, we miss the consideration of nature. No nature-songs are to be found in the folk-poetry of the Ghetto dwellers, the urban inhabitants, who were forced to that life throughout many centuries. The same people who created the Song of Songs—that hymn on nature and love, saturated with the rays of the sun, with the morning dew and the fragrance of roses—were doomed to suffocate behind the mouldy walls of their environment, the Ghetto, or to rot in the mud of the "Jewish alley," the *Jüdische Gass*. "Centuries of city life have incapacitated them for any other occupation than commerce and artisanship, and have entirely estranged them from nature." [18]   However, this statement of thirty years ago no longer holds true, for the "back to the soil" movement which started recently among the Jews in Russia and Palestine gives evidence of the deeply rooted love for nature that has resisted nineteen centuries of privation.

The contents of the religious songs of the Eastern Ashkenazim is identical with that of the German Ashkenazim, notably, the *Zemiroth* in Hebrew which were taken over in toto. However, the texts alone were taken over, while the tunes were replaced by others with Jewish-Oriental flavor, as we shall see later on. In table XXXII, 1-2, we give the song *Eliyohu Hannovi* in two tunes, both very popular; and in No. 3—a tune for *Hammavdil,* for the outgoing of the Sabbath. In addition, several new songs in Hebrew were created, usually in alphabetical acrostics and of folk-character, based on Biblical or prayer texts, as *Omar Adonoy leyaakov,* No. 4.

As in the Orient, so also in Germany and Eastern Europe, there developed bi-lingual songs in Hebrew-Yiddish, mostly of a religious character. They are either in the form of translations, i.e., the Yiddish interpreting the Hebrew or alternately a line in Hebrew and one in Yiddish. For the first form, table XXXII, 4 may serve as an illustration:

Omar adonoy leyyakov:	Said God unto Jacob:
Al tiroh, avdi Yaakov	Do not fear, my servant Jacob!
Hob nit kein forcht,	Do not fear, my servant
Mein knecht Yaakov!	Jacob!
Nein, Foterl, nein!	No, Father, no!
Ch'hob nit kein forcht far keinem.	I fear nobody,
Nor far dir allein!	But Thee!

No. 5 of table XXXII illustrates the second form:

Yovo addir veyigolenu,	May the mighty one come and redeem us,
Yovo eliyohu vivasrenu.	May Elijah come and bring us good tidings.
Un vos vet er uns mevasser sein?	What message will he bring us?
Ki yovo moschiach tzidkenu,	That the Messiah our righteous one will come,
G'vald, venn vet er kumen?!	Alas! when will he come?!
Sha, nit shrei, er vet shon kumen,	Hush! Do not cry! He will come.
Venn zshe, vet dos sein?	But when will that be?
Bimheroh veyomenu!	Speedily in our days!
Un vos far a tog vet damals sein?	And what kind of day will that be?
Yom gilloh, yom rinnoh, yom ditzoh,	A day of joy, a day of song, a day of rejoicing,
Yom chedvoh.—Haleluyoh.	A day of happiness.—Haleluyoh.

Both examples have the alphabetical acrostic.

The greatest part of the folk-songs is in Yiddish, especially cradle and love songs, and songs relating to family life, for the simple reason that they were sung and probably likewise composed by women, who did not know any other language. Some of these songs are very popular, such as the cradle song given in table XXXII, 6:

Unter dem kind's wigele	Beneath the baby's cradle,
Steht a waisse tzigele.	There stands a white kid.
Tzigele is geforen handlen,	The kid has gone a-bartering.
Rosinkes mit mandlen	Raisins and almonds

Rosinkes mit mandlen	Raisins and almonds
Is die beste s'choroh,	Are the best goods.
Mein kind vet kennen lernen	My baby will know the study
toroh.	of Torah.

It was the ideal of the mother that her boy should become a scholar in Jewish lore, and the next ideal was that her son should be a skillful merchant, since free trade was the only occupation left open to the Jew.

Both occupations were for the men only. Women were generally kept at home, excluded from instruction in Hebrew lore. They received their religious and ethical education orally from their mothers and from books in Yiddish, and awaited the ideal marriage to young men well versed in the Torah but utterly unprepared and ignorant in worldly matters. The bride knew that in most cases she would be doomed to help her husband earn a living. Besides so many calamities might strike her, as, for instance, the tyrannic law issued by Emperor Nicholas I, compelling Jewish youths to serve in the army for twenty-five years. Even later, after that law was abolished by Emperor Alexander II, the service in the Russian army was looked upon with terror. At the age of twenty-one the Jew was already married; thus, serving in the army meant to him leaving his wife and children without support, and sacrificing his best years for a government which refused to grant him full rights as a citizen. Furthermore, the suffocating restrictions against the Jew robbed him of all possibilities of making a living, and he was finally compelled to leave his native home and emigrate to another land, leaving his family in poverty. In order to help the young couple in their first steps on the path of life, one of the parents used to take them into his home and provide them with their necessities for a certain period. But family love was not always ideal, and the young woman had to suffer most, from the proverbial mother-in-law as well as from her own mother. At times, religious struggles caused the break-up of the family. A young man limited to the study of Hebrew lore was caught by the modern spirit. As a result, he could no longer get along with his "fanatic" wife, and left her.

All these bitter experiences of life struck the Jewish woman primarily, and found utterance in her song. Thus, we find bridal songs, wedding songs, laments of the young disappointed wife, of the young woman who had to stay with her mother-in-law. There are mother-songs, soldier-songs, grass-widow-songs, orphan-songs, woman's-trade-songs, accusations against and curses upon the heretic husband. These songs are in a pathetic style and in a desperate sadness.

Sad and sentimental as the songs of actual Jewish life may sound, they do not comprise the entire material of Eastern folk-songs, for there exists a considerable part of joyous songs. As soon as the subject matter is religious—the Torah, Messiah, Israel and its past, the festivals, etc.—the tone becomes brighter. Furthermore, we find a great number of humorous and witty jingles, at times of subtle satire and sarcasm against both Jew and gentile. At times, peculiar conditions of Jewish life find expression in biting irony in which tears mingle with laughter.

The forms of the songs are partly in the German four-foot meter either in trochee or in dactyl; seldom, however, in the iambic meter. They have rhyme, and consist mostly of four lines to the stanza. Some are written in alphabetical acrostics without meter. The language of the humorous and satiric songs is interspersed with Hebrew terms and Biblical quotations, with prayers and post-Biblical literature. Often Hebrew poems are paraphrased or interpreted in Yiddish or in one of the Slavic languages.

Aside from the Yiddish and Hebrew-Yiddish song, there developed a type of song composed of Hebrew-Ukrainian, Yiddish-Ukrainian or Russian, and Hebrew-Yiddish-Ukrainian, in similar manner as the Jewish-Oriental songs are composed of Hebrew-Arabic, or Hebrew-Aramaic-Arabic, as explained in the previous chapter. Those songs were composed by Jews who lived in a Slavic environment, or by those Jewish soldiers, who, cast away in the remote Russian districts, were Russified to the extent that their vernacular became more Russian than Yiddish. There are also imitations of Ukrainian folk-songs in a Judaized form, Jewish themes being inserted into shepherd and love-songs. The religious songs have the responsive form mostly, while the love-songs and those dealing with social problems are for solo—the outpouring of a single soul in solitude and despair.

The texts of the folk-songs, in so far as they have been retained, seem to be of no earlier date than the beginning of the nineteenth century, for the songs reflect events which occurred during that century. But no song is to be found, at least not in the material published, which refers to events of previous times, such as the Chmelnitzki pogroms or the pseudo-messianic movement of the seventeenth century. No doubt, there were folk-songs created which voiced those tribulations, but they were forgotten, or superseded by new poems bewailing new tragedies.

Following this survey of the texts, we turn to the musical part of the songs, to their tunes. Upon examination of the musical material employed in the Eastern folk-songs, we find these elements:

Group (A) BIBLICAL AND PRAYER MODES are employed either in their original unrhythmical form, or are shaped in rhythmical melodies. This type of music is usually employed for texts of a religious and serious nature, or for texts with humorous intent. Example 7 in table XXXII is a song in the three languages, in Ukrainian-Hebrew-Yiddish, called *Cheshbon tzedek* (the righteous account).[19]

(UKRAINIAN)

Hei, piv ya u niediliu	I have drunk all week
I propiv ya vsu nadiliu,	And spent all my possessions,
Oj, treba znati yak huliati,	One has to know how to rejoice,
Yak boha pochvaliati.	How to praise God.

(YIDDISH)

Iber hundert yor	After one hundred years I
(Ukrainian) Yak umirati,	will have to die,

(HEBREW)

cheshbon tzedek	And to give a righteous account.
(Ukrainian) otdavati,	

(UKRAINIAN)

A mi piom tai huliam	But we drink and rejoice.

(HEBREW)

Veatoh tishma min hasho-mayim.	And mayest Thou hear from the heavens.

The tune is based upon the prophetic mode (table VII, 6), but finishes in the *Ahavoh-Rabboh* mode. Example 8 is a love-song,[20] and it is based upon the mode of Lamentations (table VIII, 3); while No. 9 has the Psalm mode modified for *Akdomus* (table XXIII, 7).[21] No. 10[22] has the *Tal-Geshem* tune (table XXIII, 4, II). No. 11 is the widely known humorous song A chazzandl auf *Shabbos,* based upon the *Adonoy-Moloch Steiger* (table XII, 4). No. 12 has the character of the *Mogen-Ovos Steiger,* as applied for the study of the Talmud (table XIV). The text is a parody on the superstitious beliefs of the chassidim. No. 13—a love-song[23] and No. 14—the familiar "philosophical" song *Fregt die velt an alte kashe,* are based upon the *Ahavoh-*

Rabboh steiger (table XV). On this mode there are likewise founded
No. 3—*Hammavdil*—and No. 6—a cradle song—and many other
religious and secular folk-songs.

Group (B) The bulk of the folk-songs, however, is in the
MINOR SCALE, partly with the minor and partly with the major
seventh. Out of one hundred forty tunes in Kipnis' collection ninety-one are in minor, while in Cahan's collection one
hundred twenty-eight out of one hundred sixty-eight melodies
have this scale. As a whole, the minor tunes in the Eastern
folk-song exceed the tunes in other scales (*Hedjaz* and major)
by a great majority, while the greater number of tunes of the
Slavic folk-song are in major or Church-Phrygian.[24] On the
other hand, the old Spanish folk-songs are mostly in minor.[25]
The same is true with the Arabic and the modern Greek folk-
song.[26] This relation of minor and major changes entirely as
soon as we turn to the German song. In the collection of
German folk-song of the eighteenth and nineteenth centuries
published by F. Boehme,[27] out of seven hundred eighty, only
nineteen are in minor, all the rest being in major. Considering all these facts we are prompted to accept the opinion that
the preference of scale is a RACIAL EXPRESSION rather than the
result of conditions of life. In other words, the folk-psychol-
ogy is voiced in the scale, not the economic and social conditions, be they miserable or favorable. Major for joy, Minor
for sadness, is apparently a significance which the German nations read into these scales; while the Semitic, Latin, and Slavic
nations do not share this conception. Therefore we find so
many joyous dance and humorous tunes in minor among the
folk-songs of these nations.

The minor tunes employed in the Jewish folk-song have kinship to the Slavic as well as to the Spanish-Oriental tunes in
minor. The melodic lines of Nos. 1, 2, 4, 5, 15 and 16 (in

table XXXII) resemble those of Polish, Ukrainian, Spanish, Arabic, and old French tunes. At times it is impossible to identify the source of a melody without words, to decide whether it be of Jewish, Spanish, French, Polish, or Ukrainian origin. Such examples as 28-31 stand as evidence that a melody can be found in any of the above-mentioned folk-songs, yet No. 28 is of Polish origin.[28] Likewise can the origin of the melody No. 29 be argued, though it is a Portuguese folk-song.[29] A motive like No. 30 is very familiar in the Yiddish folk-song. In Chapter XX we will meet it in a tune by E. Zunser; yet it is, nevertheless, in an old Spanish folk-song of the fifteenth century which was published in 1575 by Francesco di Salinas of Burgos, and which was set to a satiric text dealing with the expelled Jews from Spain in 1492.[30] No. 31 could be taken as a typical Russian dance-motive. Nobody would think it a folk-tune originated in Bretagne (Northern France).[31]

This kinship in scale, melodic line, and structure may account for the fact that it is difficult to distinguish between Jewish, Slavic, and Roman tunes, if there are no Synagogal motives interwoven in them which point to an ancient Semitic-Oriental origin. Thus, Nos. 2, 5 and 15 may with equal justification be considered either Jewish creations or adoptions from the Slavic song. There are a great number of such tunes adopted from Ukrainian, Polish, and other Slavic sources of which Nos. 17-27 are further examples. Folk-tunes thus taken over show interesting changes. No. 17, a love-song, originated in the Slovak national anthem *Over Tatra,* as illustrated in No. 18.[32] A comparison of the two shows that in order to suit its iambic text, the Jewish version changed the rhythm of the tune to ¾, and extended the second period of it from three to four bars by creating a resting point on the fourth bar. In similar manner were Nos. 19-20 adjusted to text and taste. The latter is an Ukrainian folk-song,[33] considerably abbreviated and reshaped. In Nos. 22-23 the original tune is developed by the addition of a sequence built on the first period.[34] Nos. 26-27 are Ukrainian tunes, embellished, arranged in 4/4 rhythm instead of 2/4, and concluded with a coda.[35] Many tunes, suiting Jewish text and taste, were retained in their original form, as for example Nos. 24-25. Here, both the Yiddish and the Ukrainian texts are based upon four-feet trochee.[36]

Group (C) This group contains tunes in the Ukrainian "Dorian" scale. This scale, which first crept into Synagogue song (Chapter IX), entered to a small degree also into the folk-song of the Jews in the Southeastern districts. No. 21 illustrates this type of tune.[37] It has the typical Ukrainian melodic line.

Group (D) This group comprises a small number of tunes in major, all of which are adopted from German or Slavic sources, and they are all of recent date. They spring from the time when the Jewish population in the East came into closer contact with its surroundings.

The Jewish rhythmical folk-tunes are in 2/4, 3/4, 4/4, and 6/8 time. None of the intricate rhythms employed in the Oriental song are used; neither will 5/4 or 7/8 time be found. The structure, too, is simple, logical. The tunes consist of 1½, 2, 2½, or 3 periods, making 12, 16, 20, or 24 bars.

In summary, Jewish folk-song in Eastern Europe is based primarily upon types (A) and (B). It developed a style of its own, influenced by that in Slavic song which is Oriental. This accretion strengthened the Oriental foundation of the Jewish music.

The most noteworthy collections thus far published are:

S. M. GUINSBOURG and P. S. MAREK, *Yevreiskia Narodnia Pesni*, Petersburg, 1901. This collection contains three hun-

TABLE XXXII
Tunes of the Eastern Ashkenazic folk-song

4. O-mar a-do-noy le - ya-cov, nein fo-te-rl, nein, al ti-roh av-di ya-a-cov, hob nit kein forcht main knecht ya-a-cov, nein fo-terl, nein, ch'hob nit kain forcht far kain, nor far dir a - lain. lain.

5. Slowly
Yo - vo a-dir ve - yig-o-le-nu, yo - vo e-li-yo-hu vi-vas-re - nu. un vos vet er me-va-ser sein? ki yo-vo mo-shi-ach tzid-ke - nu. gvald, gvald ven vet er ku-men, ven zshe, ven zshe sha! nit shrei er vet shon ku-men, vet dos sein, bim - he-roh ve-yo-me - nu. un vos far a tog vet da mols sein? yom gi-loh, yom ri-noh, yom di-tzoh, yom ched-voh, gi - loh, ri - noh, di - tzo ched-voh, ha - le - lu - yoh.

Slowly

6.

Un-ter mein kinds vi-ga-le stet a vei-se
tzi-ga-le, di tzi-ga-le is ge-fo-ren hand-len
ro-sin-kes mit mand-len, ro-sin-kes mit mand-len is di
bes-te s'cho-roh, mein kind vet ken-nen ler-nen to-roh. *etc.*

Recitando

7.

Hei, piv ya u-nie-di-liu i pro-
piv ya vsu na-di-liu, oj tre-ba zna-ti yak hu-lia-ti,
yak bo-ha po-chva-lia-ti, i-ber hun-dert yor yak u-mi-ra-ti
chesh-bon tze-dek ot-da-va-ti, a mi piom tai hu-
lia-em, ve-a-toh ti-she-ma min ha-sho-ma-yim.

8.

Un as du forst a-vek, main
ta-ier sis le-ben, oif ve-men los-tu mich du i-ber

oj, vej, ot cha-lesh ich! oj, vej, ot starb ieh.

9. Recitando

A - lef, in - di - kes est der no - gid,

beis, bein - da - lech gri - zet der o - rim - man.

10. Recit.

Af bri. S'is ni - to vos tzu ge-ben es sen di kü. Der

Süm-mer geht a - vek ün der vin-ter kumt tzu-rik,

un kain gelt i ni-to. di sti-vel sai-nen tzü-ris-sen oj, oj, di

kush-me is tzü-shmis-sen, oj, oj, oj, oj, ün kain gelt is alz ni-to.

11. Recitando

Is ge - ku-men tzu-fo-ren a chaz-zan in a ste - tl

da - ve - nen a sha - bos, da - ve - nen a sha - bos. *etc.*

12. Recitando

Sog zshe re-be-niu. vos vet sein as mo-shi-ach vet ku-men? as mo-

shi - ach vet ku - men vel - n mir ma-chen a se - u - doh.

vos veln mir es - sen auf der s'u - doh? dem

shor ha bar mitn liv-yo-son, dem shor ha-bar mitn liv-yo-son, dem

shor ha-bar mitn liv-yo-son veln mir es-sen auf der s'u-doh. *etc.*

13.

Ich steh mir un klar, vos toig mir mein leben, as far-

vo-gelt bin ich fun der velt, oj, ich seh far mir, veh is mir,

mein tai-er le-ben, as un-ser lie-be is shon far-stert.

14.

Fregt di velt di al-te ka-she: tra-la tra-di-ri-di-ra.

ent-fert men: ta-da-ra-da-ram, oj, oj, ta-ra-ta-ra-ra.

unas, men vill ken men doch so-gen: ta-ram.

bleibt doch alz di al-te ka-she, ta-ra ta-da-ra-da-ram!

15.

Pa-pir is doch vais un tint is doch shvartz, tzu dir main sîs

Allegretto

22.

Yan-ke-le mit Riv-ke-len hal-ten sich de-rin-ter,

Yan-ke-le is a-vek ge-fo-ren oif a-gan-tzen vin-ter.

Riv-ke-le hot ge-meint si vet a-lein blei-ben,

hot si tzu ihm on-ge-hoi-ben bri-ve-lach tzu shrei-ben.

Vivace

23.

Ko-ti-li sia vo-zi zgo-ri, po-lo-ma-li shpi-tzi,

a vzshe-zme-ni ne cho-di-ti na ti ve-cher-ni-tzi.

24.

Is ge-ku-men der fet-ter no-son shein, fain, der

fet-ter no-son hot ge-bracht dem shei-nem cho-son.

25.

Na go-ro-di kirt-ki viut-sia Ne bij-te sia,

ne-ma za-sh'cho chot-ia gar-na, to lia-da-shcho.

26. Andantino

27. Moderato

Du solst nit   gen   mit kein   an - de - re

mei - de - lach, du   solst nor gen mit   mir,   Du solst nit

gen tzu dein ma-me in stü - be - le, nor ku-men sol-stu tzu mir.

Tra - ra - ra - ram.

28.

29.

30.

31. Allegretto

dred seventy-six poems in Hebrew characters with Latin transliteration without music.

M. KIPNIS, one hundred forty *Folkslieder*, Warsaw, in two volumes (without date of publication). Vol. I contains sixty songs and Vol. II eighty. The texts are printed in Hebrew characters; the melodies are given without accompaniment.

I. L. CAHAN, *Yiddish Folk-songs*, in two volumes, New York, 1912, containing three hundred twenty-four poems and one hundred eighty-six tunes. In a long introduction Cahan gives an interesting characterization of Jewish folk-song. A considerable number of songs of this collection are also incorporated in the two previous collections.

FRITZ MORDECHAI KAUFMANN edited *Die schönsten Lieder der Ostjuden*, containing forty-seven songs with a phonetical transliteration and explanations of each song. Jüdischer Verlag, Berlin, 1920.

Much material was published in various Jewish periodicals and magazines, especially in the proceedings of the ethnographical *Mitteilungen für jüdische Volkskunde* (editor M. GRUNWALD), Hamburg-Vienna, 1898-1926.

Muzykaliszer Pinkos, Vol. I, a collection of two hundred forty-three *Zemiroth* and *chassidic* songs, edited by A. M. BERNSTEIN, Wilna, 1927.

Ganovim Lieder (Songs of Thieves) and love songs, a collection of one hundred thirty songs with music, edited by SAMUEL LEJMAN, Warsaw, 1928.

In Chapter XXI account will be given of the collections and publications arranged for instruments.

CHAPTER XIX

In addition to its distinctive *chazzanuth* and folk-song, Eastern Europe made another contribution to Jewish music. The Jews in Poland and the Ukraine produced an original type of song which in its aim and composition has no counterpart elsewhere. It is generally called CHASSIDIC SONG, because it was created out of the spirit of Chassidism.

Chassidism is usually linked up with Cabbala, with mysticism. Indeed, Chassidism is a derivation of and a new phase in the development of the never completely lost mystic strain in the Jewish people. When we glance over the long history of Judaism, we become aware of the continuation of a hidden mystic stream flowing through Jewish life from ancient times on. And music is and always has been an important means wherewith to procure the mystic's inspiration and to express his ideas. The Neo-mystics in Safed, Palestine, under the leadership of the genius Isaac Luria—known by the abbreviation *Ari* (Chapter XVII)—made singing their duty and counted it a condition of inspiration and devotion.[1] From that time onward the rivulet of mysticism pushed its way ahead without pausing, winding through many changing fields and emptying into the stream of CHASSIDISM.

The mystic movement in Palestine created a special kind of cabbalistic song, peculiar not only in its text but also in its type of melody. These tunes have a taste of unearthliness—like a swaying mist which loses itself in infinity (*en sof*).[2]

We digress here for a moment to call attention to table XXXIII, 1-3, presenting a few songs of the Palestinian cabbalists. No. 1 is

the intonation for *Barechu* for the Evening service of "New Year."
We notice in this tune the long embellishment on the word *Adonay*
(Yahwe, see note 2). The tune is in the Psalm mode (Chapter
III c). No. 2—*Yedid Nefesh*—is a poem by Eleazar Azkari, who
was a disciple of Isaac Luria.[3] This poem became very popular among
the cabbalists and later among the chassidim. The tune is in modal
form, in the *makam Sabba* (Chapter II). No. 3—*Azammer bishvachin* by Isaac Luria in Aramaic became likewise very popular. This
tune has strict rhythm and is in the makam *Nawa* (Chapter II).[4]

Although this cabbalism was, as stated above, the basis of
the later chassidic movement, yet it alone never became popular, in spite of efforts made to spread it among the people. It,
therefore, remained only for world-forsakers in Palestine. But
what the Palestinian mysticism could not achieve *Chassidism*
did.

The code of the *Shulchan Aruch*, a program of Jewish life
formulated for the purpose of keeping before the people
through their daily practices the religious and ethical intent of
the Commandments, had become in the course of time an end
in itself, rather than a tool to achieve a spiritual goal; it had
become a rigid system of laws and commandments. This decadent state roused emotional spirits among the Jewish people
to infuse into Judaism new vision, or rather to re-awaken the
dormant emotionalism and mystic strain.

The founder of this movement was ISRAEL BAAL-SHEM-TOV,
known by the abbreviation *Besht*. He lived in Galicia and
Podolia (1700-1760). After his death, his disciples and followers continued his work, and at the end of the eighteenth
century, through the influence of several prominent and inspired leaders, the movement reached its height. These leaders
were called *tzadikim*—Righteous ones—in the sense of saints.
The most outstanding among them were BER OF MESERITSH

(1710-1772), Levi Yitzchok of Berditschev (1740-1810), Shneor Zalman of Ladi (1747-1813), and Nachman of Brasslaw (1772-1811). The two latter, being fine thinkers, attempted to formulate the ideas of Chassidism into a philosophical system.

The *tzadikim* founded residences, called "courts" by their adherents, whereto the chassidim—the pious ones—used to pilgrim in order to receive inspiration and salvation and to be instructed in the mysticism of the chassidic doctrine. Every chassid used to bring gifts to his *tzadik,* so that the earthly prosperity of the "saints" depended upon the number of their adherents.

Like other religious mystic movements, Chassidism is affected by and mixed with superstition. Its atmosphere is filled with good and evil spirits, with angels and ghosts, heaven and hell.

The *tzadik* is a thaumaturge and has exclusive access to the upper spheres. Only he, through his prayers, can obtain the things desired.

Throughout the nineteenth century this movement remained untouched by the realistic and materialistic *Weltanschauung* of Central and Western Europe. Secluded from the outer world in remote villages, the *tzadikim* continued their mystic work amidst their pious ones.

The chassidim were separated from the other Ashkenazic Jews by the establishment of their own synagogues in which they introduced the Sephardic ritual, according to the version sanctioned by I. Luria.[5] They made some minor changes in Jewish religious customs. Their opponents, called *misnagdim,* fought them bitterly, accusing them of pantheism, even of paganism, excommunicating them, burning the books on Chassidism,[6] and going to the extreme of effecting the imprisonment of one of their leaders, Rabbi Shneor Zalman of Ladi. Never-

theless, the movement grew in Eastern Europe, and toward the
end of the nineteenth century its adherents numbered from
three to four million.

Chassidism set piety above learning and regarded the expression of exuberant joy as a chief religious duty. The chassidic leaders believed that vocal music is the best medium of
rising to salvation. "All melodies are derived from the source
of sanctity, from the Temple of music. Impurity knows no
song, because it knows no joy; for it is the source of all melancholy." "Through song calamities can be removed." "Music
originates from the prophetic spirit, and has the power to elevate one to prophetic inspiration." [7]

Song is the soul of the universe. The realm of heaven
sings; the Throne of God breathes music; even the tetragram-
maton *Yahve* is composed of four musical notes. "Every
science, every religion, every philosophy, even atheism has
its particular song. The loftier the religion or the science, the
more exalted is its music." [8]

The *tzadik*, as the only representative of his flock, has sole
admission to the heavenly spring of music. He receives the
holy magic song from that source and uses it as a tool to purify
the fallen soul, heal the sick, and perform all sorts of miracles. [9]
The *tzadik* receives the most exalted music of the Divine
wherewith he destroys all songs of the pagan religions and of
heresy. [10] Some of the saints believed that they could achieve
more in the heavens through the power of their song than
through that of their prayers. [11] "In the high spheres there
exist temples that can be opened through song only." [12] Some
held that the sphere of music is near to the sphere of peni-
tence. [13]

Since the *tzadik* was the only divine singer, it is evident that
he was also the creator of the holy tunes by heavenly inspiration. Several melodies still circulate among the chassidim as

compositions of *tzadikim*. It is, however, uncertain whether these are inventions of the sainted leaders or adopted tunes reshaped in accord with their emotions. Almost every "court" had its original style in music, its preferred mode, or at least a special tune, expressing the individuality and train of thought of the "reigning" *tzadik*. In case the *tzadik* lacked creative musical ability, he engaged a court-singer whose task it was to study the nature of the "saint," his feelings and ideas, and give them tonal utterance. The function of the court-singer was to sing tunes with or without words at the public Sabbath-meals in order to inspire the *tzadik*. But as soon as the singer dared to intone melodies belonging to another "court," i.e., to another *tzadik*, he was immediately dismissed, because in singing other tunes he desecrated the holy impulse of this *tzadik*.[14] The *tzadik* also had his court synagogue in which he frequently functioned as precentor.[15] Because their song was largely inspirational and extemporaneous, chassidim paid but little attention to the musical tradition of the Synagogue. The *tzadik* of Gor, Isaac Meyer, used to say: "Were I blessed with a sweet voice, I could sing you new hymns and songs every day, for with the daily rejuvenation of the world new songs are created."[16] Some *tzadikim* opposed prayers and tunes "from yesterday."[17] Following their inspiration, they would invent new meditations and set them to tunes. Their texts were often a mixture of Hebrew and Yiddish, such as those of Levi Yitzchok of Berditschev, given in table XXXIII, 6.[18] This procedure stimulated the antagonism of the *misnagdim*.[19] Only Rabbi Jacob Joseph Katz, one of the outstanding disciples of Israel Besht (died 1782), favored traditional songs, at least those for the High Holidays.[20]

The songs were first rendered at the public meals of the "court." The chassidim present would memorize them and carry them into their homes, teaching them to the pious ones until the tunes became widely known. At least twice a year, on the High Holidays and *Shavuoth*, large pilgrimages to the "courts" were customary, on which occasions, as a rule, new melodies would be invented and sung.[21]

Israel Besht, so folklore has it, used to perceive words out of the tones of a melody. He was likewise able to follow the thoughts of the singer. Another saint believed that he could hear the confession of the singer, though no words were uttered.[22] Shneor Zalman was of the opinion that melody is the outpouring of the soul, but that words interrupt the stream of the emotions. "For the songs of the souls—at the time they are swaying in the high regions to drink from the well of the Almighty King—consist of tones only, dismantled of words."[23] A melody with text is, to his mind, limited to time, because with the conclusion of the words the melody, too, comes to an end; whereas a tune without words can be repeated endlessly. As a result of this attitude, most *chassidic* tunes are sung without words.

The characteristics of the early *chassidic* melodies were governed by the preferences of the *tzadikim*. Some delighted in lyric-sentimental tunes which voiced yearning and revery;[24] while others liked subtle rhythms, syncopations and tempo vivace.[25] Some would pour out their emotions in soft minor-tunes; others would give utterance to emotionalism and indulge in dance and march rhythms. Once the *chazzan* Nissi Belzer (Chapter XIV) gave a concert in the court of Rabbi Dovidl, *tzadik* of Talno. He selected his best compositions for the High Holidays in order to delight the Rabbi. But when the choir started to sing a touching tune, the *tzadik* interrupted the singing, exclaiming, "Oh, you want to move me to tears. Stop!"[26]

The material for their songs and melodies the *chassidic* singers drew from the Synagogue modes, from the Oriental elements in the Ukrainian or Slavic folk-song, and from Cossack dances and military marches. As a whole, we see here the same procedure of acquiring the material as we saw in the previous chapter. However, in the *chassidic* song the adopted melodies were reworked, for borrowed tunes, sprung forth in an entirely different *milieu*, could not satisfactorily express the *chassidic* spirit. Consequently, there developed gradually a typical style, a *chassidic* melodic line. This style branched itself out into subdivisions, in compliance with the spirit of the various "courts," voicing one or the other feature within *Chassidism*. But despite the emphasis laid by the *tzadikim* upon their individuality, they remained within the *chassidic* realm as it was framed by the first leaders of that movement.

Like the zealous Christians in the Middle Ages, some of the *tzadikim* considered it their holy duty to save secular tunes for sacred purposes. It is related of "Leib Sarah's" (1730-1791) and of his disciple the *tzadik* of Kalif, Hungary, that they used to stroll through woods and meadows to listen to the songs of the shepherds and to rework these songs into religious meditations. Once, upon listening to the love-song of a shepherd, the *tzadik* of Kalif immediately copied the ditty and paraphrased it in Yiddish. Both versions are circulating among the people, the secular and the reworked religious one: [27]

Secular	*Religious*
Ros', Ros', wie weit bist du!	Shechina, Shechina, wie weit bist du!
Wald, wald, wie gross bist du!	Golus, Golus, wie lang bist du!
Wolt die Ros' nit aso weit gewe'n,	Wolt die Shechina nit aso weit gewe'n,
Wolt der Wald nit aso gross gewe'n.	Wolt der Golus nit aso lang gewe'n.

Rose, rose, how far you are! Woods, woods, how large you are! The rose would not have been so far, Were the woods not so large.

The *tzadik* substituted *Shechina* (Divine Presence) for "rose" and *Golus* (exile) for "woods." In this sanctified form the song lived among the chassidim for about a century and a half, until lately, when it was written down and published. In table XXXIII, 4, this song is illustrated.

In the course of its development, the chassidic movement branched out in two directions: the one called "the system of Besht" with most of its adherents in Poland, Southern Russia, Roumania, and Hungary. The followers of this system claimed to be the real disciples of the founder, Israel Besht, and of his descendants. The other system was called *Chabad*, an abbreviation of *Chochma*—Wisdom, *Bina*—Insight, and *Daath* —Knowledge. This system was founded by the above-mentioned Shneor Zalman of Ladi, with its adherents mostly in Lithuania and White Russia,[28] and with its centre in Liubawitz, in the Government of Mohilev. Here the descendants of Shneor Zalman resided for about a century, establishing a dynasty of five generations, called "the Shneorsons." [29] This system, although reaching toward the same purpose of attaining divine bliss, has another approach to the goal. It is impossible, the *Chabad* contends, to leap immediately from extreme melancholy to extreme joy. It is impossible for a human being to rise from the lowest to the highest degree without proceeding through the whole scale of the intermediate states of the soul. Great stress is laid upon each progressive stage of the development, as significant for the education of the soul and for the improvement of the spirit. It is, *Chabad*-chassidism says, as if someone who had never seen the interior of a palace suddenly stepped into its bewildering splendor without having first passed through the corridors. Such a person will never be able to feel fully the glory of the palace. Therefore, the APPROACH to joy, the corridor of the palace, is very important. Every step must be achieved through deep meditation. These steps for the elevation of the spirit begin with the lowest, called *hishtapchuth hannefesh*—the outpouring of the soul and its effort to rise out of the mire of sin, out of the shell of the evil spirit, the *klippah*, and to reach the second stage, *hithoreruth*, spiritual awakening. Thence the devotee rises to *hithpaaluth*, a stage in which he is possessed by his thought; and from this state he reaches *dveikuth*, communion with God. Then he progresses to *hithlahavuth*, a flaming ecstasy; and finally he attains the highest step, *hithpashtuth hagashmiyuth*, a stage when the soul casts off its garment of flesh and becomes a disembodied spirit.

For this purpose the *Chabad*-chassidim, with even less success than the Besht sect, might seek tunes from without, because none of the gentiles has such a program underlying his folksongs. Therefore, they were compelled to create original tunes which express the meanings and the thoughts of all these stages in the elevation of the soul, tunes to be used as means for the attainment of their purpose. The founder of the *Chabad* system himself composed a tune, called *Dem Rebbens Niggun*—the Rabbi's tune—constructed to conform to his system. We give this popular melody in table XXXIII, 5. The tune starts in *largo* and voices the first stage, the outpouring of the soul. With the fifth bar, *con moto*, the tune progresses to the second stage, the spiritual awakening. The third part, beginning with the ninth bar, aims to express the steps of *hithpaaluth* and *dveikuth*, until it reaches the stage of ecstasy. And the fourth part, from bar thirteen on, presents the stage of the "disembodied soul." According to a later interpretation, however, "the Rabbi's tune" gives tonal expression to the four realms of the universe.[30] Starting at the bottom with *briah*—

the creation of the lowest elements of minerals, the tune next voices the second higher realm, *yetzirah*—the creation of living beings. Proceeding to the third realm *asiyah*—the creation of man, the tune finally reaches the goal in the fourth realm, *atziluth*—emanation, the Heavenly region. Every *Chabad* tune aims to voice either all the stages of the elevation of the soul or only some phases of them. Thus, there are tunes expressing *dveikuth, hishtapchuth hannefesh, hithlahavuth, hithoreruth,* and so on. The latter two stages are also called *Rikud* —dance. The illustrations Nos. 4, 6, 14-18 in table XXXIII are *dveikuth* or *hishtapchuth* tunes, while Nos. 7-10, 19-22, 23-28 give tonal expression to the other stages. No. 23 consists of seven parts in Rondo form and aims to express all the stages explained. The melodies voicing *dveikuth,* etc., have the free unrhythmical form, or are in a slow rhythm. The tunes for "awakening," etc., are built upon vigorous syncopated and dancing rhythms.

The melodies are based either upon the *Ahavoh-Rabboh* scale or upon the minor scale with minor or major seventh. Tunes based upon the major scale are very few and are adopted. In the *Ahavoh-Rabboh* scale are the tunes: Nos. 5, 7-13. In the minor scale are: Nos. 14-17, 19-23. Nos. 25 and 27 are in major.

No. 6 is attributed to the above-mentioned Levi Yitzchok of Berditschev. The tune is partly unrhythmical and partly rhythmical. Its text is mixed, Hebrew-Yiddish. The name *A Dudule* refers to the playing on the primitive shepherd's instrument, *Dudelsack*—bagpipe. *Dudeln* in German means "to tootle." Here, however, the name is used as a play upon the word *du-du-le*—Thou, Thou! The *tzadik* addresses himself to God with the endearing German diminutive "le." The contents of the text are as follows: "O Lord of the world, I shall sing to Thee a 'du-du-le'; where can I find Thee, and where can I not find Thee? Wherever I go Thou art present,

TABLE XXXIII
Cabbalistic and Chassidic Songs

Lento

1 Ba - re - chuet a-do-nay ha-me-vo - rach.

Recit.

2 Ye-did ne - fesh av ha - ra - cha-man me -

shoch av - dach el re - tzo - nach. ya-rutz av -

dach ke-mo a - yal____ yish-ta____

cha-we el mul ha - da - - - - rach.

Andantino

3 A - zam-mer bish-va - chin le-me - al go pi - te-chin, de -

rit.

va cha-kal tap-pu - chin de - in - nun kad-di - shin.

Largo

4 Sh'chi-noh, sh'chi-noh, vie veit bist du, go-lus, go-lus, vie lang bist du,

volt die shchi-noh nit 'so veit ge-ve'n, volt der go-lus nit 'so lang ge-ve'n.

a) Tunes in Ahavoh-Rabboh Mode

A Dudele

Ri - bo - no schel o - lom, Ri - bo - no schel o - lom, Ri - bo - no schel o - lom,

Ri - bo - no schel o - lom. Ri - bo - no schel o - lom ich wel dir a du - de - le

sin - gen, du - du - du - du - du. a - ye em - zo - e - choh we - a - ye

lo em zo - e - choh, wo kan man dich yo ge - fi - nen, un wo kan man dich

nit ge - fi - nen? du - du - du - du - du. as wo ich geh is doch du, un
wo ich steh is doch du

rak du, nor du wie - der du, o - ber du - du - du - du - du - du. is

Recit.

e-mi-zen gut, is doch dn, we-cho-li-loh schlecht, oj   du.

Con fuoco

oj, du-du-du du-du-du, du - du - du - du.   a-toh du, ho yoh du
                                                     - - - - mo-loch -

ho-we du yih-ye du   du-du-du-du - du. - du. scho-mayim du, e-rez du,
me-lech - yim-loch-

Maestoso

ma-loh du,   ma-toh du - du,   du - du - du - du.   du-du-du-du-

poco a poco rit. e dim.

du - du - du.   wo ich kehr mich, wo ich wend mich du!   du!

Allegro

7

Amyis-ro-el chay,   amyis-ro-el chay   ad be-li   day

ad be-li -day,   ad be-li   day,   amyis-ro-el chayl

Allegro

8

Ve - ta-her li-be-nu, ve - ta-her li-be-nu le - ov-de-choh be-e-mes.

Rondo
Allegro moderato

13

Fine

D.C.a F.

b) Tunes in Minor

Recit.
Con moto, mysterioso

14

Be-ne he-cho-loh dich-si-fin

le-nech-ze ziv diz-er an-pin   oj

oj   ye-hon ho-choh   oj   be-hay ta-koh

oj   oj de-ve mal-koh   be-gi-lu-fin.

Lento

15

19 *Recitando* *mf* *Solo*

Gott mus man die-nen un man we tihm die-nen,   o-ber nit wie a -go-lom,ha-

Lento   *Andante*
Choir

don ye-chi - di   le - vo - e   o -lom.   Die-nen mus man Gott,

Gott mus man die-nen, der for wos er hot uns   aus-ge-weilt zum die-nen.

20 *Allegro*
f

1   *2*   *1*   *2*
Fine

D.C.a.F.

21 *Andante*
f

22 *Andante* *with ecstasy*
f
1   *2*

c) Tunes in Major

Allegro moderato

25

Ash-re-chem, ash-re-chem, ash-re-chemyis-ro-el, ash-re-chemyis-ro-el,

ash-re-chemyis-ro-el, ash-re-chemyis-ro-el, ash-re-chemyis-ro - el.

Allegro

26

Ash-re a -yïn ver hotdos ge - sehn.

Allegro

27

Moderato

28

29 Vos vet zein mit dem rebben dem fru - men, bim - he-roh ve-yo - me - nu, az mo-shi-ach vet ku - men, fon vein un fon bron-fen vet gehn a re-gen, un dos vet zein far die ch'ssi - dim ve-gen, bim-he-roh ve-yo-me-nu vie der - lebt men dos shoin.

30 Ef-fent reb-bi-tzin, ch'ssi-dim ge-hen, ch'ssi-dim ge-hen, vil-len sich fre-hen, ch'ssi-dim ge-hen zei vil-len doch tzu gan-ve-nen die in pan-tof-fel zil-ber-ne lef-fel! ch'ssi dim ge-hen zei vil-len doch tzu gan-ve-nen die in pan-tof-fel zil-ber-ne lef - fel reb-be-tzin, reb-be-tzin, hot kein moi-roh, ch'ssi-dim ge - hen ler-nen toi - roh. ler-nen toi - roh.

and wherever I stand Thou art present. Thou, only Thou, always Thou! Prosperity is from Thee; and suffering, oh, it, too, comes from Thee! Thou art, Thou hast been, and Thou wilt be! Thou didst reign, Thou reignest, and Thou wilt reign. Thine is Heaven, Thine is earth. Thou fillest the high and the low regions. Whithersoever I turn, Thou art there!"

The tune starts in minor (g), modulates to *Ahavoh-Rabboh* (g), turns toward the end to the major on the sub-dominant (c) and concludes in minor (g).

No. 14 is by the above-mentioned Dovidl of Talno; it is a *dveikuth* tune in free modal form. Its scale is f minor, though the fifth (c) is frequently diminished, in fashion similar to the *Makam Mustaar* [31] which makes a mystical impression. The text is an Aramaic poem by I. Luria *B'nei Hechalah* for the third meal of the Sabbath, and is very popular among the chassidim.

No. 28 is a typical major-minor tune with no stable scale, beginning in major and finishing in minor. This type is known in the Oriental and in the Slavic folk-song. No. 26 starts in E major, modulates to the *Adonoy-Moloch* mode in E with the minor seventh, turns then to the Ukrainian-Dorian in E, and finishes in major. Only two bars have a text consisting of a few Hebrew and Yiddish words: Fortunate is the eye that has seen this (wonder). The remainder of the tune is sung without words.

In No. 18 only an inclination toward the Ukrainian scale is noticeable, while Nos. 12 and 24 are based entirely upon this scale. These two tunes, as well as Nos. 11 and 13 were written down in 1809-10 in Berlin by I. Löb Wolf and in Amsterdam by Sholom Friede (Chapter XI), and they prove that chassidic tunes were spread all over Central Europe at the beginning of the nineteenth century.

We find a strict form in the rhythmical chassidic tunes, even as in the Yiddish folk-songs. The tunes have symmetrical structure of one to three periods, eight bars to the period. Some of them, such as No. 23, have larger forms: the compound *Lied* form (A.B.A.; A.B.C.A.) and the Rondo form. We also notice that the principle of modulating to the subdominant is observed.

The rhythmical tunes are usually sung in unison by the groups, while unrhythmical songs are rendered by single voices.

The chassidic song, though religious in purport, is not used for the worship proper, but for inspiration and preparation of the "pious ones" for worship. It aims to elevate the troubled soul to approach the Source of all goodness, happiness and joy, in prayer and in communion.

As long as the chassidic movement flourished its song naturally developed. But toward the end of the nineteenth century, Chassidism began to deteriorate, and as a consequence, its song likewise decayed. Hence, those chassidic tunes created in the last few decades sound like caricatures of the old and genuine ones. The opponents of Chassidism took delight in imitating and caricaturing chassidic song, setting to the garbled melodies satiric words. Two examples, Nos. 29 and 30, illustrate that type of song. No. 29 recounts the miracles the *tzadik* will perform at the time when Messiah will come. The tune has the form of an unrhythmical *dveikuth* melody in the *Ahavoh-Rabboh* mode. No. 30 is a dialogue between the chassidim who seek to enter the house of the *tzadik* in order to be instructed by the "saint," and his wife, who hesitates to let them in out of fear that they might steal the silver dishes.

Chassidic song exerted a strong influence upon the *chazzanuth* of Eastern Europe. Almost all the prominent *chazzanim* treated in Chapter XIV were reared in the chassidic atmosphere and were imbued with its mystical spirit and its emotionalism. These characteristics are reflected in their musical creations. Apart from those cited in Chapter XIV, we mention here some of the *chazzanim* who served at the "courts" or were for some time connected with them.

JOSHUA FINESINGER in Lontshitz gained much popularity

for his compositions for the *piyyutim* for the Sabbaths between Passover and *Shavuoth*. Of great merit are his settings of *Shechuloh achuloh*,[32] *Yokush beonyo*, *Shviyoh aniyoh*. LEIZER OF LODZ (died 1887) was a noted *chazzan* and likewise a great Talmudist.[33] ISRAEL JAFFA of Suvalk, later *chazzan* in Kalish, was also a remarkable Hebrew scholar. MOSHE MICHEL EICHLER, *chazzan* in Praga near Warsaw is the composer of the tune in table XXXIII, 20. HERSH OF PRZSHEV (1798-1892) served for seventy-seven years as *chazzan* at the courts of Gor, Kotzk, and Alexandria. Others of ability were ZALMAN OF POLTOSK, *chazzan* at the court in Kotzk; CHAYYIM CHAYKL, a court-singer in Gor; HERSHELE TOLCZYNER, YOSELE DEM REBBINS, both court-singers in Talno; and JACOB TELECHANER, court-singer in Koydanov.[34] RABBI BER OF RADOSHITZ, called "the Little Ber," in contradistinction to Ber of Mezeritsh, "the Great Ber," became a *tzadik* through the magic of his wonderful singing.

The most gifted *chazzan* who grew out of the chassidic environment is JACOB SAMUEL MARGOWSKY, called "Zeidel Rovner." He was born in Radomishl, in the government of Kiev, in 1856, and was destined early for the career of rabbi. He sang at various occasions to the delight of the chassidim in his native village. These admirers once took the youth to the *tzadik* of Makarov, asking that Zeidel be permitted to sing in his presence. This request the saint granted. After hearing the lad, the *tzadik* ORDERED him to officiate as *chazzan* in the synagogue on the High Holidays. Zeidel's pleadings and arguments that he had neither *chazzanic* training nor knowledge of the traditional tunes were of no avail. He officiated, and by merit of the *tzadik*, with great success. After that, Zeidel engaged himself in business and continued for many years to act as High Holiday *chazzan*. He obtained rudimentary knowledge of music from the *klezmer* (instru-

mentalists) (Chapter XX). Once, while he was visiting the
tzadik, the latter suddenly ordered him to abandon his business and become a professional *chazzan*. This order Zeidel
faithfully, though reluctantly, obeyed. Thereafter he occupied
various posts and became famous through his compositions
which follow the style of Nissi Belzer's creations in structure
but which excel them in LENGTH. Seidel's compositions are
markedly instrumental in character. Under other circumstances
he might have become a prominent composer for the orchestra.
In the Synagogue his orchestra was the *a capella* choir, and his
singers, human instruments. Zeidel wrote voluminously.
After officiating in Rovno, Kishinev, and Berditshev, he left
for Lemberg. Later he traveled to London, and finally settled in New York.[35]

Chassidic song, like that of the Yemenite Jews (Chapter
XVII) is rendered exclusively by men. It is a masculine song.
Thus, we see that Jewish folk-song has both a feminine (Chapter XVIII) and masculine song. They grew out of the circumstances of Jewish life.

CHAPTER XX

A. *Badchonim* and SINGERS

Jewish folksingers were called *badchonim*—merry-makers, also *leitzim* or *leitzonim*—comedians, jesters. In Germany they were also called *marshalks, marshaliks*.[2] It was a custom of old that, though secular song and instrumental music were prohibited in Israel after the Destruction (Chapters V and VI), both were permitted at weddings and on Purim. It was even considered a merit to sing and dance and make merry in order to cheer the bride by praising her beauty and good qualities. Prominent Talmudists counted such conduct not beneath their dignity. It is reported of Rabbi Juda bar Ilai that he would dance and sing before the bride with a palm-branch in his hand —the refrain of his song being: "Oh, beautiful and virtuous bride!" The same is reported of the disciples of Hillel. The scholars would suspend their study to dance and sing at weddings in the presence of the bride.[3]

The people grasped this opportunity for rejoicing in order to give vent to their suppressed longing for music and amusement, song and dance. It became a hard task for the spiritual leaders to check this passion (Chapter V) and to direct the singers and merry-makers to songs of religious and ethical content. Hence, the singers and merry-makers used to interweave their couplets and jingles with Biblical phrases and Talmudic sayings.

Already in the first centuries of the Common Era there

existed professional *badchonim,* whose task it was to cheer the sad and to make peace between enemies,[4] an aim indicating the high conception that the *badchonim* had of their profession. They sought to elevate and to instruct the masses while entertaining them. This goal they attempted to achieve primarily through witty and subtle satire of which the Jewish people were always fond. Their songs, the *badchonim* invented extemporaneously according to the particular conditions at each wedding.

"In the Middle Ages we find among the Jews traveling merry-makers, who probably patterned themselves after the troubadours, and took the place of former voluntary entertainers at weddings. Their task was by jest, music, and humorous song to provoke joviality. The name given them originally in Jewish writing is *leitzim,* a term which occurs . . . in the early part of the thirteenth century. The jesters were obliged to possess not only comic ability, but also a certain deal of learning, since those jokes were appreciated most which were connected with Scriptural verses or Talmudic passages. Such scholarly comedians were in vogue largely in the Middle Ages. As the clouds of persecution, however, continued to gather round the Jew, merriment was discouraged. R. David Levy (1680) . . . inveighs against the fashion of engaging *lezim* for wedding festivities."[5] In Germany and Poland the standard of the *badchon* deteriorated. Singing and merry-making at weddings instead of being counted a merit were considered unfitting for a scholar. Rabbi Yair Bachrach (seventeenth century) stigmatized the professional jester as "a man playing the fool in order to provoke laughter; such a wedding is called a seat of scoffers (*leitzim,* Ps. I: 1), for it is not real rejoicing, but hilarity and folly."[6]

On *Purim,* song, merry-making, and rejoicing were permitted already in the Talmudic age.[7] The celebration consisted of special humorous *Purim*-songs in the vernacular of each country. Many of these songs are still retained, in Judeo-Italian,[8] Judeo-Spanish[9] and Judeo-German. Of the latter there are two poems in the collection of songs by E. Walich, treated in Chapter XVIII, the one relating the story of Esther and the other, a merry song by Jewish Talmud students, who would visit the Jewish homes in disguise and obtain food and gifts.[10]

The *Purim* rejoicing brought about the creation of Jewish folk-comedies. While as a usual thing a dramatic performance was considered frivolous, an exception was made with regard to *Purim*. In Gaonic times the dramatization of the story of Esther was a well-established custom among the Jews in the Orient. The central figure of these plays was a dummy representing Haman, which was burned, while the spectators jested and sang. Similar amusements are reported of the Jews of other countries during the Middle Ages.[11] The real *Purim* play, however, the Judeo-German *Purim-Spiel*, did not make its appearance until the first decade of the eighteenth century. There were, it is true, some productions on the subject of the Book of Esther and the Feast of *Purim* long before that time, such as the drama *Esther* by Solomon Usque and Lazaro Gratiano (1567)—the first Spanish drama written by a Jew. But these dramas were probably intended for the general stage, since there is no record that they were ever performed by the Jews.[12]

The first *Purim* play intended for and actually performed on the stage during the days of *Purim* was the *Ahasweros Spiel*, published in Frankfort in 1708.[13] The play was performed with music and had a special tune which became popular. Apparently this was a tune of a serious character, for it was later (in 1712) set to a lamentation on the conflagration of Frankfort, written by David Saugers of Prague.[14]

In 1720 the play *Acta Esther* was performed on the stage by Talmud students of Prague, "beautifully decorated with orchestral accompaniment." In 1780 a tragi-comedy in five acts, called *The Salvation of the Jews by Esther and Mordecai* (in Yiddish), was published in Amsterdam by Jacob of Prague. In 1828 the play *Esther* or *Belohnende Tugend* was published in Fürth by Joseph Herz.[15]

The *Purim* play was the beginning of the Jewish Theatre and melodrama, of which we shall treat later.

The *badchonim* were not solely merry-makers and jesters. Many a tear would mingle in the cup of joy that they presented to the young couples and the wedding-guests. They utilized this opportunity to keep before the eyes of their people the unpleasant conditions of the Jew as well as the Jew's inner troubles. But a tone of love was felt in the *badchon's* reproach, the challenge of a friend, of a true son of his people. This circumstance contributed considerably to the popularity of the *badchonim* and their *badchonus*—songs. Hence *badchon* became synonomous with folksinger.

Some singers published their poetry, or at least set it in writing, by reason of which circumstance their names and works were retained. Thus we hear of Eisik Walich, cited in Chapter XVIII, of Jacob Heilprin Dick in Frankfort in the sixteenth century,[16] of Hershel Weinshenk-Tausik in Prague, who in 1655 wrote a necrology on the *chazzan* Lippman Popper,[17] of Mose Stendal, who in 1586 translated the Psalms in verse, of Nathan Bach, the translator and publisher of the above-mentioned *Book-Samuel*. Jacob Kopelman of Brisk, Lithuania, paraphrased in verse the Aramaic translations of the five scrolls, to be sung to the *Book-Samuel* tune (Chapter XVIII); Elchonon Kohen paraphrased *Judith* in verse, under the name *Dos Chanukah Büchel* (Frankfort, 1712). Leib Sofer of Posen paraphrased, in verse, the great poem *Kether Mal-*

chuth by Solomon ibn Gabirol (Dessau, 1698). The *Zemiroth* were translated by Abraham Bookhandler (Basel, 1600). In 1614 Elchonon Heln wrote the *Scroll Vinz*, a narration of the expulsion of the Jews from Frankfort in 1614, to the tune of the *Battle of Pavia*.[18] The above-mentioned scholar Eliyahu Bachur was likewise a prolific verse-writer. From among his many poems, his lamentation on the conflagration of Venice should be mentioned. Concerning a similar calamity which befell Frankfort, David Schweigers wrote an elegy "to the tune of Haman in the Ahashwerosh play" mentioned above; the destruction of the community in Worms, set to "the tune of Rabbi Simon of Prague" was elegized by Isaac Liberman of Worms (1696); the Chmelnitzki pogroms in Ukraine, Joseph Ashkenazi lamented to the tune of *Adir oyom venoroh* (Prague, 1648); on the expulsion of the Jewish community from Vienna, the *chazzan* Jacob Koppel wrote an elegy to the tune of the *Akeda* (Prague, 1670); of the plague in Prague Jacob Horvitz sang to the tune of *Shochne bote chomer* (1714); Jacob Tausik composed a poem about the pseudo-Messiah Sabbathai Zebi (Amsterdam, 1666). Solomon Singer Kristal wrote many songs, of which that concerning Emperor Leopold I was well known (Prague, 1658); Selig *Chazzan* sang a hymn about the same Emperor to the tune of *Halb schwarz, halb weiss* (Prague, 1678). Leib Walich composed a hymn about King Charles (Prague, 1704). Wolf of Cracow wrote a song *Conduct of Life* to the tune of *Ach Gott wie bin ich ein verirrter Mann* (Prague, 1692). Another Solomon Singer of Prague sang a song of the fear of God to the tune of *Wie in der Tora steht geschrieben* (1692). A special type of *Torah* songs was developed, praising the Law. Noah Abraham Altshul published wedding and bridal songs as well as *Chanukah* and *Purim* songs (Prague, 1676). Zalman *Chazzan*, Samuel Pifert and Elchonan Katz of Kremnitz likewise

wrote *Chanukah* and *Purim* songs. Eliyahu Luanz wrote a
song *A Dispute Between Wine and Water* to the tune of *Diet-rich of Bern;* Zalman Sofer and Menachem Alendorf com-posed jingles on the passion for money to the tune *Hoch rief der Wächter.* From Leib Kutner "who is famed throughout
the countries" several popular verses were retained.

Among the folksingers also women appear who wrote and
published several songs. We hear of Rivka Tiktiner, Taube,
wife of Jacob Pan (Prague, 1609); of Bela, wife of Joseph
Chazzan Horvitz, who wrote *Techinoth*—supplications for
women (Prague, 1705); of Rachel, daughter of Mordecai
Sofer of Pintshof (Frankfort, 1723); of Seril, the daughter
of Jacob of Dubno (1783); and of Friedchen, the wife of
Mose Leib of Anklam (1782).[19]

From the list we gather that the field of the *badchonim* was
not limited to merry-making only. The songs reflected all
phases and vicissitudes of Jewish life.

The *badchon* vanished in Central Europe after the middle of
the nineteenth century,[20] whereas in Eastern Europe he sur-vived until recently. During the last century a few singers
(*badchonim*) arose in the Eastern countries who were probably
the most gifted of their guild, and who, before the disap-pearance of their profession, raised it considerably. We shall
speak of but the most outstanding ones. They were at once
poets and composers and performers of their own products,
some of which became very popular and were published.

(1) BERL MARGULIES, called *Broder.* He was born in
Brody, Galicia, in 1817, studied Talmud and became a bristle-worker. In 1857 he organized a troupe of *badchonim* and
toured Southern Russia, performing his songs at weddings or in
public gatherings. Later he returned to Brody and sang there
in a coffee-house, accompanying his performance with mimicry.
His themes were all taken from Jewish life and his tunes

adopted from and based on Synagogue modes and melodies.
Later he went to Bucharest, Roumania. He died there in 1880.
A collection of 30 songs in Yiddish he published in Lemberg
in 1876.[21]

(2) BENJAMIN WOLF EHRENKRANZ, called *Wölwel
Zbarazer*. This most talented Jewish singer of Galicia was
born in 1826 in the little village Zbarazh. His father was a
shochet (ritual slaughterer). He received a good Jewish education, acquiring the Hebrew language and Rabbinic knowledge. Especially was he imbued with Biblical poetry which
aroused in him his own poetical instinct. He was early caught
by the spirit of enlightenment that swept Galicia at that time.
At the age of 18 he was married against his wish, and, as a
consequence, disappeared a few days after his wedding. He
escaped to Roumania, at that time the haven for all Jews of
Galicia and Russia, who were not comfortable in their native
places. There Ehrenkranz remained for 25 years, a wandering singer, performing his songs not at weddings, as had been
customary, but in coffee-houses and at public gatherings, at
inns and saloons before the mob. His songs are distinguished
for their biting satire and humor. They are saturated with
love for the singer's people and with a deep sorrow for their
troubles and shortcomings. His greatest strength lay in his
ability to extemporize on any theme given to him or suggested
by the public. His satires on current events gained a wide
reputation. Especially bitter was he against the *chassidim* and
their *tzadikim-cult*. He was equally master of Yiddish and
Hebrew, and wrote almost all his poems in both languages.
At the urgent request of his friends, he published a selection
of his songs in 1865, in Hebrew, under the name of *Makkal
Noam* (The Staff of Pleasantness), and in Yiddish *Makkal
Chovlim* (The Staff of Severity), names taken in altered meaning from Zechariah 11, 7. His tunes he drew from the Syna-

gogal modes. But since he was not a technically trained
musician, he did not write his tunes, and, consequently, the
most of them were forgotten. Only some of them were orally
retained and written down. In table XXXIV, 1, we give a
song by Ehrenkranz, *Moshiachszeiten* (The Messianic Age),
a satire on that orthodox belief.[22] The tune is in the *Ahavoh-
Rabboh* mode. According to his statement in the preface of
his publication of 1865, his activity as professional singer began
in 1858. After a sojourn of 25 years in Roumania, he returned to Galicia. However, he could not establish himself in
his native country. The ultra-orthodox party considered him
an *Epykoros* (heretic). He was pursued by the *chassidim*,
while the "intelligenzia" saw in him a menace to their assimilative efforts. To them Yiddish was a handicap, a relic of
medievalism, to be forgotten, and to be replaced with German
and Polish. Only the masses, the artisans and laborers, clung
to him and filled the coffee-houses where he performed his art.
Soon Ehrenkranz had to realize that there was no future for
him in Galicia, and he left for Constantinople. There he married a woman, who supported him during the last years of his
life, to his death in 1883. A tombstone with a dignified in-
scription in Hebrew marks his grave: "In the Hebrew tongue
thou hast created glorious values, thy sweet songs captured all
hearts; thou hast descended from the heights to the poor
people, to enlighten their darkness, and by the whip of thy
tongue many hypocrites were chastised." [23] Those who witnessed his performances of his extemporized verses and tunes,
and those who knew his songs, testify that text and melody
constituted a unit. His tunes breathed a deep melancholy and
were seldom brightened by even a feeble smile. His melody
to his song *The Nightingale* used to draw tears from the people even 40 years after the death of the composer.[24]

(3) ELYOKUM ZUNSER was a native of the Lithuanian cen-

TABLE XXXIV

MOSHIACHSZEITEN

WOLWEL EHRENKRANZ

1 Passionate

Die a‑pi‑kor‑sim mo‑gen tzu‑setz‑ter‑heit re‑den, mir

velln es der‑tze‑len in frei‑den. Ich hoff tzu Gott, se

vel‑len bald ver‑stu‑men, vo‑ren mo‑shi‑ach vet ku‑men. Sei vel‑len

sehn, fun ve‑men sei ho‑ben ge‑lacht, fun ve‑men sei ho‑ben

choi‑zek ge‑macht, sei vel‑len sehn, fun ve‑men sei ho‑ben ge‑lacht, fun

ve‑men sei ho‑ben choi‑zek ge‑mach! Oy! vie der‑lebt man shon dos.

E. ZUNSER

2

tre, Wilna, which during the eighteenth and nineteenth centuries brought forth a great number of sages and scholars,
thinkers and leaders, poets and musicians and artists. Born in
1840 in poverty, son of a carpenter, Zunser had but little
education. While still a boy, he lost his father and was compelled to abandon his study of Talmud for a trade. At times
he sang with *chazzanim*. At the age of 14 he became private
teacher to the children of a farmer, who instead of paying him
his salary handed him over to the Russian "catchers," to be
"trained" as a soldier, according to the iron régime of Nicholas I. He was confined in the army barracks together with
several other Jewish boys. During this imprisonment he composed his first song, both text and tune, and taught it to his fellow sufferers, arranging a choir of ten boys. Through an unexpected order of Alexander II, newly ascended to the throne,
he was released from prison. He wandered to Kovno, where
he engaged in the embroidery trade. From that time on his
talent blossomed. Zunser was a very prolific composer. According to his statement, he wrote about 600 songs. One of
the most popular, *Die Blum* (The Flower), he composed at
the age of 15. His songs became much liked by the masses in
Kovno, so that in 1861 he was encouraged to abandon his trade
and devote himself to his muse. He became a *badchon*, returned to Wilna, and published a collection of *New Songs*
(1861). Zunser's popularity spread quickly, and he was invited to weddings, where he would sing his songs and improvise,
to the accompaniment of the Jewish "music-makers" (*klezmer*), of whom we shall speak presently. His fame spread all
over Lithuania and the North Russian districts, and he was
called to weddings throughout the country. While Zunser
had but a poor education, his striving toward self-education
and enlightenment brought him into contact with the outstanding scholars of Wilna, under whose influence he studied

Hebrew literature and history. He became an ardent Jew and later a nationalist. In 1862 he married, but in 1871 his wife and children died of the cholera. He then settled in Minsk, married again, and remained in that place until 1889.

In addition to his songs Zunser wrote a drama *Mechirath Yosef* (The Sale of Joseph), based on the Biblical story. It was published in 1868 and was repeatedly performed.[25] Zunser's popularity grew more and more, until he became a national figure among the Jewish people. By reason of this fame, he was suspected in governmental circles of being a disguised agitator of the revolutionary party. Becoming aware of his dangerous situation, he left Russia and settled in New York, where for a while he continued his profession. In his more advanced age he withdrew from public appearances and opened a printing office on East Broadway, which he maintained until his death in 1913. In 1904 he published his autobiography. It was translated into English and published in 1905. A selection of his songs in three volumes was published in 1920 by his family.

His tunes are all for solo; some of them were arranged with a poor piano accompaniment. They have partly the Jewish folksong character and partly the form of the German-French *couplets*.[26] His melodic line is influenced by the Synagogue song from which source, according to his own statement, he first used to draw; but includes, also, German features, as felt in his songs *Die Kontrasten, Nach dem neuesten Journal, Die Antwort, Ich bin schon sicher* and *Klug, edel und still.* Some of his tunes show Slavic influence, for example, *Die Socha.* Some remain strictly faithful to genuine Jewish melodic line, such as *The Lament on Lewando,* which has similarity to the Spanish tune given in XXXII, 30. In XXXIV, 2, we give Zunser's tune. Genuinely Jewish are also *Der Peddler, Das Neunzente Yahrhundert* and *Der Aristocrat.* This last song became endeared to the Jewish masses in Lithuania, and was sung for many years.

Zunser was the first *badchon* who acquired some rudimentary knowledge of music. During his lifetime he published several of his songs, both text and music, for solo and accompaniment. From these we gain an idea of the nature of his music.

The themes of his poems are the same as those of Ehrenkranz, i.e., subjects from Jewish life, reflections on Jewish social and cultural conditions. He conceived of the Jewish people collectively. Never does he take moments of the individual's life for his subject matter. He never sang lovesongs or voiced private griefs or joys. But he always touches the problems of the *House of Israel* (*Klal Yisroel*). Superstition, abnormal political and cultural circumstances, are the main sources from which he draws his themes. He favors enlightenment, but criticizes assimilation. He pleads with his people to awaken from apathetic slumber and to become aware of their misery. He tries to awaken in them self-respect and reverence for their own spiritual culture; and last but not least, to turn back to their territorial home, to regain their lost independence and their country—Palestine. His language is simple; he employs the Lithuanian Yiddish idiom with some Germanisms, and uses modern European names of cultural achievements. At times he is compelled, out of fear of the Russian censor, to choose an allegorical form of presentation of his subject matter. Zunser, in contradistinction to Ehrenkranz and Margulies, always strikes a mild and noble tone. He is never harsh, satiric and sarcastic, he never mocks at the shortcomings of his people. With a fatherly, warm challenge he tries to instruct and to elevate his brethren to a better understanding. No wonder that he was so much beloved and greatly venerated during almost a half-century. In the scale of art standard neither his verse nor his music reached any considerable height, and vocally he had but limited quality. But it is Zunser's intense Jewish sentiment that is his most striking characteristic. That wholesome sentiment is the magnetic power which, more than his poetic and musical talent, captured the hearts of his people.

Through his personal qualities, Zunser raised the low level of the *badchon* to the dignified standard of a singer to the people, of the people's life and struggle. He was the last JEWISH BARD of note.

(4) ABRAHAM GOLDFADEN (originally Goldenfodim) was born in Altkonstantin, Wohlynia, in 1840. His father, a watch maker, was a liberal-minded man. When Tzar Nicholas I issued the order that those Jewish children who attend the public schools, established especially for them, should be exempted from army service, his father was one of the first to make most of the alternative, and sent him to school. From this elementary school, his father sent him in 1857 to the Rabbinical Seminary in Zhitomir, from which institute he was graduated in 1866. While still a student Goldfaden started his activity as popular poet-singer. In his reminiscences he relates how he used to compose songs which the students eagerly sang. His first publication was a collection of Hebrew songs (Zhitomir, 1865) *Tzitzim Ufrachim* ("Blossoms and Flowers"). Not being rabbinically inclined he became a public-school teacher first in Simferopel and later in Odessa. In 1868 he published a collection of Yiddish songs, *Dos Yuedele*. Although he occasionally has recourse to the style of Ehrenkranz, in striking the satiric note, or, forshadowing his future career, even descending to the use of theatre *couplets*, yet most of his poems have an individual character, distinct from those of his predecessors.[27] A year later he published another collection *Die Yuedene* (The Jewess), touching the problems of the Jewish woman. For these lyrics he adopted melodies. With-

out any technical knowledge of music, he merely marked the names of the adopted tunes to be sung: popular Russian lullabies, Ukrainian melodies, or Jewish folk-songs. In 1875 he quit his post as teacher and went to Lemberg, where he started publishing a humorous journal, *Yisrolic*, for Russian Jews. But after half a year the Russian Government prohibited its circulation, and as a consequence the paper ceased to appear. He then went to Tschernowitz and started a *Folksblatt*. Upon the advice of a friend he transplanted his paper to Jassy, Roumania. "At that time," Goldfaden narrates in his reminiscences, "the Jewish public used to be entertained by popular singers-jesters, who performed their songs in saloons. They had in their repertoire also my songs, which became very popular. Once, while listening to these singers for the first time, the idea flashed in my mind to combine these songs of mine by the connecting links of prose into a tale that would make a theatrical piece. I immediately set to work and on the Feast of Tabernacles I laid the cornerstone of the Jewish Theatre." [28]

The Jewish population in Roumania at that time, in great part refugees from Russia, stood on a low cultural level. Young boys were sent over the borders by their parents to rescue them from the tyrannic army law of Nicholas I. These grew up in ignorance, without Jewish or general education, and were employed as laborers and artisans. For entertainment they frequented saloons where Jewish singers, *badchonim*, delighted their public with trivial jingles and jests. "My heart was filled with pain," Goldfaden says, "to see my people in such a low state of spiritual development and in such vulgarity. . . . I realized that it was utterly ignorant of the holy spark of its nationality, which I had thus far tried to infuse in its hearts by my songs. . . . The people needed a school! They needed to understand their own life. They needed a means by which their own life with all its deficiencies should be reflected and brought before their eyes. . . . Historic pieces should be given that they learn their history . . . and find out who they were. . . ." This was Goldfaden's train of thought when he conceived the idea of creating a Jewish theatre for melodrama or operetta.

Indeed, the Jewish play is not Goldfaden's innovation, for, as we have already seen, centuries before him there existed not only *Purim* plays but also dramas on other subjects such as the story of the sacrifice of Isaac (*Akedath Yizchac*), the story of Joseph, by Leb Ginsburg, published in Frankfort in 1712. Its performance on the stage attracted attention on account of the satire on the Catholic clergy. There were further *The Action of King David and Goliath*, published in 1711 in Hanau; *The Greatness of Joseph (Gedulath Joseph)*, 1801; *Jonah in Nineveh* (MS.); *Rabbi Henich* by Isaac Eichel, a satire on educational conditions at the end of the eighteenth century; *Leichtsin und Fromelei* (Frivolity and Hypocrisy) by Wolfsohn, published in Breslau, 1786; *The Wedding at Heichelheim*, MS. written in 1810.[29] These plays are all provided with songs and *couplets*. Finally there was already Zunser's *Mechirath Yosef* mentioned above.

Neither was the Jewish theatre Goldfaden's innovation. Already in the sixteenth and seventeenth centuries permanent stages existed in the Ghetto of Venice, for which Leon of Modena wrote plays and of which he was the director (Chapter X). Likewise in Frankfort and in other Ghettos Jewish plays were frequently performed in the "Dance-houses." Jewish professional actors and singers distinguished themselves throughout the Middle Ages in European and Oriental countries.[30] Even organized troups were acting in Germany in the seventeenth and eighteenth centuries. We mention the troup of Süsskind of Offenbach and his wife Michaele, the daughter of the *chazzan* Salmele of Frankfort and the mother of the famous Joseph Süss Oppenheim.[31]

However, in Eastern Europe there was no trace of all this, and when Goldfaden started, he had at hand neither actors nor stage. The first actor-singer at Goldfaden's disposal was Yisroel Grodner in Jassy, a *badchon*, his second, Sochor Goldstein, a harness-maker by profession, who, disguised as a young Jewish girl, played the part of the wife of a *chassid* in a concoction which Goldfaden manufactured in the form of a comedy in two acts, a caricature of the meanest order. He did it with reluctance, as he later confessed, in order to attract the Roumanian Jewish public to his ideal. He descended to them in order to elevate them gradually. Goldfaden recounts in his reminiscences his hardships and troubles in acquiring dramatic and musical talent and in training it, in constructing stages and screens, in procuring stage directors and prompters, and above all, in training the Jewish public—the mob as well as the "intelligenzia." The latter opposed the idea of a Jewish theatre as a breeding place of frivolity, joviality and blasphemy, and as an agency of reactionary nationalism, medievalism and so on. "I came to Jassy," he says, "from the big world, well acquainted with the classic literature, the drama and the opera. I already knew Meyerbeer's, Halévy's and Verdi's operas, and had heard the greatest artists. Jewish history and literature were open before me; my mind was filled with subjects such as King Solomon, the Maccabees, Yehuda Halevi, David Al-roi, Rabbi Akiba, Bar-kochba and others. Nonetheless I had to descend from my height, compelled by sheer necessity, to themes such as *Ni-be-ni-me*, *Shmendrik* and the like, appearing heedless of the scoffing of antagonists, who pointed to these products as proof of my ignorance of better subject-matter."

After many disappointments and failures, Goldfaden succeeded in organizing a troup of actor-singers, and above all in engaging some Jewish actresses. These were a real innovation in Eastern Europe, the first since the time of "Madam Europe," the sister of Salomon Rossi (Chapter X), and the above-mentioned Michaele. At that time the Russian-Turkish war started, and Bucharest became the seat of the Russian staff, surrounded with Jewish agents, contractors and traders. The invasion of this swarm of fortune-seekers stimulated Goldfaden's ambition. With their easy gotten gains the transients sought amusements, and the coffee-houses were crowded by Jews who came to listen to the songs of ballad singers. Reckoning with the Jews' fondness for music, Goldfaden abandoned for the time his ideals of historic dramas and started writing light burlesques, mostly imitation of French originals, in which the songs written and set to music by him were the most important things. "There is no other merit whatsoever in the plays, as their Jewish setting is merely such in name, and as otherwise the plot is too trivial. But the songs have survived in the form of popular ballads." [32] After the conclusion of the war, in 1878, Goldfaden returned to Odessa, where he established a regular Jewish theatre and from where he toured the country, playing in every large city.

Finally he began to near his goal, the creation of historical melodramas. He wrote *Shulamith*, a romantic melodrama of the last period of the Second Temple; *Bar-Kochba*, based on the story of the Jewish revolt against the Roman Empire in c. 135 C.E., and *Doctor Almosado*, a tale of the Jewish life in Palermo. These plays are in the style of the operetta, though they are more serious than the German *Sing-spiel*. Due to his lack of musical training, Goldfaden really wrote dramas with interspersed songs, in the form of *couplets*, arias and choruses, with primitive orchestral accompaniment. The number of the songs he used to increase or reduce, according to the vocal ability of the actors. The tunes Goldfaden drew from all sources procurable; from the Synagogue, from the Jewish, Ukrainian and Roumanian folk-song, taking also snatches from French, Italian and Russian *couplets*, marches, operas and potpourris.

The motley origin of the music is best understood through detailed analysis of the operettas. On examination we find that *Shulamith*, according to the latest edition, consists of twenty-five music-pieces.[33] No. 1, "The March to Jerusalem," is taken from Naumbourg's *Zemiroth Israel*, p. 79 (*Lechoh adonoy*). No. 2 is likewise from Naumbourg, ibid., p. 196 (*Mi hu ze melech*). No. 3 is in the *Mogen-Ovos* mode with the ending motive of the traditional tune of *Ledovid boruch* (Chapter VIII), while the motive which Goldfaden uses for the word *darkechoh* in this song is similar to a Yemenite folk motive.[34] No. 5 is a typical Italian "aria." No. 6 is a Jewish folktune, and became very popular in Goldfaden's words and setting. No. 8, too, seems to be taken from an Italian source, while Nos. 9-10 were adopted from Schestapol's setting of Psalm 114 (*Adonay Zechoronu*), who on his part adopted the aria of Verdi's *La Traviata*, No. 6 (The Aria of Violetta). Of Italian source, likewise, No. 11 appears. No. 12, a "Ballet," is an imitation of a *Mazurka*. No. 13 is Ukrainian, while No. 14 is a chassidic dance in *Adonoy-Moloch* mode, and No. 15 is chassidic in the Gipsy-scale. It became very popular. In No. 16 we recognize an imitation of Eleazar's famous aria in *La Juive* beginning "Recha, when God." No. 17 is the Ukrainian tune given in table XXXII, 24-25, and discussed in Chapter XVIII. Nos. 18-19 are a compilation of German and Ukrainian motives. No. 20 is a typical Turkish *Hedjaz* tune. Nos. 21-22 are a popular Jewish folktune with another text, No. 23 is a chassidic tune of the type called *dveikuth* (Chapter XIX), No. 24 is in the Ukrainian Dorian scale, and No. 25 is a Russian march or an imitation thereof.

The latest edition of *Bar-Kochba* contains seventeen musical numbers.[35] No. 1 is a chassidic *dveikuth* melody with a touch of *chazzanic* flavor. No. 2 is a very popular Jewish folk-song. No. 3 is a duet and solo adapted from French or Italian sources. Of the same source apparently are No. 4 and No. 5, while No. 6, a charming march, shows the Ukrainian scale. Nos. 9-10 are a concoction of *chazzanic* motives of Schestapol and others. No. 11 starts in the usual German march style and modulates to the Hedjaz scale. Nos. 12-13 are in the mixed Ukrainian scale, and became very popular. No. 14 is a *bravura*-aria in Italian style. No. 15 is in the style of Jewish folk-song, and became a favorite of the people, while No. 17 is a chassidic tune.

Though Goldfaden cannot be credited with original creations of music in these two operettas analyzed, he showed much dramatic skill and musical taste in adopting fascinating tunes which would appeal to the Jewish masses. The tunes are well chosen, also with regard to their dramatic effectiveness. It goes without saying that the accompaniment is very primitive, and that there is no musical style, with exception of that of a potpourri. Upon the more developed taste of the present Jewish public, Goldfaden's operettas do not make much impression, but a half century ago his plays were a revelation to the people in Eastern Europe and caused a furor throughout the Jewish settlement in Russia. The two melodramas were even translated into Polish. The officials of the Russian Government became suspicious of that institution which seemed to strengthen nationalistic sentiments among Jews, and in 1883 all Jewish theatres were closed. The troup had to leave Russia for Galicia. From there it proceeded to London and finally settled in New York. Goldfaden continued to compose and compile dramas and musical plays. He is accredited with 26 pieces, of which, however, only eight are of any value. Never did he again reach the climax of the two pieces discussed.

Apart from his dramatic creations, Goldfaden was a prolific song writer, composing both text and tunes. Some of his songs gained wide popularity and were published in sheet form. We name only *Yankele geht in Shul arain, Dos pintele Yüd, Yisrolik kum ahaim*. He died in New York in 1908.

Of later composers of Jewish musical plays we mention JOSEPH RUMSHINSKY (born in Wilna in 1879), who gained

popularity in New York. His music is based upon folk motives
and influenced by "Jazz" rhythms and melodic curves.

(5) MARK WARSCHAWSKI was a lawyer by profession and
a folksinger by nature (Zhitomir 1845–Kiev 1907). Many
of his songs became real folk-songs, especially *Aufn Pripitshok*,
in the *Mogen-Ovos* mode. His tunes were partly composed,
partly adopted, by him. Some of them are genuine Jewish
melodies. A collection of 25 of his poems, *Jüdische Volkslieder*, was published in 1900 (second edition, New York
1918). Some of his tunes were published in sheet form and in
various magazines.

The last few decades continued the creative stream of Jewish song that gained popularity. In most cases, the composers
of these songs, in true folk-style, remained unknown. Such
anonymous pieces are *Dos Talissl* (The Prayer Shawl), *Gott
und sein Mishpot ist Gerecht* (God and His Judgment are
Righteous) and especially *Eili, Eili*, which became so widely
known in the last fifteen years. The tune of the latter is in the
Ahavoh-Rabboh mode, expressing deep Jewish emotions. In
content and character these songs are a continuation of the
Jewish folk-song of Eastern Europe, though more intricate.
We may classify them as songs in FOLKSTYLE (*Volkstümlich*).

Of quite another character are the songs in modern Hebrew
which sprang forth in the last forty years. Their content is
nationalism, the call to rejuvenation, to the rebuilding of the
Jewish people as a nation in Palestine. They were created by
the Zionist movement, and voice its ideals. Of these songs
Hatikvah (The Hope) became the Zionist national anthem in
1897. The text was written by Naftali Herz Imber (1856-
1911) and was published in a collection of his poems called
Barkai (The Morning Star) in Jerusalem, 1886. The tune is
similar to the Dew tune of the Portuguese Jews given in table
XXVIII. Another famous song is *Birkath Am* which is by

Ch. N. Bialik. The tune has Slavic flavor. Some songs were created in Palestine, such as *Shir Avoda* (Labor Song), the text by Bar-Nash of Jerusalem, the tune of Arabic origin. The tunes are, in general, adaptations from Jewish Ashkenazic, Arabic or Sephardic-Oriental and Slavic originals; yet a Jewish spirit has been breathed into them, and they are distinguished by a vigorous, hopeful note.

B. *Klezmorim* = Music-makers

This word is a corruption of the Hebrew *kle-zemer*—musical instruments.

Already in Chapters I and V we saw that after the destruction of the Second Temple in Jerusalem music-making on instruments was restricted to weddings. Exception was made in the case of those poor people who earned their livelihood by making music for Gentiles.[36] Instrumental music was allowed at the celebration of the dedication of a synagogue or of a Scroll. In the Orient it became customary to sing hymns with musical accompaniment in the synagogues on the intermediary days of *Pesach* and *Sukkoth*. This custom was in practice already in the twelfth century [37] and has continued until the present day.

During the Middle Ages music-making became a standard profession among the Jews in the Orient as well as in the Occident. In almost every city there were professional Jewish *klezmorim*. We hear of musicians who gained fame and were court musicians of sultans and caliphs, of dukes and kings and even of Popes (Chapter X).[38] In some places the Jewish musicians were the main music suppliers, and functioned even in Christian religious ceremonies.

Thus, we hear, for example, that in Constantinople there were 500 Jewish musicians toward the middle of the nineteenth century.[39] In the fifteenth century there were in Europe organized Jewish music bands in which also women were active.[40] These bands traveled throughout the country, concertizing at Christian festivities, and were often preferred to Christian musicians on account of their art and because of their modesty and sobriety. This preference combined with prejudice caused the issuing of restrictions with regard to the Jewish musicians and the laying of heavy taxes upon them. Hence, after the sixteenth century no Jew was allowed to perform his art as a profession without a permit of the local governmental authorities, and since such governments were as many as there were cities in Germany, the hardships these musicians had to bear are easily imaginable.[41] Further restrictions were issued as to the days on which the Jews were permitted to make music even in their family celebrations, such as weddings. We hear already in the fifteenth century of cases in which Jews were punished for having made music at weddings on days prohibited to them. Many Jews were compelled to celebrate their weddings in other districts, where these prohibitions were not effective. Rabbi Jacob Mölin (*Maharil*), considering instrumental music essential for the wedding ceremony, ordered such temporary removals in cases of local restrictions.[42]

Even at times when music was permissible, the government set limits to the NUMBER of the musicians that might be employed. For quite other reasons Jewish religious authorities, too, restricted the size of the orchestra. They sought to erect a "fence" against hilarity and gaiety, out of respect for their ever remembered "Destruction." After every new disaster and each renewed outbreak of persecution Jewish authorities would reenforce interdictions against music-making. We hear, for example, that in Worms, or Brest-Litowsk, Selz and in many other communities, music-making, even at weddings, was forbidden on account of calamities.[43] In Metz, only three musicians as a rule—for weddings a quartet—were permitted, but those without legal right of residence in Metz might employ only one even for a wedding. In Frankfort a quartet was permitted, but the *klezmer* had no permission to play after midnight. In Fürth, the number was restricted to three instruments, and similarly in many other cities.

Nevertheless, the organized Jewish bands developed more and more. In some places there were no other musicians but Jews.[44] We hear of a large Jewish guild of *klezmorim* in Prague, whose emblem was a violin. They would volunteer their service for religious celebrations in the synagogue at the regular Friday evening service, before the traditional ritual would start (Chapter XI). They volunteered, also, at celebrations which the Jewish community arranged in honor of the reigning Emperor. Of one such celebration in 1716 a detailed description has been preserved.[45] There is a description for the same year of a celebration in Offenbach in the synagogue which reports the accompaniment of Jewish *klezmorim*, and another detailing a similar performance in Worms in 1790.[46]

There are also many descriptions caricaturing the nature of the music performed by the Jewish musicians and casting aspersion on their musical ability.[47] A description of a Jewish band of five, in 1800, in a small German town, seems to be objective. According to this description the five musicians engaged in other trades in addition to their playing. Two of them were violinists, one played the clarinet, one the violoncello and one the *Hackbrett* (Dulcimer). "Only the first violinist played from written music, the others following by ear. The cellist, an old man, played with especial skill. He knew nothing of notes, but had an excellent ear, observed each turn of the leading melody and was able to add accompaniment in perfect harmony."[48] The *Hackbrett* was very much in favor with the Jewish *klezmorim*. Already in 1694 this instrument was used by travelling Jewish music-makers.[49]

Next in skill to those of Prague and Fürth were the *klez-morim* of Frankfort and Berlin. They used to tour the country despite heavy taxes, visit fairs, such as the "masses" in Leipzig, making music in inns and wine-saloons, and would perform at summer resorts. These bands, however, vanished gradually with the emancipation of the Jews in Central Europe, while in Eastern Europe the *klezmorim* continued as a guild until lately.

Many distinguished Jewish musicians and virtuosos of the nineteenth century were descendants of these music-makers. But some of the *klezmorim* gained reputation and fame even as *klezmorim*. One of these was MICHAEL JOSEPH GUSIKOW. He was born in Shklow in 1806, in a family of *klezmorim*, and learned the profession of his father, the playing of the flute. Defective lungs forced him to abandon the flute in 1831 for the *Hackbrett*. Out of this he constructed the so-called "straw-fiddle." In a very short time he gained a marvelous virtuosity on this invention of his. He left his home, and toured the principal cities of Russia (in the beginning on foot). In Kiev he gained the admiration of musicians. In Odessa he gave a concert in the Italian Opera house, in 1832. His reputation spread rapidly after his appearance in Vienna. Prominent journalists, such as Saphir, described Gusikow's unique art with great enthusiasm. "See this man," writes Saphir. "Here he appears in the national costume of his Polish coreligionists, wrapped in a black 'talar,' with his black hair and the two curls *peios* (side locks), his head covered with a black cap. He relates to us a touching elegy through his features, and this elegy he sets to music. . . . Out of wood and straw he charms forth tones of deep melancholy, of profound emotion. Out of wood and straw he knows how to produce the finest vibrations, sounds of most tender softness. How painful and tender sound his national tunes." In 1836 he gave a concert in Leipzig. Felix Mendelssohn-Bartholdy, who attended, wrote to his mother thus: "I am curious to learn whether Gusikow pleased you as much as he did me. He is quite a phenomenon, a famous fellow, inferior to no virtuoso in the world, both in execution and facility. He, therefore, delights me more with his instrument of wood and straw than many with their pianofortes, just because it is such a thankless kind of instrument. . . . It is long since I so much enjoyed any concert as this, for the man is a true genius." [50] After his tour of Germany and France his malady, consumption, overpowered him and in 1837 he died in Aix-la-Chapelle. A tune of his for Psalm 126, in the *Ahavoh-Rabboh* mode, is still preserved. [51]

A similarly gifted musician was the *klezmer* MORDCHELE ROSENTHAL, whose name was later changed to Rozsavölgyi Mark (1787-1848). He was the creator of the Gipsy-Hungarian national music and the composer of the Hungarian Rakoczy march. JOSEPH SCHLESINGER (born 1794), in order to escape the occupation his father had selected for him, fled to the just-mentioned Rosenthal and became a flutist in his "Gipsy band," which consisted entirely of Jews disguised as Gipsies. [52]

Some of the artists among the *klezmorim* communicated their art to gentile musicians. [53]

Among the Jews in Poland, too, music was much cultivated. Reports of the sixteenth century inform us of talented Polish artists who came to Silesia and were recommended to the German nobleman. [54] Occasionally Jewish *klezmorim* served in military bands of the German armies. A certain Chayyim Cimbalist of Poland served in Wallenstein's army, and died in the war in 1637. [55] The influx of Jewish musicians from

Poland into Germany continued throughout the last three centuries.[56]

The music which the *klezmorim* used to perform was of Jewish as well as of non-Jewish origin—music of all the various styles, according to the demand of their audiences, from elegiac tunes to frivolous dances. Especially were their stirring and subtle rhythms much liked by their gentile employers.[57] The competition of the Jews raised the wrath of the Christian musicians, and in Bohemia they petitioned the authorities repeatedly, in 1641 and 1651, to prohibit the Jewish musicians from playing at Christian festivities, "because they confuse the music in that they are incapable of keeping strict rhythm or tempo, and vulgarize our noble and graceful music." The Jewish musicians were likewise accused of possessing no music of their own, but only imitating Christian music in a miserable manner. In their reply, the Jewish musicians attempted no vindication of their musicianship, but only appealed to the human sentiments of the authorities, declaring that inasmuch as they had no other profession by which they could earn their livelihood, the interdiction to practice their music would cause their ruin.[58]

The prejudice seems to have been one-sided, for we find that Jews employed Christian musicians not only on Sabbaths and festivals, when music-making was forbidden to Jews [59] (Chapters I and V), but even on week days Christian musicians were invited to play together with the Jewish *klezmorim*. Christian musicians were known to come to Jewish weddings uninvited.[60]

Thus, we see that the *klezmorim* in Central and Eastern Europe were the forerunners of the host of musicians of Jewish extraction, both composers and performers, who, from the beginning of the nineteenth century on, contributed enormously toward the upbuilding of European art-music.

CHAPTER XXI

Almost a century after European artistic achievements in the field of music had been employed for the song of the Synagogue, these were applied also to the Jewish folk-song. Though, occasionally, Jewish folk motives had been utilized for artistic works, as, for example, by Anton Rubinstein in his opera *The Maccabees* (in 1875), it was only toward the end of the nineteenth century that some Jewish musicians, trained in European art-music, discovered artistic possibilities in the folk-song of their people, and set themselves to systematic artistic endeavors. These young men were of East European origin, educated in a Jewish atmosphere, saturated with the sounds of Jewish folk-song. They were stimulated by the newly revived Jewish national movement which stirred up their Jewish self-consciousness, and turned their interest to their people's song. They devoted themselves to cultivating Jewish folk-songs: first, in ARRANGING them mostly for solo with piano accompaniment; but also for choir or for instruments—and, secondly, in utilizing folk motives and tunes for ORIGINAL compositions in the classic forms of European music. The creations of the second type are both vocal (for solo or choir) and instrumental (for violin, violoncello, piano; duets, trios, quartets and for small orchestras).

The new undertaking involved difficulties of technique and spirit not apparent on the surface. Artistically successful arrangement of folk-song depends not merely upon faithful adherence to the melody—vitally important as is this care of

461

the tune's genuineness. The musician must have absorbed the spirit of the tune, and be moved by the emotions which gave it birth, so that, instead of caricaturing the melody by reason of unsuited harmonization, he give it fuller expression through instrumental accompaniment. He needs must preserve the simplicity of the folktune, must subordinate the instrument to the melody, and must employ only such modulation, progressions and harmonic combinations as spring from the character of the song. The value of all artistic labor in the realm of folk music rests with the composer's regard for and preservation of the song's own character.

If with mere "arrangement," when guided by the established melody, the musician face so complicated a problem, how much more intricate, how much greater, the hazards of creating original compositions in which folk motives are utilized as themes. The artist is not free for a moment to forget the source of the theme, to violate the atmosphere that there surrounded it and gave it color; he is never privileged to abduct it to realms of foreign emotions. So imbued must he be with the spirit of the song from which his theme sprang, that his artistic product breathe forth the atmosphere of that theme's origin, and that from the theme in its new setting there flow the expression of the sentiments and emotions of the people who conceived it.

I. ARRANGEMENTS

In 1887 H. B. GOLOMB, a music teacher in Wilna, published ten Jewish folk-tunes for weddings, arranged for piano, under the name *Kol Yehuda*—Klänge der Juden. BOGUMIL ZEPLER (Breslau, 1858—Berlin, 1918), after considerable success as operetta composer and writer on music, took to cultivating Jewish folk-song. Several of his arrangements were

published in sheet form and in the monthly *Ost und West* in
Berlin. JULIUS (YOEL) ENGEL (1868 Verjansk, Tauria-
Crimea—died, Tel Aviv 1927), was music teacher and music
critic in Moscow and an ardent cultivator of Jewish song. He
composed and published several collections of songs for children and adults with piano accompaniment, in Hebrew and
Yiddish, also numbers for piano and choir. He also attempted
solo and piano arrangement for Yemenite songs,[1] but being
unacquainted with their Oriental atmosphere, gave to their
accompaniment an inappropriate harmony. PLATON BROU-
NOFF (1868 Russia—1924 New York) in 1911 published in
New York a volume of 50 Jewish folk-songs with piano accompaniment. This collection contains valuable material.
His accompaniment is in the routine style. Brounoff likewise
published several original works based upon Jewish motives,
in which he tries to give Oriental color.

In the above-mentioned *Ost und West* about 70 songs for
voice with piano or for violin and piano were printed during
the existence of this monthly: 1901-1922. Among the contributors ARNO NADEL was the most productive (born in
Wilna 1878. Is now choir leader at a synagogue in Berlin).
He further published a few collections of folk-songs with
piano accompaniment: *Juedische Volkslieder* and *Jontefflieder*,
Juedischer Verlag, Berlin.

In 1908 a "Society for Jewish Folk Music" was organized in
Petersburg, with the aim of collecting folk-songs and arranging them in artistic forms. The founders and coworkers
were trained musicians. In 1911 this society published *A Collection of Songs for School and Home.* The songster includes 62 Jewish songs for solo and three-part chorus with
simple but appropriate piano accompaniment; and 23 songs
selected from German and Russian classical music.[2] In an appendix some examples of the Biblical and Synagogal modes

are given. The same society published several songs arranged
for voice with piano accompaniment and some for choir or
for instruments, by M. Gnessin, M. Milner, S. Kisselgof, P.
Lwow, I. Achron, L. Saminsky, M. Schalit, A. Schitomirsky,
L. Zeitlin, S. Gurowitsch, I. Schulman, E. Sklar, I. Kaplan and
H. Kopit.

The activity of this society was cut short by the World
War. With reestablished peace some members of the original group organized the Juwal Publishing Company for Jewish music in Berlin; and since 1922 have put out several works
among which is a number of folk-songs in arrangements.

In 1918 a "Chamber-Music-Ensemble"—*Zimro* ("Song")
was organized in Petrograd by G. Mistechkin (first violin),
G. Besrodney (second violin), K. Moldavan (viola), I. Cher-
niavski (cello), S. Bellison (clarinet) and L. Berdichevski
(piano), trained at the conservatories of Petrograd and Leipzig, with the following objects in view:

"(1) To propagate Jewish Folk Music artistically cultivated.
(2) To collect means by subsidy and percentage from income of concerts, for the *fund* which the 'Zimro'
Ensemble established for the purpose of building
a Temple of Art in Palestine.
(3) To unite all Jews, who are active in the field of art
and literature, in one common bond under the name
of *Omonuth* (Art), in order that they may contribute potentially to the revival of the Jewish Nation
and cooperate in the development of Jewish Art in
Palestine."

To materialize their ideal they started out on a concert tour
through Siberia, China, Japan, via America to Palestine. After
concertizing in all these countries the troup published a book-

let relating its aims and activities (New York, 1919). Some of the members of this "Ensemble" arranged Jewish folk-songs for quintette (string quartette and clarinet), and solos for cello, clarinet and violin.

Many more workers are now collecting and arranging: JANOT S. ROSKIN, Berlin, has given a considerable number of songs in sheet form. HENRY GIDEON published *From the Cradle to the Chuppe*, Boston, 1923, containing 15 songs; and LAZAR SAMINSKY, *Ten Hebrew Folk-songs and Folkdances*, New York, 1924. SARAH PITKOWSKY-SCHACK collected 50 Yiddish Folk-songs which were arranged for piano by ETHEL SILVERMAN COHEN, New York, 1924, 2nd edition 1927.

ZAVEL ZILBERTS (Pinsk, 1881), the violinist EFREM ZIMBALIST (Rostov-on-Don, 1889), JOSEPH CHERNIAVSKY and A. W. BINDER, all living in America, arranged several folk-songs and utilized folk motives in their compositions.

Among the songs favored with several arrangements are *Dem Rebbins Niggun* (table XXXIII, 5), *Kaddish* and *A Dudule* (ibid., 6), *Alte Kashe* (XXXII, 14), *A Chazzandl auf Shabbos* (ibid., ii) and *Eili, Eili*.

Occasionally musicians of European reputation interested themselves in the arrangements of Jewish folk-song, as in the instance of MAX BRUCH's *Hebräische Gesänge* or MAURICE RAVEL's *Deux Mélodies Hébraïques*, Paris, 1915, containing *Kaddish* (table XXIII, 4) and *An Alte Kashe*. In most such cases the composer's lack of familiarity with the spirit of the songs and the atmosphere out of which they sprang precluded the possibility of his offering appropriate arrangements.

II. ORIGINAL COMPOSITIONS

A classic illustration of the use of Jewish motives without the production of a Jewish composition is the *Kol nidré* concerto for cello and orchestra, op. 47, by Max Bruch.   In Chapter XIII (note 22) it was related that Bruch became interested in Jewish songs through the *chazzan* Lichtenstein. Bruch utilized the *Kol nidré* theme to create a fine piece of music but one that is *German-European* in spirit and style. He did not express as a background of the tune the *milieu* out of which it sprang, the religious emotions which it voices: awe, repentance and hope.   In Bruch's conception the melody was an interesting theme for a brilliant secular concerto.   In his presentation, the melody entirely lost its original character.   Bruch displayed a fine art, masterly technique and fantasy, but not Jewish sentiments.   It is not a JEWISH *Kol nidré* which Bruch composed.

Quite different are some of the artistic endeavors by Jewish composers of Eastern Europe.   Out of the nucleus of the motive, they develop an artistic composition.   Saturated with Jewish sentiments, they feel the emotions which gave birth to these tunes with the intense and profound sense of artists; and they try to pour these sentiments into artistic moulds.

The above-mentioned J. Engel composed 50 children-songs with piano accompaniment, utilizing folk motives.   In his accompaniment he breaks with the routine manner of applying arpeggio-figures, passages and runs, and adheres to the harmonic support of the melody.   His accompaniment, while it gives primarily a basis for the tune, has an expression of its own through modulative and rhythmic combinations.

SOLOMON GOLUB (born in Russia 1888—now living in New York) in some of his published Yiddish songs with piano accompaniment has succeeded in creating artistic music based upon the genuine Jewish folktune.   His songs *Tanchum*, in the mode of Talmud-study (Chapter XIV), "The Old Watchman," "The Cup," "A Cradle Song" and *Burikes af*

Pessach rank as successful achievements in the field of Jewish art-songs in *folkstyle*. Golub certainly absorbed the spirit of Jewish song, in the motives, melodic line and in the modulations he employs. In the accompaniment of "The Old Watchman" and *Tanchum* he displays original features. In his later publications, however, his attempt to compose in EUROPEAN style led him to imitate in melody and in form the German *Lied*, notably such songs as those of Schubert, Schumann, Franz and Wolf. The compositions are consequently weak.

Among many songs of Jewish value we mention *In Cheder* by M. MILNER. The tune is in the mode of the Talmud-study, worked out in a dramatic manner.

In the field of instrumental music JOSEPH ACHRON (1886 in the Government of Suvalki—now lives in New York) was successful with his "Hebrew Melody" for violin and piano, published by the above-mentioned Petersburg Society in 1914. This composition is based upon a folk-tune in minor, with the Ukrainian augmentation on the 4 and 6 toward the end. He developed this melody in the violin and the piano part according to Jewish ways: by the sudden transferring of the tune to the upper third, giving vent to the outburst of suppressed pain and emotion, and then, toward the end, falling back exhausted to the first state of depression. His "Hebrew Dance" is another solo for violin and piano, based upon a *chassidic* tune in the *Ahavoh-Rabboh* mode. In this piece the Jewish-Oriental fiery temperament is expressed in masterly fashion. The same feature is to be found in *Märchen* (Fairy tale) for violin and piano.

Of a similar character is a "Fantastic Dance" of the *Chabad chassidim* (Chapter XIX), for piano, violin and cello by SOLOMON ROSOWSKY. The tune is based upon the Gipsy scale explained in Chapter IX, which is seldom used in Jewish music.

On the other hand there are some works, such as "Variations on a Jewish Theme, for String Quartet" by M. GNESSIN and a "Romance for Violin and Piano" by I. WEINBERG, which do not show Jewish characteristics.

These endeavors are but a beginning in the building up of a Jewish art-music, in which the vibrations of the Jewish pulse will be reechoed.

PART III

CHAPTER XXII

THE JEW IN GENERAL MUSIC.

We have thus far treated Jewish music created by Jews for Jews. But apart from the musicians who served the Jewish cause in creating Jewish music, the Jewish people produced throughout the ages hosts of professional musicians, who were active in the music of their gentile neighbors. The question naturally arises as to whether or not Jewish musical sounds vibrate in their compositions or in their performances; whether they brought to the music of the general world a distinctively Jewish contribution.

It is generally known that a composer creates his music on the established premises of the music prevalent in his immediate environment. His tonal elements he instinctively chooses from the folk- and art-music with which he is filled from his childhood. Since every historical nation has its peculiar folk-song, and, to a certain degree, also its original style in art-music, the new composition generally makes an additional contribution toward the music of the artist's nation. Despite the professed tendency in the classical music of Europe toward INTERNATIONALISM, toward a European music for all European peoples and for those of European extraction, the classic music created by Germans has the imprint of German folk-song and character; while the Russian music unmistakably bears the marks of Russian folk-song and character. We find, likewise, Anglo-Saxon and Gaelic folk-song features in English music, and in Scandinavian music its people's folk-motives. We know of many cases in which musicians of one nation were

attracted to the musical style of another people and sought
to create in that adopted style. The result, however, was different from what they had originally anticipated. Handel,
Gluck, and Mozart, despite being enamored of Italian music,
created German music with some Italian flavor.[1] Verdi, in
his *Aïda*, made an effort to introduce Wagner's style into Italian music. The result was an Italian opera with some German flavor. In either case childhood training and environ-
mental influence proved to be stronger than foreign models
and personal effort.

Musicians of Jewish origin, due to their scattered places of
residence and the often preponderant influence of the non-
Jewish majority, present a phenomenon apparently unique but
genuinely in line with the facts just presented. They created
or performed music in the style of their neighbors and were
considered good composers in the field of their neighbors'
music. The participation of the Jews in European music increased tremendously since the beginning of the nineteenth
century after their admittance into the social and cultural life
of Europe. An innumerable host of musicians filled the musical world, creators and especially performers—virtuosos on
various instruments, but notably on the violin. They cultivated all styles and branches in music: opera, oratorio, concerto, symphony, sonata, vocal and instrumental music from
sacred Church music to the comic opera and Jazz hits. They
became distinguished theoreticians and teachers, musical critics
and essayists, directors, publishers and promoters of music.
The following list of the most important and successful musicians of Jewish extraction, who contributed enormously toward
the upbuilding of European classic and popular music, may
suffice to illustrate their activity during the last century up
to the present day: Jacob (Giacomo) Liebmann Meyerbeer
(Berlin 1791–Paris 1864); Jacques Fromental Halévy (Paris

1799–Nizza 1862); Felix Jacob Mendelssohn-Bartholdy (Hamburg 1809–Leipzig 1847); Ignaz Moscheles (Prague 1794–Leipzig 1870); Jacques Offenbach (Cologne 1819–Paris 1880); Sir Michael Costa (Naples 1810–Brighton 1884); Ferdinand David (Hamburg 1810–Switzerland 1873); Ferdinand Hiller (Frankfort 1811–Cologne 1885); Anton Rubinstein (Wechotynetz 1829–Peterhof 1894); Karl Goldmark (Hungary 1830–Vienna 1915); Joseph Joachim (Kitsee, near Pressburg, 1831–Berlin 1907); Leopold Damrosch (Posen 1832–New York 1885); Gustav Mahler (Kalisch 1860–Vienna 1911); Hermann Levy (Giessen 1839–Munich 1900); Adolph Bernhard Marx (Halle 1795–Berlin 1866); Salomon Jadassohn (Breslau 1831–Leipzig 1902); Leopold Auer (Veszprém 1845–Loschwitz 1930); Arnold Schönberg (Vienna 1874–Los Angeles 1951); Ernest Bloch (Geneva 1880–Portland, Ore. 1959); Ignace Friedman (Cracow 1882–Sydney 1948); Irving Berlin (Israel Baline) (Temun 1888–New York 1989); George Gershwin (New York 1898–Hollywood 1937); Erich Korngold (Brno 1897–Hollywood 1957); Mischa Elman (Talnoye 1891–New York 1967); Jascha Heifetz (Vilna 1901–Los Angeles 1987).

All these musicians created or performed European music for the European people. Almost none of them had been reared in a distinctly Jewish environment, or had been given a positive Jewish education and knowledge. As a result several of these musicians became converts to the dominant Christian faith; some attempted assimilation in the society they had adopted. Indeed, Mendelssohn's and Rubinstein's parents had carefully kept them away from Jewish influence, and educated them in the culture of their Christian environment. There were musicians of the younger generation whose only knowledge of their Jewishness was the bare fact of their extraction. In any case, very few knew anything of Jewish Synagogue and folk-song. The most conscious Jew among the earlier of these musicians,

Halévy, only once (for the aria of Eleazar, in his *La Juive*, Act IV) utilized a Jewish motive, while Goldmark and Offenbach—both sons of *chazzanim*—never employed Jewish motives in their compositions. These Jewish composers drew their material from the wells of the music of their adopted peoples.

On examination of their creations we discover not a single element that bears Jewish features that might be reckoned a distinctly Jewish contribution. Of them all, it was Rubinstein who occasionally and with conscious intent used Jewish motives in connection with Jewish or Oriental episodes in his operas and in his songs. But he, likewise, utilized other Oriental material, such as Persian and Tartaric motives. Some claim that a certain inclination toward melody—lyricism—is a pronounced feature in the music of Jews.[2] But the music of Mozart, Haydn and Schubert has also the same feature. There is no standard or measure by which we can distinguish a German song by Mendelssohn from hundreds of other German songs; or a jazz song by Berlin from the other innumerable modern Anglo-Saxon popular "hits." Neither by their motives and form, nor by their style and spirit, can they be identified.

Ernest Bloch's music is designated "Jewish." Its Jewishness, however, consists in an abundance of augmented steps, and, according to the opinion of some, in a certain heavy melancholy. But, these characteristics are NOT exclusively Jewish, for all the Semitic and Tartarian peoples have the same characteristic step, and as to the melancholy impression Oriental music makes on the Occidental hearer, we have seen in the course of our discussion that such an impression is based upon the difference of taste of Orientals and Occidentals. At best, Bloch's music may be said to have a touch of Orientalism. A. Einstein says of him: "Determined to create Jewish music, he does not turn to the real Oriental or Jewish music for themes, but tries to construct the character and spirit of his race out of himself." [3] In a similar way an Englishman, German or Russian, born and reared in the Orient in an Arabian atmosphere, would try to compose English, German or Russian music, without actual knowledge of his people's song. In music such as Bloch's, we find the refutation of the lightly conceived and unthinkingly accepted present-day opinion that the musician, unconscious and ignorant though he be of his people's music and folklore, yet instinctively manifests these racial expressions. Seductive as is the theory, for rational nationalists, there is in music not only no tangible proofs of it, but positive evidence against it. Not through composers without Jewish background, and without being imbued with their people's folk-song, has Jewish music left any unique impress upon general art-music. For the Jew his lore and his faith substitute national atmosphere. [4]

We shall not discuss all the arguments and accusations brought forth in the course of the last century as to the genuineness of the creation of Jewish composers. Opinions of that type are created out of subjective impressions, without any real basis, and are often in line with the cheap and malicious attacks of Richard Wagner, which sprang forth not out of analysis and conviction, but out of bitterness and envy. He obviously had forgotten the enthusiastic laudations of Meyerbeer, Mendelssohn and Halévy which he had written when he was in need of their support. At that time he had proclaimed Meyerbeer and Mendelssohn the greatest and *purest* German composers. [5]

Nor can we give more than passing attention to another opinion expressed lately, that the Jews are revolutionaries in music, that they destroy established forms and are the protagonists of all that is new and ultra-modern. [6] As examples we are shown: Schönberg, Korngold, etc. However, but a glance through the above list suffices to prove the superficiality of such a viewpoint. Alongside of the few musicians who became adherents of the revolutionary music doctrines of modern times, we find the majority of Jewish composers holding to the established principles of classic music without admitting any sidestep. Were not Mendelssohn, Halévy, Goldmark, Joachim, Moscheles, Rubinstein and others strict classicists? Did not the latter, in his zeal for classical forms, make the statement that after Schumann and Chopin there are no new creations worthy of the name "music." "*Finis musicae!*" he exclaimed.[7] Were not the great theoreticians, Marx and Jadassohn, pious adherents of the style established by Bach—Mozart—Beethoven, recognizing no later innovations in harmony and form? For about eighty years these two men taught nothing but the classic music of the eighteenth and of the beginning of the nineteenth centuries.

Jewish musicians did contribute much toward the internationalization of art-music. Since Meyerbeer, the Jewish composer has learned to merge different styles into a composite one, and the virtuoso has rendered Italian, German or Russian music in the genuine temperament of each people, giving expression to the spirit of the people whose music he presents, penetrating into the very core of that people's scale of emotions. Further, the Jewish musicians contributed NUMBERS. The list of Jews among the great in general music is out of all proportion to the comparative numbers of the Jews and gentiles of the nations whose songs we have considered. Musical talent is undoubtedly a pronounced feature of the Jewish people.

Verily, history teaches us that RACE alone does not make for originality in music. It serves merely as fertile soil which, when sown with seeds of the spiritual culture of that race, bears distinctive fruits. The Jew in general music has written not as a JEW, but has produced out of and contributed to the culture in which he happened to be reared.

The place for an evaluation of the musical creations of these Jewish musicians is, therefore, not in a treatise on JEWISH music, but in the history of GENERAL art-music. Indeed, such evaluation has been repeatedly made. Here we need only demonstrate the fact that music composed by JEWS is not always JEWISH music.

CHAPTER XXIII

HARMONY.

More than two centuries (from Salomon Rossi to Salomon Sulzer) were required to stabilize harmony in the Synagogue song of Europe. Almost three centuries passed before this art was applied to Jewish folk-song. Apparently insurmountable obstacles stood in the way of employing harmony for a song, the primary features of which sharply contradicted the established principles of classical harmony. First in importance stands the problem of the SCALES. As explained in Chapter II, and frequently discussed in this book, Synagogue song is based upon THREE principal scales.

First, the tetrachord e—f—g—a, conjunctively repeated: e—f—g—a—b♭—c—d becomes a heptachord, while disjunctively: e—f—g—a+b—c—d—e constitutes an octachord. Out of this scale the Ashkenazim developed the scale of the *Adonoy-Moloch* mode, by adding two tones below the tonic (d—c) and by lowering e in the octave (e♭), thus creating the following succession of notes: c—d—e—f—g—a—b♭—c—d—e♭. The second scale consists of the minor tetrachord d—e—f—g, which, if conjunctively repeated: d—e—f—g—a—b♭—c, produces a heptachord, and by its disjunctive repetition: d—e—f—g+a—b—c—d, forms an octachord. The third scale: d—e♭—f♯—g+a—b♭—c—d, the basis for the *Ahavoh-Rabboh* mode, is formulated of two disjunctive tetrachords.

None of the scales has the elements requisite for the accepted system of harmony. The basic variances are six, designated (a through f) as follows: (a) The scales of Jewish music have no "Leading-note" in the seventh (i.e., a semi-tone between 7 and 8), and in their heptachordal form have no octave at all. This circumstance precludes the forming of a major triad on the fifth tone. (b) In none of the scales is the fifth dominating, the classical importance of the dominant being transferred to the sub-dominant, the fourth, because the SCALES, and as a consequence, the melodic line of the *modes* have the tetrachordal form. (c) In scale 1, in its heptachordal form, the fifth (b^b) is diminished, thus preventing the forming of a common triad upon the tonic (e). (d) The second in the scales 1 and 3 being minor, semitones, makes the forming of a triad upon the fifth a diminished cord. Thus, for example, in scale 1 the triad upon the fifth will be b—d—f and that of scale 3 will be a—c—e^b. (e) The second in scale 3 is augmented (e^b—$f^\#$), a step which is forbidden in classic harmony. (f) The third in the scale of the *Adonoy-Moloch* mode is, in its octave, flat (E—e^b), and the sixth in scale 3 is major below the tonic and minor above it (B—b^b). Both cases make a permanent system of diatonic harmony impossible.

The tetrachordal character of the ancient part of Synagogue song, in giving the fourth the dominating rôle calls not only for the plagal cadence, but causes a change in the whole system of modulation. The tendency toward the TETRACHORDAL CIRCLE involves departure from the circle of the fifth and its related keys, and makes a system of modulation to the related keys of the sub-dominant. Thus, scale 3 has the following modulations: the sub-dominant minor or major, or *Ahavoh-Rabboh;* the upper-mediant (flat) major or minor; the sub-second minor and major; the sub-mediant major. Scale 2 has: The sub-dominant minor; the fifth *Ahavoh-Rabboh;* the upper-mediant major; the sub-mediant major; the sub-second major; the upper-second *Ahavoh-Rabboh.* Scale 1 in the *Adonoy-Moloch* form has: the sub-dominant major; the fifth minor and *Ahavoh-Rabboh;* the tonic minor; the upper-mediant *Ahavoh-Rabboh.* In the original form of scale 1 the nearest modulations are: to the upper-mediant in minor; to the sub-mediant major; to the sub-dominant in the same scale, and to the tonic in *Ahavoh-Rabboh.*

These obstacles faced the first harmonizers of Synagogal song. The problem was the same as that of the first harmonists of the Gregorian chant three or four centuries earlier, except that the workers in Synagogue music had the more dif-

ficult task of coping with scale 3, which has no counterpart in
the eight old Church modes. The Church musicians, as is
known, cut the Gordian knot: reduced the eight scales to two,
Major and Minor; and reshaped the latter by creating in it
the "leading-note" of the major seventh. Needless to comment, in so doing, they violated all that was unique in the
Church song, sacrificing its character to the rules of the science
of European music. What they intended was the beautifica-
tion of a revered inheritance. What they did was to lop off
the individualities of their chants to fit the Procrustean bed
of accepted classical harmony. They lacked the knowledge,
the art and the daring to recast the technique of harmony to
conform to the artistic demands of another song.

The first harmonists of the Synagogue fell into the same
manner of meeting their difficulty. The structure of Oriental song succumbed to the rules of harmony. The *Adonoy-
moloch* scale they reshaped to major; and scale 2 to minor
in its "harmonic" and "melodic" succession; scale 3 appeared
too "exotic" for the application of harmony; therefore, they
often employed for that scale harmony of the major scale.
Had they been fully aware of the affront to the integrity of
the Synagogue song, some among them might have preferred
violating the rules of harmony. As it was they (Jew and
gentile alike) believed that they were "modernizing" the traditional scales and modes.

We shall now examine the harmony of the first prominent
composers for the Synagogue. Their work was of two-fold
character: the creating of new compositions for choir and solo,
and the harmonizing of old modes and tunes. Their *new*
creations were based entirely upon European music, in melody
and in harmony, without the employment of any Jewish material whatsoever. The only problem of which they were at
all conscious was the harmonization of traditional material.

On examination of the *Schir Zion* by S. SULZER we find that he has turned the *Adonoy-moloch* mode into major (Nos. 19-38), and the *Ahavoh-Rabboh*, likewise, to major (Nos. 56-75, 82-92). He harmonizes the responses for the three festivals in major (Nos. 164-174; 237; *Anhang* I, No. 21). The test of the man's ability to utilize harmony in accord with the character of Jewish song would have been the *Ahavoh-Rabboh* mode. But not a single item did Sulzer compose in the *Ahavoh-Rabboh* in harmonic setting. He uses minor as a basis and modulates occasionally to the *Ahavoh-Rabboh*. The minor he employs for short items in which, however, no tetrachordal melodic line is utilized. The old traditional tunes, with but two exceptions, Sulzer gave either in solo or in unison, without any harmony. These exceptions are: No. 435, in *Adonoy-moloch* mode, in which Sulzer retained the minor seventh and added organ accompaniment "ad libitum," and No. 461, a minor tune, the tetrachordal line of which Sulzer retained. Sulzer's harmony expresses depth and exaltation. In it he voices his Jewishness only through his inclination toward interrupted ("deceptive") cadences, through modulations in minor, and the avoiding of too frequent modulations to the dominant.

S. NAUMBOURG's harmony is inferior in depth and in originality to that of Sulzer. The *Ahavoh-Rabboh* he did not use at all. Scale 1 he, like Sulzer, "modernized" to major. In his harmonization of traditional ancient tunes he not always preserved their integrity, as proved by these numbers from his *Zemiroth Israel*: Nos. 136, 148, 169, 182, 183, 226, 229, 233, 246, 282, 292, and these from his *Agudath Schirim*: Nos. 1, 3, 7, 11, 13, 14, 15, 27, 42, 48, 50, 52. He generally selected those tunes the scale and melodic structure of which were easily adjustable in the major or minor key. Most of the other tunes he rendered as Sulzer did, without harmony. In some items in his *Agudath Schirim* Naumbourg succeeded in giving harmony not discordant with the characteristics of the Jewish melodic curve. For example, there are No. 31, in which modulations to the second in *Ahavoh-Rabboh*, and to the upper mediant are made; and No. 35 (*Adonoy, Adonoy*), in which the turn toward the sub-dominant is noticeable.

After this scrutinizing search through the entire works of the two most prominent first Synagogue composers for the few harmonical progressions that merit attention as adjustments to the character of the song, we conclude that the most that these men achieved even in these rather insignificant exceptions was the avoidance of jarring modulations; and that through their work they nowhere deviated from the strictest adherence to classical harmony.

The first who met the problem, first as a Jew and secondly as a harmonist, who either by conscious planning or by an inspirational leap (We shall never know which.), devised a system of harmonization for Jewish modes, was H. WEINTRAUB (Chapter XIII). Rooted deeply in Synagogue song, technician and artist enough to manipulate with freedom the tools of the science of harmony, he turned to the advantage of Synagogue song, his acquaintance with the work of J. S. Bach, with the classics of Church and secular music. The soundness of his knowledge of classical forms and usages he evidences in his employment of the "Cantus Firmus" with contrapuntal embellishments, which he was first to introduce into Synagogue song, and further in his composition of fugues (see his work *Tempelgesänge*, Nos. 31, 81, 119). Strongly influenced by Sulzer, he follows his prototype in the harmonization of simple responses in major. But in his handling of scales 1 and 3 he demonstrates his mastery, his bold independence. In his harmonization of the Synagogue modes he leaves Sulzer behind, he breaks the fetters of classical harmony, and strikes out, forcing for himself a new and untried path. Note numbers 33, 35, 38, 134, 145, 182, 183 in his above-mentioned work. But Weintraub's crowning achievement is the creation of a harmonic system for the *Ahavoh-Rabboh* mode.

He sanctioned the augmented second as a DIATONICAL STEP, and set the perfect cadence of that mode in two forms: (1) by means of the sub-dominant, and (2) by the sub-second, or by the diminished fifth in its first inversion (table XXXV, 1). He gave ample illustrations of ways the *Ahavoh-Rabboh* mode should be harmonized, such as Nos. 163, 172, 183, 185, 186, 187, 191, 192, 193, 194, 195, 196, 201, 202, 219-223, 229-231, 236-239, 241. Even his numbers in the minor modes, in the *Selicha* or *Mogen-ovos* modes are interspersed with modulations into *Ahavoh-Rabboh*, such as numbers 188, 189, 190, 197, 198, 199, 200, 207, 209, 210, 211, 213, 216, 232, 234. He was first to introduce the system of transcribing the *Ahavoh-Rabboh* scale in the key of its sub-dominant minor as, for example, for *Ahavoh-Rabboh* in "e" the "a" minor key, with individual marking of sharps for the third tone: g♯; for "g" *Ahavoh-Rabboh* the "c" minor key, with the separate marking of b♮ for the third, etc. Similarly he applied for *Adonoy-moloch* the key of its sub-dominant, as, for instance, for *Adonoy-moloch* in "c" the key of F Major; for *Adonoy-moloch* in "d" the key of G Major is employed, etc. Weintraub was the first to render the *Adonoy-moloch* mode in harmonic setting, retaining in its scale the minor seventh (Nos. 215, 217).

Extracting Weintraub's harmonic scheme from his published work and preserved MSS., we may formulate thus its progressions, combinations and modulations.

(a) *Ahavoh-Rabboh or Hedjaz,* or Phrygian as Weintraub wrongly called it: (1) 1. Hedjaz—4 minor—1. Hedjaz. (2) 1. Hedjaz—4. Hedjaz—1. Hedjaz. (3) 1. Hedjaz—sub-second minor, then Dorian—1. Hedjaz. (4) 1. Hedjaz—3. major—4. Hedjaz—1. Hedjaz (see No. 186). (5) 1. Hedjaz—3. major—3. Dorian—4. Hedjaz—4. major—4. minor—1. Hedjaz. (6) 1. Hedjaz—1. minor—1. Hedjaz—2. major—2. Dorian—3. Hedjaz—3. major—sub-second Dorian—1. Hedjaz. (7) 1. Hedjaz—4. Hedjaz—6. major—4. Hedjaz. (8) 1. Hedjaz—3. major—4. Hedjaz—5. Hedjaz—4. minor (see No. 193). (9) 1. Hedjaz—4. minor—4. Hedjaz—6. Dorian—sub-second minor+Hedjaz+minor—1. Hedjaz (see No. 201). (10) 1. Hedjaz—4. minor—sub-second minor+major—3. major—sub-second major+minor—1. Hedjaz. (11) 1. Hedjaz—sub-second major—3. major—4. minor—6. Dorian—6. major—4. minor—4. Hedjaz—1. Hedjaz (see No. 201). (12) 1. Hedjaz—4. minor—6. major—4. Hedjaz—4. minor—sub-second Hedjaz+minor—4. Hedjaz—1. Hedjaz (see No. 241).

(b) Minor, or *Æolian* as Weintraub called it: (1) 1. minor—4. minor—4. Hedjaz—1. minor. (2) 1. minor—3. major—1. minor.

(3) 1. minor—5. Hedjaz—3. major—1. minor. (4) 1. minor—3. major—sub-second major—4. major (see No. 206). (5) 1. minor—5. Hedjaz—3. major—sub-second major—5. major—1. minor (see No. 195). (6) 1. minor—3. Dorian—4. Hedjaz—4. minor—3. major—sub-second major—1. minor. (7) 1. minor—3. major—5. Hedjaz—1. minor—5. Hedjaz—1. minor—3. Dorian—5. Hedjaz—1. Hedjaz—4. minor—1. minor—3. major—1. minor (see No. 197). (8) 1. minor—5. Hedjaz—sub-second major—3. major—4. minor—upper-second Hedjaz—3. Dorian—3. Major—1. Dorian—1. minor (see No. 198). (9) 1. minor—3. major—1. Hedjaz—sub-second major—3. Dorian—1. Hedjaz—3. Dorian—3. minor (see No. 200).

(c) *Adonoy-moloch, or Mixolydian* according to Weintraub: (1) 1. A.M.—4. major—5. minor—1. minor—4. Dorian—1. A.M. (2) 1. A.M.—1. minor—1. Dorian—1. A.M.—5. minor—1. Dorian—1. A.M.—4. major—1. A.M.—sub-second major—1. A.M.—1. Dorian—2. Hedjaz—1. A.M.—1. Dorian—2. Hedjaz—sub-second major—2. A.M.—5. minor—4. major—1. A.M. (see No. 205). (3) 1. A.M.—4. major—5. major—5. minor—4. minor—5. major—4. major—sub-second major—5. major—1. A.M.—4. major—5. major—1. A.M. (see No. 215).

Weintraub's compositions in the old Synagogue modes are all for cantor solo and choir, so that a good part of the modulations are executed by one voice. Weintraub's harmonic art has not been superseded by any subsequent composer.

L. LEWANDOWSKI had no more Jewishness in his harmony than had Sulzer or Naumbourg. True, he succeeded in creating some fine Jewish items, like No. 91 in his *Todah Wesimrah* I, which he developed out of the traditional *Ledovid-Boruch* tune. Likewise, No. 198 *Zocharti loch* and No. 202 for Psalm 150. In his harmony he was an adherent of Mendelssohn's school, whose oratorio-style for vocal music he adopted. His music is based, as already pointed out in Chapter XIII, on the German *Lied* of the nineteenth century and is, therefore, in major with German harmony. The latter feature is expressed in the preference for the progression of major chords and modulation into major keys and in an avoidance for minor chords and modulations. Furthermore, there is the predominant striving toward the major dominant. In minor, Lewandowski composed but a very few numbers, while in *Ahavoh-Rabboh* he has but one composition (No. 218). Noteworthy are his fine organ accompaniments of some traditional tunes, such as Nos. 109, 120, 122, 164, 181, 222, 244 in his above-quoted work. As a whole he adopted the policy of Sulzer, to give traditional tunes and modes without harmony. The other Synagogal composers in Central and Western Europe stood entirely upon the basis óf European harmony, and in only very rare cases we find harmonic progressions of Jewish character.

For this artistic Jewishness we have to turn to the works of East European *chazzanim*. In the collections of E. GERO-WITSCH (Chapter XIV) there is a wealth of Jewish harmony. Both his treatment of traditional material and his original compositions in the Synagogal modes are remarkable for their genuineness and their fine artistic conception. The same holds true with regard to the works of DAVID NOWAKOWSKY, P. MINKOWSKY, A. M. RABINOWITZ (Wilna, 1855—Cantor in Libau), and several others. They evolved either through Weintraub's influence, or independently, the same manner of harmonic treatment of the *Ahavoh-Rabboh, Mogen-ovos* and *Selicha* modes, a system unlike anything to be found in European music.

In table XXXV several examples of harmonic progressions are given. No. 2 is from a composition by D. Nowakowsky.[1] This selection is in the *Ahavoh-Rabboh* in "g" and modulates to the sub-second in major (F). No. 3 is by Weintraub from his work No. 220. It modulates into the sub-dominant (c), to the third flatted (b♭) and to the sub-second in major, and finishes on the tonic (g) in *Ahavoh-Rabboh*. No. 4 is from Gerowitsch's work *Shire Tefilla* No. 36, in which the same progression is observed, namely, the turn toward the sub-dominant and the cadence with the sub-second in minor.

The same system was later applied for the harmonization of folk-songs in *Ahavoh-Rabboh*. No. 5 furnishes an example of the harmonization of the tune *Alte Kashe* by A. Shitomirski, given in table XXXII, 14.[2] The same tune was harmonized by Maurice Ravel in ultra-modern style, without regard for its scale and the nature of the mode.[3]

Among the latest composers S. ALMAN, in his above-mentioned work for the Synagogue (Chapter XIV), does justice to the *Ahavoh-Rabboh* mode in numbers 25, 26, 32. In the latter he modulates to the sub-dominant in minor and in the *Ahavoh-Rabboh* scale; to the sub-second in minor, to the sixth in major, and finishes on the tonic in *Ahavoh-Rabboh*. In No. 47 he modulates into the 6th and 3rd major.

In a period of 80 years (the oldest composition by Weintraub dates from 1842) the Jewish composers of East European extraction developed a system of harmonization of the *Ahavoh-Rabboh* mode, which is based on the tonality of its scale and accords with the characteristics of its melodic curves. The consistency with which they have adhered to the system gives us the possibility of establishing certain rudiments of harmony for that mode.

(A) The Harmony of "Ahavoh-Rabboh"

In XXXV, 6, we give the chords applied in the diatonic scale. In this example we find three major chords upon the first, second and sixth degrees; two minor chords upon the fourth and the seventh, and two diminished chords upon the third and the fifth degrees. The third is at times altered to major, in lowering it a semi-tone (II), while the sixth is, as a rule, applied in major only, taking the third or its octave (tenth) flat. The triads are used in the first and second inversions. The seventh 7th chord, in all inversions, is the one most frequently used. Next in order come the third 7th and the fifth 7th (No. 7). Also on the first and on the fourth degree, the chords of seventh are built, while on the second and sixth, seventh chords occur but seldom. As has been explained above, the leading-note of the *Ahavoh-Rabboh* mode is not a semi-tone from the seventh to the eighth. Its leading-tones are the sub-second (a whole tone) ascending, or the upper second (semi-tone) descending to the tonic.

(B) The Harmony of the Minor Modes

The modes in minor are harmonized in two forms, (1) in the harmonic minor, and (2) in the Æolian minor. In the first case the harmonic progressions are like those used in classic harmony. The exceptions lie in the modulations. These never occur to the dominant major or minor, but to the dominant *Ahavoh-Rabboh*, to the subdominant minor and major, to the upper mediant major and minor, to the sub-second major, to the upper second and sub-dominant *Ahavoh-Rabboh*. The cadence is effected through the dominant chord. In the (2), Æolian form, the dominating power is given to the subdominant, through which cadences and modulations occur. Cadences are effected also by the major chord on the seventh, as, for example, in Sulzer's *Mogen-ovos* (No. 43). The use of that form of minor is extensive both in the Synagogue and in folk-songs. We give two examples of harmonization in the Æolian minor scale. One is No. 8 in XXXV, a lullaby arranged by P. Lwow.[4] The second is No. 9, which is a harmonization of XXXIII, 15. In both examples we clearly see the predominance of the sub-dominant and the lack of the semi-tonal leading-note. In No. 8 the cadence occurs through the sub-second major mentioned above.

At times minor tunes end in the *Ahavoh-Rabboh* scale on the tonic of the minor in which they begin. In this instance the harmony at the end is in accordance with the *Ahavoh-Rabboh*.

(C) The Harmony of the "Adonoy-moloch"

This mode has been comparatively seldom set to harmony. In addition to Weintraub, Gerowitsch, in his above-mentioned work, p. 61, made use of it. XXXV, No. 10 affords an example. Here we see the seventh consistently minor. However, the dominant is regularly applied as leading major chord, owing to the fact that the seventh is major when BELOW the tonic. Thus the harmonization leaves the impression of a major scale in which modulation is continuously made to

the sub-dominant, rather than of the *Adonoy-moloch* scale with the
lowered seventh a regular diatonic step.

The chords are, as furnished in No. 11, three major-chords upon
the first, fourth and seventh; three minor-chords upon the second,
fifth and sixth, and one diminished chord upon the third degree. The
seventh, when occurring below the tonic, is major and the chord upon
it is a diminished triad. In this case the seventh serves as leading-note
and as third in the chord upon the fifth, which chord in this case receives the major dominant character. From all described we see that
the chords upon the fifth and the seventh are applied in twofold manner, and these, if properly employed, add a great deal of color and
variety to the harmony. The modulations are: to the sub-dominant
major, to the fifth minor and *Ahavoh-Rabboh* scale, to the tonic in
Ukrainian Dorian (see S. Alman, No. 7 in his above-mentioned work),
and to the sub-second major.

Harmony has adapted itself to Jewish song. Not only has
a beginning been made, but a complete system lies before us,
the success of which is best attested by the character of the
works from which the formulæ have been extracted. Masters have blazed a path. They employed the IDEA of harmony rather than its established RULES. For what they laid
the foundation must depend upon the knowledge and the
art of those who now approach Jewish music, upon the degree to which composers will remain faithful to the unique
character of Synagogue and folk-song.

TABLE XXXV
Harmony
a) Ahavoh-Rabboh

CONCLUSION

As a result of our treatise, we see that the Jewish people has created a special type of music, an interpretation of the spiritual and social life, of its ideals and emotions. In this music we find the employment of particular scales, motives, modes, rhythms, and forms, based on definite musical principles. These run through the music like a golden thread. Elements which do not conform to them have no hold on the music and consequently vanish from the body of that song.

Jewish song voices the spirit and the history of a people who for three thousand years has been fighting bitterly but hopefully for its existence, scattered in thousands of small groups among the millions having diverse tongues, cultures, and creeds. Its history has shown Jewish music always to be a genuine echo of Jewish religion, ethics, history, of the inner life of the Jews and of their external vicissitudes.

Wherever a Jewish group maintained Jewish spiritual culture, there Jewish song was cultivated. Wherever the group upheld its historic integrity, Jewish song flourished. It is a song created by the people of Semitic-Oriental stock, the same who created the other Jewish spiritual values and upheld them. It is the product of those imbued with the fundamental and genuine elements of that song. Often have our pages recounted of musicians of foreign origin as well as of Jews without knowledge of Jewish music, who were unable to create music genuinely Jewish. That great song, born of Jews, preserved by them, and in the course of centuries developed by them, can continue to grow only through musicians, born Jews, reared in Jewish environment, steeped in Jewish folklore and folk-song, vibrant with Jewish emotion, sensitive to Jewish sorrows, joys, hopes, and convictions—faithful sons of Israel.

NOTES

1. Ambros, A. W., *Geschichte der Musik*, Vol. I, 3rd edition. Leipzig 1887, p. 365.
2. Ambros, o.c., p. 347-8.—Ambros' presumption that Herodotus referred to a folk song cannot be correct, because the song being a lamentation had a religious character.—Maneros was the only son of the first Egyptian king. On the instruments of the ancient Orient see Curt Sachs, *Reallexikon der Musikinstrumente*, Berlin 1914; *Handbuch der Musikinstrumente*, Berlin 1920.
3. Ambros, o.c., p. 388; Chayne, Encycl. Biblica s. v. Music.
4. *B. Sabbath*, 56 b.
5. *Jer. Sukka* V, 6. Maimonides, *Kelé Hamikdash.*
6. *Midrash Shocher-tob*, Ed. S. Buber, p. 406.
7. Josephus, *Antiquities of the Jews*, VII, 12, 3.
8. Muss-Arnold, *Assyrisch-Deutsches Handwörterbuch*, Berlin 1905, p. 1093.
9. *B. Rosh Hashanah*, 34 b; 16 a.
10. *Saadiah*, quoted by Abudraham, Ed. Warsaw 1878, p. 145.
11. Maimonides, *Hilchoth Teshuvah*, Chap. III, IV.
12. *B. Rosh Hashanah*, 34 a; Jewish Encycl. s. v. *Shofar.* The form of blowing explained is the Sephardic-Oriental, whereas the Ashkenazim changed the *terua* to a short staccato note, and the *shevarim* to three long abrupt notes. Up to the present day Arabic shepherds in Palestine call their sheep and cattle with a *tekia-terua-tekia* sound of a *Shofar*, in Arabic also *Shafur.*
13. Ambros, o.c., p. 389.
14. How much of exaggeration there is in that number we cannot determine.
15. Josephus, o.c., III, 12, 6.
16. *Mishna Rosh Hashanah*, III, 3-4.
17. The list of instruments is given in *Mishna Arachin* II.
18. *Targum Onkelos* to Genesis 4, 21; *Targum Jonathan* to Psalms 150, 4.
19. *B. Arachin*, 10 b; *Jer. Sukka*, V, 6.
20. *Mishna Arachin*, II, 3.
21. l.c.
22. *B. Arachin*, 10 b; *Jer. Sukka*, V, 6.
23. For list of instruments of the First Temple see I Chronicles 15, 16, 25; II, 5: 29, 25-30.
24. *Mishna Sukka*, V, 1; *B. Sukka*, 50 b.
25. *Mishna Bikkurim* III.
26. *Mishna Kethuboth* IV, 4.
27. Maimonides' commentary to *Mishna Arachin* II.
28. Rashi's commentary to *Arachin* II, 10 a, gives for *Halil* the French *chalumeau* which was the ancestor of the present oboe. The origin of *chalumeau* is the Latin *calamus*—reed. In Babylon the *Aulos* was known and called *malilu*, and was considered a lamenting instrument par excellence. See M.

495

Jastrow, *Die Religion Babyloniens u. Assyriens*, II, 1. Giessen 1912, p. 4. *Ḥalil*, from *ḥalal*—to hollow out, may have a relation to the Assyrian *chalalu*—flute, from which *muttachalilu*—the flute player is derived. See Muss-Arnold, o.c., p. 314. The Greek name *Aulos* may be borrowed from the Semitic *ḥalalu*, by dropping the "h" and adding the Greek suffix "os." It is agreed that the Aulos was brought to Asia Minor from Assyria, from where Olympus introduced it into Greece about 800 B.C.E. Ambros, o.c., pp. 388, 399, 401; H. Abert, in G. Adler's *Hdb. M. G.* 1924, pp. 44, 47.

29. *M. Tamid* III, 8. In like manner it is reported in the same place that the tone of the *Magrepha*, of the Cymbal, of the Levitical song, of the *Shofar*, of the voice of the High Priest when he chanted his confession on the Day of Atonement, and of the call to service, that all these voices were heard in Jericho.

30. Writers like Dio Cassius (born 155 C.E.) stated the fact that the tetrachordal system was borrowed by the Greeks from Asia. Even the halftone system was not of Greek origin, but was also taken over from the Egyptians, who knew it as early as 1200 B.C.E. According to H. Abert, l.c., it was most likely imported into Egypt by the Semites.

31. In Arabic *Alama* means "open lips," "parted lips," figuratively for teacher, orator, or sage.—On *elymos* see Abert, o.c., p. 41.

32. On *Magrepha* see *Mishna Tamid* V, 6; *B. Arachin*, 10 b.—*Magrepha* is derived from the Hebrew "grophith"—reed.

33. *B. Arachin*, l.c.; *Jer. Sukka*, V, 6.

34. *Mishna Tamid* VII, 3.

35. *Mishna Arachin* II, 5.

36. Ambros, o.c., p. 364.

37. *Mishna Sukka* V, 4. Rabbi Simeon ben Gamaliel, who was killed during the fall of Jerusalem, is reported to have been a skillful dancer. See *B. Sukka*, 53 a; *Jer. Sukka*, V, 4.

38. *Mishna Sukka*, IV, 5.

39. *Alamoth* is translated "soprano" or "falsetto," and in conjunction with our explanation of *Alamoth* (double-pipe) it may refer to a soprano pipe instrument. We know that the Greeks had *Aulos* of soprano, alto, tenor, and bass register. See H. Abert, l.c.

40. Already around 100 C.E. Rabbi Meir explained that the female singers mentioned in the Bible referred to the women of the Levites, whereas Rabbi Simeon entertained the opinion that they were "talented women" in general. *Pirke R. Eliezar*, Chap. XVII.

41. Jeremias, A., *Das Alte Testament im Lichte des alten Orients*, Leipzig 1906, p. 527.

42. *Mishna Kethuboth* IV, 4.

43. *Mishna Arachin* II, 3; *Sukka* IV, V.

44. *Mishna Sukka* V, 4.

45. *Mishna Arachin* II, 6.

46. *B. Chullin* 24.

47. *Arachin*, l.c.; *B. Arachin*, 13 b, tells that the boys caused embarrassment to the adults on account of their sweet voices, and were nicknamed "pain causers"—"*Tsoare*" instead of "assistants"—"*Soade*."

48. *Mishna Arachin*, II; *B. Arachin*, 11 a.

49. *B. Sukka*, 50 b-51 a; *Arachin*, 11 a.

50. *Mishna Yoma* III, 11. He used to press his thumb in his mouth; while

his fingers he pressed "between the voice-chords," i.e., on the Adam's apple. On the Assyrian bas-relief, quoted above, we see a female singer in like manner pressing her hand against her cheek and neck. The same is to be seen on the Egyptian wall-pictures.

51. *Mishna Tamid V.*

52. Deut. 32, 1-43; *B. Rosh Hashanah*, 31 a; even the laymen read from the Pentateuch. *Mishna Taanith*, IV, 2-3. *Baraitha Yoma*, vii a; *B. Yoma*, 69 b; *Mishna Sota* VII, 7-8.

53. According to tradition there were 480 synagogues in Jerusalem at the time of its conquest by the Romans. *Jer. Megilla* III, 1; while according to another tradition there were 390. *B. Kethuboth*, 105 a.

54. *Mishna Taanith* IV, 2. The *Anshe Maamad* were selected from the different districts of the country as representatives of the people to be present at the offerings and pray for their people. They were divided into 24 groups, each group serving two weeks a year in turn, or rather one week each half-year. See Elbogen, o.c., pp. 237, 553. During the week that their representatives were on duty in Jerusalem, the congregations of the respective districts used to gather, hold public services, and read from Genesis I.

55. *B. Sota*, 30 b; Tosefta ed. *Zuckermandel*, p. 303; *Jerus. Sota*, V, 4; *Mechilta*, ed. I. H. Weis, p. 42; Maimonides, *Hilchoth Megilla*, etc. Chapter III. § 12-13.

56. Hastings, *Encyl. of Religion & Ethics*, Vol. X, p. 160 ff.

57. *Mishna Sota* VII, 5.

58. Josephus reports that Herod introduced in Jerusalem Greek musicians for the theater. *Ant. Jud.* XV, 8, 1.

59. *Midrash Ruth Rabba*, 6; *B. Hagiga*, 15 b, reports about Elisha ben Abuya called "Acher," who was fond of Greek song.

60. L.c., *Midrash Shir Hashirim Rabba*, 8. end.

61. All the traditional material of the song of these communities I have collected and explained in my *Thesaurus of Hebrew-Oriental Melodies*.

NOTES TO CHAPTER II

1. On Semitic-Oriental music see *Thesaurus*, etc., o.c., Vol. IV, German edition, Berlin 1923, pp. 52-112.

2. The creation of compositions of European folk-song and even art music is essentially also an arrangement and variation of motives *traditional* in a folk-song of a certain people or race. Many motives are common to the musics of the different European peoples. Not only are the creations of the classics based upon melodies or motives which the composers have consciously taken from their folk-song, but they have likewise been unconsciously influenced by the motives of the music of their people. The fundamental difference between the manner of composition in the Orient and in the Occident is that in the Orient a motive is employed in its mode and in a customary position with relation to the other motives of that mode; whereas in Occidental music, a motive is a unit unbound to mode, scale, or position.

3. A detailed account of the various modes and scales is given in *Thesaurus*, etc., o.c., IV, pp. 53-112.

4. *Thesaurus*, l.c.
5. *Thesaurus*, l.c.
6. The illustrations in table I are taken from *Thesaurus*, o.c.
7. The illustrations 1-7 of table II are taken from *Der Kirchengesang der Jakobiten* by A. Z. Idelsohn, published in *Archiv fuer Musikwissenschaft*, Berlin 1922, III; No. 8 from D. J. Parisot, *Rapport sur une mission scientifique*, etc., Paris 1899, No. 62.
8. The illustrations of table III are from J. B. Rebours, *Traité de Psaltique*, Jerusalem-Paris 1906, pp. 148-163.

NOTES TO CHAPTER III

1. *B. Megilla*, 32 a.
2. *B. Sanhedrin*, 101 a.
3. Luke 4:17; Elbogen, o.c., p. 176; J. E. *Haftora* VI, p. 136.
4. Elbogen, *Der Jüd. Gottesdienst*, etc., 1913, p. 533; *Tosefta Megilla*, 1-6, quotes a decision regarding the reading of Esther on Purim in the name of Rabbi Zacharia, the Priest, who lived long before the destruction of the Second Temple. See J. E. *Megillot*, the five X, p. 431. *Purim* is mentioned in the second book of Maccabees XV: 43.
5. Though the usage of their public reading is mentioned only in the late source of *Soferim* XIV: 18.
6. D. Pinna's notation was printed in the introduction to the Bible. Ed. Jablonsky, Berlin 1699.
7. The notation was prepared by J. Boeschenstein, who was a pupil of a Jewish scholar and mingled with Jews (1472-1540); and was printed in Reuchlin's *De accentibus et Orthographia Hebræorum*, Hagenau 1518.—All other oriental examples are taken from my *Thesaurus*, Vols. I-V.
8. These communities are remnants of the old Jewish settlements in Provence and France. At present only sixty families survive in Avignon and twenty in Carpentras, many of them having moved to Marseilles, where they established a community. In 1885, they published their traditional tunes and modes, called *Chants Hebraiques* (*Zemiroth Israel*) by Jules and Mardochee Cremieu. The example 6 is taken from that collection, p. 153.
9. For example, R. Gershom, "the light of the exile," who was a native of Norbonne and settled in Mayence toward the end of the tenth century.
10. Such as the Kalonymos family, originally from Luca, which settled in Germany about 870 or 970.
11. See for example P. Wagner, o.c., I, Chapters I-III.
12. About the way in which the Biblical modes could be made attractive and palatable for modern taste, see Chapter XXIII.
13. The Ashkenazim chant the Song of Songs, Ruth, and Ecclesiastes in the same mode.
14. *B. Megilla*, 16 b; *Soferim*, Chapters XII and XIII. However, Deut. 33 is considered a song only in the Yemenite tradition.
15. L.c.
16. See illustrations in table II; Gardiner, W. H. T., *Egyptian Hymn-tunes*. London, No. 43; *Der Kirchengesang d. Jakobiten*, o.c., No. 32.
17. The Arabic Dictionary, *Muchit-il-Muchit*, s. v. Rehaw.
18. P. Wagner, o.c., III, Leipzig 1921, p. 236.
19. According to P. Wagner, o.c., I, Chapter I.

20. P. D. Johner, *Neue Schule d. Greg. Choralges.*, Regensburg 1913, II, p. 154.
21. P. Wagner, o.c., I, p. 36.
22. More details about these local modes are given in my *Thesaurus*, Vols. I-V, o.c.
23. On the *cheironomia* compare P. Wagner, o.c., II, Chapter I, Leipzig 1912.
24. *B. Berachoth*, 62 a, for which the second finger was used. The statement is reported in the name of Rabbi Akiba (40-135 C.E.).
25. Rashi's commentary to *B. Berachoth*, l.c.
26. In the ninth century only nineteen accents were known, twelve disjunctives and seven conjunctives. Compare *Dikduke Taamim*, S. Baer and H. Strack, Leipzig 1879.
27. P. Wagner, o.c., p. 18.
28. P. Wagner, o.c., Chapter II.
29. Neumos = sign in Greek, seems to have relation to the Hebrew *Neima* = tune (sweetness), mentioned in *B. Megilla*, 32.
30. A detailed account of the accents, as well as all Hebrew sources referring to their description, is given in my *Hebrew History of Jewish Music* I, Berlin 1924, pp. 95-117.
31. See my *Hebrew History*, o.c., J. E. Accents, cantillation.
32. The system of accents for chanting was employed also for the Mishna and Talmud, accentuated parts of which are retained in MS. in several libraries. Compare J. E., o.c.; my *Hebrew History*, o.c. On the system of accents of Job, Proverbs and Psalms, compare *History*, o.c., and *Thesaurus* II, p. 13.

NOTES TO CHAPTER IV

1. *Mishna Tamid*, V; *Mishna Berachoth*, I; *B. Berachoth*, 12 a.
2. The introductory six Psalms 95-99, 29, for the Friday evening service as well as the hymn *Lechoh dodi* were introduced into the service by Isaac Luria in Safed (Palestine) about 1570 and became generally used at the beginning of the seventeenth century. Up to that time the service started with Psalms 92-93.
3. P. D. Johner, *Neue Schule des Greg. Choralgesanges*, Regensburg 1913, I, p. 46. In the English transl., I, pp. 56, 217.
4. *B. Sabbath*, 24 a-b; 119 b.
5. Hammanhig, Lemberg 1858, *Sabbath*, 7. See also *Machsor*, Vitry, Berlin 1893, pp. 82-83.

NOTES TO CHAPTER V

1. *Ben Sira* IX, 4; "The hearing of a woman's voice is indecency." *B. Berachoth*, 24 a.
2. *B. Chagiga*, 15 b.
3. *Ruth Rabba*, Chapter VI.
4. *Yalkut Mishle*, § 932, 3.
5. *Psikta Rabbathi*, Chapter XXIII; *Tanchuma*, Reé, § 9.
6. *Shir Hashirim Rabba*, Chapter VIII end.
7. L.c.

8. *B. Gittin*, 7 a; *Orach Chayyim*, § 560.
9. All quotations cited are from *B. Sota*, 48 a. See M. Jastrow's Dictionary, p. 919.
10. (I quote from the English translation by G. M. Butterworth.) *The Instructor*, Book II, Chapter IV. According to H. Windisch in *Zeitschrift für Palästina-Kunde*, 1925, p. 152, Clement had a Jewish teacher during his sojourn in Palestine about 180-200.
11. In the Egyptian cult, too, after its destruction by Cambyses of Persia, instrumental and choral music were interdicted. The song was limited to one soloist—a priest. Ambros, o.c., p. 381.
12. P. Wagner, *Gregorianische Melodien*, I, p. 16. Havelock Ellis in his *The Dance of Life* II, "The Art of Dancing," is entirely on a wrong track in stating that Christianity and Judaism retained dancing at worship. He either fails to take account of or ignores historic facts. Not only was it the tendency of Synagogue and Church to abolish all bodily motions, but this reform was actually carried out in practice. Only here and there in provincial places, as a remnant of paganism, dances occasionally accompanied worship. Similarly reads a Jewish source of the preference of vocal music. *Midrash Tehilim*, ed. Buber, p. 204.
13. *B. Sota*, l.c.
14. Though the origin of that custom may be rooted in the superstitious belief of frightening away evil spirits. Compare *B. Berachoth*, 30 b-31 a.
15. *B. Berachoth*, 30-31. At the same place it is related that upon the request of the guests of *Rab Hamnuna Zuta* to sing, he started to eulogize, "Woe unto us, we have to die," and he taught his guests the response, "Study and obeying the commandments will protect us."
16. *B. Gittin*, l.c.
17. *Shir Hashirim Rabba*, Chapter VIII end, in the manner of the singing of which, God finds great delight and he says, "Oh, let me hear thy voice for it is sweet" (Canticles 2, 15), but when they sing in confusion in shouting one before the other, then God says, "Let us run away."
18. P. Wagner, l.c.
19. H. Burgess, *Selected Metrical Hymns*, etc., of Ephraim Syrus, London 1853, gives in his introduction a detailed description of Ephraim's poetry.
20. Thus do we notice a meter of 3-4 words in Genesis 49: 2-26; Exodus 15: 1-19; Deuteronomy 32; Judges 5: 2-31; 1 Samuel 2: 2-10; 2 Samuel 22: 2-51, etc., besides, of course, the poetical books Psalms, Proverbs and Job.

NOTES TO CHAPTER VI

1. On Babylonian liturgy, see M. Jastrow, *Die Religion der Assyrier und Babylonier* I, l.c., Chapter XVII, "Gebete und Hymnen."
2. "We have no one on whom to rely but our Father in Heaven," *B. Sota*, 49 a-b.
3. Such as *Honi Hammeagel, B. Taanith*, 23 a-b; his grandson Abba Hilkia and his wife; Rabbi Akiba, o.c., 25 b; Rabbi Chiya, o.c., 24 a, and many others, on whose power in prayer many legends are related in the *Talmud Taanith*, 23-25.
4. "Those who write down prayers are like those who burn the Scripture." *Tosefta Sabbath*, Chapter XIII; *Tania Rabbathi*, Warsaw 1879, 7.

5. *Tosefta Megilla,* Chapter IV; *Sofrim,* Chapter XIV; *Pesikta,* Ed. Buber F. 22; *Pirke R. Eliezar,* 44; *Jerushalmi, Megilla,* Chapter IV.

6. L.c., the assistants were also called *Mutznafim*—Aramaic, assistants, *Pachad Yitzchak,* letter "shin," p. 223. In the *Machzor Sepharad,* Livorno 1822, I, 81 b, there is still the regulation that beginning with *Nishmath* the precentor must have two assistants, *somchim.*

7. *B. Taanith,* 16 a.

8. *Pesikta Rabbathi,* Chapter XXIII; *Tanchuma,* Reé, § 9.

9. *B. Megilla,* 24.

10. *Tosefta, Megilla,* 4.

11. L.c.; *Siddur,* Amram Ed. Koronel F. 35; Meyer of Rothenburg in *Yam Shel Shlomo* to *B. Chullin,* Chapter I, § 48.

12. *B. Berachoth,* 10 b.

13. *Jerus. Yebamoth,* Chapter XII; *B. Sukkah,* 51 b; Jer. ibid., V, 1.

14. On the origin of *chazzan:* Jewish Encycl., VI, p. 284; *B. Kethuboth,* 8; *Tosefta,* IV; *B. Makkoth,* 23; *Mishna Tamid,* V, 3; *B. Joma,* 7 a; *Jerus. Berachoth,* V, 3; *B. Taanith,* 16; *Tanchuma,* Jethro; *Wayyikra Rabba,* 6; *Tosefta, Bikkurim,* II; *B. Sota,* 5 b. Already around 200 C.E. some communities were compelled to engage a permanent *chazzan* who was able to render also other communal services. *Jerus. Yebamoth,* Chapter XII, reports that the community in Simonia asked Jehuda Hannasi to recommend them a man who should be capable of functioning as Judge, *chazzan,* and Scribe; and of performing all communal tasks. And he sent Levy ben Sisi.

15. The *chazzan* had no right to read the portion of the Pentateuch without special permission from the elders of the Synagogue, *Tosefta, Megilla* III, and only at a later time he became the permanent reader or lektor, *Sofrim* ii. He likewise became the instructor of children in the Mishnaic time, *Sabbath* I, 3. On the custom of appointing two precentors *B. Megilla,* 24; *M. Rosh Hashanah* IV, *Teshuvoth Hag'onim,* Lyck 1864, § 9.

16. *Jerus. Berachoth* IV a.

17. *Jerus. Berachoth,* III a; *Sofrim* XIII.

18. *Midrash Tehillim,* ed. Buber F. 29.

19. *Siddur Amram,* o.c., F. ii.

20. *M. Taanith* I.

21. Maimonides, *Hilchoth Tefilla* VIII.

22. W. Oesterley, *The Jewish Background of the Christian Liturgy,* Oxford 1924.

23. P. Wagner, o.c., I, pp. 16-17, 19-20.

24. O.c., pp. 20, 29-30, 81-87, 95.

NOTES TO CHAPTER VII

1. W. Bäumker, o.c., I, pp. 6-7, etc.; P. Wagner, o.c., I, p. 30, etc., is of the opinion that rhythmical singing in the Church was practiced already in the fourth century. H. Riemann goes further and decides that the Church hymns were based upon Greek art and had strict rhythm, *Hdb. M.* I, 2, Chapter VIII; he finds also rhythm in the "Sequences" (Prosae), o.c., § 36. Indeed, being aware of the fact that the Sequences have modal structure, he compromises in saying that only the older ones have rhythm, while LATER, rhythm and form were neglected. O.c., pp. 124-125.—The *Lais* of the

French and the *Leiche* of the Germans are products of Gregorian song intermingled with folk elements. Riemann, o.c., § 37. The same is true of the *Minnesong* and of the song of the *Troubadours*, compare H. Riemann, o.c., Chapter XV.

2. Franz M. Boehme, *Altdeutsches Liederbuch*, 2 Ed., Leipzig 1913, p. lxvii.
3. *M. Berachoth* IV; *B. Berachoth*, 29 b; *M. Aboth* II, 18.
4. Compare my *Thesaurus* I: "The Song of the Yemenite Jews," 1925. Ibid., II: "The Songs of the Persian," etc. Jews, 1923.
5. On Arabic meter compare Martin Hartmann, *Metrum und Rhythmus*, Giessen 1896, p. 4, etc.; on the different metrical forms, his *Das Arabische Strophengedicht*, Weimar 1897, pp. 200-201.
6. S. Duran, *Magen Aboth*, Livorno 1785 F. 55; S. Archevalti, *Arugoth Habosem*, Venice 1602, F. 100. M. Lonsano, *Sheté Yadoth*, Venice 1617, F. 140.
7. J. Elbogen, o.c., pp. 283-4.
8. *Tachkemoni (Makames)* XXIV Ed. A. Kaminka, Warsaw 1899, pp. 220-27.
9. *Hay Gaon, Responsa of the Gaonim*, Ed. Miller, p. 208. Isaac Alfasi, *Responsa*, § 281. Jehuda of Barcelona, *Sefer Haitim*, F. 173, p. 253.
10. Maimonides, Responsa, *Pe'er Hador*, Lemberg 1849, § 129.
11. *Kusari* II, § 70-78.

NOTES TO CHAPTER VIII

1. Zunz, *Ritus*, Berlin 1858, p. 66; Jewish Encycl., II, pp. 191-3.
2. Graetz, *Geschichte der Juden*, 2 edition, Leipzig 1871, Vol. V, p. 195 ff.
3. Ibid., Gross, *Galia Judaica*, Paris 1879, p. 401.
4. *B. Megilla*, 17 b; *Matzref Lachochma*, Warsaw 1890, p. 64.
5. D. Kaufmann in *Monatsschrift f. W. J.* 1896 s. v. "Achiamaaz."
6. Zunz, o.c., p. 67.
7. *B. Taanith*, 10 a.
8. Agobard's letters were translated from Latin into German by Emanuel Samostz, Leipzig 1852, which translation I used here. The same fact is stated in Hebrew sources of the twelfth century. *Shibbole Halleket*, Ed. Buber, Wilna 1887 F. 113.
9. Ibid.
10. Reissmann, *Das Deutsche Lied*, Cassel 1862, p. 2.
11. W. Bäumker, *Das katholische deutsche Kirchenlied* I, Freiberg i/B., 1886, p. 6.
12. Ibid.
13. M. Güdemann, *Geschichte des Erziehungswesens u. der Kultur*, etc., I, p. 14 (Hebrew).
14. *Sefer Chassidim*, Ed. Freimann, Frankfort 1924, p. 332.
15. Ibid., p. 106.
16. O.c., Berlin, p. 85.
17. A. Epstein, *Die Wormser Minhagbücher* (reprint) Breslau 1900, p. XXII. On hymns on "Maria Magdalena" of the twelfth century, see Boehme, o.c., Nos. 560, 618; p. 654.
18. Epstein, o.c., p. XXIV.
19. *Yosif Ometz*, Frankfort 1727 F. 77.
20. Mose ben Ezra (eleventh century) in his work on Hebrew poetry makes the

statement that in Arabic poetry each poem has a tune, but not each tune a separate poem. *Shirath Israel*, Leipzig 1924, p. 110. (Hebrew translation by B. Halper.)

21. *Sefer Chassidim*, § 302, interprets the phrase in Exodus 19:19, "And God answered him by a voice"—God taught Moses the Biblical modes.

22. The term *Steiger* may be interpreted either with the German *Weise* (way, wise, mode) or as a derivation from *steigen*—ascending, i.e., scale or curve or succession of tones.

23. The sharp on the f being an alteration, influenced by the *Ahavoh-Rabboh* mode.

24. Boehme, o.c., No. 513.

25. H. Riemann, o.c., I, 2, p. 29.

26. V. d. Hagen, *Der Minnegesang*, Hannover 1841, Vol. IV, p. 792. The rhythmization is mine.

27. W. Bäumker, l.c., II, p. 203.

28. F. Pedrell, *Cancionero*, etc. Cataluna 1920, introduction.

29. F. Consolo, o.c., No. 17.

30. P. Wagner, o.c., III, pp. 140-141.

31. Ibid.

32. This change caused the medieval theoreticians to identify this mode with the fifth Gregorian mode which corresponds to the Lydian. However, the artificial classification of Semitic-Jewish modes according to the scheme of the Greek scales killed their vitality by this Procrustean procedure.

33. A. Schubiger, *Die Sängerschule St. Gallens*, 1858, p. 3; P. Wagner, o.c., I, p. 164. Illustration 8 is taken from H. Riemann, o.c., I, 2, p. 27.

34. V. d. Hagen, o.c., p. 826; *Die Jenaer Handschrift*, Leipzig 1901, ed. E. Bernoulli and Saran II, p. 42.

35. These special modes are mentioned in *Siddur Rashi, Machzor Vitry, Shibbole Halleket, Rokeach, Sefer Chassidim*, etc.

36. *Emek Habbacha*, Leipzig 1858, p. 8 (Hebrew) and p. 31 (German). The translation cited is by K. Kohler in Jewish Encycl. s.v. Alenu.

37. In his prayerbook, *Malěa Haaretz Dea*, Thiengen, 1560, F. 172 a. R. Mordecai Jaffa in Prague (1530-1612) explains the reason why the *Olenu* should be sung on these days in a solemn tune, in his work *Lewush*, Prague 1622-24, § 133. In like manner another author in Frankfort of the seventeenth century, Joseph Nordlingen, in his work *Noheg Katzon Josef*, Hanau 1718 F. 72 ff. reports of that tune.

38. Tashbetz, § 245; *Machzor Maagle Tzedek*, Venice 1568 I, F. 22.

39. Compare my essay, *Der Missinai Gesang der Deutschen Synagoge*, in Z. M. G. 1926, p. 466.

40. *Maharil, Rosh Hashanah*, ed. Warsaw 1874, F. 38 b.

41. *Machzor Maagle*, etc., o.c., Purim.

42. *Noheg*, etc., F. 52 b. The tune for the verse in Esther is retained in MS. L. Sänger.

43. *Tashbetz*, l.c.

44. *Noheg*, etc., l.c.

45. *Tashbetz*, l.c.; *Maharil*, o.c., F. 38 b; *Siddur Troyes*, in Bloch's Jubilee Volume, Budapest 1905, p. 97 ff.

46. *Noheg*, etc., F. 63.

47. *Chibbure Likkutim*, Venice 1715, F. 4; *Reshith Bikkurim*, Frankfort 1708, F. 29.

48. *Shire Yehuda*, Amsterdam 1697, introduction.
49. *Chorgesänge der Synagoge in München*, 1839, No. 74.
50. *Baal Tefillah*, Frankfort 1901, No. 1442, P. W.
51. Ahron Beer and Goldstein use it for *Vechach hoyoh omer.*
52. MS. Goldstein, while others used a part of the Kol-nidré tune. *Baal Tefillah*, No. 851, W. 1.
53. *Machzor Vitry*, o.c., p. 388; Raban (thirteenth century), Prague 1610, F. 70 testifies to the same usage customary in the Slavic countries.
54. *Machzor Nürnberg*, ed. B. Ziemlich, Berlin 1886, p. 50.
55. *Maharil*, o.c., F. 45 b: "*Yaarich bo beniggunim.*"
56. *Lewush*, o.c., § 619.
57. *Sefer Chassidim*, o.c., § 414; *Machzor Vitry*, p. 210.
58. Compare my *Thesaurus* II, pp. 71-72; IV, p. 157.
59. *Machzor Vitry*, p. 154.
60. *Maharil, Sabbath.*
61. S. Geiger, *Divre Kehilloth*, Frankfort 1862, p. 67; Baer, *Baal Tefillah*, No. 504.
62. *Maharil*, l.c.
63. *Rokeach*, Lemberg 1858, § 49; *Maagle Tzedek*, o.c., II; *Noheg*, etc., F. 57.
64. *Noheg*, etc., F. 72.
65. *Siddur Troyes* l.c.; in B. *Rosh Hashanah*, 32 b, Rabbi Abbahu of Cesarea (fourth century) states as the reason why on the High Holidays no *Hallel* (Laudation Ps. 113-118) is recited, that Israel stands trembling on trial on the Day of Judgment, in which state of mind the joyous singing of laudation is impossible.
66. *Maharil, Rosh Hashanah; Noheg*, etc., F. 76.
67. *Maharil*, l.c.; *Maagle* II, l.c.; *Noheg*, etc., l.c.
68. *Baal Tefillah*, No. 713 W. 2; Jewish Encycl. s. v. Ledavid.
69. F. Consolo, o.c., No. 143.
70. Zunz, *Lit. d. syn. Poesie*, Berlin 1865, p. 240.
71. Volume IV, p. 86, Psalm 21.
72. Nos. 3, 4, are taken from J. Zahn, *Die Melodien der deutschen evangelischen Kirchenlieder*, III Gütersloh 1890, Nos. 4533-4.
73. Bäumker, o.c., I, p. 496.
74. F. Pedrell, *Cancionero*, etc., No. 46.
75. J. Malát, *Tschechische und Moldaische Gesänge*, Prague 1871, Vol. I.
76. Compare W. Tappert's interesting study *Wandernde Melodien*, Berlin 1890.
77. The chorale was composed in 1523 and published in Wittenberg in 1524. Boehme, o.c., Nos. 623, 635.
78. Boehme, o.c., No. 381.
79. *Ha-asif*, Warsaw 1885, p. 298.
80. *Responsa Chawoth Yair*, § 238.
81. Vol. III, p. xii, Psalm 15.
82. The illustrations in example 11 are taken as follows: I from the *Hagada* of Johann Stephan Rittangel, Koenigsberg i/P. 1644; II from the *Hagada Zewach Pesach* by Friedrich Albrecht Christian, Leipzig 1677. He was *chazzan* in Bruchsal, his Jewish name having been Moshe of Prossnitz; III from the periodical *Der Jude* published by the convert Gottfried Selig, Leipzig 1769; IV from M. Kohn MS., written probably about 1840.
83. Boehme, o.c., No. 521 a; 569 a.
84. Bäumker, o.c., II, p. 133; No. 363.

85. Ibid., IV, p. 481; No. 79.
86. Ambros, o.c., II, p. 516, etc.; ibid., III, p. 477; H. Riemann, o.c., II, 2; pp. 329-339 ff.
87. From the many references collected in my Hebrew history II, Chapter XIII, but a few sources shall be given, such as *Shire Yehuda*, o.c., F. 5; *Reshith Bikkurim*, o.c., F. 29; and in the Judeo-German Songster *Simchath Hannefesh*, Fürth 1727.
88. Responsa, Jacob Weil, Venice 1549, § 140, § 147, § 152; *Pachad Yitzchak*, letter *Mem*, F. 137.
89. Eckstein, *Geschichte der jüdischen Gemeinde in Bamberg*, p. 149.
90. Responsa, Mose Minz, Salonica 1615, § 81.
91. *Yosif Ometz*, o.c., F. 87 b.

NOTES TO CHAPTER IX

1. Philaret Kolessa, *Phonographierte Melodien der Ukrainischen rezitierenden Gesaenge* (Dumy), in *Beitraege zur Ukrainischen Ethnologie* B. XIII, Lemberg 1910, introduction, p. lxxv.
2. O.c., part II, Lemberg 1913, p. xxix.
3. O.c.
4. O.c., part II, p. xxxi-ii.
5. O.c., part I, p. lxxxi.
6. The Ukrainian examples are taken from Kolessa, ibid., as follows: No. 1— part I, No. 21; 3—No. 15; 4—pp. 91, 102; 5—part II, 57; 6—part II, No. 10; 7—part II, No. 11. The Jewish example 2 is taken from E. Schnipelisky *Tefillath Eliyahu*, New York 1924, p. 38.
7. Kolessa, l.c., part I, p. lxxvi.
8. Béla Bartók, *Volksmusik der Rumaenen von Maramures*, Munich 1923, Drei Masken Verlag.
9. Ibid., p. xxix.
10. Ibid., p. xx. The Roumanian examples in table XXVII are taken from Bartók's collection: 8—21 e; 11—52; 15—23 a; 16—23 c.
11. Bartók in his *Das Ungarische Volkslied*, Berlin 1925, p. 24, denies the existence of this scale in the Hungarian folk-song.
12. F. Liszt, *Die Zigeuner und ihre Musik*, Leipzig 1883, pp. 20-81. More on this subject in Chapter XIII.
13. The example of Dovidl Brod is taken from the musical appendix to *Oester.-Ungar. Cantoren-Zeitung*, 1886, No. 17.
14. Kolessa, l.c., Bartók, o.c., p. 22.
15. A. P. Berggreen, *Folkivisor, Folkesange og Melidier*, 2nd Ed. 1864, Vol. 10.
16. Bartók, o.c., p. x; Kolessa II, p. xxxii.
17. Example 17 is taken from *Tefillath Eliyahu*, o.c., No. 19, with some changes.
18. We meet such orders in the community of Brisk in 1623: "No *chazzan* shall sing on Sabbaths more than three selections, and on distinguished Sabbaths no more than four tunes, and this not before 'Shema' in the morning service." In Selz after the persecutions of 1650 it was agreed that in no Jewish home should there be heard music except at weddings (see Chapter V): "In 1655 the rule was accepted to mourn the destruction of our country, that no music should be heard in Jewish homes, not even at weddings, for a period of a year." *Ha-asif* VI, p. 172.

19. Nathan Hanover, *Yevén Metzula*, Cracow 1896, p. 9.
20. In his book *Chibburé Likkutim*, Venice 1715, F. 4-5.
21. J. G. Frazer, *The Golden Bough*, part IV, *Adonis Attis Osiris*, I, London 1914, pp. 53-54.

NOTES TO CHAPTER X

1. See Ed. Birnbaum, *Jüdische Musiker am Hofe von Mantua von 1542-1628*, Vienna 1893. Reprint of the *Kalender für Israeliten für das Jahr 5684*. Already at the court of the art-loving Pope Leo X (1513-1521) two Jewish musicians were much in favor. The one was Jacobo Sansecondo, who stood as a model in Raphael's "Apollo on Mount Parnassus." The other musician was Giovani Maria, who in honor of the Pope adopted the name "de Medicis," and who was the model of the "Violinist" by Sebastiano del Piombo. Among the oldest theoreticians of the dance was Guglielmo da Pesaro, who at the end of the sixteenth century was considered foremost. "His treatise *Trattato del arte del ballo* is the basis upon which all the choreographical works are founded." Paul Nettl, *Alte jüd. Spielleute und Musiker*, Prague 1923, pp. 4-5.

2. Birnbaum, o.c., p. 14. The title page reads as follows: *Premite armoniche a tre voci de Davit Civita Hebreo. Al Serenissimo Signor Signor, e Patron mio Collendissimo il Sig. D. Ferdinando Gonzaga Duca di Mantova di Monte ferato*, etc. In Venetia, Appresso Giacomo Vincenti MDCXVI. The sheets are marked: *Madrigali Ebrei*.

3. The Hebrew name of Allegro was, according to Birnbaum, o.c., p. 16, note 23, *Simcha*.

4. Grove's *Dictionary of Music*, s. v. Rossi.

5. H. Riemann, o.c., II, 2, p. 88.

6. Idem., o.c., pp. 94-95.

7. Birnbaum, o.c., pp. 19-34, gives a detailed list of his works.

8. The title of the opera is *Musiche de alcuni eccellentissimi Musici, composte per la Maddalena, sacra Rapresentazione de Gio Battista Andreini, Fiorentino*, Venice 1617, with a *Balleto á tre, vá contato & Sonato con 3 Viole da Braccio*. The last item was by Rossi. See P. Nettl, o.c., p. 14.

9. Birnbaum, o.c., p. 22, gives the ducal order verbatim. Grove, l.c.

10. In his autobiography *Chaye Yehuda*, Kiev 1912, p. 64.

11. The verbal translation of the Hebrew reads "in the arrangement and according to the relation of voices to each other, based on THAT SCIENCE."

12. The Responsa on that controversy were published by Modena, and republished several times. Compare *Teudath Sh'lomo*, by the *chazzan* Sh'lomo Lifshitz, Offenbach 1718 F. 13 ff.

13. L.c.

14. The Sullam family was one of the most cultured Jewish families in Italy at that time. The daughter-in-law of Mose Sullam, Sara Copia Sullam, was a highly educated and gifted woman (d. 1641 in Venice), musician, poetess, and renowned writer. She knew Italian, Hebrew, Spanish, Latin, and Greek. She fought for her religion, and was very active as an author. S. Naumbourg in his introduction, o.c., p. 16.

15. The collection of Madrigals for five voices is drawn in part from R's Madrigals *Libro* I (11 numbers) and in part from his Libro II (11 num-

bers). As an appendix, d'Indy gave R's song *Spazziam pronto o vecchia velle.*

16. Naumbourg, o.c., p. 16.

17. In order to prove his innocence, that man, Nehemia Cohen, published an apology in Hebrew *Metzitz Umelitz*, Mantua 1715, where he states all details.

18. See Catalog Halberstam *Kehillath Sh'lomo*, Vienna 1890, No. 227. From that collection only one page has been preserved. It contains the mode of Psalms.

19. *Divre Agor*, Venice 1603.

20. J. Moscato devoted his first sermon to music. The collection of his sermons is called *Nefutzoth Yehuda*. Porteleone published his work *Shilté Haggibborim* in Mantua 1612, in which he devoted several chapters to the music of the Temple.

21. This Hebrew theory is but a fragment in MS. in the Bibliotheque Nationale in Paris. A copy of it is in the H. U. C. Library in Cincinnati.

22. His description of his travel was published in the *Israelit. Letterbode* in Amsterdam 1884.

23. B. Marcello's Psalms *Esto poetico-armonico* were published in eight volumes in Venice 1724-1727. On the Jewish tunes chosen by M. Josef Singer gives a detailed account in his article "Marcello Benedetto" in the *Kalender für Israeliten*, Vienna 1900.

NOTES TO CHAPTER XI

1. In his above-mentioned (Chapter VIII) commentary to the prayer-book Diengen 1560; preface to the *Kaddish*.

2. H. Riemann, o.c., II 2, p. 239 ff.

3. Sabbathai Bass, *Sifthei Yeshenim*, Amsterdam 1680 end; A. Levy's *Travels in Israel. Letterbode*, l.c.

4. *Bikkure Haitim*, 1824, p. 257; Nettl, o.c., p. 39.

5. A. Levy's *Travels*, l.c.

6. *Shivche Ari.*

7. *Kevod Chachamim*, Venice 1700, Chapter VIII, F. 15; *Noheg*, etc., f. 39.

8. Grove I, p. 457; H. Riemann, o.c., II 2, p. 308; II 3, p. 5; Ambros IV, p. 218.

9. *Maharil*, Ed. Warsaw 1874, p. 64.

10. More in detail compare Albert Wolf, *Fahrende Leute bei den Juden*, in *Mitteilungen Z. Jüd. Volkskunde XI*, Leipzig 1908, 3.

11. *Yosif Ometz*, F. 13 b; Yoel Sirkish in his responsa § 103 reports of a certain Chayim Cimbalist of Turbin (Poland) who served in Wallenstein's army in 1637 as cymbal player, and who embraced Christianity.

12. *Sefer Chassidim* reports of a Jewish musician who would play and sing Christian music while among Christians. Ed. Freimann, Frankfort 1924, p. 85.

13. P. Nettl, o.c., p. 33.

14. P. Nettl, o.c., p. 39. The bass singer Isaac composed a German song in 1716.

15. Ibid., pp. 41, 64-65.

16. *Éle Divre Habrith*, Dessau 1818, F. 5.

17. Wagenseil in his work *Sota* appendix, p. 85; on the *chazzanim* in Prague compare my essay in *Reshumoth* V, pp. 354-6; further below.

18. Schudt, *Jüd. Merkwürdigkeiten* II, pp. 51, 284, 323. Süss is the hero of the famous novel *Power* by L. Feuchtwanger.

19. In a pamphlet called *Shloshoh Tzoakim*, see note 46, Chapter IX.

20. V. Sluys: *De Oudste Synagogen der Hoogduitsch-joodsche Gemmente Te Amsterdam* (1635-1671), Amsterdam 1921, p. 27.

21. *Mitteilungen*, etc., 1903. *Jahrbuch der Jüdischen Literaturgesellschaft* VI, p. 18 ff., concerning the minutes of the Portuguese community of the year 1652.

22. V. Schudt: *Merkwürdigkeiten der Juden* 1714, part IV.

23. V. L. Geiger: *Geschichte der Juden in Berlin* I, Berlin 1871, pp. 45, 68.

24. Michael of Kempen was appointed *chazzan* in Prosnitz 1764. His agreement (*Chazzanuth-brief*) is still preserved in the archives of that community. Therein it is stated that the bachelor Samuel was appointed bass on the salary of one-half *Taler* per week; the community had to supply him with Sabbath meals, while the *chazzan* was to provide his food for the week-days. *V. Oest. Ung. Zeit.* 1894, No. 26.

25. The "Great Singer," Rabbi Josef of Bixheim was appointed *chazzan* in Hildesheim in 1780. In the still retained agreement the community urges him to have a bass singer, for whose salary the community and the *chazzan* are responsible.

26. Community regulations (*Tekanoth*) of Worms from 1641; *Blätter für Jüd. Gesch. u. Lit.*, Mayence 1903, No. 10, §§ 31, 33.

27. *Mitteilungen*, etc. M. Grunwald, 1923, p. 231; idem., 1903, VII, p. 13.

28. There is a legend about evil spirits which were called forth by the bass during his singing in the Synagogue in Izborz. Compare A. Kahana, *Sefer Hachasiduth*, Warsaw 1922, p. 40.

29. *Reshith Bikkurim*, Frankfort 1708, F. 29.

30. Cantor in Osterode, Minden in Western Germany, then in Altona and Hamburg, originally from Poland. His book *Shire Yehuda* was published in Amsterdam 1697, XIV.

31. In his book on the conduct of the *chazzan*, *Teudath Sh'lomo*, Offenbach, 1718, F. 20.

32. Responsa (*Bach Yeshanoth*) Frankfort 1697, § 127.

33. *Shtei Yadoth*, Venice 1618, F. 142.

34. *Yosif Ometz*, Frankfort 1627, F. 77.

35. *Reshith Bikkurim*, l.c.

36. The custom of singing *Boruch Sheomar* was an old one. V. Tur *O. CH.*, § 51, v. also *Machzor Maagle Tzedek*, Venice 1568, Vol. I. Introduction. Already Reb Samson ben Eleazar the Scribe was called *Boruch Sheomar* and that same name he gave his book, Shklow 1805. He lived in the fourteenth century. In his introduction he tells that, as a boy of eight, he was brought from Saxony to Prague, where he lost his parents and remained an orphan. There, every morning, in the Synagogue, he used to sing *Boruch Sheomar* with a loud and sweet voice. Every Synagogue in Prague had a special society called *Mezamrei B'sh*. On the tombstones of the members of those choral societies is marked *Mezamrei B'sh*, v. Hock: *Epitaphs of Prague*, ed. D. Kaufmann, Pressburg 1892. There were also orchestral societies which played in the Synagogue before the beginning of

the Friday evening service. Abraham Levy, in his *Reisebeschreibungen*, speaks of Prague thus: "In Prague are famous *chazzanim*. Among them I found one who is a great artist and famous throughout Europe. His name is Yokele *Chazzan*. The chazzanim use 'singers' and also flutes and organs and violins and cymbals and various instruments of percussion for every Friday to receive the Sabbath. With the help of these instruments, they sing not only Lechoh dodi, but after they finish that poem, they continue to sing several sweet tunes for about an hour's time." See Ant. Margarite's (born 1500) report in Mitteilungen, etc., 1909, p. 60; also Elbogen, *Der jüd. Gottesdienst*, etc., p. 506. Of the famous *chazzan* Lipman Poppers (d. 1649) it is reported in the Necrologue of Hirschele Tausig Weinschenk, which was printed in the introduction to *Sota*, Wagenseil 1614, p. 83 ff.; *Von Schnitzen und Mahlen will ich schweigen still, dazu alle Seitenspiel Schalmeien und Tromete.*

37. Riemann, o.c., II 3, p. 71.
38. L.c.
39. Idem., p. 78.
40. Bäumker, o.c., II, p. 5.
41. Idem., III, p. 11.
42. L.c.
43. Idem., III, p. 144.
44. O.c., II, p. 5.
45. O.c., III, p. 11.
46. First in MS. found in a book (*Klei Yakar*) published 1602 in Lublin, then printed in Amsterdam as a placard (1709?). Heb. Bibl. II, pp. 155-158.
47. *Chibbure Likkutim*, l.c.
48. Levy's *Travels*, l.c.
49. In the memoirs of Glickel von Hammeln, Ed. D. Kaufmann, p. 325; Benjamin Kreilsheim in his pamphlet, *Chelkath Binjamin*, Berlin 1722.
50. Jacob Emden, *Megillath Sefer*, Warsaw 1903, p. 27 ff.; Sluys, *De Oudste Synagogen der Hoogduitsch-joodsche Gemeente Te Amsterdam* (1627-1671), 1921, p. 27.
51. *Hammaor Hakkaton*, Fürth, 1679, by Meier Tarnopol, who was rabbi in Oettingen, and whose father-in-law, Chayim Zelig, was *chazzan* in Fürth. The latter was originally *chazzan* in Lemberg in Poland, and in 1660 was compelled to emigrate by reason of the Chmelnitzki pogroms. The author states also that all the Polish rabbis and their disciples emigrated to Moravia and Southern Germany. P. Ch. Kirchner, *Jüdisches Ceremoniel*, etc., Nürnberg 1724, p. 177, tells that the *chazzan* sings with four singers; p. 189 speaks of ten singers not less than thirteen years of age.
52. MS. copied by Birnbaum.
53. V. Memoirs in *Oesterreichisch-Ungarische Cantoren-Zeitung*. Jhrg. 3, Nos. 6-8.
54. The traditional tune of the so-called Sefira *Lechoh-dodi* is claimed to be an imitation of an aria in Mozart's "The Wedding of Figaro," No. 3. In reality the tune of *Lechoh-dodi* has also very much similarity to a German folk-song of Paderborn of the year 1765 (v. W. Bäumker, *Das Katolische-Deutsche Kirchenlied*, Vol. III, No. 121). The basis seems to be an older German folk-song, utilized both by Mozart in the aria mentioned and by some *chazzanim*. That the *chazzanim* did not take the tune from Mozart is evident from the fact that Mozart composed his Figaro in 1785, while

the *Lechoh dodi* tune was well known a long time before that, as proved by the manuscripts.

55. James Piccioto, *Sketches of Anglo-Jewish History*, London 1875, pp. 147-8.
56. *Jewish Chronicle*, 1873: 642. The Leoni tune is to be found in the *Church Hymnal* . . . *of the Protestant Episcopal Church*, Boston 1925, No. 460, and in *The Hymnal* . . . *of the Protestant Episcopal Church*, New York 1916, No. 253.
57. F. Pedrell II, No. 186.
58. Noskowski, S. *Piessn Ludu*, 1892, p. 218.
59. Salaberry, J. D. J., *Chants populaires du Pays basques*, Bayonne 1870, pp. 236-238, 260.
60. Kirchner, o.c., pp. 177, 189. See note 51.
61. A. Levy's *Travel*, o.c., 1884, No. 10, p. 148 ff.

NOTES TO CHAPTER XII

1. David Friedländer published a circular in 1799 addressed to *Oberconsistorialrat* Teller, in which he together with several Jewish families "agreed to accept Christianity and even baptism, if they were not required to believe in Jesus and might evade certain ceremonies."—In 1813 he proposed a plan by which he intended "to reduce Judaism to a mere colorless code of ethics." Jewish Encycl. V, p. 515.
2. Bäumker, o.c., III, p. 12.
3. Idem., III, p. 15; idem., p. 160.
4. *Hebräische und Deutsche Gesänge zur Andacht und Erbauung, zunächst für die neuen Schulen der Israelitischen Jugend in Westphalen.* Kassel 1810. This Hymnal contains 26 German and 4 Hebrew hymns to be sung according to 17 Church-tunes.
5. See note 14, Chapter XIII.
6. The title of the collection is *Gesaenge fuer Synagogen.* It became very popular and experienced several enlarged editions.
7. *Allg. Zeit. d. Judenthums*, 1842, p. 412; 680.
8. Nos. 1 and 3 are taken from W. Bäumker, o.c., III, pp. 285-6; No. 2 from J. Zahn, o.c., III, No. 3495.
9. Of Ashkenazic origin are: Nos. 6, 20, 24, 25 a-b, 27, 28 b, 34, 39, 42 c, 44, 48, 52, 53, 54, 55, 56 b, 57, 58, 59, 60, 63 (*Kol Nidré* with the German text *O Tag des Herrn*). Of Sephardic origin are: Nos. 11, 12, 14 d, 16, 18, 19, 21 a, 26, 33, 35, 42, 49, 50, 51. The "Chorale-book" entitled *Gesänge und Melodien für die Jacobson Schule in Seesen* was reedited later in Wolfenbüttel without date of print. In addition to the 106 tunes 110 new chorales and 20 traditional melodies were added, making a total of 236.
10. This was not the first Jewish-German Hymnal, for the Songster of Cassel *Religiöse Lieder und Gesaenge für Israeliten*, 1816, preceded it.
11. *Festschrift zum hundertjährigen Bestehen des Israel. Tempels in Hamburg*, 1918, pp. 68-70.
12. L.c.
13. O.c., pp. 68, 84.
14. In his letter to the author dated 7/15/27/ he says, "When I was appointed in 1913 successor to M. Henle, I had no interest to republish the chorale-

book (referring to the Hamburg songbook originated by Kley and in 1887 republished by Henle), because my intention was to abolish entirely the "chorale singing," i.e., to create a Jewish musical service. I succeeded in overcoming the strong opposition. And now for several years no chorale is sung with the exception of 'My soul, why art thou cast down' for the Memorial service, which became traditional." This song was composed by the organist I. H. Stoewing, o.c., p. 69. The text has been paraphrased in English in the U. P. B. II, p. 327. In the Union Hymnal, No. 184, this hymn is set to the "El nora" tune.

15. See the *Hymnal . . . of the Protestant Episcopal Church*, New York 1916, No. 158.
16. F. Boehme, o.c., No. 622; *Hymnal . . .* o.c., No. 424.
17. The reports and discussions of that fight have been published in Hebrew: *Éle Divré Habrith* and *Noga Hatzedek*, Dessau 1818.
18. *Protokolle der 2. Rabbiner Versammlung in Frankfurt*, 1845, p. 149; 354, 360.
19. Idem., p. 133.
20. I. Nathan, *Musurgia Vocalis*, London 1836, p. 102. The traveller was Thomas Rees (1777-1864), who wrote about his travels in 1800-1810.
21. An attitude again and again expressed at the Conference at Frankfort in 1845, o.c.

NOTES TO CHAPTER XIII

1. Born in Nikolsburg, 1769. He continued later as second *chazzan* with Sulzer. Died 1848. See G. Wolf, *Wiener Friedhof*, p. 33, Vienna 1879.
2. Moscheles was born in Prague. His grandfather was Isaac Schulhof Moscheles. His great-grandfather, Zalman Schulhof, *Dayyan* in Prague, was burned in 1689. He composed a cantata for the Vienna Congregation in 1814; and on the occasion of the victory over Napoleon, he conducted a thanksgiving service of which this cantata formed a part. His wife was of the Emden family in Hamburg. His son Felix, named after his godfather, Felix Mendelssohn-Bartholdy, was a painter in London. See *Aus I. Moscheles Leben*, Leipzig 1872, v. I, p. 16; 254; 261 ff.
3. Paul Nettl, *Alte jüd. Spielleute u. Musiker*, Prag, 1923, p. 43, says: "Emil Breslaur (*Sind originale Synagogen - und Volks-Melodien bei den Juden geschichtlich nachweisbar?* Leipzig 1898, p. 35), discovers a remarkable similarity between the *Kol Nidré* and the beginning of Beethoven's Quartet in C♯ Minor, opus 131 (Movement 6. Adagio quasi un poco andante, measures 1-5). I wish to add the following remark, in order to set forth the relation of Beethoven to the Synagogue: Beethoven composed his abovementioned quartet in 1826. In the previous year (1825), Beethoven was asked by the Israelitic Community (in Vienna) to compose a cantata on the occasion of the dedication of the new Temple. As a matter of fact, Beethoven was considering complying with the request. Finally, it was not Beethoven who wrote it, but Drechsler." Nettl presumes that Beethoven might have occupied himself with Synagogue tunes in order to become acquainted with the style. It is noteworthy that at one time Beethoven was near to Jewish atmosphere, for in 1792 he fell in love with Rachel Löwenstein, whose Jewish faith prevented her acceptance of Beethoven's offer of marriage. *Wahrheit*, Vienna 1901, No. 21.

4. Noah Mannheimer (1754-1824) was originally from Hungary. He had been for a certain time *chazzan* in Mannheim, from where in 1795 he went to Copenhagen, remaining there until his death. In Copenhagen he arranged a somewhat modernized musical service. Mannheimer composed some numbers for the Synagogue, one of which was adopted by Lewandowski in his *Todah Wesimrah* I, No. 51, without mention of Mannheimer's name. See also the biography of his son by M. Rosemann, Vienna 1922, p. 22.

5. Of these composers, Franz Schubert, the most distinguished, contributed one number, Psalm 92, while Seyfried, Drechsler, etc., were the main collaborators with Sulzer.

6. Part I of the *Schir Zion* was published in 1840, though the preface was written in 1838; Part II in 1866. The compositions of the Christian musicians were not specified in Part I, apparently to avoid arousing the antagonism of the Orthodox party. Part II does not include non-Jewish contributions. Herein we see that Sulzer later somehow considered Christian participation inappropriate. A second edition in 1905, with some eliminations and some additions, was published by Sulzer's son Joseph (1850-1927), who was the musical conductor at the Temple in Vienna for many years. In this edition, the names of the Christian contributors to Part I are given.

7. French 1859. Quotation from the German edition: *Die Zigeuner und ihre Musik in Ungarn*, translated by L. Ramann, Leipzig 1883, p. 51 ff.

8. See the above-mentioned second edition of the *Schir Zion*.

9. P. Wagner, *Gregor. Mel.* I. Leipzig 1911, p. 30 ff.; R. Lach, *Studien zur Entwickelungsgeschichte der ornamentalen Melopöie*, Leipzig 1913, p. 195.

10. He utilized recitatives and themes of Bezalel Schulsinger of Odessa, of Dovidl Brod, and H. Weintraub.

11. A title adopted from the Church. However, already at the beginning of the eighteenth century the *chazzan* used to be called so, compare Kirchner, o.c., p. 209.

12. *Allgemeine Zeitung d. Judenthums* 1865, pp. 620, 635.

13. H. Graetz, *Geschichte d. Juden* (German), Leipzig 1870, V. XI, p. 239 ff.

14. *Kindergebet*, published by Schlesinger, Berlin. Meyerbeer, as far as is known, never wrote for the Synagogue. L. A. Frankl, secretary of the Vienna Community, asked Meyerbeer to compose a special number on the occasion of the dedication of a Temple in Vienna, which request Meyerbeer refused on the ground that, inasmuch as they had Sulzer, they should not approach him. At the same time, Meyerbeer added the hope that no organ would be installed in the new synagogue, because it is a "pure Christian instrument: and I consider it my merit that, in accordance with Mendelssohn-Bartholdy, I arranged in Berlin an a cappella choir only. The praying man should approach his God without any intermediary. The Jews have maintained that opinion since the destruction of the Temple, and we should not introduce any innovation. But, if any music is required, then— according to my opinion—flutes and horns should be used, similar to those used in Solomon's Temple. However, the human voice is the most moving." *Der Jüd. Cantor*, Bromberg 1879, No. 26. The musical service to which he referred was most likely the attempt made by Meyerbeer's father, J. H. Beer, who arranged such a service in his private home in 1815-17. Surely the opinion of Felix Mendelssohn-Bartholdy, in the earlier years of that

service, when Mendelssohn was a boy of seven or eight years, could not have been of great value.

15. That valuable manuscript prepared in 1839-40 is still preserved; and I am publishing it in the second part of the sixth volume of my *Thesaurus of Hebrew Oriental Melodies.*

16. In his pamphlet, *Das Judentum in d. Musik,* 1850, Wagner's *Gesam. Schriften,* Hesse and Becker, Leipzig V. XIII. To Wagner's anti-semitic attitude, which, as is generally known, sprang from envy, his writings testify: *Über Meyerbeer's Hugenotten,* Ibid., V, VIII,—in which these Jewish composers are considered by Wagner as great geniuses; Meyerbeer and Mendelssohn especially as pure and genuine *Germans!* In V. VIII, p. 86, he protects the Jews against the attacks of Rossini in Paris.

17. As an item in operatic style, *Seu Sheorim, Zemiroth Yisroel* v. II., No. 162. *Uvnucho Yomar,* according to Meyerbeer's tune in *Zemiroth Yisrael* v. II, No. 166.

18. *Recueil de Chants Religieux et populaires des Israelites.* See Group I.

19. H. Steinthal, *Ueber Juden und Judentum,* Berlin 1925, p. 284.

20. H. Weintraub's biography of his father, *Hammagid,* Lyck 1875.

21. *Der Jüdische Cantor* 1882, p. 18 ff.

22. Extracts from Max Bruch's letter to E. Birnbaum: Breslau 4/12/89/ . . . "Ich habe schon als junger Mann, namentlich in den Jahren 1861-63, Volkslieder aller Nationen mit grosser Vorliebe studiert, weil das Volkslied die Quelle aller wahren Melodik ist—ein Jungbrunnen, an dem man sich wieder erfrischen und erhaben muss—wenn man sich nicht zu dem absurden Glauben einer gewissen Parthei bekennt: Die Melodie sei 'ein überwundener Standpunkt.' So lag denn auch das Studium Hebräischer Nationalgesänge auf meinem Wege—Kol Nidre und einige andere Lieder (u. A. 'Arabiens Kamele') habe ich in Berlin durch die mir befreundete Familie *Lichtenstein* kennen gelernt. Obgleich ich Protestant bin, habe ich doch als Künstler die ausserordentliche Schönheit dieser Gesänge tief empfunden und sie desshalb durch meine Bearbeitungen gerne verbreitet. . . .

"Ihr ergebener
"MAX BRUCH."

23. Preserved in the Hebrew Union College Library.

24. Zunz, *Gesam. Schriften.* Vol. II, Berlin 1870, p. 135 ff. Speaking of Lewandowski's endeavor to give new form to old songs, Zunz makes the following statement (p. 142): "Ist Israel's Geschichte unbekannt, bleibt jüdische Literatur vernachlässigt, wird die hebräische Sprache vergessen und das Judentum geringgeschätzt, so helfen weder alte Texte noch neue Melodien. . . ."

25. Sulzer originally had the idea of compiling a handbook for *chazzanim,* of which he speaks already in the preface to his *Schir Zion* I, in 1838; but he never carried out his intention.

26. Kirschner in his above-mentioned work, Vol. II, *Sh'ma.*

NOTES TO CHAPTER XIV

1. An account of his rendition of the service at the dedication of the Brody-Synagogue in Leipzig in 1818 was given in the newspaper *Weimarische Zeitung,* May 14, 1818.

2. *Oester.-Ungar. Cantoren-Zeitung* 1883, Nos. 6-8. Dovidl Brod's biography was written in Hebrew by his son, entitled *Zecher Olam*, Lemberg 1849.

3. The description is given by Wolf Privin, cantor in Graudenz (1843-1895), who for twelve years sang with Sender, in *Der Jüdische Cantor* 1886.

4. The agreement (*Ksav-chazzanuth*) made with the Wilna community was published in the Hebrew magazine *Talpiyoth*, Berditschev 1895, by Hillel Noah Steinschneider, who also gave a short biography of Yoel Dovid of Wilna.

5. Ibid., the name of his father-in-law was Mordecai Strashum (Raines). Compare *Ir Hatzedek*, p. 190.

6. On Stanislaus Moniuszko compare the *Musical Quarterly*, 1928, No. 1, G. Schirmer, New York.

7. The author of an important collection of Synagogue tunes frequently quoted in this book.

8. *Der Jüdische Cantor*, 1892, p. 75.

9. Some of his tunes were printed, as *Vahavienu* and a tune for *Chanukah* in Golomb's *Zimrath Ya*, Wilna 1885; *Habbet mishomayim* in Grunwald's *Mitteilungen*, etc., 1923, p. 244 and in my *Manual*, etc., 1926, No. 104.

10. A vivid description of Boruch Karliner is given in the Hebrew annual for ethnology and folklore *Reshumoth*, Vol. II, pp. 71-74.

11. A detailed characterization of Nissi Belzer as well as of the prominent *chazzanim* in Southern Russia in the nineteenth century is given by P. Minkowsky in the above-mentioned *Reshumoth*, Vols. I, II, IV, V.

12. Its first *chazzan*, Schpitzberg, was a disciple of Sulzer who served him as prototype. P. Minkowsky, ibid.

13. His biography was published in the *History of Chazzanuth* (Yiddish), New York 1924, pp. 89-91.

14. On this scale compare *Thesaurus*, Vol. IV, p. 69 (German).

15. This statement in the biographical sketch in the publication of his compositions edited by his son is incorrect since Tschaikowsky was from 1866 engaged as teacher of Theory at the conservatory in Moscow, and during his stay in Petersburg in 1868 he was already starting his career as composer. Compare Grove's *Dictionary of Music* s.v.

NOTES TO CHAPTER XV

1. I. M. Wise in his *Reminiscences*, Cincinnati 1901, pp. 21-23, describes the condition of the Synagogue Service in America at the time of his arrival in the United States in 1846.

2. Compare D. Philipson, *The Reform Movement in Judaism*, New York 1907, p. 468.

3. Ibid., p. 478.

4. According to the statement of Rabbi A. S. Moses, Mobile, in a letter to the author, dated February 21, 1928.

5. D. Philipson, l.c., p. 474. On the history of the Orthodox congregations in New York compare I. D. Eisenstein, "The History of the First Russian American Jewish Congregation," in the *Publications of the American-Jewish Historical Society*, Vol. 9, 1901, pp. 63-74.

NOTES TO CHAPTER XVI

1. *Catalogue Halberstam*, Vienna, 1890, No. 227.

2. Of the Spanish period we may consider the numbers: 6, 8, 9, 11, 12, 14, 16, 18, 27, 28, 30, 31, 32, 33, 34, 36, 42, 51, 54, 56, 59, 62, 68. The collection contains seventy numbers.

3. Published in Emmerich, 1868. It contains: (a) material of the eighteenth century, as, e.g., in Part I; p. 9, p. 15, p. 17, p. 18, p. 19, p. 24, p. 25, p. 27, p. 28, p. 31, p. 37, p. 39, p. 41, p. 43, p. 48, p. 51. In Part II: p. 24, p. 53, p. 60, p. 87, p. 88; (b) compositions or adaptations by the compilers. In Part I, p. 46, p. 51; in Part II, p. 6, p. 37, p. 39-45; p. 60, p. 63, p. 64, p. 29, are of Sephardic origin. See De Sola-Aguilar, ibid.; Machsor H. Gaster, London 1904, Vol. III, p. 273.

4. Portuguese tunes are Nos. 937-943. The last edition: Leipzig 1901. I. Kaufmann, Frankfort A/M.

5. On the history of this community see I. Loeb, *Les Juifs de Carpentras*, D. d. E. J. Vol. XII, Paris 1886; I. Cohen in *B'nai B'rith Magazine*, Cincinnati, 1927, Nos. 5-6.

6. Ibid. However, the Sephardic songs had but little influence upon them. See my *History of Jewish Music* (in Hebrew), Vol. II, Chapter IX.

7. Graetz, *Gesch. d. Juden*, Leipzig 1900, Vol. XI, Chapter VI, pp. 46, 146 (Hebrew translation, Wilna 1900); S. M. Dubnow, *Die Neueste Geschichte des Jüd. Volkes*, Vol. I, Berlin, 1920, pp. 93-97.

8. On the origin and originality of their Syn. songs, see my above-mentioned *History*, Chapter IX.

9. There are some other collections to be mentioned, e.g., S. SCHEUERMANN, Frankfort A/M., 1912; JACOB ROSENHAUPT, *Schiré Ohel Yaakov*, I-III, 1879-1886. In Vol. II a tune for the chanting of *Vechoraus* is given, which according to tradition dates back to *Maharil.*

10. Birnbaum's collection consists of musical material in MS., mainly Ashkenazic Synagogue songs of Europe of the eighteenth and nineteenth centuries. Of Portuguese origin, his collection contains a MS. of Rome of the early part of the eighteenth century, another MS. of Amsterdam by Abraham Caceres written in 1739, and one of Bayonne in Southern France. A detailed description of Birnbaum's musical MSS. is to be found in the above-mentioned H. U. C. Jubilee Vol., in my essay, "Songs and Singers of the Synagogue in the Eighteenth Century." A considerable number of Birnbaum's MSS. are inserted in the sixth volume of my *Thesaurus* mentioned above. His collection is now in the possession of the Hebrew Union College Library, Cincinnati.

11. Boeschenstein was teaching Hebrew in various Christian institutions in Germany. See Jewish Encyclopedia III, s. v. Compare also Chapters III, VIII. Bäumker, o.c., III, p. 348.

12. Partly collected in the *Pachad Yitzchak: zemer, chazzan, Naggen, Shirah, Shaliach tzibur;* in my *Hebrew History*, etc., Chapters VI-XVII.

13. *Pachad Yitzchak*, l.c., *History*, etc.; *Hachazzan Beyisroel* in the Hebrew monthly *Hatoren*, New York, 1923-5.

14. See A. W. Ambros, *Musikgeschichte*, Vol. I, Leipzig, 1887, p. 425 ff.; J. Moscato in his work, *Nefutzoth Yehuda.*

15. Such as Arthur Bedford, *The Temple Musick*, or an essay concerning the method of singing the Psalms in the Temple before the Babylonian captiv-

ity, wherein the music of our Cathedrals is vindicated. London, Motlock, 1706. An account of these theories is given in A. Baer's *Baal Tefillah*, mentioned above. See, *The Occident*, vol. XIII, pp. 373-381.

16. In the introduction to Psalms, though it is to a great extent based on the explanation of A. Porteleone in his quoted work.

17. *Haolam*, Berlin, 1908.

NOTES TO CHAPTER XVII

1. *Aboth de'rabbi Nathan*, I, Ed. S. Schechter, Vienna 1887, p. 2.
2. M. *Yadayim* III, 5; B. *Megilla*, 7 a; *Midrash Shir Hashirim* I, Verses 11-12 ff.
3. B. *Sanhedrin*, 101 a.
4. *Midrash Shir Hashirim*, I, 8.
5. *Hammanhig, Sabbath*, § 71.
6. B. *Sabbath*, 119 a.
7. For more detail concerning those poets, see *Thesaurus*, Vol. IV.
8. O.c. (Hebrew edition), p. 19 ff.
9. O.c., pp. 19-28.
10. *Nashad* is the name given in Yemen to a certain type of beggars who acquire their alms by singing. They are popular singers and fortune tellers, and exert a great influence chiefly on the women. Hence their songs are sung with predilection. For this reason, the *Neshid* poetry has come to be accredited to the feminine muse. For more detail about the Yemenite poetry and music, see *Thesaurus*, Vol. I.
11. F. Consolo, o.c., No. 142.
12. *Thesaurus*, Vol. IV, p. 29 (Hebrew), p. 14 (German).
13. Some of these old Castilian songs current among the Jews were recently collected and published by various Spanish authors. Compare, for example, Manuel L. Ortega, *Los Hebreos En Marruecos*, Madrid 1919, where 22 old "Romances" are given.
14. In *Thesaurus*, Vol. IV, Nos. 476-500, 25 Judeo-Spanish songs of religious and secular nature are given.

NOTES TO CHAPTER XVIII

1. A second edition was published by Libraire Lipschutz, Paris, 1927.
2. Ibid., p. 16, a list of the adopted French tunes is given.
3. This collection, a manuscript in the Bodleiana, Oxford, was treated by F. Rosenberg in his essay *Ueber eine Sammlung deutscher Volks- und Gesellschafts-Lieder in hebräischen Lettern*, published in L. Geiger's *Zeitschrift für die Geschichte der Juden in Deutschland*, Berlin 1888-1889. See Neubauer, Catalogue of Hebrew Manuscripts, No. 2420.
4. F. Rosenberg, o.c., No. 46.
5. F. Boehme, o.c., No. 266.
6. F. Boehme, o.c., p. 697.
7. Similarly in Persia Mula Shahin of Shiraz translated the Pentateuch into Persian in verse and rhythm. This translation became popular among the

Persian and Bokharian Jews to such a degree that it was and still is sung every Saturday to a special tune. Compare *Thesaurus*, Vol. III (German), pp. 7, 45-46.

8. The *Bovo-book* was translated by Eliyahu Bachur Ashkenazi, a distinguished Ashkenazic scholar who lived in Italy. His translation he prepared from an Italian translation of the English story *Bevis of Hampton*, which in Italian became *Bovo d'Antona*, and in Judeo-German it was changed to *Bovo*—or *Baba-book*, i.e., "Grandmother's tales." E. Bachur, according to his own statement, adopted a "Welshtune," i.e., an Italian melody.

9. The names quoted are gathered from A. Schulman's treatise on Judeo-German Literature from the sixteenth to the end of the eighteenth centuries (Hebrew), Riga, 1913.

10. A. Schulman, o.c., p. 201.

11. A copy of this rare print is preserved in the H. U. C. Library. A photostatic copy with an introduction was published by J. Schatzky, New York, 1926.

12. Example 14 is taken from F. Boehme, o.c., No. 650.

13. F. Boehme, o.c., No. 399 c.

14. Rabbi Joseph Hahn of Frankfort, in the first half of the seventeenth century, opposed the custom of singing Zemiroth and especially *Kol Mekaddesh* to the tunes of the gentiles. *Yosif Omets*, o.c., § 602, F. 77.

15. The tune with Stein's German text is to be found in Baer's *Baal Tefillah*, No. 417.

16. *Yosif Ometz*, o.c., §§ 603, 619.

17. *Shire Yehuda*, introduction, l.c., *Simchath Hannefesh*, l.c.

18. L. Wiener, *The History of Yiddish Literature*, etc., New York, 1899, p. 53.

19. M. Kipnis, *Volkslieder*, Warsaw, Vol. I, p. 131.

20. L. Cahan, *Jüdische Volkslied*, New York, 1920, Vol. I, p. 93.

21. M. Kipnis, o.c., Vol. II, p. 119.

22. L. Cahan, o.c., Vol. II, p. 270.

23. Ibid., I, p. 189.

24. In my *Thesaurus*, Vol. IV (German), p. 118, a detailed account of melodies in major and minor of the Slavic folk-songs is given from which we may deduce that the minor scale is by no means predominant. Thus, out of 1600 Southern Slavic folk-tunes in the collection published by Kuhac, c. 1000 are in major; out of 700 Czechoslovakian tunes edited by J. Malat, 387 are in major; and out of 300 Ukrainian rhythmical tunes in the collection of F. Kolessa, o.c. (Chapter IX, note 1), over a half are in major.

25. In the *Cancionero Musical*, published by F. Pedrell (Chapter VIII, note 28) 160 are in minor and 96 in major.

26. In the collection of 260 Greek melodies published by G. D. Pachtikos, Athens, 1905, 145 are in minor, 38 in Hedjaz, 13 in the Third Church-scale, and 23 tunes have the Lydian scale.

27. Leipzig 1882.

28. No. 28 is taken from the collection *Folk Songs of Many Peoples*, The Woman's Press, New York 1921, Vol. I, p. 73.

29. No. 29 is taken from *Cancionero Salamantino*, etc., Madrid 1907, p. 60.

30. Compare F. Pedrell, *Folk-lore Musical Castillan du XVI siècle*, in I.M.G., Vol. I, pp. 372-400.

31. *Chants Populaires de la Bretagne*, by H. de la Willemarqué, Paris 1867, Appendix.

32. No. 18 is taken from *Folk Songs of Many Peoples*, o.c., Vol. I, p. 150. No. 17—from L. Cahan, o.c., Vol. I, p. 231.
33. *Folk Songs*, etc., o.c., I, p. 110.
34. No. 22 is taken from L. Cahan, o.c., I, p. 51. No. 23 from F. Kolessa, o.c., III, Lemberg 1916, No. 127.
35. No. 26 is taken from F. Kolessa, ibid., IV. No. 70, No. 27 from L. Cahan, Vol. I, p. 27.
36. No. 24 is from L. Cahan, II, p. 50. No. 25 from Kolessa, o.c., No. 112.
37. M. Kipnis, I, p. 38.

NOTES TO CHAPTER XIX

1. In *Shivche Ari* it is related that "once on the eve of a Sabbath the Rabbi (I. Luria) went out of the city of Safed, followed by his disciples . . . to receive the Sabbath, and started singing special Sabbath songs in sweet tunes." Compare also *Sefer Charedim*, Venice 1601, Chapter VII.
2. A remainder of that Palestinian cabbalistic movement still persists in Jerusalem in the Synagogue Beth El as a special congregation, called *Mechavnim* —The Meditators. According to their doctrine, every law or custom should be observed not in meaningless manner, but with devotion, accompanied by thinking upon its religious and ethical purpose and upon its additional mystic meanings introduced by these cabbalists. In the reading of the daily prayers, the worshipper must think not only upon the meaning of every word, but must likewise recall an entire historic event, or a complete cabbalistic or ethical meditation. The greatest stress is laid on the name *Yahve*. Whenever this name occurs during the prayers, it has a certain shade of meaning which must be thought over. During this contemplation of the meaning of the word, its pronunciation must be prolonged until the meditation (*kavanah*) is finished. And naturally, this prolongation is executed through melodic curves, through tunes.
3. This poem was first published in his work *Sefer Charedim*, l.c.
4. The three examples are taken from *Thesaurus* IV, Nos. 188, 363, 377.
5. The most important prayer-book was edited by Shneor Salman, called *Dem Rebbins Siddur*, and was published by his son Ber, Kopust 1830 (?).
6. Rabbi Elija of Wilna (1720-1798) ordered in 1772 the excommunication of the *chassidic* sect, and in 1777 the burning of their books. He repeated his orders in 1781 and in 1797. V. M. Teitelbaum, *The Rabbi of Ljadi* (Hebrew), Vols. I-II, Warsaw 1913.
7. *Likkute Moharan*, a collection of sermons by Nachman of Brasslaw, Jerusalem 1874, F. 54 a ff.; 62 b.
8. *Likkute*, etc., F. 18 a, 79 a.
9. Ibid., F. 79 a.
10. Ibid., F. 79 b.
11. A. B. Birnbaum in his essay "The song in the courts of the *tzadikim* in Poland" (Hebrew), *Haolam*, 1908.
12. Teitelbaum, o.c., I, p. 19.
13. Attributed to Rabbi Pinchas of Koretz, Birnbaum, l.c.
14. Birnbaum, l.c.
15. L.c., such as Rabbi Shlomele of Radomsk, who used to sing accompanied by a choir of his adherents, or Rabbi Meirl of Apta, and Rabbi Avrohom Moshe of Prshischa.

16. Birnbaum, l.c.
17. This saying is attributed to Rabbi Mendel of Kotzk, ibid.
18. Nachman of Brasslaw in his above-mentioned work *Likkute*, etc., II, F. 23 a, says: "Seclusion is the highest stage in which man can attain divine inspiration, where he can pour out his heart to his God in a free and intimate way, and in the language familiar to him, in his native tongue. In our country this is Yiddish, for Hebrew is little known to the average man, and consequently it is difficult for him to express himself in it fluently. Therefore, whenever Hebrew is used as a medium of prayer, the ears do not hear what the mouth utters."
19. Among the reasons for the issuance of an excommunication of the *chassidim* in Cracow in 1786 was also the accusation that they changed the traditional form of the ritual and disregarded the traditional tunes. Wetstein, *Kadmoniyoth*, etc., Cracow 1892, p. 62.
20. *Toldoth Yaacov Yoseph*, quoted by A. Kahana, o.c., p. 139. However, already in *Sefer Chassidim* of the thirteenth century § 158, ed. Warsaw, 1902, the advice is given that if one cannot invent new prayers or meditations, he should choose the tune which appeals to him most and chant in it his prayers. In so doing his heart will be filled with meditation. Soft minor-tunes should be selected for supplications, while for laudations joyous ones should be chosen.
21. Birnbaum, l.c.
22. A statement of the *Maggid* (preacher) *of Koznitza*, Birnbaum, l.c.
23. *Kontros Hahithpaaluth*, Warsaw 1876, F. 5; Teitelbaum, o.c., I, p. 19 ff. The same opinion was expressed by Anton Rubinstein: *Die Musik und ihre Musiker*, Leipzig 1891, pp. 2-3.
24. To that type belonged the "court" of Borka, Birnbaum, l.c.
25. This type of song was cherished in Talno, Kotzk, and Gor.
26. P. Minkowsky in *Reshumoth*, o.c., I, p. 114.
27. Kahana, o.c., pp. 284-286.
28. The best work on the founder of the *Chabad* system is by M. Teitelbaum, cited in the text.
29. The last living Rabbi of Liubawitz and the sixth generation of Shneor Salman was forced by the Bolshevik Government in 1927 to leave his residence and to emigrate. He settled in Riga, Latvia.
30. A. S. Rabinowitsh, *Derech Haruach*, in *Hashiloach*, Vol. XXI, Odessa 1909, p. 468.
31. Compare *Thesaurus* (German), Vol. IV, p. 105.
32. This composition, however, is by others attributed to Joshua Feinsinger, *chazzan* of Wilna (1839-1872). Printed in my *Manual*, etc., No. 103.
33. *Kneseth Israel*, II, Warsaw 1887, p. 359.
34. Some of his tunes are printed in *Der Kuzykaliszer Pinkos*, Wilna 1927.
35. *Die Geschichte fun Chazzanuth*, l.c., pp. 92-93.

NOTES TO CHAPTER XX

1. "Songs in folk style" is here used for *Volkstümlich* in German. According to Grove, o.c., IV, p. 608, "This term defies exact translation; but, speaking broadly, it means a simple and popular form of the art-song. . . . The *Volkstümliches Lied* is, in short, a combination of the *Volkslied* and the

Kunstlied, and its area of capacity is a very wide one. It may rise to a high level of poetic beauty, and may descend to low depths of stupidity or triviality without ceasing to be *volkstümlich*."—The form of *Volkstümliches Lied* became very popular in Germany since the seventeenth century, and many of them were converted into folk-songs. Of many songs the authorship is wholly unknown. Some composers wrote nothing but *volkstümliche Lieder*. Grove, ibid., p. 609.

2. Compare *Jewish Encycl.*, II, p. 427.

3. In Palestine, the popular wedding song was: "Precious without powder or rouge, or hair dye."—Rav Acha used to dance with the bride on his shoulders. When questioned by his disciples as to whether they should do the same, he answered: "Only if you can withhold yourselves from base thoughts." *B. Kethuboth*, 17 a; *Aboth de Rabbi Nathan*, § 4.

4. *B. Taanith*, 22 a.

5. In his commentary *Ture Zahav* to *Orach Chayyim*, § 560, 3. See also I. Abrahams, *Jewish Life in the Middle Ages*, Philadelphia 1898, pp. 135, 197. *Jewish Encycl.*, II, p. 427.

6. *Jewish Encycl.*, o.c., A. Schulman, o.c., p. viii. *Noheg*, etc., F. 17 calls *Klezmorim* the *Letzanim*. Albert Wolf, *Fahrende Leute bei den Juden*, in M. Grunwald's *Mitteilungen*, etc., 1908, p. 151 ff.

7. *B. Megilla*, 7 b.

8. *Mitteilungen*, etc., o.c., 1901, p. 156.

9. *Thesaurus*, Vol. IV, No. 491.

10. F. Rosenberg, o.c., pp. 278-281. A long *Purim* song is also printed in *Mitteilungen*, etc., o.c., 1909, pp. 33-36.

11. *Abudraham*, Warsaw 1878, p. 112; *Jewish Encycl.*, X, p. 279.

12. *Jewish Encycl.*, l.c.

13. I. Abrahams, o.c., pp. 265-6.

14. *Beniggun Haman of the Ahashverosh-Spiel*, A. Schulman, o.c., p. 133.

15. On *Purim* celebration in Italy see M. Güdemann, *Leben und Erziehungswesen*, etc., Vol. II, Chapter VII; III, Chapter III. I. Abrahams, o.c., p. 254, Chapter XIV.

16. *Yosef Ometz*, o.c., F. 45 b.

17. Published by Wagenseil in *Sota* 1674, p. 85 ff.

18. *Megillas Vinz* was first printed in Frankfort 1696, 2nd edition Berlin 1916, Louis Lamm, publisher. On the event of Vinz (Vincenz Fettmilch) compare *Yosef Ometz*, o.c., § 953; J. E., V, pp. 378-79.

19. Compare A. Schulman, l.c.

20. A. Wolf, o.c., *Mitteilungen*, etc., 1909, p. 40 ff.

21. On his biography in details and on his poetry see *Mitteilungen*, etc., 1913, III, pp. 1-8, IV, pp. 1-12.

22. G. Dalman, in his *Jüdische Melodien aus Galizien und Russland*, Leipzig, No. 3.

23. His biography was written by M. Fried, *Mitteilungen*, etc., 1917, pp. 1-25. A characterization of his poetry is given in *Mitteilungen*, etc., 1909, pp. 65-89, 103-121, by M. Weissberg.

24. M. Weissberg, o.c., p. 73; p. 115.

25. A list of his publications is given by Guinsbourg and Marek (Chapter XVIII), appendix pp. ix-xiii. A new edition of 49 of his songs is now in press in New York.

26. In French and German, the term *couplet* signifies a type of song dealing in

a satiric manner with topics of current events. V. Brockhaus' *Konversations Lexikon*, item "couplet."

27. L. Wiener, o.c., p. 87.
28. A selection of his reminiscences was published in Jewish *Forward* (*Vorwärts*), New York 1927, April 24.
29. A. Schulman, o.c., pp. 76-77.
30. A. Wolf, o.c., p. 40 ff., 1909.
31. A. Wolf, o.c., p. 57.
32. L. Wiener, o.c., p. 237.
33. Published by the Hebrew Publishing Co., New York, arranged for piano by H. A. Russotto.
34. Compare *Thesaurus*, Vol. I, No. 191 end.
35. According to A. Garfinkel's arrangement, R. Mazin Co., London 1904.
36. *Noheg*, etc., o.c., F. 17, quoted from Yosif Ometz.
37. *Sibbuv Rabbi Petachya*, ed. Grünhut, Jerusalem 1905 (Hebrew), p. 24 (German), p. 33.
38. A detailed account is given by A. Wolf, o.c.; Paul Nettl, *Alte Jüdische Spielleute und Musiker*, Prag 1923, pp. 49-55.
39. A. Wolf, o.c., p. 53 ff., 1909.
40. Ibid., p. 93, 1908.
41. Compare A. Wolf and P. Nettl, l.c.
42. *Maharil*, ed. Warsaw 1874, F. 31 b.
43. See Chapter IX, note 18.
44. A. Wolf, o.c., p. 154.
45. A. Wolf, o.c., 1908, p. 93 ff.
46. Ibid.
47. Ibid., P. Nettl, o.c., p. 64, gives caricatured Jewish dances of the sixteenth century.
48. A. Wolf, o.c., p. 154.
49. Ibid., p. 155.
50. Mendelssohn's Letters from 1833 to 1847, English translation by Wallace, Boston 1863, pp. 98-99. On Gusikow in details compare Mendel's *Mus. Conver. Lexicon*, Vol. IV, p. 460.
51. *Allgemeine Zeitung d. Judenthums*, October 1837. His tune for Psalm 126 was published in *Muzykaliszer Pinkos*, o.c., No. 114.
52. A. Wolf, o.c., 1909, p. 6. Grove, Vol. III, p. 27, discussing the Rakoczy-march does not mention Rozsavölgyi's name. W. S. Pratt, in *The New Encycl. of Music and Musicians*, New York 1924, p. 703, quotes his name as the father of Julius Rozsavölgyi, the founder of the Royal Music Publishing House in Pest.
53. We hear, for example, of a blind Jewish violinist, Löbel, in the eighteenth century who was the teacher of the famous violinist Franz Benda. The latter was grateful to the Jewish *klezmer* all his life for the perfect and wonderful production of tone he taught him. Compare Mendel's *Lexicon*, Vol. I, p. 537. However, the later encyclopedists, such as Grove and Riemann, omit the story of his blind Jewish teacher. A Bohemian poetess used this episode as a subject for the novel *Judith-Mary*, published 1867.
54. A. Wolf, o.c., 1909, p. 19.
55. *Responsa Bach* (Yoel Sirkish) § 103.
56. In 1842 a Jewish family, Kantorowitz of Grodno or Wilna, came to Berlin and concertized at the royal court. A. Wolf, o.c., p. 57.

57. P. Nettl, o.c., p. 37, cited a statement of 1580 by Wenzel Brezam that a Jewish band played at a Christian wedding and delighted the people with its music.
58. P. Nettl, o.c., p. 38.
59. *Orach Chayyim,* § 338, 2; I. Abrahams, o.c., p. 197. In the fifteenth century the employment of Christian musicians on Sabbath and festivals was already customary. See *Maharil,* o.c., F. 31 a.
60. *Radbaz, Responsa,* § 132; *Magen Abraham* to *Orach Chayyim,* § 338, 2; I. Abrahams, ibid.

NOTES TO CHAPTER XXI

1. Selected from *Thesaurus,* Vol. I, Nos. 155, 174.
2. Fourth edition Berlin Juwal Publishing Co., 1923.

NOTES TO CHAPTER XXII

1. A. Rubinstein, *Die Musik und ihre Meister,* Leipzig 1891, pp. 64-65.
2. Heinrich Berl, *Das Judentum in der Musik,* Berlin und Leipzig 1926.
3. Alfred Einstein, *Das Neue Musiklexikon,* Berlin 1926, p. 58.
4. Richard Wagner's *Gesammelte Schriften,* Hesse & Becker, Leipzig. On Meyerbeer compare Vol. VII, pp. 48-58; Vol. XI, pp. 83-97. On Halévy and Mendelssohn, Vol. VIII, pp. 65-96. Wagner's well-known attack on these Jewish composers *Das Judentum in der Musik* and *Aufklärungen über das Judentum in der Musik,* see in Vol. XIII, pp. 7-50. In this connection the opinion of Friedrich Nietzsche may be quoted according to which Wagner was strongly influenced by French music and folklore. Compare Friedrich Herz, *Rasse und Kultur,* Leipzig 1925, p. 367.
5. Compare Max Brod and F. Weltsch, *Zionismus als Weltanschauung,* 1925, pp. 96-107.
6. H. Berl, o.c.
7. A. Rubinstein, o.c., p. 92.

NOTES TO CHAPTER XXIII

1. Published in *Avodas Habore,* Wilna 1914, p. 15 ff.
2. Published in *Lieder-Sammelbuch,* etc., cited in Chapter XXI, No. 50.
3. *Deux Mélodies Hébraïque,* avec accompagnement de Piano, par Maurice Ravel, A. Durand & Fils, Paris 1915.
4. *Lieder-Sammelbuch,* o.c., No. 19.

INDEX

Aapid, tune of, 170
Abahu in Cæsarea, 10
Abba Areka (Rab), 93
Abbub, Abobas, 11
Abelov, Jacob Moshe of Trocki (J. M.), 150, 158
Abert, H., 496
Abobas, 6
Abraham (bar) ben Ezra, 126, 360
Abramino dall' Arpa Ebreo, 196
Abrass, Osias (Joshua), 289
accents, 68; Greek-Byzantine, 68; Hebrew, 69
A Chazzandl auf Shabbos (song), 397
Acher. See Elisha ben Abuya
Achron, I., 464; Joseph, 467
Ackermann, Aron, 294, 351
acutus, 67, 68
Acta Esther (play), 438
Addir bimluchoh, 188
Addir hu (tune of), 168, 174, 341, 361
Adon olam (tune of), 116
Adonay bekol Shofar (music), 122 f., 127
Adonoy-Moloch mode, Steiger, 73, 285, 478; scale, 480
A Dudule, 420
Æolian, 483
Af bri (music), 404
Agada, 105
Agades (Hagros), 18
Agala, 70
Agathon, 113
Agobard of Lion, bishop, 130
Agudath Schirim, 265, 346, 348
Aguilar, Emanuel Abraham, 292-3, 338, 348
Ahasweros spiel, 437
Ahavoh-rabboh, 88; mode, 84 ff., 285, 478; music, 90 f., 422 ff.; scale, 26
Akdomus, 160; tune of, 156
Akeda, 170
Akiba, Rabbi, 20
Alamoth, 13, 496
Alcharizi, 371
Alef indikes (music), 404
Alendorf, Menachem, 440
Alfasi, Isaac, 125
Alkabetz, Solomon, 126, 361
Allegro Porto Hebreo, 196

Allgemeine Zeitung des Judentums, 338
Allmächtiger Gott (Baugesang), 174
Alman, Samuel, 313, 486, 488
"Alt-Neu-Schul," 205
Altshul, Joseph (Yoshe Slonimer), 299
Ambros, A. W., 4, 7, 351, 495
Amen, 21
Amida, 78, 108
Amran Gaon, 108
Am Yisroel chay (music), 423
Ancient Liturgical music, 350
anenu, 21
Anglo-Saxon song in the Synagogue, 316 ff.
anshada, 25, 367
Anshe Maamad, 20, 497
antiphonal singing, 21
anudata, 67
Aolodia, 13
Arabic melodies in the Synagogue, 125; meter, 113, 115, 124
Arabic Tunes, secular, 29; religious, 30
Ari. See Isaac Luria
ariach all gabbe levena, 50
Armianus Mercelinus, 131
ars nova, 162, 201, 210
artistic endeavors, 461 ff.
Asaf, 15
Asher, Aaron ben, 68
Asher, Simon, 314
Ashkenazi, Joseph, 439
Ashkenaz, 129
Ashkenazic Modes in Major, 145 f.; in Minor, 138 ff.
Ashkenazic-Pentateuch for the High Holidays, 59
Ashkenazic Song of the Synagogue in the seventeenth and eighteenth centuries, 204 ff.; song, 133
"Ashkenazim," Synagogue song of the, 129 ff.
Ashkenazic tunes for individual poetical texts, 166 ff.; prose, 148 ff.
Ashrechem (music), 429
Asia Minor, 87
Asor, 8
Assyria, music of, 7
Athanasius, bishop of Alexandria, 60

Athkinu seudathah, 362
Athnah, Ethnachta, 67, 68
Auer, Leopold, 473
Aufn Pripitshok, 454
augmented second as a Diatonical step, 482
Aulos, 4, 12, 26, 87
Av-horachamim Steiger, 185; (music), 186
Avignon, 43
Avoda, 159
Avodath Yisrael, 345
Azammer Bishvachin, 362, 412
Azkari, Eleazar, 412

Baal-Shem-Tob, Israel (Besht), 412. See Besht I.
Baal Tefillah, 307, 339, 346, 348
Babylonia, 23, 97; Babylonian, 43; music, 7
Bach, Johann Sebastian, 235, 476, 482
Bach, Nathan, 438
Bachmann, Jacob, 290
Bachrach, Rabbi Yair, 436
Bachur, Eliyahu, 439
badchon, badchonim (merry-makers), 380, 435 ff.
badchonus, 438
Baer, Abraham, 292, 339, 348
baith, 28
Balkan, 87
de Balmes, Abraham, 345
bands, Jewish music, 456
Bardaisan of Edessa, 99
"bards," 125
Bar-Kochba, opera, 451
Bar-Nash of Jerusalem, 455
barock style, 165, 213, 384
Bartók, Béla, 190, 505
Baruch of Kalisch, 194
Bashraw (Pashraw), 27
Basit meter, 114
Bass, Lipman, 215
Battle of Pavia tune, 439
Bauer, Jacob, 294
Baum, Solomon, 336
Bäumker, W., 210, 501
Bayat-Huseni, 84; -*Nawa,* 84
Bayati (makam), 29, 34, 50
Bedford, Arthur, 515
Beer, Ahron, in Berlin (A.), 148, 149, 154, 157, 158, 159, 193, 217, 218, 236, 278
Beer, Jacob Herz, 236, 512
Beethoven, L., 247, 331, 476; Quartet in C♯ Minor, 511
Belzer, Nisson Spivak (Nissi), 275, 303, 306, 313, 314

Bema, 106
Ben Asher, 345
Ben Azra, 19
Benda, Franz, 521
Benjamin ben Yerach, 170
Ben Naftali, 68
Benei Hechalah, 362, 425
Benzenauer, 171
Berdichevski, L., 464
Ber of Meseritsh, 412
Ber of Radoshitz, Rabbi, 433
Berggreen, A. P., 191
Berl, Heinrich, 353
Berliyn, Anton (Ahron Wolf), 289
Berlin, Irving (Israel), 473
Bernstein, A. W., 411
Berthold von Regensburg, 164
Besht, Israel, 415, 416, 418
Besrodney, G., 464
Beth-Hak'neseth, 19
Bethuel, 240
Bevis of Hampton, 517
Bialik, Ch. N., 455
Biblical and Post-Biblical, 35 ff.; modes, 38
Bibliotica Rabbinica, 346
bi-lingual songs, 392
Binder, A. W., 465
Birkath am, 454
Birnbaum, Abraham Ber, 294, 351
Birnbaum, Eduard (Asher Ensel), 293, 350; collection, 513
Blaustein, Abraham, 294
Bloch, Ernest, 473; music, 474
Blumenthal, Nisson, 307
Boehme, Franz M., 111, 390
Bokharian, 43
Book of Samuel tune, 382, 438
Bookhandler, Abraham, 439
Borchu tune, 158, 161
Boruch-sheomar tune, 170; custom of singing, 508
Böschenstein, Johann, 346
Bovo-book, tune of the, 382, 517
Braham, John, 226, 338
Breslaur, Emil, 350
Brod, Dovidl, 216
Brunoff, Platon, 463
Bruch, Max, 276, 465; Max Bruch's letter, 513
Bruder Veit's tune, 384; music, 390
Butstedt, 210
butu, 67
Byzantian system, 69

Cabbala, 412; cabbalistic movement, Palestinian, 518; song (music), 421 ff.

Cahan, I. L., 411
calamus, 495
canciones, 376
cantor, 109
cantus firmus, 201
Caceres, Abraham, 515
Carian muse, 94
Carpentras, 43
Castilian dialect, 376
Cenni Sull'origine, 349
Chabad songs, 418
Chad gadyoh, 361
Chalumeau, 495
"Chamber-Music-Ensemble," 464
Chanukah tune. See Mooz tzur, hymn, 171
Chants Hebraique, 340
Charlemagne, 129, 131
Chassidic singers, 416; song, 412 ff.; (music), 421 ff.; style, 230; tunes in Major, 429 f.; in Minor, 425 ff.
Chassidim, 419, 467; tune, 420
Chassidism, 412
Chatzotzera (Trumpet), 10, 11
Chaykl, Chayyim, 432
chazah, 106
Chazzan, Origin of, 501; Rise and Development of the, 101 ff.
Chazzanim, 133; and Chazzanuth in Eastern Europe, 296 ff.
Chazzanuth-brief, 215
Chazzanya, 125
Chazarian proselytes, 87
cheironomia, 67
Cherniavsky, I., 464
Cherniavsky, Joseph, 465
chidduyoth form, 366
Chmelnitzki pogroms, 195, 213
Chopin, 476
chor-chazzanim, 306; *-schul*, 306, 307
chorus (employed in the Temple), 17
chromatic, 13, 34; -harmonies, 95
Chronicles, 38
Chronoi (*ta'amim*), 68
chronos protos, 28
Church style, 244
Cimbalist, Chayyim, 459, 507
circumflex, 67, 68
City-chazzan, 305
classical style, 165
Clement of Alexandria, 93
Coblentz, Meier, 219
Cohen, Elkan, 215
Cohen, Ethel Silverman, 465
Cohen, Francis Lyon, 291, 293, 351
Cohen-Linaru, M., 292
Cohon, A. Irma, 352

comparative table of accent motives for the intoning of the Pentateuch, 44 ff., 70
congregational singing, 98
conjunctives (*ta'amim*), 38, 70
Consolo, Federigo, 202, 293, 341, 349
Costa, Sir Michael, 473
Cremieu, Jules Salomon, 293, 340
Cremieu, Mardochee, 293
cymbal, 17
couplet (*s*), 451, 452, 520; German-French, 445

Damrosch, Leopold, 473
dance, 15; dancing at worship, 500; religious, 16
Daniel, 61
darbaka, 370
darga, 70
Das Hamburger Familienblatt, 349
Das Pavierlied, 383
Das Schloss in Oestereich, 383
David, Ernest, 349
David, Ferdinand, 473
David (son of Jacob), Futeralmacher, 217
David, King, 9, 14, 15, 192
David, Samuel, 290
Davis, A. J., 328, 331
Davit da Civita Hebreo, 196
Day of Atonement, 57
Dem Rebbins niggun, 419
Der Jüdische Cantor, 348
Der Lehrer und cantor, 349
De Sola, David, 292, 338
Der Synagogale Gesang, 351
Der Tod als Schnitter, tune of, 384; (music), 389
Deutsch, Moritz, 288, 292, 339
Diaconus, John, 131
Diaconus, Paulus, 144
Dick, Jacob Heilprin, 438
Die Geschichte von Chazzanuth, 352
Die mame hot mir geshikt (music), 407
Dietrich von Bern, 383, 440
d'Indy, Vincent, 199
diminished fifth, 482
Die Wahrheit, 349
Die Oestereichische-Ungarische Can-toren-Zeitung, 348
Dio Cassius, 496
Disjunctives (*ta'amim*), 38, 70
Doctor Almosado, 451
Dorian, 47, 56, 60; (Greek), 25; scale, 43
Dort vo die zeder, 221
Dos Tallis'l, 454

double-flute, 4, 13
double-pipe, 14
Dovidl of Talno, 431
Dovidl, Rabbi, 416
drong, 216
Dudaim, 255
duf, 370
Dukes in Mantua, 196
Dulcimer. See Hackbrett
Dunash ben Labrat, 361
Dunham, Arthur, 328
Duran, Simon, 346
Du solst nit gen (music), 409
dveikuth, 419; melody, 432

ear-marks, 27
Eastern Europe, 23
Ecclesiastes, 36, 38, 47
Echod mi yodea, 361
Eder vohod, 170
Effent rebbitzin (music), 429
Egypt, 87; song of the Copts in, 56;
  Egyptian music, 3
Ehrenkranz, Benjamin Wolf (Wölwel
  Zbarazer), 441
Ehrlich, Hermann, 294, 338
Eichberg, Salmon, 248
Eichel, Isaac, 449
Eichler, Moshe Michel, 432
Eisenstadt, Abraham, 342
elamu, 13
Eliazar, Rabbi (son of Joseph Ha-
  galili), 20
Eliezer ben Meshullam "the Great,"
  161
Elijah of Wilna, Rabbi, 518
Elijah-songs, 360
Elisha ben Abuyah, 92, 359
Eli tziyon, tune of, 168, 171
Eliyohu Hanovi, tunes of, 392; music,
  401
Ellis, Havelock, 500
Elman, Mischa, 473
El Mole Rachamim, 194
Elymos, 13
Emechoh nososi, 165
Endel, Edmond Sereno, 328
Engel, Julius Yoel, 463, 466
En kelohenu, 238; (music), 239
Ensel, G. S., 350
Ephraim of Nisibis, 99
Es is geflogen (music), 406
Es ist kein grosser freud (music), 390
Esoh dei, tune of, 167, 170
Esser, P., 329
Esther, 36; the Book of, 38; mode of,
  65; (music), 66
Ethnachta, athnah, 70

Eth shaare ratzon, 127
Ett, 262
Etz Chayim, melody, 241; tune for,
  239
European art-music, 461; folk-song,
  497; music, 471; style, 467
Ezra, 38

fa-i-lan, 114; *fa-i-la-tun,* 113; *fa-u-
  lun,* 114
Feinsinger, Joshua, 164, 432
female singers, 496
Finzi, Jacob, 201, 337
Fischof, 249
Fisk, Frank T., 327
Fleischer, Oskar, 353
Folk character, 27
Folk-song of the Ashkenazim, 379 ff.;
  in Germany, 379 ff.; in Eastern Europe, 385 ff.; tunes of the Ashkenazic, 401 ff.
Folk-song in the Biblical and Prayer
  modes, 396; in Minor scale, 398
Folk-song, Jewish, 50; "secular," 435
Folk-song of the Oriental Jews,
  357 ff.; Hebrew-Yiddish, 396; Uk-
  rainian, 396; Hebrew-Yiddish-Uk-
  rainian, 396
Folk-songs in Arabic, 371; Aramaic,
  370; Hebrew-Arabic, 371, 396; He-
  brew-Aramaic, 371, 396
folk style, 467; motives, 471
Foot, Arthur, 328
Forkel, 348; Forkel's history, 351
form, 27; in which the Psalms and
  prayers were rendered, 20
Fraenkel, Jacob, 322
Frankel, Isaac Seckl, 240
Frankl, L. A., 512
Franz, 467
Frazer, J. G., 195, 245
Fregt di velt (music), 405
Freudenthal, Julius, 238
Friedchen, wife of Moses Leib, 440
Friede, Sholom, 229, 431
Friedländer, David, 235, 510
Friedman, Ignace, 473
Friedmann, Aron, 286, 293, 350

galchish, 254
Gamaliel in Jamnia, Rabban, 107, 129
Garte tarzunae (music), 173
Geh ich mir spatziren (music), 407
Geiger, Abraham, 242
Geiger, Salomon, 352-3
General art-music, 477
Genung, C. G., 329-30
gereshin (see *Tarsa*), 70

German Jews, 23; Lied, 467, 484; music, 133; song, 131
Gerovitsch, Eliezer, 310, 487, 485
Gershwin, George, 473
Gervelyn, Meister, 142
Gibraltarian, 43
Gideon, Henry, 331, 465
Ginsburg, Leb, 449
Gipsy music, 190, 191
girdle-form, 368
Glogow, Yitzchok, 226
Gloria patri, etc. (music), 146
Gluck, 330, 472
Gnessin, M., 464, 468
God of Abraham, Praise," "The, 220
Goldberg, Hirsch, 238, 289
Goldfaden, Abraham, 229, 449, 453; operettas, 453
Goldfarb, Israel and Samuel E., 336
Goldmark, Karl, 473, 476
Goldstein, Joseph H., 151, 153, 159, 230, 290, 337
Goldstein, Morriz, 323
Golomb, H. B., 462
Golub, Solomon, 466
Gott mus man dienen (music), 427
Gott un sein mishpot is gerecht, 454
gova, 68
Grauman, M., 327
gravis, 67, 68
Greek art-music, 96
Greek Churches, 96; tunes, 33
Greek Dorian, 39
Greek song, 92; penetrated into Palestine, 22
Gregorian chant, 56, 61, 111, 132; Lamentations, 4:16, 55, 1:59, 5:1, 59; (Prima lectio), 55
Gregorian mode, 47; and Minnesong, Motives of the, 163; song, 42, 47, 73, 210
Gregory I, 177
Grimm, Carl, 328
Groenland, F. J., 240
Grodner, Yisroel, 450
Grünzweig, Adolf, 291
Guido of Arezzo, 69
Guinsbourg, S. M., 400
Guinsbourg, Theodor, 331
Gurowitsch, S., 464
Gusikow, Michael Joseph, 458
Gut Shabbos, 383

Haarbleicher, M., 241
Hackbrett, 457, 458
Haftara, Haftora, 38, 51
Hagada, 174

Hahn, Joseph, 132, 180, 209, 385
Hakkol Yoduchoh, 160
Hakofoth, 137
Halaka, 105
Halb schwarz halb weiss, 383, 439
Halévy, Jacques Fromental, 262, 263, 473, 475
Halevi, Jehuda, 126, 363
Halil, Chalil, 11, 12, 17, 495; Halilim players, 12
Hallel, 20, 73, 361
Haleloth, 366
Halleluyah, 21
Halpern, M., 336
Hamavdil (music), 402
Hamburg Temple, 246; Reform, 252, 320
Hammelech, 148, 157, 158
Hammithpallel, 342
Hamshorer Hagodol, 217
Hamishoyoh (mode), 31
Handel, G., 472
Hand-marks, 67
Haolam, 351
Happakoli, Simeon, 129
Harmony, 26, 478 ff.; (music), 489 ff.; classical, 482; harmonists of the Synagogue, 480; harmonizers of Synagogal song, 479
Harmony of the modes, Adonoy Moloch, 487 f.; (music), 491; Ahavoh Rabboh, 486 f.; (music), 489; Mogen-ovos, 486; minor, 487
Hashirim asher Lishlomo (S. Rossi), 199
Hashkivenu, tunes for, 116
Hassler, Hans Leo, 241
Hast, Marcus, 286, 291, 314
Hatikva, Zionist hymn, 221, 454
Hausman, Rosalie, 329
Hawkes, H. W., 331
Haydn, 474
Hay Gaon, 125
Hayyuj, Jehudah, 345
hazag (meter), 114
Hebräisch-Orientalischer Melodienschatz, 343
Hebrew songs, Babylonian (music), 372 f. Sephardic-Syrian, 373; Yemenite (music), 374 f.
Hecht, Rev. Simon, 329, 348
Hedjaz (mode), 30, 34; scale, 88
Heifetz, Jascha, 473
Hei piv ya (music), 403
Heine, Salomon, 246
Heinroth, J. A. G., 240
Henle, Elchonon, 439
Helfere, Marx, 328

Heller, Josef, 291
Henle, Moritz, 240, 292
heptachord, 478
Herodotus, 5, 495
Hersh of Przshev, 432
Hershman, Mordecai, 334
Herz, Joseph, 438
Hessel, David, 261
Hiller, Ferdinand, 240, 473
Hirsch, S. R., 284
Hirsch of Ziviotov, 194
Hisda, Rab, 97
hishtapchuth hannefesh, 50, 419
hithlahavuth, 419
hithpaaluth, 419
hithpashtuth hagashmiyuth, 419
Hoch rief der Wächter, 383, 440
Horace, 6
Horvitz, Jacob, 439
Hoshanah Rabbah, 159
Hoshianah, 21
Huna, Rab, 97
Hungary, 87; Hungarian Rakoczy
    march, 459
Hurenlieder, 385   [34
Huseni, Bayat-Huseni (makam), 30,
Hypodorian, 50, 51, 56, 61, 73
Hypolydian, 61
Hypophrygian, 61

Ich hob gelibt (music), 406
Ich steh mir un klar (music), 405
Idelsohn, A. Z., 498
Imber, Naftali Herz, 454
Immanuel of Rome, 181
Improvisation, 26
In cheder (song), 467
Influence of Moderate Reform upon
    Synagogal Song, 246 ff.
Influence of the Reform Movement
    on the Synagogal Song, 232
instruments employed in the Temple,
    16
interrupted ("deceptive") cadences,
    481
Introduction of Harmony and Polyph-
    ony into the Synagogue in Italy,
    196 ff.
invitatorium, 144
Ionian, 56
Isaac of Prosnitz, 226
Isacchino or Jacchino Massarano, 196
Isaacs, Louis M., 336
Is gekumen der fetter (music), 408
Is gekumen tzuforen a chazzan (mu-
    sic), 404
Israel Baal Shem-tob, 208. See Besht
    I., Baal-Shem-Tob

Isr. Wochenschrift und freie Lehrer
    und Cantorzeitung, 349
Isidor of Sevilla, 61
Iste confessor, 146
Italian, 23
Italy, 43

Jablonski, 346
Jacob of Prague, Rabbi, 438
Jacob the son of Peretz, 217
Jacobite, 96; Church song, unrhyth-
    mical, 31; rhythmical, 32
Jacobson, Israel, 235, 236, 240; reform
    of, 241; Songbook of, 241
Jadassohn, Salomon, 473, 476
Jadlowker, 312
Jaffa, Israel, 432
Jaffa, Rabbi Mordecai (M.), of
    Prague, 159
Japhet, Israel Meyer, 284 ff., 289
Jazz hits, 472; song by Berlin, 474
Jehuda of Barcelona, 125
Jellinek, A., 259
Jessurum, 341
Jesus, 38
Jew in General Music, The, 471 ff.
Jewish dance music, 206
Jewish Encyclopedia, 346
"Jewish Ministers Cantors Association
    of America," 352
Jewish Music, Rise and Development
    of, 351
Jewish Song, Oldest Unrhythmical ele-
    ments of, 35 ff., 72 ff.
Jewish theatre, 449
Jischac, Jehudah ben, 202
Joachim, Joseph, 473, 476
Job, 36; (music), 59; "Job mode," 57;
    mode of, 56
Joel, Chazzan in Leipa, 352
Johlson, Joseph, 241
Jokele of Rzeszow, *chazzan,* 213
Jonas, Emile, 290
Joseph, Rab, 93
Joseph of Bixheim, 508
Joseph the son of Benjamin, 380
Josephus Flavius, 8, 11
"Jubilation," 147; (chants), 131
Judah bar Illai, Rabbi, 105, 435
Judeo-French folk-song, 380
Judeo-German song, 133, 380; Ash-
    kenazic of seventeenth century (mu-
    sic), 386 ff.
Judeo-Italian song, 437
Judeo-Spanish song (Ladino), 376 ff.;
    (music), 377
*Juedische Musiker am Hofe von Man-
    tua,* 350

Juedische Presse, 349
Julianus, Emperor, 131

Kaddiah, 158; tunes for, 116, 151, 152
Kadma, 67, 68, 70
kadmoyoh (mode), 31
Kahal-singers, 207
Kaiser, Alois, 322, 350
Kallir, Eleazar, 113, 170
Kalonymos, 134, 345; family, 129
Kamil (meter), 114
Kanun, 25
Kaplan, I., 464
Karliner, Boruch, 302, 303
Kashtan, Nochum Leb, 298
Kashtan, Salomon, 193, 266, 267, 271, 297
Kasida, 367
Katz, Elchonon, 439
Katz, Rabbi Jacob Joseph, 415
Katz, N. H., 292
Kaufmann, Fritz Mordechai, 411
Kedusha, musaf, 88
kelei-chomos, 207
kelim, 192
kiddush, 160
Ki lo noe, 361
kina, 73
Kinnor, 5, 8, 12, 16
Kinnura, 5
Kipnis, M., 411
Kircher, Athanasius, 346
Kirchhain, Rabbi Elchonon-Henle, 227, 383
Kirschner, Emanuel, 286, 291, 324
Kithara, 4
Kitzinger, Fred E., 327
Kley, Israel Eduard, 236, 238
klezmer, klezmorin (music-makers), 435 ff., 455 ff.
klippah, 419
Kobsari, 185; Ukrainian, 297
Kohn, Maier (M.), 159, 174, 260 ff., 288
Kohen, Elchonon, 438
Kolessa, Philaret, 185, 505
Kol mekadesh shevii (music), 389; tune of, 384
Kol-Nidré, I, II, III, IV, 154-155; tune, 160, 226; Max Bruch's, 276
Kopelman, Jacob, 438
Kopit, H., 464
Koppel, Jacob, 439
Kol Rinnah, 160, 281; *Utefillah,* 276
kore, 104
Korngold, Erich, 473
Kornitzer, L., 241
Kotili sia (music), 408
Krebs, T. L., 328

Kristal, Solomon Singer, 439
Kunstlied, 520
kurr, 67
Kutner, Leib, 440
Kvartin, Zavel, 334
kyrie eleison, 42, 47, 131

Lach, Robert, 353
Lachmann, Isaak, 286, 292, 301, 345
La Juive, 474
Lamentations, 36, 38; (music), 54 f.
La Traviata, 309
Lazaro Gratiano, 437
Leb, Jehudah, 352
Leb, Chazzan Nahum, 219, 267
Lebensbilder Berühmter Cantoren, 350
Lechoh dodi, 116, 362; Sefira, 509
Ledovid boruch, 170
Legarme, 70
"Leib Sarah's," 417
Leitner, Franz, 353
Leitzim, Leitzonim, see *badchonim*
leitzim, leitzonim, 435
Leizer of Lodz, 432
lektor, 109
Lejman, Samuel, 411
Leon of Modena, 198, 205, 265, 350
Leon, Meier, 220
"Leoni," 220
Lern-steiger, 191
Levi, Hirsch Bochur, 299
Levinsohn, Yoel Dovid, 299
Lewandowski, Louis (Eliezer), 155, 160, 269 ff., 276, 288, 324, 484
Levy, Abraham (of Amsterdam), 202
Levy, Heniot, 329
Levy, Hermann, 473
Liberman, Isaac, 439
Libro de canti D'Israele, etc., 341
Lichtenstein, Abraham Jacob (*chazzan*), 275, 276, 466   [282
Lied-form, 431; -style, German, 275,
Lifshitz, Moses, 215
Lifshitz, Salomon, 209, 215, 217
Lifschutz, Shlomo, 352
Linos, 5
Lion, Asher, 236, 269
Liszt, Franz, 191, 253, 265, 353
Liturgische Zeitschrift, 338, 348
Lob, Otto, 329
Löbel, a blind violinist, 521
Lobt Gott den Herrn (music), 172
Loewe in Strassburg, *chazzan* Karl, 262, 276
Louis the Pious, 130
Lovy, Israel (I. Levy, Lowy), 219, 226, 255, 287
Löwenstamm, Max G., 289

Löwit, I., 295
Luanz, Elijahu, 440
Lucian, 6
Liubawitz, 418
Luria, Isaac (Ari), 126, 205, 362, 365, 412
Luther, Martin, 171
Lutkin, P. C., 331
Lwow, P., 464, 487
Lydian scale, 56, 61; Greek, 26, 43

Maarich, 70
Maccabees, The (opera), 461
Machbaroth. See Imanuel of Rome
Machir, Rabbi, 129
machol, 15
Machzor, Ashkenazic, Sephardic, 57
Mackfarlane, W., 327
Madama Europa, 197, 451
mafsikim (ta'amim), 39
"Magdala," the tune of, 132
Magrepha (pipe-organ), 14, 19, 496
Maharil, Jacob Levi (Segal) Mölin, 170, 177, 206, 456
Mahler, Gustav, 473
Mahler, Maier, 205
Maimonides, M., 10, 12, 126
makam(s), 24, 34, 363
Maneros, 5, 495
Mannheimer, Isaac Noah, 246, 247, 249, 512
Marcello, Benedetto, 167, 171, 202; Marcello's Psalms, 202
Marchettus of Padua, 202
Marek, P. S., 400
Margolis, Rabbi Selig of Kalish, 194, 213
Margowsky, Jacob Samuel ("Zeidel Rovner"), 433
Margulies, Berl (Broder), 440
"Maria's cradlesong," 174
Maria, Giovani, 506
Marien ward ein bot, 146
Markbreiter, Koppel, 247
Maronite song, 32
"Marseilleuse," 383
Marshalik, marshalk. See badchonim, 435
Mar Ukba, 98
Marusya (music), 407
Mathias, Chr., 329
Marx, Adolph Bernhard, 473, 476
Mayence, 158
Mayer, Rabbi Harry H., 332
Mayer, L. M., 226
Ma yofis (song), 384; tune of, 385; (music), 390
Megilla, see Esther, 65

Meier ben Yitzchak of Worms, 159
meinyana, 60
Meldola, David, 240
melisma, 258
melody, melodies, 111; in the Hazag meter, 117 ff.; in the kámil meter, 120; in the Major and Minor, 517; in the Mutakarib meter, 120, in the Ragaz meter, 120
melos, 192
mena'anim, 15
Menahem de Lonzano, 209
Mendell of Kotzk, Rabbi, 519
Mendelssohn, Moses, 330, 331, 348
Mendelssohn-Bartholdy, Felix Jacob, 247, 459, 473, 474, 475, 476
Mensch gedenk, 384
mesayim, 104
mesharethim (ta'amim), 39
meshorer, meshorerim, 204
Meshullam ben Kalonymos, 134, 165
metrical poetry, 100
Methfessel, A. G., 240, 241
metziltayim, 15
Meyer, Joachim, 210
Meyer, Isaac, 415
Meyer of Rothenburg, Rabbi, 157, 158
Meyerbeer, Jacob Liebmann (Giacomo), 236, 264, 472, 475, 512
Michael Chosid, 218
Michael ben Nathan of Lublin, 213
Michael of Kempen, 508
Mi Chomochoh, 160
Milner, M., 464, 467
Min Hametzar, by Halévy, 263
"minhag," 180; minhag Carpentras, 340
Minkowsky, Pinchos, 293, 351, 485
Minnesinger, Minnesong, 125, 132, 147, 175
Minz, Rabbi Moses, 179
Mirkin, 272
Misheberach Steiger, 185
misnagdim, 413
Missinai melodies, tunes, 136, 177, 312
Mistechkin, G., 464
Mixolydian (scale), 73, 286
mithpallel, mithpallelim, 102, 104
Mitteilungen fur jüd. Volkskunde, 411
mode, modal, 24, 28; modes of the Bible, 35; modes or Steiger in Major, 143 f.; in Minor, 137; for Sabbath Mincha, 137
modulations in minor, 481; to the dominant, 481
Mogen-Ovos, 285; mode, 78, 483; (music), 85-6
Moise, Penina, 320

Moldavan, K., 464
Mölin, Rabbi and *chazzan*, 157, 159
Mombach, Israel Lazarus, 286, 288, 314
mono-aulos, 12
Moniuszko, Stanislaus, 300
Mooz tzur, tune of, 168, 171
Moravia, 221
Moroccan, 43
Moscato, Jehuda, 201
Moses ben Ezra, 126, 502
Moses de Lion, 57
Moses, Rabbi Isaac S., 330
Moscheles, Ignaz, 247, 285, 473, 476, 511
Moshe of Prshischa, Rabbi Avrohom, 518
Moshiachszeiten, song, 442
Mosley, B. L., 291
motive(s), 24; and tunes of German religious and secular folk-song, 172 f.
Mozart, 330, 331, 472, 474, 476
Muezzin, 28
mu-fa-i-lun, 113, 114
music, sacred, 21; secular, 21
musical performances at the Temple service, 18
Musaf, 108; *Kedusha*, 159
mustaar (*makam*), 431
mus-taf-i-lun, 114
Musurgia Universalis, 346
mutakarib (meter), 114
Muzmar, 12

Nabla, 4; Sidonian, 5
Naboth, 92
Nadel, Arno, 463
Nachman of Brasslaw, 413, 519
nagen, 9
naghana, 24
Na gorodi (music), 408
Najara, Israel, 126, 362
nashwad (plu.) *neshid*, 367; form, 366; songs, 367
nashad, 516
Nasi, Joseph, 371
Nathan, Isaac, 338
Naumbourg, Samuel, 199, 229, 230, 260 ff., 280, 288, 292, 337, 348, 350; Naumbourg's harmony, 481
Nawa, 29, 34, 412
neginoth, 69
Nehemiah, 38
Nehemiah, Rabbi, 21
Neidlinger, W. H., 328
Neila, 308; Kaddish, tune of, 170
Ne'im Zemiroth, 192

Neo-mystics, 412
Nestorian, 96
Nettl, Paul, 506, 511
Neuberger, 261
Neumeister of Weissenfels, Erdman, 210
Nevel, 5, 8, 12, 16
Nezwizshki, A. A., 342
Ni-be-ni-me, 450
Nicholas I, Emperor, 394
Noheg Katzon Yosef, 352
Nordlinger, Joseph Hahn, 352
North Africa, 23
Northern European music, 110, 111
Northern Germany, 87
Nowakowsky, David, 308, 485
Nun freut Euch Ihr lieben Christen, 171; (music), 173
Nun wend is horen (music), 173

Occident, Jews of, 26
Ochiloh loel, 170
octachord, 478
Odessaer, Bezalel, 298, 303
Odo, Archbishop, 132
Offenbach, Jacques, 473
Olenu (tune), 147, 148, 157
Olivers, Thomas, 220
Olympus, 13, 87
Omar adonoy leyaakov, tune of, 392; (music), 402
Oppenheim, David, 215
organ-builder, Jewish, 205
"Organ" congregations, 244
ornament, oriental, 25
Ortega, Manuel L., 516
Oschoh edrosh, tune of, 165
Osisi, tune of, 170
Ost und West, 349, 463
Ottenhofer, 327
Otzar Neginoth Yisrael, 343
Over Tatra, 399; (music), 406
Ovos (tune), 149, 150
Owst, W. G., 328
"*Oz shesh meos*," 159

Paamonim, 15
Pachtikos, G. D., 517
Palestine, 87
Pan, Moshe, 219
Papir is doch vais (music), 405
Parisot, Dom J., 344
Pashraw, 27
Pashta, 68
paytanim, 134
Pazer, 70
Pedrell, F., 517
pentameter, 51

Pentateuch, 36; mode, 39; reading of the, 38; (music), 40 ff.
pentachordal, 25
percussive instruments, 14
Perl, Joseph, 245
Persia, Persian, 23, 43
Phœnicians, music of the, 5
Phrygian (Greek), 25, 483
Piccioto, James, 220
Pifert, Samuel, 439
Pilpul, pilpulistic, 184
Pindar, 13
Pinkos, Muzykaliszer, 411
Pinna, David, 39, 346
Pitkowsky-Schak, Sarah, 465
piyyut, 87, 106
"Plain Chant," 47
Plutarch, 15
Pneumata (ta'amim), 68, 70
Poetical Portions of the Pentateuch, modes of the, 47
Poetry of the Pentateuch, tunes for the, 49
Poland, 87
Polatshik, Sender, 298; "Sender Minsker," 302
Polnisch, 182
Popper, Lipman Katz, 207, 217, 438
Portuguese songs, 348
Porush, 301
Porteleone, Abraham ben David, 201, 346
Prayers, the modes of the, 72 ff.
precentor (in the church), 109; Rise and Development of the, 101 ff.
pronunciator psalmi, 109
Prophets, 36; mode of, 50; (music), 52 f.
prosodia, 68
Provence, 47
Proverbs, 36, 61
Psalms, 36; modes of the, 58; (music), 62 ff.
Purcell, Henry, 234
Purim-Spiel, spieler (play), 437
Purim songs, 437
Pythagoras, 5

quarter-tone system, 25, 26

Raba, 93
Rabbi Henich, 449
rabbis-chazzanim, 135
Rabinowitz, A. M., 485
Raff, Moshe, 230
ragaz (meter), 114
ramal (meter), 114
Rashi, 130

Ravel, Maurice, 465, 486
Rebia, 70
"Reform Society of Israelites," 320
Reform Temple in Seesen, 96
rehaw (makam), 57
Renaissance in Italy, 196
responsive form, 7
Reuchlin, Johannes, 43, 346
rhythm, 28
rhythmical music, 100, 124; set to unmetrical text, 121; song, 110 ff.
rhythmical music, Oriental, 25
Ribono schel olom (music), 422
Riemann, H., 197
Rikud, 420
Rimsky-Korsakow, 254
Rittangel, J. S., 174
rococo style, 272
Rogers, James H., 327
Romanos (of Homs), 100
rondo-form, 431
Rosenblatt, Joseph, 334
Rosenthal, Mordchele (klezmer), 459
Rosenstein, Gerson, 238
Rosh Hashana, 57
Roskin, Janot S., 465
Rosowsky, Boruch Leib, 311
Rosowsky, Solomon, 312, 467
Rossi, Anselmi, 196
Rossi, Salomon, 196, 197, 265, 336, 350, 478
Rossini, 331
Roumania, 87; Roumanian folk-song, 190; (music), 187 ff.
Rubin, David, 290
Rubinstein, Anton, 311, 461, 473, 476
rum, 68
Ruth, 36, 38; mode of, 47; (music), 48

St. Jacobs-tune, 143
St. Jerome, 60
Saadia, 10
"Sabba" (mode), 26, 412
Sabel, S., 331
Sachs, Curt, 495
Sagri, Abraham, 201, 337
Saint-Saëns, 254
di Salinas of Burgos, Francesco, 399
Salman in Frankfort, 207
Salmele of Frankfort, chazzan, 450
Salue mundi (music), 172
Saminsky, Lazar, 464, 465
Sänger, Loew, 148, 150, 158, 230, 260, 264, 337
Sangers of Prague, David, 437
Sanseconda, Jacobo, 506
saria (meter), 114

Sasgar (*makam*), 29, 34
scales, minor, 27; major, 27; problem of the, 478
Schalit, M., 464
scarbove, 136
Schaz, Rabbi Meir, 221
Schechter, Mathilda S., 336
Scheuermann, S., 515
Schink, 240
Schir Zion, I, 250, 255, 257; II, 251, 258, 481
Schire Beth Adonai, 348
Schir Haschirim asher lischlomo, 265
Schitomirsky, A., 464
Schlesinger, Joseph, 459
Schlesinger, Sigmund, 325
Schlome of Prague, 380
Schönberg, Arnold, 473
Schorr, Boruch, 286, 290, 309
Schorr, Israel, 310
Schubert, F., 249, 331, 467, 474
Schulman, I., 464
Schulsinger, Bezalel of Odessa, 267, 298
Schumann, 331, 467, 476
Schwartz, Joseph, 312
Schweigers, David, 439
Schwenke, I. F., 240, 241
Scroll Vinz, 439
Seder service, 174, 361
Sefer shire Yisrael, 341
Selicha, 73; mode, comparative table of, 79 ff.
Selig, *Chazzan*, 439
Semetic-Oriental characteristics, 24; song, 24 ff., 38
Sender Polatschik, "Minsker," 298, 344
Sephardic in Amsterdam, 43; in France, 43; in Egypt, 43; in Palestine, 43; Sephardim, 23
sequence (chants), 147
Seril, daughter of Jacob of Dubno, 440
Seyfried, 249
Shabbatai Zevi, 365, 439
Shabzi, Sholem, 364
Shachrith, 108
shafur, 495
Shahin, mula, 516
shaliach-tzibur, 102
shalishim, 15
shalsheleth, 70
shapparu, 9
shechitah, 182
Shechina, wie weit bist du, 417
Shechuloh achuloh, 432
Shefal berech, 127
shehiya, 68
shekalim, 160

Shema, 18, 21, 103, 108
sheminith, 8
shesht, 67
Shestapol, Wolf, 308
shira, shiroh, Yemenite song, 367; form, 366; stanza, 368
Shir avodah, 455
Shire Yehuda, 352
Shitomirski, A., 486
Shlomele of Radomsk, Rabbi, 518
Shmendrik, 450
shofar, shofaroth, 9, 10, 11, 495; *mehuppach*, 70; *munach*, 70
Shofet kol hooretz, tune of, 167, 202
sholom aleichem, 384; (music), 390
sh'titoyoh (mode), 31
shuar, 125
Shulchan Aruch, 333, 412
Shulamith, 309, 451, 452
Shviyoh aniyoh, 433
Siddur, 108, 361
siga (*makam*), 29, 34
silluk, 70
Simchath Hannefesh, 227, 383
Simchath Torah, 137
Simeon the Great, Rabbi, 132
Simon bar Abbun, 134, 165, 170
Simon bar Yochai, 371
Simon of Prague, tune of *rabbi*, 383, 439
Sind originale Synagogen-und Volksmelodien, 350
Singer, Abraham, 226, 338
Singer, Josef, 292, 349
Singer, Leon, 220
Sirkas, Rabbi Joel, 209
Sistrum, 4, 15
Sklar, E., 464
skolion, 95
Slavs, Southern, 111
Smetana, 221
"Soade," 496
"Society for Jewish Folk Music," 463
sof, 67, 68; *-passuk*, 70
Sofer of Pintshof, Mordecai, 440
Sofer, Leib, 438
Sofer, Zalman, 440
sofer, 103
sogachts, 183
Sog zshe rebeniu (music), 404
Solomon of France, 171
Solomon ibn Gabirol, 126, 439
Solomon Usque, 437
Songs of the *Ashkenazim*, 344
Songs of the Babylonian Jews, 343; Moroccan Jews, 344; Persian, Bokharian and Daghestan Jews, 343; Yemenite Jews, 343

Songs of the Oriental Sephardim, 344
Song of the Sea, 124; Song of Songs,
  36, 38; intonation of, 48
song and singers in Folk-style, 435 ff.
Souvenir Volume, 350
Sparger, William, 324, 327
Spicker, M., 327
Spivak, Nisson, 303
Spohr, 331
Stadt-chazzan, 182
Stark, Edward, 326
Stark, Joseph, 326
Stendal, Mose, 438
Stein, Rabbi Leopold, 385
Steinthal, Hyman, 265
Stoewing, I. H. G., 240
"straw-fiddle," 458
Strelisker, Dovidl Brod, 297 f.
String instruments, 8
Sullam family, 506; Mose, 198, 506;
  Sara Copia, 506
Sulzer, Salomon, 246 ff., 287, 324, 478,
  481; music, 279; style, 327
Süsskind of Offenbach, 207, 449
suz-nak (*makam*), 310
svarita, 67
Synagogue Song after the Destruc-
  tion of the Second Temple, a histor-
  ical survey of the, 92 ff.; Eastern
  European, 181 ff.; Collections of and
  Literature of, 337 ff.; in the United
  States, 316 ff.
Syria, 87; Syriac, 93; church, 99;
  Syriac, 43
syrinx, 14

Ta'amim, the (musical notation) of
  the Bible, 35, 65, 69
Tachanun, 73
Tal-and-*geshem* mode, 137; tune, 241
Talbott, L., 292
talsha, 70
tarsa (*gerishin*), 70
Tartaric-Altaic, 13; Tartaric Oriental
  mode, 88 ·
Tartil, 25
Taube, wife of Jacob Pan, 440
taushish, 367
Tausik, Jacob, 439
tawil (meter), 114
tebir, 70
Techinna, Techinnoth, 73, 440
Tefilla, 73; mode, 73; (music), for
  the High holidays, 75 f., 137
tekia, 10
Telechaner, Jacob, 433
Teller, Oberconsistorialrat, 510
Temple in Jerusalem, music of the, 7

"Temple Verein," 238
terua, 9
tetrachord, tetrachordal, 25, 39, 478;
  circle, 479; form, 479
Teudath Shlomo, 352
Thatcher, Howard, 328
Thesaurus of Hebrew Oriental Melo-
  dies, 343
tifha, 67, 68, 70
Tinker, M. Z., 329
Tochter Zion, 210
Todah Wesimrah, 227, 282
Tof, 14
Tolczyner, Hershele, 432
tomechim, 104
tonality, 8, 26; in Oriental music, 25;
  scales and modes of ancient Jewish
  song, 22
tonoi (*ta'amim*), 68, 70
Tosefta Megillah, 498
tradition, musical, 22
Treves, Herz, 176, 204
Trobadors, Troubadours, 125, 132
trumpet, 4
Tumas tzurom, tune of, 167
Tunes for Individual Texts, 144 ff.
Tylor, Abram Ray, 328
tzadik, tzadikim, 412, 413, 415
Tzadik of Kalif, the, 417
Tzadik of Makarov, 433
tzalzal, tziltzal-cymbal, 15

Ud, 25
udata, 67
Uggav, 11, 12
Ukraine, Ukrainian, 87; "Dorian,"
  314, 400; folk-song, 184, 185, 399;
  Gipsy-scale, 298; motives in Dorian
  ending on the second, 186; (music),
  186 f.; song, 183
Ultra-Reform, 246
ultra-reform movement, 244-5
Un as du forst (music), 403
*Ungarische isr. Kultus-Beamtenzei-
  tung,* 349
Union Hymnal, 331
Unison singing, 21
Unrhythmical (elements), 25; music
  set to metrical text, 121
Unter dem kinds vigele, tune of, 393;
  (music), 403

Van der-Stucken, Frank, 327
Vaychullu, 84
Vehakohanim, 159; (tune), I, 153,
  II, 153, III, 153
Venite exultemus, 146
Verdi, 254

Vetaher libenu (music), 424
Viddui, 73; comparative table of mode, 78, 82-3
de Villers, M. A., 342
Villoteau, 344
vocal music, 17, 19; song of the Temple, 20
"voice-chords," 497
Volhynia, 87
Volkstümlich, 454
Vom jungen Grafen, 383
Vorbeterschule, 339, 348
Vos vet zein mit dem rebben dem frumen (music), 430
Vrowenlop, Heinrich, 164
Vulpius, M., 171

Wachenheimer, Abele, 221
wafir (meter), 114
Wagenseil, 217
Wagner, Peter, 353, 500
Wagner, Richard, 111, 265, 475, 476; attack on Jewish composers, 522
Wald, Franz, 327
Waley, Simon, 291
Walich, Eisik, 380, 438
Walich, Leib, 439
Warschawsky, Mark, 454
Wasserzug, Chaim, 289
"water libation," 16, 17
water-organ (organon hydraulium), 14
Weber, 331
Weinberg, I., 468
Weinshenk-Tausik, Hershel, 438
Weinstein, L., 331, 348
Weintraub, Hirsch (Alter), 266 ff., 271, 286, 288, 482, 486, 487; chazzanuth of, 311; harmonic scheme, 483
Weiss, Jacob Leopold (Leib), 290
Welsch, Samuel, 323
"Welwele Chersoner," 308
Wie in der Tora steht geschrieben, 383
Wilnaer Baalhabessil (Yoel Dovid Levinsohn), 299
de la Willemarque, H., 517
Wimmelbacher, 261
Wind instruments, 9; musical, 11
Wodak, M., 342
Woelflin von Locham, 206
Wolf of Cracow, 439, 467
Wolf, I. Löb, 431
Women in religious music, 27; in the Temple choir, 16

Yah Ribbon Alam, 362, 370
Yankele geht in Shul arain, 453
Yankele mit Rivkelen (music), 408
Yarchon Lechazzanim, 351
Yedid Refesh, 412
Yehudah Charizi, 125
Yehudah Leb ben Moses, 209
Yekel Bass, Singer (I. Lehman), 221
Yekuthiel ben Moshe, 170
Yemen, Yemenite, 23; folk-song of Jews, 364
Yeruchom Hakoton, Blindman, 302, 303, 314
Yeshivah, 215
Yesli te (music), 173
yethib, 70
Yigdal, tune, 221; Table of Folk-songs compared with the, 222 ff.
Yisrolik kum ahaim, 453
Yisroel in Prosnitz, 215
Yitzchok Chazzan, 219
Yitzchok of Berditschev, Levi, 413, 420
Yokush beonyo, 432
Yoreisi, 170
Yosef of Bicksheim, chazzan, 215
Yossele dem Rebbins, 432
Yotzer, 160; mode for the three Festivals, 142
Yovo addir, tune of, 393; (music), 402

Zafát form, 366
Zakef, 67, 70
Zalman of Ladi, Shneor, 413, 416, 418
Zalman of Poltosk, chazzan, 432, 439
Zarfati, Rabbi Benzion, 198
Zarka, segol, 70
Zeidel Rovner. See Margowsky, J. L.
Zeitlin, L., 464
Zemiroth (songs), 73, 361, 384; in Hebrew, 392; Israel, 263, 363; Yisroel, 340
Zenon, Rabbi, 107
Zepler, Bogumil, 462
"Zevach Pesach," 174
Zilberts, Zavel, 465
Zimbalist, Efrem, 465
Zimro (organization), 464
Zoelner, J., 327
Zohar, the, 57
Zunz, L., 279
Zunzer, Elyokum Badchan, 399, 442; (music), 443; popularity of, 444

A CATALOG OF SELECTED DOVER
BOOKS IN ALL FIELDS OF INTEREST

DRAWINGS OF REMBRANDT, edited by Seymour Slive. Updated Lippmann, Hofstede de Groot edition, with definitive scholarly apparatus. All portraits, biblical sketches, landscapes, nudes. Oriental figures, classical studies, together with selection of work by followers. 550 illustrations. Total of 630pp. 9⅛ × 12¼.
21485-0, 21486-9 Pa., Two-vol. set $29.90

GHOST AND HORROR STORIES OF AMBROSE BIERCE, Ambrose Bierce. 24 tales vividly imagined, strangely prophetic, and decades ahead of their time in technical skill: "The Damned Thing," "An Inhabitant of Carcosa," "The Eyes of the Panther," "Moxon's Master," and 20 more. 199pp. 5⅜ × 8½. 20767-6 Pa. $4.95

ETHICAL WRITINGS OF MAIMONIDES, Maimonides. Most significant ethical works of great medieval sage, newly translated for utmost precision, readability. Laws Concerning Character Traits, Eight Chapters, more. 192pp. 5⅜ × 8½.
24522-5 Pa. $4.50

THE EXPLORATION OF THE COLORADO RIVER AND ITS CANYONS, J. W. Powell. Full text of Powell's 1,000-mile expedition down the fabled Colorado in 1869. Superb account of terrain, geology, vegetation, Indians, famine, mutiny, treacherous rapids, mighty canyons, during exploration of last unknown part of continental U.S. 400pp. 5⅜ × 8½. 20094-9 Pa. $7.95

HISTORY OF PHILOSOPHY, Julián Marías. Clearest one-volume history on the market. Every major philosopher and dozens of others, to Existentialism and later. 505pp. 5⅜ × 8½. 21739-6 Pa. $9.95

ALL ABOUT LIGHTNING, Martin A. Uman. Highly readable non-technical survey of nature and causes of lightning, thunderstorms, ball lightning, St. Elmo's Fire, much more. Illustrated. 192pp. 5⅜ × 8½. 25237-X Pa. $5.95

SAILING ALONE AROUND THE WORLD, Captain Joshua Slocum. First man to sail around the world, alone, in small boat. One of great feats of seamanship told in delightful manner. 67 illustrations. 294pp. 5⅜ × 8½. 20326-3 Pa. $4.95

LETTERS AND NOTES ON THE MANNERS, CUSTOMS AND CONDITIONS OF THE NORTH AMERICAN INDIANS, George Catlin. Classic account of life among Plains Indians: ceremonies, hunt, warfare, etc. 312 plates. 572pp. of text. 6⅛ × 9¼. 22118-0, 22119-9, Pa. Two-vol. set $17.90

ALASKA: The Harriman Expedition, 1899, John Burroughs, John Muir, et al. Informative, engrossing accounts of two-month, 9,000-mile expedition. Native peoples, wildlife, forests, geography, salmon industry, glaciers, more. Profusely illustrated. 240 black-and-white line drawings. 124 black-and-white photographs. 3 maps. Index. 576pp. 5⅜ × 8½. 25109-8 Pa. $11.95

THE BOOK OF BEASTS: Being a Translation from a Latin Bestiary of the Twelfth Century, T. H. White. Wonderful catalog real and fanciful beasts: manticore, griffin, phoenix, amphivius, jaculus, many more. White's witty erudite commentary on scientific, historical aspects. Fascinating glimpse of medieval mind. Illustrated. 296pp. 5⅜ × 8¼. (Available in U.S. only) 24609-4 Pa. $6.95

FRANK LLOYD WRIGHT: ARCHITECTURE AND NATURE With 160 Illustrations, Donald Hoffmann. Profusely illustrated study of influence of nature—especially prairie—on Wright's designs for Fallingwater, Robie House, Guggenheim Museum, other masterpieces. 96pp. 9¼ × 10¾. 25098-9 Pa. $8.95

FRANK LLOYD WRIGHT'S FALLINGWATER, Donald Hoffmann. Wright's famous waterfall house: planning and construction of organic idea. History of site, owners, Wright's personal involvement. Photographs of various stages of building. Preface by Edgar Kaufmann, Jr. 100 illustrations. 112pp. 9¼ × 10. 23671-4 Pa. $8.95

YEARS WITH FRANK LLOYD WRIGHT: Apprentice to Genius, Edgar Tafel. Insightful memoir by a former apprentice presents a revealing portrait of Wright the man, the inspired teacher, the greatest American architect. 372 black-and-white illustrations. Preface. Index. vi + 228pp. 8¼ × 11. 24801-1 Pa. $10.95

THE STORY OF KING ARTHUR AND HIS KNIGHTS, Howard Pyle. Enchanting version of King Arthur fable has delighted generations with imaginative narratives of exciting adventures and unforgettable illustrations by the author. 41 illustrations. xviii + 313pp. 6⅛ × 9¼. 21445-1 Pa. $6.95

THE GODS OF THE EGYPTIANS, E. A. Wallis Budge. Thorough coverage of numerous gods of ancient Egypt by foremost Egyptologist. Information on evolution of cults, rites and gods; the cult of Osiris; the Book of the Dead and its rites; the sacred animals and birds; Heaven and Hell; and more. 956pp. 6⅛ × 9¼. 22055-9, 22056-7 Pa., Two-vol. set $21.90

A THEOLOGICO-POLITICAL TREATISE, Benedict Spinoza. Also contains unfinished *Political Treatise*. Great classic on religious liberty, theory of government on common consent. R. Elwes translation. Total of 421pp. 5⅜ × 8½. 20249-6 Pa. $7.95

INCIDENTS OF TRAVEL IN CENTRAL AMERICA, CHIAPAS, AND YUCATAN, John L. Stephens. Almost single-handed discovery of Maya culture; exploration of ruined cities, monuments, temples; customs of Indians. 115 drawings. 892pp. 5⅜ × 8½. 22404-X, 22405-8 Pa., Two-vol. set $15.90

LOS CAPRICHOS, Francisco Goya. 80 plates of wild, grotesque monsters and caricatures. Prado manuscript included. 183pp. 6⅝ × 9⅝. 22384-1 Pa. $5.95

AUTOBIOGRAPHY: The Story of My Experiments with Truth, Mohandas K. Gandhi. Not hagiography, but Gandhi in his own words. Boyhood, legal studies, purification, the growth of the Satyagraha (nonviolent protest) movement. Critical, inspiring work of the man who freed India. 480pp. 5⅜ × 8½. (Available in U.S. only) 24593-4 Pa. $6.95

HOW TO WRITE, Gertrude Stein. Gertrude Stein claimed anyone could understand her unconventional writing—here are clues to help. Fascinating improvisations, language experiments, explanations illuminate Stein's craft and the art of writing. Total of 414pp. 4⅝ × 6⅜. 23144-5 Pa. $6.95

ADVENTURES AT SEA IN THE GREAT AGE OF SAIL: Five Firsthand Narratives, edited by Elliot Snow. Rare true accounts of exploration, whaling, shipwreck, fierce natives, trade, shipboard life, more. 33 illustrations. Introduction. 353pp. 5⅜ × 8½. 25177-2 Pa. $8.95

THE HERBAL OR GENERAL HISTORY OF PLANTS, John Gerard. Classic descriptions of about 2,850 plants—with over 2,700 illustrations—includes Latin and English names, physical descriptions, varieties, time and place of growth, more. 2,706 illustrations. xlv + 1,678pp. 8½ × 12¼. 23147-X Cloth. $75.00

DOROTHY AND THE WIZARD IN OZ, L. Frank Baum. Dorothy and the Wizard visit the center of the Earth, where people are vegetables, glass houses grow and Oz characters reappear. Classic sequel to *Wizard of Oz*. 256pp. 5⅜ × 8.
24714-7 Pa. $5.95

SONGS OF EXPERIENCE: Facsimile Reproduction with 26 Plates in Full Color, William Blake. This facsimile of Blake's original "Illuminated Book" reproduces 26 full-color plates from a rare 1826 edition. Includes "The Tyger," "London," "Holy Thursday," and other immortal poems. 26 color plates. Printed text of poems. 48pp. 5¼ × 7. 24636-1 Pa. $3.95

SONGS OF INNOCENCE, William Blake. The first and most popular of Blake's famous "Illuminated Books," in a facsimile edition reproducing all 31 brightly colored plates. Additional printed text of each poem. 64pp. 5¼ × 7.
22764-2 Pa. $3.95

PRECIOUS STONES, Max Bauer. Classic, thorough study of diamonds, rubies, emeralds, garnets, etc.: physical character, occurrence, properties, use, similar topics. 20 plates, 8 in color. 94 figures. 659pp. 6⅛ × 9¼.
21910-0, 21911-9 Pa., Two-vol. set $15.90

ENCYCLOPEDIA OF VICTORIAN NEEDLEWORK, S. F. A. Caulfeild and Blanche Saward. Full, precise descriptions of stitches, techniques for dozens of needlecrafts—most exhaustive reference of its kind. Over 800 figures. Total of 679pp. 8⅛ × 11. Two volumes. Vol. 1 22800-2 Pa. $11.95
Vol. 2 22801-0 Pa. $11.95

THE MARVELOUS LAND OF OZ, L. Frank Baum. Second Oz book, the Scarecrow and Tin Woodman are back with hero named Tip, Oz magic. 136 illustrations. 287pp. 5⅜ × 8½. 20692-0 Pa. $5.95

WILD FOWL DECOYS, Joel Barber. Basic book on the subject, by foremost authority and collector. Reveals history of decoy making and rigging, place in American culture, different kinds of decoys, how to make them, and how to use them. 140 plates. 156pp. 7⅞ × 10¾. 20011-6 Pa. $8.95

HISTORY OF LACE, Mrs. Bury Palliser. Definitive, profusely illustrated chronicle of lace from earliest times to late 19th century. Laces of Italy, Greece, England, France, Belgium, etc. Landmark of needlework scholarship. 266 illustrations. 672pp. 6⅛ × 9¼. 24742-2 Pa. $14.95

ILLUSTRATED GUIDE TO SHAKER FURNITURE, Robert Meader. All furniture and appurtenances, with much on unknown local styles. 235 photos. 146pp. 9 × 12. 22819-3 Pa. $8.95

WHALE SHIPS AND WHALING: A Pictorial Survey, George Francis Dow. Over 200 vintage engravings, drawings, photographs of barks, brigs, cutters, other vessels. Also harpoons, lances, whaling guns, many other artifacts. Comprehensive text by foremost authority. 207 black-and-white illustrations. 288pp. 6 × 9. 24808-9 Pa. $9.95

THE BERTRAMS, Anthony Trollope. Powerful portrayal of blind self-will and thwarted ambition includes one of Trollope's most heartrending love stories. 497pp. 5⅜ × 8½. 25119-5 Pa. $9.95

ADVENTURES WITH A HAND LENS, Richard Headstrom. Clearly written guide to observing and studying flowers and grasses, fish scales, moth and insect wings, egg cases, buds, feathers, seeds, leaf scars, moss, molds, ferns, common crystals, etc.—all with an ordinary, inexpensive magnifying glass. 209 exact line drawings aid in your discoveries. 220pp. 5⅜ × 8½. 23330-8 Pa. $4.95

RODIN ON ART AND ARTISTS, Auguste Rodin. Great sculptor's candid, wide-ranging comments on meaning of art; great artists; relation of sculpture to poetry, painting, music; philosophy of life, more. 76 superb black-and-white illustrations of Rodin's sculpture, drawings and prints. 119pp. 8⅜ × 11¼. 24487-3 Pa. $7.95

FIFTY CLASSIC FRENCH FILMS, 1912–1982: A Pictorial Record, Anthony Slide. Memorable stills from Grand Illusion, Beauty and the Beast, Hiroshima, Mon Amour, many more. Credits, plot synopses, reviews, etc. 160pp. 8¼ × 11. 25256-6 Pa. $11.95

THE PRINCIPLES OF PSYCHOLOGY, William James. Famous long course complete, unabridged. Stream of thought, time perception, memory, experimental methods; great work decades ahead of its time. 94 figures. 1,391pp. 5⅜ × 8½. 20381-6, 20382-4 Pa., Two-vol. set $23.90

BODIES IN A BOOKSHOP, R. T. Campbell. Challenging mystery of blackmail and murder with ingenious plot and superbly drawn characters. In the best tradition of British suspense fiction. 192pp. 5⅜ × 8½. 24720-1 Pa. $4.95

CALLAS: PORTRAIT OF A PRIMA DONNA, George Jellinek. Renowned commentator on the musical scene chronicles incredible career and life of the most controversial, fascinating, influential operatic personality of our time. 64 black-and-white photographs. 416pp. 5⅜ × 8¼. 25047-4 Pa. $8.95

GEOMETRY, RELATIVITY AND THE FOURTH DIMENSION, Rudolph Rucker. Exposition of fourth dimension, concepts of relativity as Flatland characters continue adventures. Popular, easily followed yet accurate, profound. 141 illustrations. 133pp. 5⅜ × 8½. 23400-2 Pa. $4.95

HOUSEHOLD STORIES BY THE BROTHERS GRIMM, with pictures by Walter Crane. 53 classic stories—Rumpelstiltskin, Rapunzel, Hansel and Gretel, the Fisherman and his Wife, Snow White, Tom Thumb, Sleeping Beauty, Cinderella, and so much more—lavishly illustrated with original 19th century drawings. 114 illustrations. x + 269pp. 5⅜ × 8½. 21080-4 Pa. $4.95

SUNDIALS, Albert Waugh. Far and away the best, most thorough coverage of ideas, mathematics concerned, types, construction, adjusting anywhere. Over 100 illustrations. 230pp. 5⅜ × 8½. 22947-5 Pa. $5.95

PICTURE HISTORY OF THE NORMANDIE: With 190 Illustrations, Frank O. Braynard. Full story of legendary French ocean liner: Art Deco interiors, design innovations, furnishings, celebrities, maiden voyage, tragic fire, much more. Extensive text. 144pp. 8⅜ × 11¾. 25257-4 Pa. $10.95

THE FIRST AMERICAN COOKBOOK: A Facsimile of "American Cookery," 1796, Amelia Simmons. Facsimile of the first American-written cookbook published in the United States contains authentic recipes for colonial favorites—pumpkin pudding, winter squash pudding, spruce beer, Indian slapjacks, and more. Introductory Essay and Glossary of colonial cooking terms. 80pp. 5⅜ × 8½. 24710-4 Pa. $3.50

101 PUZZLES IN THOUGHT AND LOGIC, C. R. Wylie, Jr. Solve murders and robberies, find out which fishermen are liars, how a blind man could possibly identify a color—purely by your own reasoning! 107pp. 5⅜ × 8½. 20367-0 Pa. $2.50

ANCIENT EGYPTIAN MYTHS AND LEGENDS, Lewis Spence. Examines animism, totemism, fetishism, creation myths, deities, alchemy, art and magic, other topics. Over 50 illustrations. 432pp. 5⅜ × 8½. 26525-0 Pa. $8.95

ANTHROPOLOGY AND MODERN LIFE, Franz Boas. Great anthropologist's classic treatise on race and culture. Introduction by Ruth Bunzel. Only inexpensive paperback edition. 255pp. 5⅜ × 8½. 25245-0 Pa. $6.95

THE TALE OF PETER RABBIT, Beatrix Potter. The inimitable Peter's terrifying adventure in Mr. McGregor's garden, with all 27 wonderful, full-color Potter illustrations. 55pp. 4¼ × 5½. (Available in U.S. only) 22827-4 Pa. $1.75

THREE PROPHETIC SCIENCE FICTION NOVELS, H. G. Wells. *When the Sleeper Wakes, A Story of the Days to Come* and *The Time Machine* (full version). 335pp. 5⅜ × 8½. (Available in U.S. only) 20605-X Pa. $6.95

APICIUS COOKERY AND DINING IN IMPERIAL ROME, edited and translated by Joseph Dommers Vehling. Oldest known cookbook in existence offers readers a clear picture of what foods Romans ate, how they prepared them, etc. 49 illustrations. 301pp. 6⅛ × 9¼. 23563-7 Pa. $7.95

SHAKESPEARE LEXICON AND QUOTATION DICTIONARY, Alexander Schmidt. Full definitions, locations, shades of meaning of every word in plays and poems. More than 50,000 exact quotations. 1,485pp. 6½ × 9¼. 22726-X, 22727-8 Pa., Two-vol. set $31.90

THE WORLD'S GREAT SPEECHES, edited by Lewis Copeland and Lawrence W. Lamm. Vast collection of 278 speeches from Greeks to 1970. Powerful and effective models; unique look at history. 842pp. 5⅜ × 8½. 20468-5 Pa. $12.95

THE BLUE FAIRY BOOK, Andrew Lang. The first, most famous collection, with many familiar tales: Little Red Riding Hood, Aladdin and the Wonderful Lamp, Puss in Boots, Sleeping Beauty, Hansel and Gretel, Rumpelstiltskin; 37 in all. 138 illustrations. 390pp. 5⅜ × 8½. 21437-0 Pa. $6.95

THE STORY OF THE CHAMPIONS OF THE ROUND TABLE, Howard Pyle. Sir Launcelot, Sir Tristram and Sir Percival in spirited adventures of love and triumph retold in Pyle's inimitable style. 50 drawings, 31 full-page. xviii + 329pp. 6½ × 9¼. 21883-X Pa. $7.95

THE MYTHS OF THE NORTH AMERICAN INDIANS, Lewis Spence. Myths and legends of the Algonquins, Iroquois, Pawnees and Sioux with comprehensive historical and ethnological commentary. 36 illustrations. 5⅜ × 8½. 25967-6 Pa. $8.95

GREAT DINOSAUR HUNTERS AND THEIR DISCOVERIES, Edwin H. Colbert. Fascinating, lavishly illustrated chronicle of dinosaur research, 1820's to 1960. Achievements of Cope, Marsh, Brown, Buckland, Mantell, Huxley, many others. 384pp. 5¼ × 8¼. 24701-5 Pa. $7.95

THE TASTEMAKERS, Russell Lynes. Informal, illustrated social history of American taste 1850's–1950's. First popularized categories Highbrow, Lowbrow, Middlebrow. 129 illustrations. New (1979) afterword. 384pp. 6 × 9. 23993-4 Pa. $8.95

DOUBLE CROSS PURPOSES, Ronald A. Knox. A treasure hunt in the Scottish Highlands, an old map, unidentified corpse, surprise discoveries keep reader guessing in this cleverly intricate tale of financial skullduggery. 2 black-and-white maps. 320pp. 5⅜ × 8½. (Available in U.S. only) 25032-6 Pa. $6.95

AUTHENTIC VICTORIAN DECORATION AND ORNAMENTATION IN FULL COLOR: 46 Plates from "Studies in Design," Christopher Dresser. Superb full-color lithographs reproduced from rare original portfolio of a major Victorian designer. 48pp. 9¼ × 12¼. 25083-0 Pa. $7.95

PRIMITIVE ART, Franz Boas. Remains the best text ever prepared on subject, thoroughly discussing Indian, African, Asian, Australian, and, especially, Northern American primitive art. Over 950 illustrations show ceramics, masks, totem poles, weapons, textiles, paintings, much more. 376pp. 5⅜ × 8. 20025-6 Pa. $7.95

SIDELIGHTS ON RELATIVITY, Albert Einstein. Unabridged republication of two lectures delivered by the great physicist in 1920–21. *Ether and Relativity* and *Geometry and Experience.* Elegant ideas in non-mathematical form, accessible to intelligent layman. vi + 56pp. 5⅜ × 8½. 24511-X Pa. $2.95

THE WIT AND HUMOR OF OSCAR WILDE, edited by Alvin Redman. More than 1,000 ripostes, paradoxes, wisecracks: Work is the curse of the drinking classes, I can resist everything except temptation, etc. 258pp. 5⅜ × 8½. 20602-5 Pa. $4.95

ADVENTURES WITH A MICROSCOPE, Richard Headstrom. 59 adventures with clothing fibers, protozoa, ferns and lichens, roots and leaves, much more. 142 illustrations. 232pp. 5⅜ × 8½. 23471-1 Pa. $3.95

PLANTS OF THE BIBLE, Harold N. Moldenke and Alma L. Moldenke. Standard reference to all 230 plants mentioned in Scriptures. Latin name, biblical reference, uses, modern identity, much more. Unsurpassed encyclopedic resource for scholars, botanists, nature lovers, students of Bible. Bibliography. Indexes. 123 black-and-white illustrations. 384pp. 6 × 9. 25069-5 Pa. $8.95

FAMOUS AMERICAN WOMEN: A Biographical Dictionary from Colonial Times to the Present, Robert McHenry, ed. From Pocahontas to Rosa Parks, 1,035 distinguished American women documented in separate biographical entries. Accurate, up-to-date data, numerous categories, spans 400 years. Indices. 493pp. 6½ × 9¼. 24523-3 Pa. $10.95

THE FABULOUS INTERIORS OF THE GREAT OCEAN LINERS IN HISTORIC PHOTOGRAPHS, William H. Miller, Jr. Some 200 superb photographs capture exquisite interiors of world's great "floating palaces"—1890's to 1980's: *Titanic, Ile de France, Queen Elizabeth, United States, Europa,* more. Approx. 200 black-and-white photographs. Captions. Text. Introduction. 160pp. 8⅞ × 11¾. 24756-2 Pa. $9.95

THE GREAT LUXURY LINERS, 1927–1954: A Photographic Record, William H. Miller, Jr. Nostalgic tribute to heyday of ocean liners. 186 photos of Ile de France, Normandie, Leviathan, Queen Elizabeth, United States, many others. Interior and exterior views. Introduction. Captions. 160pp. 9 × 12. 24056-8 Pa. $10.95

A NATURAL HISTORY OF THE DUCKS, John Charles Phillips. Great landmark of ornithology offers complete detailed coverage of nearly 200 species and subspecies of ducks: gadwall, sheldrake, merganser, pintail, many more. 74 full-color plates, 102 black-and-white. Bibliography. Total of 1,920pp. 8⅝ × 11¼. 25141-1, 25142-X Cloth. Two-vol. set $100.00

THE SEAWEED HANDBOOK: An Illustrated Guide to Seaweeds from North Carolina to Canada, Thomas F. Lee. Concise reference covers 78 species. Scientific and common names, habitat, distribution, more. Finding keys for easy identification. 224pp. 5⅜ × 8½. 25215-9 Pa. $6.95

THE TEN BOOKS OF ARCHITECTURE: The 1755 Leoni Edition, Leon Battista Alberti. Rare classic helped introduce the glories of ancient architecture to the Renaissance. 68 black-and-white plates. 336pp. 8⅜ × 11¼. 25239-6 Pa. $14.95

MISS MACKENZIE, Anthony Trollope. Minor masterpieces by Victorian master unmasks many truths about life in 19th-century England. First inexpensive edition in years. 392pp. 5⅜ × 8½. 25201-9 Pa. $8.95

THE RIME OF THE ANCIENT MARINER, Gustave Doré, Samuel Taylor Coleridge. Dramatic engravings considered by many to be his greatest work. The terrifying space of the open sea, the storms and whirlpools of an unknown ocean, the ice of Antarctica, more—all rendered in a powerful, chilling manner. Full text. 38 plates. 77pp. 9¼ × 12. 22305-1 Pa. $4.95

THE EXPEDITIONS OF ZEBULON MONTGOMERY PIKE, Zebulon Montgomery Pike. Fascinating first-hand accounts (1805–6) of exploration of Mississippi River, Indian wars, capture by Spanish dragoons, much more. 1,088pp. 5⅜ × 8½. 25254-X, 25255-8 Pa. Two-vol. set $25.90

CATALOG OF DOVER BOOKS

A CONCISE HISTORY OF PHOTOGRAPHY: Third Revised Edition, Helmut Gernsheim. Best one-volume history—camera obscura, photochemistry, daguerreotypes, evolution of cameras, film, more. Also artistic aspects—landscape, portraits, fine art, etc. 281 black-and-white photographs. 26 in color. 176pp. 8⅜ × 11¼. 25128-4 Pa. $13.95

THE DORÉ BIBLE ILLUSTRATIONS, Gustave Doré. 241 detailed plates from the Bible: the Creation scenes, Adam and Eve, Flood, Babylon, battle sequences, life of Jesus, etc. Each plate is accompanied by the verses from the King James version of the Bible. 241pp. 9 × 12. 23004-X Pa. $9.95

WANDERINGS IN WEST AFRICA, Richard F. Burton. Great Victorian scholar/adventurer's invaluable descriptions of African tribal rituals, fetishism, culture, art, much more. Fascinating 19th-century account. 624pp. 5⅜ × 8½. 26890-X Pa. $12.95

FLATLAND, E. A. Abbott. Intriguing and enormously popular science-fiction classic explores the complexities of trying to survive as a two-dimensional being in a three-dimensional world. Amusingly illustrated by the author. 16 illustrations. 103pp. 5⅜ × 8½. 20001-9 Pa. $2.50

THE HISTORY OF THE LEWIS AND CLARK EXPEDITION, Meriwether Lewis and William Clark, edited by Elliott Coues. Classic edition of Lewis and Clark's day-by-day journals that later became the basis for U.S. claims to Oregon and the West. Accurate and invaluable geographical, botanical, biological, meteorological and anthropological material. Total of 1,508pp. 5⅜ × 8½.
21268-8, 21269-6, 21270-X Pa. Three-vol. set $26.85

LANGUAGE, TRUTH AND LOGIC, Alfred J. Ayer. Famous, clear introduction to Vienna, Cambridge schools of Logical Positivism. Role of philosophy, elimination of metaphysics, nature of analysis, etc. 160pp. 5⅜ × 8½. (Available in U.S. and Canada only) 20010-8 Pa. $3.95

MATHEMATICS FOR THE NONMATHEMATICIAN, Morris Kline. Detailed, college-level treatment of mathematics in cultural and historical context, with numerous exercises. For liberal arts students. Preface. Recommended Reading Lists. Tables. Index. Numerous black-and-white figures. xvi + 641pp. 5⅜ × 8½.
24823-2 Pa. $11.95

HANDBOOK OF PICTORIAL SYMBOLS, Rudolph Modley. 3,250 signs and symbols, many systems in full; official or heavy commercial use. Arranged by subject. Most in Pictorial Archive series. 143pp. 8⅛ × 11. 23357-X Pa. $6.95

INCIDENTS OF TRAVEL IN YUCATAN, John L. Stephens. Classic (1843) exploration of jungles of Yucatan, looking for evidences of Maya civilization. Travel adventures, Mexican and Indian culture, etc. Total of 669pp. 5⅜ × 8½.
20926-1, 20927-X Pa., Two-vol. set $11.90

DEGAS: An Intimate Portrait, Ambroise Vollard. Charming, anecdotal memoir by famous art dealer of one of the greatest 19th-century French painters. 14 black-and-white illustrations. Introduction by Harold L. Van Doren. 96pp. 5⅜ × 8½.
25131-4 Pa. $4.95

PERSONAL NARRATIVE OF A PILGRIMAGE TO ALMANDINAH AND MECCAH, Richard Burton. Great travel classic by remarkably colorful personality. Burton, disguised as a Moroccan, visited sacred shrines of Islam, narrowly escaping death. 47 illustrations. 959pp. 5⅜ × 8½.   21217-3, 21218-1 Pa., Two-vol. set $19.90

PHRASE AND WORD ORIGINS, A. H. Holt. Entertaining, reliable, modern study of more than 1,200 colorful words, phrases, origins and histories. Much unexpected information. 254pp. 5⅜ × 8½.   20758-7 Pa. $5.95

THE RED THUMB MARK, R. Austin Freeman. In this first Dr. Thorndyke case, the great scientific detective draws fascinating conclusions from the nature of a single fingerprint. Exciting story, authentic science. 320pp. 5⅜ × 8½. (Available in U.S. only)   25210-8 Pa. $6.95

AN EGYPTIAN HIEROGLYPHIC DICTIONARY, E. A. Wallis Budge. Monumental work containing about 25,000 words or terms that occur in texts ranging from 3000 B.C. to 600 A.D. Each entry consists of a transliteration of the word, the word in hieroglyphs, and the meaning in English. 1,314pp. 6⅜ × 10.
23615-3, 23616-1 Pa., Two-vol. set $35.90

THE COMPLEAT STRATEGYST: Being a Primer on the Theory of Games of Strategy, J. D. Williams. Highly entertaining classic describes, with many illustrated examples, how to select best strategies in conflict situations. Prefaces. Appendices. xvi + 268pp. 5⅜ × 8½.   25101-2 Pa. $6.95

THE ROAD TO OZ, L. Frank Baum. Dorothy meets the Shaggy Man, little Button-Bright and the Rainbow's beautiful daughter in this delightful trip to the magical Land of Oz. 272pp. 5⅜ × 8.   25208-6 Pa. $5.95

POINT AND LINE TO PLANE, Wassily Kandinsky. Seminal exposition of role of point, line, other elements in non-objective painting. Essential to understanding 20th-century art. 127 illustrations. 192pp. 6½ × 9¼.   23808-3 Pa. $5.95

LADY ANNA, Anthony Trollope. Moving chronicle of Countess Lovel's bitter struggle to win for herself and daughter Anna their rightful rank and fortune—perhaps at cost of sanity itself. 384pp. 5⅜ × 8½.   24669-8 Pa. $8.95

EGYPTIAN MAGIC, E. A. Wallis Budge. Sums up all that is known about magic in Ancient Egypt: the role of magic in controlling the gods, powerful amulets that warded off evil spirits, scarabs of immortality, use of wax images, formulas and spells, the secret name, much more. 253pp. 5⅜ × 8½.   22681-6 Pa. $4.50

THE DANCE OF SIVA, Ananda Coomaraswamy. Preeminent authority unfolds the vast metaphysic of India: the revelation of her art, conception of the universe, social organization, etc. 27 reproductions of art masterpieces. 192pp. 5⅜ × 8½.
24817-8 Pa. $5.95

CHRISTMAS CUSTOMS AND TRADITIONS, Clement A. Miles. Origin, evolution, significance of religious, secular practices. Caroling, gifts, yule logs, much more. Full, scholarly yet fascinating; non-sectarian. 400pp. 5⅜ × 8½.
23354-5 Pa. $6.95

THE HUMAN FIGURE IN MOTION, Eadweard Muybridge. More than 4,500 stopped-action photos, in action series, showing undraped men, women, children jumping, lying down, throwing, sitting, wrestling, carrying, etc. 390pp. 7⅞ × 10⅝.
20204-6 Cloth. $24.95

THE MAN WHO WAS THURSDAY, Gilbert Keith Chesterton. Witty, fast-paced novel about a club of anarchists in turn-of-the-century London. Brilliant social, religious, philosophical speculations. 128pp. 5⅜ × 8½.
25121-7 Pa. $3.95

A CEZANNE SKETCHBOOK: Figures, Portraits, Landscapes and Still Lifes, Paul Cezanne. Great artist experiments with tonal effects, light, mass, other qualities in over 100 drawings. A revealing view of developing master painter, precursor of Cubism. 102 black-and-white illustrations. 144pp. 8¾ × 6⅝.
24790-2 Pa. $6.95

AN ENCYCLOPEDIA OF BATTLES: Accounts of Over 1,560 Battles from 1479 B.C. to the Present, David Eggenberger. Presents essential details of every major battle in recorded history, from the first battle of Megiddo in 1479 B.C. to Grenada in 1984. List of Battle Maps. New Appendix covering the years 1967–1984. Index. 99 illustrations. 544pp. 6½ × 9¼.
24913-1 Pa. $14.95

AN ETYMOLOGICAL DICTIONARY OF MODERN ENGLISH, Ernest Weekley. Richest, fullest work, by foremost British lexicographer. Detailed word histories. Inexhaustible. Total of 856pp. 6½ × 9¼.
21873-2, 21874-0 Pa., Two-vol. set $19.90

WEBSTER'S AMERICAN MILITARY BIOGRAPHIES, edited by Robert McHenry. Over 1,000 figures who shaped 3 centuries of American military history. Detailed biographies of Nathan Hale, Douglas MacArthur, Mary Hallaren, others. Chronologies of engagements, more. Introduction. Addenda. 1,033 entries in alphabetical order. xi + 548pp. 6½ × 9¼. (Available in U.S. only)
24758-9 Pa. $13.95

LIFE IN ANCIENT EGYPT, Adolf Erman. Detailed older account, with much not in more recent books: domestic life, religion, magic, medicine, commerce, and whatever else needed for complete picture. Many illustrations. 597pp. 5⅜ × 8½.
22632-8 Pa. $8.95

HISTORIC COSTUME IN PICTURES, Braun & Schneider. Over 1,450 costumed figures shown, covering a wide variety of peoples: kings, emperors, nobles, priests, servants, soldiers, scholars, townsfolk, peasants, merchants, courtiers, cavaliers, and more. 256pp. 8⅜ × 11¼.
23150-X Pa. $9.95

THE NOTEBOOKS OF LEONARDO DA VINCI, edited by J. P. Richter. Extracts from manuscripts reveal great genius; on painting, sculpture, anatomy, sciences, geography, etc. Both Italian and English. 186 ms. pages reproduced, plus 500 additional drawings, including studies for *Last Supper, Sforza* monument, etc. 860pp. 7⅞ × 10¾. (Available in U.S. only) 22572-0, 22573-9 Pa., Two-vol. set $31.90

CATALOG OF DOVER BOOKS

THE ART NOUVEAU STYLE BOOK OF ALPHONSE MUCHA: All 72 Plates from "Documents Decoratifs" in Original Color, Alphonse Mucha. Rare copyright-free design portfolio by high priest of Art Nouveau. Jewelry, wallpaper, stained glass, furniture, figure studies, plant and animal motifs, etc. Only complete one-volume edition. 80pp. 9⅜ × 12¼.   24044-4 Pa. $9.95

ANIMALS: 1,419 COPYRIGHT-FREE ILLUSTRATIONS OF MAMMALS, BIRDS, FISH, INSECTS, ETC., edited by Jim Harter. Clear wood engravings present, in extremely lifelike poses, over 1,000 species of animals. One of the most extensive pictorial sourcebooks of its kind. Captions. Index. 284pp. 9 × 12.
23766-4 Pa. $9.95

OBELISTS FLY HIGH, C. Daly King. Masterpiece of American detective fiction, long out of print, involves murder on a 1935 transcontinental flight—"a very thrilling story"—NY Times. Unabridged and unaltered republication of the edition published by William Collins Sons & Co. Ltd., London, 1935. 288pp. 5⅜ × 8½. (Available in U.S. only)   25036-9 Pa. $5.95

VICTORIAN AND EDWARDIAN FASHION: A Photographic Survey, Alison Gernsheim. First fashion history completely illustrated by contemporary photographs. Full text plus 235 photos, 1840–1914, in which many celebrities appear. 240pp. 6½ × 9¼.   24205-6 Pa. $8.95

THE ART OF THE FRENCH ILLUSTRATED BOOK, 1700–1914, Gordon N. Ray. Over 630 superb book illustrations by Fragonard, Delacroix, Daumier, Doré, Grandville, Manet, Mucha, Steinlen, Toulouse-Lautrec and many others. Preface. Introduction. 633 halftones. Indices of artists, authors & titles, binders and provenances. Appendices. Bibliography. 608pp. 8⅜ × 11¼.   25086-5 Pa. $24.95

THE WONDERFUL WIZARD OF OZ, L. Frank Baum. Facsimile in full color of America's finest children's classic. 143 illustrations by W. W. Denslow. 267pp. 5⅜ × 8½.   20691-2 Pa. $7.95

FOLLOWING THE EQUATOR: A Journey Around the World, Mark Twain. Great writer's 1897 account of circumnavigating the globe by steamship. Ironic humor, keen observations, vivid and fascinating descriptions of exotic places. 197 illustrations. 720pp. 5⅜ × 8½.   26113-1 Pa. $15.95

THE FRIENDLY STARS, Martha Evans Martin & Donald Howard Menzel. Classic text marshalls the stars together in an engaging, non-technical survey, presenting them as sources of beauty in night sky. 23 illustrations. Foreword. 2 star charts. Index. 147pp. 5⅜ × 8½.   21099-5 Pa. $3.95

FADS AND FALLACIES IN THE NAME OF SCIENCE, Martin Gardner. Fair, witty appraisal of cranks, quacks, and quackeries of science and pseudoscience: hollow earth, Velikovsky, orgone energy, Dianetics, flying saucers, Bridey Murphy, food and medical fads, etc. Revised, expanded In the Name of Science. "A very able and even-tempered presentation."—The New Yorker. 363pp. 5⅜ × 8.
20394-8 Pa. $6.95

ANCIENT EGYPT: ITS CULTURE AND HISTORY, J. E Manchip White. From pre-dynastics through Ptolemies: society, history, political structure, religion, daily life, literature, cultural heritage. 48 plates. 217pp. 5⅜ × 8½.   22548-8 Pa. $5.95

CATALOG OF DOVER BOOKS

SIR HARRY HOTSPUR OF HUMBLETHWAITE, Anthony Trollope. Incisive, unconventional psychological study of a conflict between a wealthy baronet, his idealistic daughter, and their scapegrace cousin. The 1870 novel in its first inexpensive edition in years. 250pp. 5⅜ × 8½. 24953-0 Pa. $6.95

LASERS AND HOLOGRAPHY, Winston E. Kock. Sound introduction to burgeoning field, expanded (1981) for second edition. Wave patterns, coherence, lasers, diffraction, zone plates, properties of holograms, recent advances. 84 illustrations. 160pp. 5⅜ × 8¼. (Except in United Kingdom) 24041-X Pa. $3.95

INTRODUCTION TO ARTIFICIAL INTELLIGENCE: SECOND, ENLARGED EDITION, Philip C. Jackson, Jr. Comprehensive survey of artificial intelligence—the study of how machines (computers) can be made to act intelligently. Includes introductory and advanced material. Extensive notes updating the main text. 132 black-and-white illustrations. 512pp. 5⅜ × 8½. 24864-X Pa. $8.95

HISTORY OF INDIAN AND INDONESIAN ART, Ananda K. Coomaraswamy. Over 400 illustrations illuminate classic study of Indian art from earliest Harappa finds to early 20th century. Provides philosophical, religious and social insights. 304pp. 6⅜ × 9⅜. 25005-9 Pa. $11.95

THE GOLEM, Gustav Meyrink. Most famous supernatural novel in modern European literature, set in Ghetto of Old Prague around 1890. Compelling story of mystical experiences, strange transformations, profound terror. 13 black-and-white illustrations. 224pp. 5⅜ × 8½. (Available in U.S. only) 25025-3 Pa. $6.95

PICTORIAL ENCYCLOPEDIA OF HISTORIC ARCHITECTURAL PLANS, DETAILS AND ELEMENTS: With 1,880 Line Drawings of Arches, Domes, Doorways, Facades, Gables, Windows, etc., John Theodore Haneman. Sourcebook of inspiration for architects, designers, others. Bibliography. Captions. 141pp. 9 × 12. 24605-1 Pa. $7.95

BENCHLEY LOST AND FOUND, Robert Benchley. Finest humor from early 30's, about pet peeves, child psychologists, post office and others. Mostly unavailable elsewhere. 73 illustrations by Peter Arno and others. 183pp. 5⅜ × 8½. 22410-4 Pa. $4.95

ERTÉ GRAPHICS, Erté. Collection of striking color graphics: *Seasons, Alphabet, Numerals, Aces* and *Precious Stones*. 50 plates, including 4 on covers. 48pp. 9⅜ × 12¼. 23580-7 Pa. $7.95

THE JOURNAL OF HENRY D. THOREAU, edited by Bradford Torrey, F. H. Allen. Complete reprinting of 14 volumes, 1837-61, over two million words; the sourcebooks for *Walden*, etc. Definitive. All original sketches, plus 75 photographs. 1,804pp. 8½ × 12¼. 20312-3, 20313-1 Cloth., Two-vol. set $125.00

CASTLES: THEIR CONSTRUCTION AND HISTORY, Sidney Toy. Traces castle development from ancient roots. Nearly 200 photographs and drawings illustrate moats, keeps, baileys, many other features. Caernarvon, Dover Castles, Hadrian's Wall, Tower of London, dozens more. 256pp. 5⅜ × 8¼. 24898-4 Pa. $6.95

CATALOG OF DOVER BOOKS

AMERICAN CLIPPER SHIPS: 1833–1858, Octavius T. Howe & Frederick C. Matthews. Fully-illustrated, encyclopedic review of 352 clipper ships from the period of America's greatest maritime supremacy. Introduction. 109 halftones. 5 black-and-white line illustrations. Index. Total of 928pp. 5⅜ × 8½.
25115-2, 25116-0 Pa., Two-vol. set $17.90

TOWARDS A NEW ARCHITECTURE, Le Corbusier. Pioneering manifesto by great architect, near legendary founder of "International School." Technical and aesthetic theories, views on industry, economics, relation of form to function, "mass-production spirit," much more. Profusely illustrated. Unabridged translation of 13th French edition. Introduction by Frederick Etchells. 320pp. 6⅛ × 9¼. (Available in U.S. only)
25023-7 Pa. $8.95

THE BOOK OF KELLS, edited by Blanche Cirker. Inexpensive collection of 32 full-color, full-page plates from the greatest illuminated manuscript of the Middle Ages, painstakingly reproduced from rare facsimile edition. Publisher's Note. Captions. 32pp. 9⅜ × 12¼.
24345-1 Pa. $4.95

BEST SCIENCE FICTION STORIES OF H. G. WELLS, H. G. Wells. Full novel The Invisible Man, plus 17 short stories: "The Crystal Egg," "Aepyornis Island," "The Strange Orchid," etc. 303pp. 5⅜ × 8½. (Available in U.S. only)
21531-8 Pa. $6.95

AMERICAN SAILING SHIPS: Their Plans and History, Charles G. Davis. Photos, construction details of schooners, frigates, clippers, other sailcraft of 18th to early 20th centuries—plus entertaining discourse on design, rigging, nautical lore, much more. 137 black-and-white illustrations. 240pp. 6⅛ × 9¼.
24658-2 Pa. $6.95

ENTERTAINING MATHEMATICAL PUZZLES, Martin Gardner. Selection of author's favorite conundrums involving arithmetic, money, speed, etc., with lively commentary. Complete solutions. 112pp. 5⅜ × 8½.
25211-6 Pa. $2.95

THE WILL TO BELIEVE, HUMAN IMMORTALITY, William James. Two books bound together. Effect of irrational on logical, and arguments for human immortality. 402pp. 5⅜ × 8½.
20291-7 Pa. $7.95

THE HAUNTED MONASTERY and THE CHINESE MAZE MURDERS, Robert Van Gulik. 2 full novels by Van Gulik continue adventures of Judge Dee and his companions. An evil Taoist monastery, seemingly supernatural events; overgrown topiary maze that hides strange crimes. Set in 7th-century China. 27 illustrations. 328pp. 5⅜ × 8½.
23502-5 Pa. $6.95

CELEBRATED CASES OF JUDGE DEE (DEE GOONG AN), translated by Robert Van Gulik. Authentic 18th-century Chinese detective novel; Dee and associates solve three interlocked cases. Led to Van Gulik's own stories with same characters. Extensive introduction. 9 illustrations. 237pp. 5⅜ × 8½.
23337-5 Pa. $5.95

Prices subject to change without notice.

Available at your book dealer or write for free catalog to Dept. GI, Dover Publications, Inc., 31 East 2nd St., Mineola, N.Y. 11501. Dover publishes more than 175 books each year on science, elementary and advanced mathematics, biology, music, art, literary history, social sciences and other areas.